Seeds of
Modern Drama

SEEDS
OF MODERN DRAMA

edited by
NORRIS HOUGHTON

APPLAUSE
NEW YORK • LONDON

SEEDS OF MODERN DRAMA
Introduced and Edited by Norris Houghton

Library of Congress Cataloging-in-Publication Data
Seeds of modern drama.
In modern translations.
Reprint. Originally published: New York: Dell Pub. Co., 1963.
(Laurel masterpieces of continental drama series; v. 3)
Contents: Thérèse Raquin / Emile Zola—An enemy of the
people / Henrik Ibsen—Miss Julie / August Strindberg—[etc.]
1. Drama—Collections. I. Houghton, Norris.
PN6112.S38 1986   808.82   86-17269
ISBN 0-936839-15-5

APPLAUSE THEATRE & CINEMA BOOKS
19 West 21st Street, Suite 201
New York, NY 10010
Phone: (212) 575-9265
Fax: (212) 575-9270
Email: info@applausepub.com
Internet: www.applausepub.com
Applause books are available through
your local bookstore, or you may
order at www.applausepub.com or
call Music Dispatch at 800-637-2852

Sales & Distribution
NORTH AMERICA:
    Hal Leonard Corp.
    7777 West Bluemound Road
    P.O. Box 13819
    Milwaukee, WI 53213
    Phone: (414) 774-3630
    Fax: (414) 774-3259
    Email: halinfo@halleonard.com
    Internet: www.halleonard.com

Norris Houghton, founder of the famous Phoenix Theatre, remains one of the most distinguished and versatile men in the American theatre. He has staged widely acclaimed productions throughout his career, including productions on Broadway such as *Macbeth* and *Billy Budd*. He has served as professor of drama and theatre at Princeton, Columbia, Barnard, SUNY Purchase and Vassar College. His other books include ADVANCE FROM BROADWAY, MOSCOW REHEARSALS, RETURN ENGAGEMENT, and ENTRANCES AND EXITS.

CONTENTS

INTRODUCTION 9

EMILE ZOLA: THERESE RAQUIN 17

HENRIK IBSEN: AN ENEMY OF THE PEOPLE 99

AUGUST STRINDBERG: MISS JULIE 193

GERHART HAUPTMANN: THE WEAVERS 249

ANTON CHEKHOV: THE SEA GULL 347

INTRODUCTION

If you had been junketing around Europe during the theatrical season of 1892-93, with that day's equivalent of *Theatre Arts* magazine or some other continental guide to playgoing in your hand, these are some of the events you might have been led to: the première in London of the first play from the pen of Bernard Shaw, *Widowers' Houses;* the premières in Paris of Maeterlinck's *Pélleas and Mélisande* and of Oscar Wilde's *Salomé;* the first performances of Ibsen's *The Master Builder,* of Gerhart Hauptmann's *The Weavers,* of Sir Arthur Wing Pinero's *The Second Mrs. Tanqueray,* of Hermann Sudermann's *Magda,* of Arthur Schnitzler's *Affairs of Anatol.*

What a season! One stage historian has dubbed it the most significant year in theatrical history since 1600, and I am inclined to agree. Certainly one would have to search far and wide to come across any other single season that contained such an outpouring of major works. Now, a season like this does not simply happen suddenly. It represents the flowering of a process that has been developing, in this case, for almost half a century. And especially must that 1892-93 season be thought of as relating to the rise of a new movement in art, one that continues to dominate our stage right up to the present day; a movement that is related in turn—as art always is—to a background of a much larger ferment in Western Europe. The new movement was called "realism" (sometimes "naturalism"), and the world in which it grew up looked something like this.

By the middle of the last century our modern system of capitalism was becoming fairly well consolidated, for the Industrial Revolution, which led to it, had been accomplished. The victory of large-scale industry was accompanied by a significant growth in world commerce. Simultaneously, and as a result of these forces, the old aristocracy began to dwindle in power and to be replaced by a dynamically ascending middle class to take over the vested interests. Simultaneously a self-conscious proletariat was emerging, which resulted in a sharpening of class lines. In 1848, there were revolutions in France and Germany, and the Chartist movement was stirring England. In the same year Karl Marx published his *Communist Manifesto.*

Probably more significant in its impact than Marx's statement was the appearance of Charles Darwin's *Origin of Species* in 1859. That was a blow from which Europe—and America too—staggered for decades. For the theory of evolution challenged, or seemed to do so at the time, almost all the religious finalities on which the Christian world had established itself. We find it hard today to take seriously the Scopes trial in Tennessee, but the recent play and motion picture, *Inherit the Wind,* have served to bring home to a generation that was not alive in 1925 the desperate struggle of faith to accept the possibility that man's progenitor was not Adam but a monkey.

Combine this revolutionary concept with the dialectical materialism of Marx and Friedrich Engels, based on the idea that nothing is final, on a denial of permanence, on a demand for an investigation of the processes of society to match those of nature, and you can see that there were real reasons for the ferment that was boiling in Europe's spiritual and intellectual life as the nineteenth century drew to a close.

How was the drama affected by this multifaceted

revolution? I do not suggest that the dramatists of the day sat down to write with copies of the *Communist Manifesto* and *Origin of Species* at their elbows. Many of them may well have never delved into either volume. But I cannot but believe that the thinking of their times became so altered that the art forms necessarily altered too, and as a direct result.

Realism has been defined as art based on that attitude which considers the reality of the observable fact as the final one. Therefore, what is of greatest import and interest is that which we are most capable of apprehending with the senses—what we can see and touch, hear and smell.

The prophet of this new art form was the French "encyclopedist," Denis Diderot. A century earlier (in 1748) he had written, "The perfection of a spectacle consists in the imitation of an action so exact, that the spectator, deceived without interruption, imagines that he is present at the action itself." Pointing out the principle of cause and effect in nature, he concluded: "So dramatic art prepares for events only to link them, and it links them in its productions only because they are linked in nature." Already, then, there was at least one voice advocating that the stage should take Hamlet's advice quite literally and "hold, as 'twere, the mirror up to nature."

Certainly the interest in the effect of environment on man, stimulated by the newly fashionable psychology, also played its part in the emergence of the new realism. Ridiculing the romantic tendency to flee from today with its drab walls and crowded streets, to the spiritual security of far-away times and exotic climes, the realists demanded that the portrayal of life should be etched in the familiar lines of daily life; that the ugly should not be glossed over; that the stage should offer a true "slice of life."

The world's foundations had just been shaken by the revelations of Darwin, whose dualistic thought was beginning to be affected by Marx and Spencer. From this world, as a consequence, a sense of finality was slipping, so that realism, with its faith in the immediately perceptible representation of outwardly observable facts, was truly attractive. The dramatists of the late nineteenth century took over the role of photographer and for the last one hundred years our Western drama has in its main stream been, whether we like it or not, essentially photographic. This volume, then, is a sort of photograph album, comprised of candid shots taken by photographers of genius who have captured their subjects in the act of coping (or of not coping) with their environment, with the pressures of daily life—men and women whom we recognize even as we recognize the images presented to us on the pages of our tabloids and picture magazines of today. This is our realistic drama.

NORRIS HOUGHTON

EMILE ZOLA

Of all people since the Romans, the French, it seems to me, are the most persistent in their desire to codify, to issue manifestoes and pronunciamentos, to formulate and regularize. As a result, every shift in artistic development, every new trend is the subject of an announcement, a preface or a newly enunciated rule. They are adept at inventing "isms": *"dadaisme," "surréalisme," "naturalisme,"* to mention but the first few that come to mind.

Stage history is full of testimony to this Gallic predilection. Corneille's *First Discourse on the Uses and Elements of Dramatic Poetry* was an early example. With it the seventeenth century's classicism was announced and defined by the author of that form's first masterpiece, *The Cid*. A couple of centuries later Victor Hugo issued his Preface to *Cromwell* and the romanticists were provided with a new testament on which to base their assault against classicism. Scarcely forty years passed before a new revolution began to take place and, as might be expected, it was also introduced by a new credo, this one laying down the lines of attack against the earlier rebels and formulating the latest "ism." Its author was Emile Zola and the banner he unfurled in 1873 was that of naturalism. The means he employed was the Preface to *Thérèse Raquin*.

"There should no longer be any school," cried Zola (as he was in the very act of announcing a new school of his own); "no more formulas, no standards of any sort: there is only life itself, an immense field where each may study and create as he likes." Going on to explain himself, he continued, "I am for no schools because I am for human truth, which excludes all sects and all systems." The model was to be life, for he wrote, "the word *art* displeases me: it contains I do not know what idea of necessary arrangement, of absolute ideal. To make art, is it not to make something which is outside of man and of nature?"

One can sympathize with Zola's desire to rid the drama—and also the novel, of course, for he was preeminently a novelist—of artificialities and conventions. But to abandon form because the flow of life so often seems formless is to give up the very thing which makes an artist an artist. One may say that the candid camera snatches bits of life in random glimpses, but on reflection one is forced to acknowledge that the photographer who focuses the lens and turns the camera to left or to right is exercising selectivity, he is choosing among alternate images, and by that very act is establishing that he is in some degree or other an arranger, an artist. So the *"tranche de vie"* or slice-of-life drama that Zola and his followers advocated was a slice of their own carving, selected to make some point about life or society, and when it was effective it was a work of art, Zola's denials notwithstanding.

Thérèse Raquin is such a work of art, despite the fact that one critic has dismissed it (and some may think with reason) as a melodrama, "romantic and old-fashioned to a degree." At the same time it does exemplify many of the characteristics of the new, revolutionary and supposedly formless naturalism. It is full of the sordid and unsavory aspects of the life of the time, of the drabness of lower middle-class environment. Zola, like Tennessee Williams who has given us the recent *Sweet Bird of Youth* and *Suddenly Last Summer*, did not mind horrifying and shocking his audience. "Given a strong man and an unsatisfied woman," Zola noted, in outlining his aim in *Thérèse:* "to seek in them the beast, to see nothing but the beast, to throw them into a violent drama and note scrupulously the sensations and acts of these creatures ... I have simply done in two living bodies the work which surgeons do on corpses."

If you seek only amusement in the theatre, keep away from this literary surgeon. But then, if that is your aim, you will have to dismiss this entire collection, for none of the early naturalist-realists was exactly a fun-maker. Ibsen and Strindberg, Zola and Hauptmann are all somber recorders of the seamy side of life; and even Chekhov, who called many of his plays comedies and who had the detachment from life that a true comic writer must always possess, fills his stage with heartbreak and frustration.

This man Zola was born a Parisian in 1840; he grew up in Aix but at eighteen returned to Paris, became a clerk for expediency's sake but determined to make his fame as a writer. This was accomplished in a major way by his novel, an epic of drink, *L'Assommoir,* which made him the most widely read, most talked of novelist of the day in France. There followed three novels *Nana, La Débâcle,* and *Germinal. Thérèse Raquin* Zola wrote first as a novel, then made his own dramatization of it.

It will be enough to mention the Dreyfus affair to remind some readers of the most sensational episode of Zola's life. At an early point in that explosive case, Zola became convinced of Dreyfus' innocence. His righteously indignant efforts in behalf of the young Jewish major catapulted him into the center of the political convulsion which followed. The Dreyfus case had not yet been completely resolved when, on a fine September morning in the autumn of 1902, the body of Emile Zola was discovered in the bedroom of his home in Paris. He had been accidentally asphyxiated during the night by the fumes of a defective flue. The arch-exponent of naturalism thus died in the kind of chance and mechanical manner that somehow seems appropriate to his preachings and view of life.

Thérèse Raquin

A Drama in Four Acts
by EMILE ZOLA

Translated by Kathleen Boutall

CHARACTERS

Laurent
Camille
Grivet
Michaud
Madame Raquin
Thérèse Raquin
Suzanne

The scene is a large bedroom, in a byway of the Pont Neuf, which serves at the same time as parlor and dining room. It is lofty, dark and dilapidated, hung with a faded greyish paper, furnished with shabby oddments and cluttered up with cardboard boxes of haberdashery. At the back is a door on the left of which is a sideboard and on the right a wardrobe. On the left wall upstage, on a slant, is an alcove in which can be seen a bed and a window looking out on a blank wall. Below this there is a small door and lower downstage a work table. On the right wall, upstage, is a flight of stairs leading down to the shop. Below this is a fireplace and on the mantelpiece are a columned clock and two bouquets of flowers under glass shades. In the middle of the room is a round table covered with oilcloth. There are two armchairs, one blue, the other green, and occasional chairs.

The setting is the same for the four acts.

ACT ONE.

The time is 8 o'clock on a summer evening. Supper is over and the table is still laid. The window is open. The atmosphere is one of peace and of middle-class comfort. CAMILLE *is seated in an armchair to the right, posing for his portrait. He is wearing an evening suit and is stiffly conscious of his best clothes.* LAURENT, *by his easel at the window, is painting. Beside him on a low chair crouches* THÉRÈSE, *her chin in her hand, her thoughts far away.* MADAME RAQUIN *is clearing the table.*

CAMILLE. Does it disturb you if I talk?

LAURENT. Of course not. So long as you keep still.

CAMILLE. I go to sleep after supper if I don't talk. You are lucky to have such good health. It doesn't matter what you eat. I ought not to have had that second helping of the custard—it upset me. I've got such a weak tummy. You're fond of custard, aren't you?

LAURENT. Yes, very. It's good stuff.

CAMILLE. They know what you like here. The custard was made specially for you—although they know it doesn't agree with me. Mama spoils you—doesn't she, Thérèse? Thérèse, doesn't Mama spoil Laurent?

THÉRÈSE [*without moving her head*]. Yes.

MME. RAQUIN [*taking up a pile of plates*]. Don't take any notice of them, Laurent. It was Camille who first told me that you preferred custard to vanilla and Thérèse who insisted on shaking the sugar over it.

CAMILLE. Mama, you know, you are a humbug.

MME. RAQUIN. Me, a humbug?

CAMILLE [to MME. RAQUIN *as she goes out smiling*]. Yes, yes, you are. [*To* LAURENT.] She's fond of you because you come from Vernon like herself. Do you remember the pennies she used to give us when we were children?

LAURENT. Yes, you used to buy heaps of apples.

CAMILLE. And you used to buy little penknives. It was lucky finding each other again in Paris. It was such a relief. I was bored to death. It was so frightfully dull here when I got back from the office. Can you still see?

LAURENT. Not very well, but I want to finish it.

CAMILLE. It's nearly eight o'clock. These summer evenings are so dreadfully long. I wish you had painted me by daylight; it would have looked nicer. You ought to have put in a country scene, instead of that grey background. But there is scarcely time in the mornings to swallow a cup of coffee before I have to go off to the office. I say, it can't be very good for the digestion to sit here after a meal without moving.

LAURENT. I'll let you go in a minute. This is the last sitting.

[MME. RAQUIN *enters, takes last things from table and wipes it over.*]

CAMILLE. You would have had a much better light by day. We don't get the sun but it shines on the wall opposite and that lights up the room. It was a queer idea of Mama's to take a place in the Pont Neuf Passage. It's so damp. On rainy days you would think it was a cellar.

LAURENT. Oh well, in business one place is as good as another.

CAMILLE. I daresay you're right. They've got the haberdashery shop downstairs to occupy themselves with. But I have nothing to do with that.

LAURENT. The flat is convenient.

CAMILLE. I'm glad you think so. Apart from this room

where we eat and sleep there is only Mama's room.
You can't count the kitchen. That's only a dark hole
like a cupboard. Nothing shuts and you freeze.
There's an abominable draught at night from that
little door on the staircase. [*Points to door.*]

MME. RAQUIN [*having finished her clearing away*]. Poor
dear Camille, you are never satisfied. I did it for the
best. It was your own idea to be a clerk in Paris. I
would have started business in Vernon again. When
you married your cousin Thérèse I had to work again
in case you had children.

CAMILLE. Well, I thought we should live in a street
where I could see plenty of people passing. I should
have sat at the window and watched the carriages.
That's fun. But now all I can see from here when
I open the window is the blank wall opposite and
the fanlight underneath. I prefer our Vernon windows. I could see the Seine flowing by—although
that wasn't much fun.

MME. RAQUIN. Well, I offered to go back there.

CAMILLE. Good Lord, no—not now that I've discovered
Laurent at the office. After all, I'm only here in the
evenings. I don't care if the passage is damp as long
as you're happy.

MME. RAQUIN. Now don't bully me any more about this
place. It's quite all right. [*Shop bell rings.*] Shop,
Thérèse. [THÉRÈSE *does not move.*] Aren't you going
down? Oh, all right. Just a minute, I'll go. [MME.
RAQUIN *goes down to shop.*]

CAMILLE. I don't want to upset her but the passage is
very unhealthy. What I'm afraid of is an attack of
pneumonia which would carry me off. I'm not as
strong as the rest of you. [*Pause.*] I say, can't I relax
for a bit? I can't feel my left arm.

LAURENT. If you like. I've practically finished.

CAMILLE. I'm sorry, but I can't stand it any longer. I
must walk about for a bit. [*He walks up and down
the stage and finally comes to where* THÉRÈSE *is sit-*

ting.] I've never been able to understand how it is my wife can sit still for hours on end without moving a finger. I should be pins and needles all over. It irritates me to see a person forever mooning. Laurent, doesn't it annoy you to feel her like that there beside you? Now then, Thérèse, wake up! Are you enjoying yourself?

THÉRÈSE [*without moving*]. Yes.

CAMILLE. Well, I hope you're happy, sitting there like a stuck pig. When her father, Captain Degans, left her with Mama her great big staring dark eyes used to frighten me. He was a captain, you know, but a dreadful man. Died in Africa, never came back to Vernon again. That's right, isn't it, Thérèse?

THÉRÈSE [*without moving*]. Yes.

CAMILLE. She's lost her tongue. Poor thing! [*Kisses her.*] Never mind, you're a good girl. We've never had a quarrel since Mama got us married. [*To* THÉRÈSE.] You're not cross with me?

THÉRÈSE. No.

LAURENT [*tapping* CAMILLE *on the shoulder with his maulstick*]. Now then, Camille. I'm only asking you for ten minutes more. [CAMILLE *sits.*] Turn your head to the left. [CAMILLE *looks left.*] That's it!—now don't move.

CAMILLE [*after a pause*]. Any news of your Father?

LAURENT. No, he's forgotten me. Besides, I never write to him.

CAMILLE. It's queer, all the same—father and son. It wouldn't do for me.

LAURENT. Papa Laurent had his own ideas. He wanted me to be a lawyer to act for him in his everlasting lawsuits with his neighbors. As soon as he found out that I was spending the money for my fees on running about the studios he cut off supplies. There's not much fun in being a lawyer.

CAMILLE. But it is a good position. You have got to have brains and it is well paid.

LAURENT. I met a man who was at college with me and who is an artist. So I studied painting too.

CAMILLE. You ought to have stuck to it. You could probably have got a decoration by now.

LAURENT. I couldn't. I was starving. So I chucked it and looked for a job.

CAMILLE. Well, at any rate, you still know how to paint.

LAURENT. I'm nothing wonderful. I liked painting because it was fun and not too much like hard work. But at first what I regretted when I started going to the office was that devil of a studio. I had a divan there and I used to sleep all the afternoon on it. I've had some gay nuptial nights there, I can tell you.

CAMILLE. Do you mean you had affairs with the models?

LAURENT. Of course. There was a magnificent blonde . . . [THÉRÈSE *rises slowly and goes down to the shop.*] We have shocked your wife.

CAMILLE. If she was listening. She hasn't much brain, poor girl, but she looks after me marvelously when I'm ill. Mama has taught her to make my camomile tea.

LAURENT. I don't think she likes me very much.

CAMILLE. Well, you know, these women . . . I say, haven't you finished?

LAURENT. Yes, you can get up now.

CAMILLE [*rises, and goes to portrait*]. Quite, quite finished?

LAURENT. It only has to be framed.

CAMILLE. Oh yes—it's a great success, isn't it? Yes, of course it is. [*Goes to door and shouts over staircase to shop.*] Mama, Thérèse, come and look. Laurent has finished the picture.

[MME. RAQUIN *and* THÉRÈSE *enter from staircase.*]

MME. RAQUIN. What, he's finished?

CAMILLE [*holding portrait*]. Yes, come and look.

MME. RAQUIN [*looking at portrait*]. Ah—yes. It's like. Especially the mouth. The mouth is strikingly like. Don't you think so, Thérèse? Now, clear away those things for Laurent. [*To* LAURENT.] You have finished, haven't you?

THÉRÈSE [*without turning to look at it*]. Yes. [*Crosses to window, leans against the window frame, her head pressed against the frame, her thoughts far away.*]

CAMILLE. And my dress suit—my wedding suit. I've only worn it four times. The cloth of the collar looks absolutely real.

MME. RAQUIN. And so does the arm of the chair.

CAMILLE. H'm, amazing. It looks like real wood. It's my own armchair too. We brought it from Vernon. No one uses it except me. [*Pointing to the other armchair.*] Mama's is blue.

MME. RAQUIN [*to* LAURENT, *who has put away his easel and painting materials*]. Why have you put that dark bit under the left eye?

LAURENT. It's the shadow.

CAMILLE [*putting portrait on easel which is leaning against the wall between the alcove and the window*]. It would probably have been nicer without the shadow, but never mind, I look distinguished—as though I were going to a party.

MME. RAQUIN. Laurent, dear, how can I thank you! And you won't even let Camille pay for the paints.

LAURENT. But it is I who should thank him for sitting.

CAMILLE. No, we can't let it go at that. I'm going out to get a bottle of something. Dash it all, we'll christen the picture.

LAURENT. Oh, all right, if you want to. I'm going out to get the frame. [*Gets coat and hat.*] Today's Thursday and Monsieur Grivet and the Michaud couple must see the portrait in its proper place. [*He goes out.*]

[CAMILLE *takes off his jacket, changes his tie, puts on his overcoat which his Mother gives him and starts to follow* LAURENT.]

CAMILLE [*turning back*]. What shall I get?

MME. RAQUIN. It must be something he likes. He's such a dear boy. He's like one of the family now.

CAMILLE. Yes, he's like a brother. What about anisette?

MME. RAQUIN. Do you think he likes anisette? Some really good wine might be better, with some cakes.

CAMILLE [to THÉRÈSE]. You're not saying anything, Thérèse. Do you remember if he likes Malaga?

THÉRÈSE. No, but I do know that he likes anything. He eats and drinks like a wolf.

MME. RAQUIN. My dear child—how can you—

CAMILLE. That's right, Mama, you scold her. She can't bear him. He has noticed it. He told me so. It's not very nice. [To THÉRÈSE.] I'm not going to let you spoil my friendships. What have you got against him?

THÉRÈSE. Nothing. He is always here. He has all his meals here. You give him the best of everything. It's Laurent here, Laurent there—it drives me wild! He's not very amusing and he's greedy and lazy.

MME. RAQUIN. Now, now, Thérèse, Laurent is not very happy. He lives in a garret and they feed him very poorly at that little café of his. I'm quite glad for him to have a good dinner here and to warm himself at the fire. He makes himself at home and has a smoke, that's what I like to see. Poor boy, he's all alone in the world.

THÉRÈSE. Oh, all right, just as you like. Pet and coddle him. It is nothing to me.

CAMILLE. Mama, I've got an idea. I'm going to get a bottle of champagne; it'll be splendid.

MME. RAQUIN. Yes, a bottle of champagne will do as payment for the picture. Don't forget the cakes.

CAMILLE. It's not half-past eight yet. Our visitors won't be here until nine o'clock. They'll have a nice surprise when they see champagne. [He goes out.]

MME. RAQUIN [to THÉRÈSE]. You'll light the lamp, won't you? [Going out.] I'm going down to the shop.

[THÉRÈSE, *left alone, stands still for a moment, then look-ing round she takes a deep breath. Coming down-stage she gives a gesture of weariness and boredom. Then, hearing* LAURENT *coming in from the little door, she smiles and thrills with sudden joy. During this scene the light becomes dim as night falls.*]

LAURENT. Thérèse.

THÉRÈSE. Laurent, my darling! My love—I felt you would come. [*Taking his hands, she leads him down-stage.*] It's eight days since I've seen you. I waited for you every afternoon. I hoped you'd manage to get away from your office. If you hadn't come I should have done something desperate. Tell me, why did you stay away for eight whole days? I can't stand it any longer. Shaking hands before the others this evening—so cold—like strangers.

LAURENT. I'll explain everything.

THÉRÈSE. You're frightened. You baby. We're quite safe here. [*Raises her voice and moves a pace or two.*] Who would believe that you and I are in love? No one would ever come and look for us here—in this room.

LAURENT [*pulling her to him and taking her in his arms*]. Now, now, don't be silly. No, of course I'm not afraid to come here.

THÉRÈSE. Then you're afraid of me. Now, own up. You're afraid that I love you too much—afraid that I shall be a nuisance.

LAURENT. Why do you doubt me? Don't you know that I can't sleep because of you? It's driving me out of my mind—and I never took women seriously before. You have wakened something in the very depths of my being, Thérèse. I'm someone I never knew ex-isted. And it frightens me because it isn't natural to love anyone as I love you—I'm terrified that it's going to take us out of our depth.

THÉRÈSE. Nothing can ever spoil our happiness; the sun will always shine for us.

LAURENT [*suddenly breaking away*]. Did you hear someone on the stairs?

THÉRÈSE. It's only the damp. It makes the stairs creak.
Let our love be without fear and without remorse.
If you knew what my life has been like. As a child
I grew up in the stuffy air of a sickroom.

LAURENT. Poor Thérèse.

THÉRÈSE. Oh, I was unhappy. I used to crouch over the
fire making his everlasting concoctions. If I moved,
his mother used to scold me. You see, Camille must
not be wakened. I used to stutter and stammer and I
moved about like a shaky old woman. I was so
clumsy that Camille used to make fun of me. But I
was strong and sturdy when I was little and I used to
clench my fists and I'd have liked to smash up everything. They told me my Mother was the daughter of
an African chief. It must have been true. I was always dreaming of running away—of escaping and
running barefoot in the dust. I would have begged
like a gypsy. You see, I felt I would rather starve
than stay and be kept by them.

[*Her voice has gradually become louder, and* LAURENT
crosses the stage to listen.]

LAURENT. Not so loud. You'll have your Aunt coming
up.

THÉRÈSE. Let her come. I don't know why I agreed to
marry Camille. It was all settled for me. My Aunt
waited until we were old enough. I was twelve when
she said to me: "You will love your poor little cousin
and take care of him." She wanted a nurse for him,
someone to make his camomile tea. He was such a
puny little thing. Over and over again she had to
fight to save his life and she brought me up to be his
servant. I never stood up for myself; they made a
coward of me. I felt sorry for him. On our wedding
night instead of going into my own bedroom on the
left of the stairs I went into Camille's room on the
right. And that was all! But you—you—oh Laurent!

LAURENT. You love me? [*Takes her in his arms and leads her gently to chair by table.*]

THÉRÈSE. I love you. I love you. I have loved you since that day when Camille brought you into the shop. Do you remember—the day when you two met again in the office? I don't know how it happened. I'm proud and I'm passionate. I don't know what sort of love it was. It seemed more like hate. The sight of you drove me mad. The moment you came in my nerves were strained to breaking-point—and yet I longed for the pain and used to wait for your coming. When you were painting I was nailed there on that stool at your feet and yet I longed to get away—hating myself . . .

LAURENT. I adore you. [*Kneeling before her.*]

THÉRÈSE. And our only amusement is our Thursday evenings. Always that silly old Grivet and Michaud. But you know all about them with their eternal dominoes. They've driven me almost mad. Thursday after Thursday the same boring jokes. But now, I'm the lucky one and I've got my revenge. When we are sitting round the table after our meal and having our friendly gossip I shall be taking a wicked delight in remembering my secret happiness. While you are all playing dominoes, there I'll be, doing my embroidery as usual—not saying a word. And in the midst of all this humdrum, I'll be counting over my precious memories and feeling again the ecstasy.

LAURENT [*listening at staircase door*]. I tell you, you are talking too loudly; we'll be caught—you'll see, your Aunt will come up. Where is my hat?

THÉRÈSE [*rising*]. Yes, you're right. I think you'd better go. What about tomorrow? You will come, won't you? At two o'clock?

LAURENT. No, don't expect me. It's impossible.

THÉRÈSE. Impossible? Why?

LAURENT. My chief is beginning to notice. He has threatened to sack me if I'm away again.

THÉRÈSE. Then we shan't see one another any more? You're leaving me. So it's come to this—all your caution—What a coward you are!

LAURENT. Listen to me—We can be happy—It's only a matter of taking our chances and being patient. So often I have dreamed of having you to myself for a whole day. Then the day becomes a month—a year— a whole lifetime of happiness. A whole lifetime to ourselves for love—to be together. I'd leave my job and I would start to paint again. You should do just whatever you wanted. We would adore one another for always. You would be happy?

THÉRÈSE [smiling, her head on his breast]. Happy? Yes— ah, yes.

LAURENT [in a low voice and backing away from her]. If only you were free—

THÉRÈSE [in a dream]. We would be married. Nothing to be afraid of. A dream come true.

LAURENT. In these shadows I can only see your eyes— your shining eyes. [Pause.] They'd drive me mad if I were not wise for the two of us—Now it must be good-bye, Thérèse—

THÉRÈSE. You won't come tomorrow?

LAURENT. Now, you must trust me. If we don't see one another for a little while you must tell yourself that we're working for our happiness. [Kisses her and leaves through the little door.]

THÉRÈSE [after a pause]. If only I were free.

MME. RAQUIN [enters]. What's this? No light yet? What a dreamer! The lamp is ready, I'll go and light it. [Goes out through door at back.]

CAMILLE [enters with bottle of champagne and a bag of cakes]. Wherever are you? Why haven't you got the light?

THÉRÈSE. Your Mother has gone for the lamp.

CAMILLE [in fright]. Oh, it's you, is it? You frightened me. Why couldn't you speak naturally? You know I don't like practical jokes played on me in the dark.

THÉRÈSE. I'm not joking.

CAMILLE. I could only just see you—looking like a ghost. Games like that are silly. Now if I wake up tonight I shall think that a woman with a white face is walking round my bed to murder me. It's all very well for you to laugh.

THÉRÈSE. I'm not laughing.

MME. RAQUIN [*enters with lamp*]. What's the matter now?

CAMILLE. Thérèse is amusing herself by frightening me. It wouldn't have taken much more to make me drop the champagne. That would have been three francs gone.

MME. RAQUIN. You only paid three francs? [*Takes bottle.*]

CAMILLE. Yes. I went to the Boulevard St. Michel where I'd seen one in a grocer's marked down. It's just as good as one at eight francs. It's a well-known fact that these shopkeepers are a lot of frauds and that it's only the label that's different. Here are the cakes, Mama.

MME. RAQUIN. Give them to me. We'll have everything on the table so that Grivet and Michaud will have a surprise when they come in. Give me a couple of plates, Thérèse. [*Puts bottle between two plates of cakes.* THÉRÈSE *goes to worktable and takes up her embroidery.*]

CAMILLE. Monsieur Grivet is punctuality personified. As nine strikes, in he will come. Be nice to him, Thérèse, won't you? And you too, Mama. He's only a senior clerk but he can be very useful to me. He's really quite important. The older men in the office swear that in twenty years he's never been a minute late. Laurent is wrong when he says he'll never make his mark.

MME. RAQUIN. Michaud is very punctual, too. When he was superintendent of police at Vernon, he used to come up at eight o'clock every night on the dot, do you remember? We used to congratulate him on it!

CAMILLE. Yes, but he seems to have gone all to pieces since he has retired to Paris with that niece of his. It has upset him. Suzanne leads him by the nose. But it really is nice to have friends to entertain once a week. It would be too expensive, of course, to do it more often. Oh, I've got a plan I wanted to tell you about before they arrive.

MME. RAQUIN. What is it?

CAMILLE. Well, you know that I promised Thérèse to take her to Saint-Ouen one Sunday before it gets too cold. She won't go out with me in the town although it's much nicer than the country. She says I tire her out and that I don't know how to walk. So I thought it would be a good idea of we went on Sunday to Saint-Ouen and took Laurent with us.

MME. RAQUIN. Very well, children, you go to Saint-Ouen. My legs are too old for me to go with you, but it's an excellent idea. That will quite square you up with Laurent for the portrait.

CAMILLE. Laurent is such fun in the country. Do you remember, Thérèse, when he came with us to Suresnes? The idiot! He's as strong as a horse. He jumps ditches full of water and he throws stones to incredible heights. When we were at Suresnes on the roundabouts, he imitated the galloping postilions and the cracking of the whips and the noise of the spurs. He was so good that a wedding party there laughed until they cried. The bride was positively ill, wasn't she, Thérèse?

THÉRÈSE. He drank enough at dinner to make him funny.

CAMILLE. Oh, you don't understand that people like to enjoy themselves. If I depended on you to make me laugh it would be pretty dreary at Saint-Ouen. Do you know what she does, Mama? She sits on the ground and looks at the water. After all, if I take Laurent he will keep me amused. Where the devil has he gone to get his frame? [*Shop bell rings.*] Ah, there he is. Monsieur Grivet won't be here for seven minutes yet.

LAURENT. That shop is hopeless. [*Sees* CAMILLE *and* MADAME RAQUIN *whispering.*] What are you two hatching between you?

CAMILLE. Guess.

LAURENT. You're going to invite me to dinner tomorrow and there will be boiled chicken.

MME. RAQUIN. Greedy!

CAMILLE. Better than that—much better. On Sunday I'm taking Thérèse to Saint-Ouen and you are coming with us. Will you?

LAURENT. Indeed I will. [*Takes picture from easel and gets hammer from* MME. RAQUIN.]

MME. RAQUIN. But you will be careful, won't you? Laurent, I entrust Camille to you. You are so strong and I am happier when I know he is with you.

CAMILLE. Mother gets on my nerves with her everlasting fuss-fuss-fussing. D'you know that I can't go to the end of the street without her imagining something awful has happened? No, I don't like always being treated like a little boy. Now, we'll take a cab to the fortifications and then we'll only have the one fare to pay. Then we'll follow the towpath. The afternoon we'll spend on the island and we'll feed in the evening at a little inn on the riverbank. Well? All right?

LAURENT [*putting canvas in frame*]. Splendid, but I can go one better.

CAMILLE. What?

LAURENT [*with a look at* THÉRÈSE]. A boat on the river.

MME. RAQUIN. No—no boat. I should be worried.

THÉRÈSE. You don't expect Camille to take any chances on the water. He's too frightened.

CAMILLE. Me frightened?

LAURENT. Of course you are. I forgot you were afraid of the water. When we used to paddle in the Seine

at Vernon you used to stay shivering on the bank.
All right then—no boat.

CAMILLE. But it's not true. I'm not afraid. We will go
boating. See? Heavens, you'll soon be making me out
an imbecile. We'll see who is the most frightened of
the three of us. It's Thérèse who's afraid.

THÉRÈSE. My poor dear, you're pale at the thought of it.

CAMILLE. That's right. Laugh at me—laugh at me. We'll
see. We'll see.

MME. RAQUIN. Camille darling, give up the idea—for my
sake.

CAMILLE. Mama, please, don't nag at me. You know it
makes me ill.

LAURENT. Well, let your wife decide.

THÉRÈSE. Accidents can happen anywhere.

LAURENT. That's very true. You can slip in the street,
or a tile can fall from a roof—

CAMILLE. Besides, you know how I adore the Seine.

LAURENT. Right! We're agreed. We go on the river. You
win.

MME. RAQUIN [to LAURENT]. I can't tell you how much
this worries me. Camille is so headstrong. You saw
how he behaved.

LAURENT. Don't worry. Don't worry. You needn't be
afraid, I shall be there. Ah! Now I'm going to hang
the portrait. [Hangs portrait above sideboard.]

CAMILLE. You're sure it's in a good light there. [Shop
bell rings and clock strikes nine.] Nine o'clock! Ah,
there's Monsieur Grivet.

GRIVET [enters]. I'm the first. Good evening, ladies and
gentlemen.

MME. RAQUIN. Good evening, Monsieur Grivet. Shall I
take your umbrella? [Taking umbrella and going to
put it in upstage corner by fireplace.] Is it raining?

GRIVET. It's threatening. Excuse me, that's not the place
for my umbrella. Not that corner, not that corner.
[Moves umbrella downstage corner.] You know my
little ways. In the other corner. There—thank you—

MME. RAQUIN. Give me your galoshes.

GRIVET. No, no. I'll see to them myself. [*Taking off galoshes.*] I look after myself. A place for everything and everything in its place. And then there's nothing to worry about. [*Puts galoshes beside umbrella.*]

CAMILLE. And what's your news, Monsieur Grivet?

GRIVET. Well, I left the office at four-thirty. I had dinner at six o'clock at the little Orleans restaurant. At seven o'clock I read my paper at the Café Saturnin and as today is Thursday, instead of going back to bed at nine o'clock as I usually do, I came here. [*Thinking.*] Yes, I think that's all.

LAURENT. Did you see anything interesting on the way, Monsieur Grivet?

GRIVET. Oh yes, how stupid of me. There was an enormous crowd in the rue St. André-des-Arts. I had to walk on the other side of the road to get by and it put me out. You know I go to the office along the left-hand pavement and come back along the other side.

MME. RAQUIN. The right-hand one.

GRIVET. No. On the left. You see, I walk along the pavement like this— [*Walking with left hand extended to indicate left-hand pavement, turns and comes back, still with left hand extended, indicating opposite side of road.*] and I come back on the other side in the evening. That makes it the left hand side, you see. I always keep to the left, just like the trains, you see. Then I know where I am.

LAURENT. But what was everybody doing on the pavement?

GRIVET. I don't know. How should I?

MME. RAQUIN. An accident of some kind, I expect.

GRIVET. Yes, of course, it must have been an accident. I never thought of that. You know, that's relieved my mind, your saying it was an accident. [*Sits in front of table.*]

MME. RAQUIN. Ah, here is Monsieur Michaud.

[*Enter* MICHAUD *and* SUZANNE. SUZANNE *takes off shawl and hat and goes to speak to* THÉRÈSE *at worktable.* MICHAUD *shakes hands all round.*]

MICHAUD. I think I'm late. [*To* MONSIEUR GRIVET, *who has his watch in his hand.*] I know, six minutes past nine. It's the child's fault. [*Indicating* SUZANNE.] We had to stop and look in every shopwindow. [*Puts his stick in same corner as* GRIVET's *umbrella.*]

GRIVET. Please forgive me, that's the place for my umbrella. You know I don't like that. I have left the other corner for your stick.

MICHAUD. Well, well, don't let's worry about it.

CAMILLE [*in an undertone to* LAURENT]. I say, I think Grivet is annoyed because there is champagne. He's looked at the bottle three times, but hasn't said a word. I'm amazed he didn't show more surprise at it.

MICHAUD [*seeing champagne*]. My word! Do you want to send us home rolling? Cakes and champagne!

GRIVET. What! Champagne! I've only tasted it four times in my life.

MICHAUD. What's the festive occasion?

MME. RAQUIN. We are celebrating Camille's portrait. Laurent finished it this evening. [*Holds lamp to show portrait.*] Look!

[*All join her except* THÉRÈSE *at worktable, and* LAURENT *who is leaning against mantelpiece.*]

CAMILLE. It's a striking likeness, isn't it? I look as if I'm off to a party.

MICHAUD. Yes, yes.

MME. RAQUIN. It's only just done. You can smell the paint.

GRIVET. Yes. I noticed a smell. That's the advantage of a photograph. It doesn't smell.

CAMILLE. Yes, but when it's dry . . .

GRIVET. Ah yes—when the paint's dry . . . It'll dry all right. There's a shop in the rue de la Harpe which took five days to dry.

MME. RAQUIN. Well, Monsieur Michaud, you like it?

MICHAUD. Very good, very good.

[*They all turn back and* MME. RAQUIN *puts lamp on table.*]

CAMILLE. Now, Mama, what about some tea? We will have the champagne after the dominoes.

GRIVET [*sitting*]. Quarter past nine. We shall have time for the conqueror.

MME. RAQUIN. I won't keep you five minutes. You stay here, Thérèse, as you don't feel well.

SUZANNE. Well, I'm bursting with health, Madame Raquin, I'll come and help you. I like being useful in the house.

[*They go out through door at back.*]

CAMILLE. And what's your news, Monsieur Michaud?

MICHAUD. On nothing. Just taking Suzanne into the Luxembourg to do her needlework. Oh, but of course, if you want news, there's the tragedy in the rue St. André-des-Arts.

CAMILLE. Tragedy, what tragedy? Monsieur Grivet said he saw a lot of people there.

MICHAUD. It's been crowded ever since this morning. [*To* GRIVET.] They were all looking up, weren't they?

GRIVET. I couldn't tell you. I had to cross over. So it was an accident then? [*Puts on a skullcap and draws cuffs over his sleeves, taking them from his pocket.*]

MICHAUD. Yes, at the Hôtel Bourgogne. They found a woman's body cut in four pieces in a trunk—in a trunk belonging to a guest who has disappeared.

GRIVET. You don't say. In four pieces? How can you cut up a woman's body into four pieces?

CAMILLE. How horrible.

GRIVET. And *I* passed the place. I remember now they were looking up in the air. Did they see anything up there?

MICHAUD. The crowd thought they could see the window of the room where the trunk was discovered. As a matter of fact they were wrong. *The* room looks on to the courtyard.

LAURENT. Have they got the murderer?

MICHAUD. No. One of my old colleagues who has the case in hand said they were completely in the dark. [GRIVET *tosses his head and laughs.*] It's going to be a bit difficult to see that justice is done.

LAURENT. Have they established the identity of the victim?

MICHAUD. No. The body was naked and the head missing.

GRIVET. The head missing? I suppose someone has mislaid it.

CAMILLE. Don't! It gives me the creeps—your woman in four pieces.

GRIVET. Oh, but you can afford to take it lightly when you're in no danger yourself. When Monsieur Michaud was superintendent of police he had some very funny stories. Do you remember the one about the gendarme who was buried and they found his fingers in a box of carrots? He told us that one last autumn. It was a good one, I thought. We know we're quite safe here; this is a God-fearing house. I shouldn't say the same thing about some places. If I were going through a dark wood with Monsieur Michaud—well—

LAURENT. Monsieur Michaud, do you think a lot of crimes go unpunished?

MICHAUD. Yes, worse luck. Disappearances, lingering deaths, stranglings, fatal falls—not a cry heard, not a drop of blood seen. The law is there but it has no clues. There's more than one murderer walking about in broad daylight.

GRIVET [*laughing loudly*]. I can't help laughing. And they're not arrested?

MICHAUD. My dear Monsieur Grivet, if they are not arrested, it's because there are no clues.

CAMILLE. Then is there something wrong with the police?

MICHAUD. Oh, the police are all right, but they can't do the impossible. Let me tell you again that there are some very lucky murderers living on the fat of the land who are both loved and respected. Don't wag your head, Monsieur Grivet.

GRIVET. Wag my head? I will wag my head. You leave me alone.

MICHAUD. It's quite possible that some acquaintance of yours is a murderer and that you shake hands with him every day.

GRIVET. Oh, I say, don't say that. You mustn't say that because you know quite well it isn't true. If I liked, I could tell you a story . . .

MICHAUD. Go on then. Tell it.

GRIVET. Very well, I will. It's the story of the thieving magpie. [MICHAUD *shrugs his shoulders.*] Perhaps you know it. You know everything. Some time ago there was a servant who was thrown into prison because he'd stolen a silver spoon. A couple of months later, the spoon was found in a magpie's nest when they were cutting down a tree—a poplar tree it was. The magpie was the thief. The servant was set at liberty. You see, the culprit is always punished!

MICHAUD [*sneering*]. Did they put the magpie in prison?

GRIVET [*annoyed*]. Magpie in prison! Magpie in prison? Michaud, you're an idiot.

CAMILLE. No, that isn't what Monsieur Grivet meant. You're getting him all mixed up.

GRIVET. The police are no good, that's all. It's all wrong.

CAMILLE. Laurent, what do you think? Is it possible for a man to kill anyone and to get away with it?

LAURENT [*goes slowly to where* THÉRÈSE *is sitting*]. Don't you see that Monsieur Michaud is pulling your leg? He's trying to frighten you with his stories. How can he know what he confesses no one knows? And if there are such clever people about, well, good luck to them. I'm sure your wife isn't so gullible. What do you say, Thérèse?

THÉRÈSE. What no one knows, doesn't exist.

CAMILLE. Let's change the subject, for goodness' sake and talk of something else.

GRIVET. I quite agree. Let's talk about something else.

CAMILLE. We haven't brought up the chairs from the shop. Will someone come and help me carry them up? [*Goes down to shop.*]

GRIVET [*gets up grumbling*]. That's what he calls talking about something else—going to fetch chairs.

MICHAUD. Are you coming, Monsieur Grivet?

GRIVET. After you! Magpie in prison! Magpie in prison . . . As if you could see such a thing! For a retired police superintendent you've made a bit of a fool of yourself, Monsieur Michaud.

[*They both go down to shop.*]

LAURENT [*in an undertone, taking* THÉRÈSE'*s hands*]. Swear you'll do as I say.

THÉRÈSE. I'm yours, all of me. You can make of me what you please—

CAMILLE [*from below*]. Now then, Laurent, you lazy-bones. Why couldn't you come down and fetch your chair instead of leaving it to these two gentlemen?

LAURENT [*answering* CAMILLE]. I stayed behind to make love to your wife. [*To* THÉRÈSE.] Keep hoping. We will be happy together yet.

CAMILLE [*from below*]. Oh, that! I give you leave to do that. Be nice to her.

LAURENT [*to* THÉRÈSE]. And remember what you said. What no one knows doesn't exist. [*Noise on stairs.*] Careful!

[*They separate quickly;* THÉRÈSE *resumes her sulky attitude at the worktable.* LAURENT *moves away. The others return each with a chair, laughing heartily.*]

CAMILLE [*to* LAURENT]. You old humbug. All that non-sense because you didn't want the trouble of going downstairs.

GRIVET. Ah, here's the tea.

[*Enter* MME. RAQUIN *and* SUZANNE *with tea.*]

MME. RAQUIN [*as* GRIVET *takes out his watch*]. Yes, I know, I've been longer than I said. Now sit down, all of you, and we'll make up for lost time.

[GRIVET *sits in front of table with* LAURENT *behind him.* MME. RAQUIN'S *chair is R. and* MICHAUD *sits behind her.* CAMILLE *is in the middle at the back in his arm-chair.* THÉRÈSE *is at her worktable.* SUZANNE *goes to join her when the tea has been served.*]

CAMILLE. Well, here I am, in my chair. Give me the dominoes, Mama.

GRIVET [*beaming*]. Now isn't this delightful! Every Thursday, when I wake up, I say to myself, "Aha! Tonight I'm going to play dominoes at the Raquins'!" You know, you can't imagine . . .

SUZANNE [*interrupting*]. Sugar, Monsieur Grivet?

GRIVET. Thank you, my dear. That's very nice of you. Two lumps—may I? [*Beginning again.*] You know, you can't imagine . . .

CAMILLE [*interrupting*]. Thérèse, aren't you coming?

MME. RAQUIN [*giving him the box of dominoes*]. Leave her alone. You know she doesn't feel well. She doesn't care for dominoes. And if anyone comes to the shop she'll go down to see to them.

CAMILLE. It's infuriating to have to look at someone who isn't enjoying the fun when everyone else is having a good time. [*To* MME. RAQUIN.] Now, Mama, aren't you going to sit down?

MME. RAQUIN [*sitting*]. Yes, yes, I'm sitting down now.

CAMILLE. Well then, is everyone all right?

MICHAUD. That we are. And tonight I'm going to wipe the floor with you. Madame Raquin, your tea is a trifle stronger than it was last Thursday. Oh, but Monsieur Grivet was saying something.

GRIVET. I was saying something? No, I don't think so.

MICHAUD. Yes, you began to say something.

GRIVET. To say something? I think you're mistaken.

MICHAUD. No, I'm not. He did, didn't he, Madame Raquin? He said "You know, you can't imagine . . ."

GRIVET. "You know, you can't imagine . . ." No, I don't remember it! If this is one of your jokes, Monsieur Michaud, I don't think it's very funny.

CAMILLE. Everyone all right? Very well, then, let's begin. [*Noisily emptying the box of dominoes.*]

[*A pause while the players shuffle and deal.*]

GRIVET. Now we each take seven. [*To* LAURENT, *who is standing at table, looking on.*] Monsieur Laurent, you're not playing, you mustn't give any advice. No peeping, you understand, Monsieur Michaud, no peeping. [*Pause.*] Ah! Double six! It's my first go.

ACT TWO.

*The time is ten o'clock at night and the lamp is lit. A
year has gone by but nothing in the room is changed.
There is the same atmosphere of peace and intimacy.*
MADAME RAQUIN *and* THÉRÈSE *are in deep mourning.
At the rise of the curtain* THÉRÈSE, GRIVET, LAURENT,
MICHAUD, MME. RAQUIN, *and* SUZANNE *are discovered in
the positions they occupied at the end of the previous
act.* THÉRÈSE, *remote, with the air of a sick woman, her
embroidery on her knees, sits by the worktable.* GRIVET,
LAURENT, *and* MICHAUD *are in the chairs in front of the
round table. Only Camille's chair is empty. There is a
pause while* MME. RAQUIN *and* SUZANNE *serve the tea, repeating exactly their actions of the previous act.*

LAURENT. Now, Madame Raquin, you must not dwell
on your grief. Give me the dominoes.
SUZANNE. Sugar, Monsieur Grivet?
GRIVET. Thank you, my dear. That's very nice of you.
Two pieces, may I? Sweets from the sweet.
LAURENT [*with box of dominoes*]. Ah, here they are.
Now, sit down, Madame Raquin. [MME. RAQUIN *sits.*]
Is everyone all right?
MICHAUD. That we are! And tonight I'm going to wipe
the floor with you. Just a minute while I put some
rum in my tea. [*Pours rum into his tea.*]
LAURENT. All right? [*Turns dominoes on to table.*]
Very well. Let's begin.
[*The players shuffle and deal.*]
GRIVET. With pleasure! Now we each take seven. No
peeping, Monsieur Michaud, d'you hear, no peeping.
[*Pause.*] No. Today it is not my first go.
MME. RAQUIN [*bursting into tears*]. I can't do it. I

can't—I can't. [LAURENT *and* MICHAUD *rise and* SU-
ZANNE *bends over* MME. RAQUIN's *armchair*.] When I
see you all round this table, just as we used to be,
I remember and it breaks my heart. Poor Camille
used to sit there.

MICHAUD. Come now, Madame Raquin, you must be
sensible.

MME. RAQUIN. Please forgive me. I can't help it. You remember how he loved to play dominoes. He always
turned them out of the box himself, exactly as Laurent did just now. He used to scold me when I
didn't sit down soon enough. I was afraid to cross
him. It made him ill. We had such happy evenings.
And now, look, his chair is empty.

MICHAUD. Dear lady, you must pull yourself together or
you will make yourself really ill.

SUZANNE [*embracing* MME. RAQUIN]. Please, please don't
cry. It hurts us so much to see you like this.

MME. RAQUIN [*still crying*]. Yes, you're right. I must be
brave.

GRIVET [*pushing dominoes away*]. Well, I suppose we'd
better not play then. It's a great pity that it affects
you like this. Your tears won't bring him back.

MICHAUD. We are all of us mortal.

MME. RAQUIN. Alas, yes.

GRIVET. We came here to play dominoes because we
hoped to distract your mind from your sorrow.

MICHAUD. You must try and forget, dear Madame.

GRIVET. He's quite right. Come now, we must cheer up.
We'll play the best out of three, shall we?

LAURENT. No—in a minute. Let Madame Raquin have
a little time to get calm. We all of us grieve for dear
Camille.

SUZANNE. Do you hear, Madame dear? We all grieve for
him. Our hearts ache for you. [*Sits down by* MME.
RAQUIN's *knees*.]

MME. RAQUIN. You are all so kind. Please don't be cross
with me for spoiling the game.

MICHAUD. We're not cross with you. But it's a year now
since it happened, and you ought to be able to think
about it more calmly.

MME. RAQUIN. I haven't counted the days. I cry because
the tears just come. Please forgive me. All the time,
I can see my poor child drifting down the rough
waters of the Seine. And I see him when he was little
—when I used to put him to bed between two blan-
kets. It was such an awful death—he must have suffered so. I had a terrible presentiment. I begged him
to give up the idea of going on the water but he
wanted to show he wasn't afraid. If you only knew
how I looked after him when he was a baby. For
three whole weeks when he had typhoid I held him
on my knees without ever going to bed.

MICHAUD. But you still have your niece. You still have
Thérèse. You mustn't distress her and you mustn't
distress the generous man who saved her. It will always be a grief to him that he wasn't able to drag
Camille to the bank too. It is selfish of you to nurse
your grief. You are upsetting Laurent.

LAURENT. These memories are so painful.

MICHAUD. You did what you could. Now—the boat cap-
sized when it crashed into a stake, didn't it?—one of
those stakes they use for fixing the eel nets, wasn't it?

LAURENT. Yes, that's what I thought. The jolt threw us
all three into the water.

MICHAUD. Then when you were in the water you managed to get hold of Thérèse.

LAURENT. I was rowing and she was beside me. All I
had to do was to grab her dress. Then I dived in after
Camille but he had disappeared. He was at the front
of the canoe; he was trailing his hands in the water.
He was making jokes about the soup being cold . . .

MICHAUD. You mustn't stir up these memories; they're
upsetting. You behaved like a hero—you went in
three times.

GRIVET. I quite agree. There was a magnificent article

in my paper about it the next day. They said that Monsieur Laurent deserved a medal. It just gave me the creeps when I read how the three people fell into the river while their dinner was waiting for them in the restaurant. And then there was another article a week later, after they had found poor Monsieur Camille's body. [*To* MICHAUD.] You remember . . . it was Monsieur Laurent who fetched you to go with him to identify the body.

[MME. RAQUIN *breaks into fresh sobs.*]

MICHAUD [*to* GRIVET]. Really, Monsieur Grivet, do hold your tongue. Madame was just calming down and then you start raking up all these details . . .

GRIVET [*in a low voice, sulkily*]. I'm sorry, but you began it. As we're not playing dominoes we must say something.

MICHAUD [*slightly louder*]. You've talked about that newspaper article of yours hundreds of times. It's in bad taste, you know. Now she's off again.

GRIVET [*rising and shouting*]. It was you who began it.

MICHAUD [*also shouting*]. Damn it all, it was you!

GRIVET [*shouting*]. All right, call me a fool!

MME. RAQUIN. Now, now, you two, don't quarrel. [*They retire muttering and grumbling.*] I am going to be sensible. I won't cry any more. I like to talk about my loss. It comforts me and it reminds me too of what I owe to all of you. Laurent, dear, give me your hand. You aren't angry?

LAURENT. Yes, with myself, because I couldn't bring both of them back to you.

MME. RAQUIN. You're my child and I love you. I pray for you every night because you tried to save my boy. I ask God to watch over you. Camille is in Heaven. He'll hear me and you will owe your happiness to him. Every time you find some joy in life, say to yourself that it's because I've prayed for you and Camille has heard my prayers.

LAURENT. Dear Madame.

MICHAUD. Hear, hear!

MME. RAQUIN [*To* SUZANNE]. And now, dear, go and sit down again. Look—I'm smiling—for you.

SUZANNE. Thank you, dear, dear Madame. [*Kisses* MME. RAQUIN *as she rises.* MME. RAQUIN, *returning to place at table.*] Now, come along. Whose turn is it?

GRIVET. You really want to play? Good! [GRIVET, LAURENT *and* MICHAUD *sit down.*] Whose turn is it?

MICHAUD. Mine. [*Plays domino.*]

SUZANNE [*goes across to* THÉRÈSE]. Thérèse, darling. Would you like me to tell you about the Blue Prince?

THÉRÈSE. The Blue Prince?

SUZANNE [*taking a stool and sitting by* THÉRÈSE]. It's quite a story. I shall whisper it—There's no need for Uncle to know anything about it. He's a young man. He wears a blue coat and has a fair moustache which suits him marvelously.

THÉRÈSE. Take care. Your Uncle is listening.

[SUZANNE *half rises and glances at the players.*]

MICHAUD [*angrily to* GRIVET]. But you passed five a minute ago and now you are putting down five all over the place.

GRIVET. I passed five? You'll excuse me but you're making a mistake.

[MICHAUD *protests and then the game continues.*]

SUZANNE [*sitting down again and speaking in a low voice*]. There's no need to worry about Uncle when he's playing dominoes. Now this young man used to come to the Luxembourg every day. Uncle always sits under the third tree on the left along the terrace, you know . . . near the newspaper kiosk. The Blue Prince used to sit under the fourth tree and read. Every time he turned the page he used to smile at me.

THÉRÈSE. Is that all?

SUZANNE. Yes. That's all that happened in the Luxembourg. Oh, but no, I was forgetting. One day he saved me from a hoop. A little girl was bowling it full tilt at me. He knocked it hard to make it go the other way. That made me smile. I thought of lovers who hurled themselves at the heads of runaway horses. The same idea must have struck him as he began to smile too when he bowed to me.

THÉRÈSE. And that is the end of the story?

SUZANNE. Oh no, that's where it begins. The day before yesterday Uncle went out and left me all alone with Hortense. She's such a boring thing, so to amuse myself I set up the big telescope—you remember the one Uncle had at Vernon? You can see more than five miles through it. From our roof we can see quite a lot of Paris, you know. I was looking in the direction of Saint Sulpice. There are some very fine statues at the foot of the large tower.

MICHAUD [testily to GRIVET]. Come, come, now, six. Hurry up.

GRIVET. A six . . . a six . . . I know, I know. Heavens alive. I must work it out.

[Game continues.]

THÉRÈSE. And the Blue Prince?

SUZANNE. Don't be impatient! I saw chimneys—chimneys —scores of them—oceans of them. When I moved the telescope a bit they looked like regiments of soldiers, marching at the double and bumping into one another. The whole telescope was full of them. Suddenly, between two chimney pots—whom do you think I saw? The Blue Prince.

THÉRÈSE. Oh, so he's a chimney sweep then?

SUZANNE. No, no, of course not. He was on the roof, the same as I was. And the funny thing is that he was looking through a telescope too. I recognized him at once, with his blue suit and his moustache . . .

THÉRÈSE. And where does he live?

SUZANNE. I don't know. I only saw him through the telescope, you see. It was certainly a long way away— very long . . . in the direction of Saint Sulpice. When I looked only with my eyes and not through the telescope, it all looked grey except for the blue of the slate roofs. I very nearly lost him too. The telescope moved and I had to do that awful journey over the chimney pots again. Now I've got a bearing—the weathercock on a house near ours.

THÉRÈSE. Have you seen him again?

SUZANNE. Yes—yesterday—today—every day! Is it wrong of me? If you knew how sweet he looks through the telescope . . . not much taller than this. Like a little china figure. I'm not a bit afraid of him. But I don't know if he's real—or just something one sees through the telescope. It's all so far away. When he does this— [*Blows a kiss.*] I draw back and then I see nothing but grey. So perhaps he never did this— [*Blows kiss.*] And then I can't see him there any longer, however hard I stare.

THÉRÈSE. You're very sweet. [*Looking at* LAURENT.] But keep him in your heart . . . forever as a Dream Prince.

SUZANNE. Oh . . . No! Sh—they've finished their game.

MICHAUD. We've beaten you, Monsieur Grivet.

GRIVET. Yes, sir, you are the better man!

[*They shuffle the dominoes.*]

MME. RAQUIN [*pushing her armchair back*]. Laurent, as you are up, will you get my basket that I keep my wool in? It should be on the chest of drawers in my room. Take a light.

LAURENT. No, I don't need one. [*Goes out through door at back.*]

MICHAUD [*to* MME. RAQUIN]. You have a real son there. He's so kind.

MME. RAQUIN. Yes, he's very good to us. I give him little jobs to do and in the evening he helps me to shut up shop.

GRIVET. The other day I saw him selling some needles like a shopgirl. He, he, he! A shopgirl with a beard! [*Laughs.*]

[*Enter* LAURENT *quickly, his eyes full of terror, as if he were being pursued: for a moment he leans against the wardrobe.*]

MME. RAQUIN. Why, whatever's the matter?

MICHAUD [*rising*]. Are you ill?

GRIVET. Did you bump into something?

LAURENT. It's nothing. It's . . . My eyes are dazzled, that's all! [*Pulling himself together slightly.*]

MME. RAQUIN. And my workbasket?

LAURENT. The basket. . . . I don't know . . . I didn't get it.

SUZANNE. What! You, a man and afraid?

LAURENT [*trying to laugh*]. Afraid? Of what? I just didn't find the basket, that's all.

SUZANNE. Just a minute, I'll find it. And if I meet your ghost I'll bring him down to you. [*Exit.*]

LAURENT [*almost normal*]. I'm sorry. I'm all right now.

GRIVET. It's the blood. You're too healthy!

LAURENT [*shivering*]. Yes, the blood.

MICHAUD. You need some cooling medicine.

MME. RAQUIN. As a matter of fact I've noticed you haven't been looking well for some time. I'll make you a tisane. [*Enter* SUZANNE *with basket.*] Ah, so you found it!

SUZANNE. It was on the chest of drawers. [*To* LAURENT.] I didn't see your ghost, Monsieur Laurent. I expect I frightened him.

GRIVET. She's a young caution, that child.

[*Shop bell rings.*]

SUZANNE. Don't worry, I'll see to it. [*Goes downstairs.*]

GRIVET. A treasure—a real treasure. [*To* MICHAUD.] We agree that I have thirty-two and you twenty-eight.

MME. RAQUIN [*after searching in basket which she puts on mantelshelf*]. There now! I haven't got the wool I wanted. I shall have to go down to the shop. [*She goes downstairs.*]

GRIVET [*to* MICHAUD]. Well, the game was nearly ruined just now. It's not such fun here as it used to be.

MICHAUD. Can you wonder? When death strikes a house
. . . But cheer up! I've discovered a way to get our
good old Thursdays back again.

[*They start a new game.*]

THÈRÉSE [*in a low voice, to* LAURENT, *who has come close
to her*]. You're afraid, aren't you?

LAURENT. Yes. Shall I come to you tonight?

THÈRÉSE. We must be discreet. We mustn't. make any
mistake.

LAURENT. A whole year we've been discreet—a whole
year I have never had you to myself. It would be so
easy—I'd come in by the little door. We are free now.
We shouldn't be afraid if we were together now in
your room.

THÈRÉSE. No, don't let us spoil the future. We need so
much happiness. Shall we ever have enough!

LAURENT. You must have faith. There will be peace
when we are in each other's arms. We shan't be frightened when we are together. When shall I come?

THÈRÉSE. On our wedding night. It won't be long now
—you'll see. Be careful. My aunt is coming back.

MME. RAQUIN [*enters. To* THÉRÈSE.] Thérèse, dear, go
down, will you? You are wanted down there.

[THÉRÈSE *goes wearily downstairs; they all watch her as
she goes.*]

MICHAUD. Have you noticed Thérèse—how pale she
looks? She can hardly hold up her head.

MME. RAQUIN. Yes. It's the same all day long. Her eyes
are sunken and her hands tremble.

LAURENT. Yes, and she has that consumptive color in
her cheeks.

MME. RAQUIN. Yes. You noticed that first, Laurent,
dear. Now I see it getting worse. It seems I'm to be
spared nothing.

MICHAUD. Rubbish! You're upsetting yourself without
any reason. It's nerves. She'll get over it.

LAURENT. No. She has been struck to the heart. Those
long silences—that sad smile. It's as if she is saying

good-bye to us. She will gradually fade away.

GRIVET. My dear man, you're not very comforting. You ought to liven her up a bit instead of piling up the gloom.

MME. RAQUIN. No, he's right. The sickness is in her heart. She doesn't want to be consoled. Every time I try to make her see reason she gets impatient—angry, even. She shuts herself away like a wounded animal.

LAURENT. We shall have to resign ourselves to it.

MME. RAQUIN. That would be the last blow. She is all I have now. I was hoping she would be there at the end to close my eyes. If she went I'd be all alone here, and I'd die in some corner alone. I'm so unhappy. I don't know what's come to this house.

GRIVET [timidly]. So we're not playing any more?

MICHAUD. Wait a minute now—dash it all. [Rises.] I want to try and find a remedy for all this. At Thérèse's age—good heavens!—one is not inconsolable. Did she cry much on the night of the tragedy at Saint-Ouen?

MME. RAQUIN. No, she doesn't cry easily. It was a kind of dumb grief, as if her mind and body were utterly exhausted. She seemed stupefied. She has become very nervous.

LAURENT [trembling]. Nervous?

MME. RAQUIN. Yes. One night— [To LAURENT.] I never told you this before—I heard stifled sobbing and of course I came down to her—she didn't recognize me. She was muttering . . .

LAURENT. It was a nightmare . . . Did she say anything? What did she say?

MME. RAQUIN. I couldn't understand. She was calling Camille. She is afraid to come in here any more after dark without a light. In the mornings she is utterly tired out—she drags herself about. It breaks my heart, it does really. I am certain she is leaving us, that she wants to be with that other poor child of mine again.

MICHAUD. Yes, yes. Well, Madame, I have finished my inquiry and now I'll tell you precisely what I think. But first of all, I'd like you all to leave us.

LAURENT. You want to be alone with Madame Raquin?

MICHAUD. Yes.

GRIVET [*rising to go*]. Very well, all right. We'll leave you. [*Comes back.*] You know you owe me two, Monsieur Michaud. Give me a call when you are ready.

[LAURENT *and* GRIVET *go out through door at back.*]

MICHAUD. Now, Madame, I'm a blunt man.

MME. RAQUIN. If only we could save her! What is your advice?

MICHAUD [*lowering his voice*]. Thérèse must be married.

MME. RAQUIN. Married! Oh, but you are cruel! It would be like losing my Camille a second time.

MICHAUD. But I mean it. I face facts. I'm a doctor if you like.

MME. RAQUIN. No, no, it's impossible. You see what a state she's in. She'd hate the idea. She hasn't forgotten my dear boy. It isn't very nice of you to suggest it, Michaud. Camille is still her husband, in her heart. She couldn't marry. It would be sacrilege.

MICHAUD. Big words, Madame. I only know that when a woman is afraid to go to her room at night, it's a husband she needs.

MME. RAQUIN. And how about the stranger we should be bringing into our home? I am old—it would worry me. We might make a bad choice, and that would spoil any chance of peace we have left. No, no! I'd rather die while we still mourn our dear boy. [*Sits in armchair.*]

MICHAUD. Naturally we'd have to look for a decent man who would be a good husband for Thérèse—and a good son to you . . . someone who would take Camille's place. . . . Laurent.

MME. RAQUIN. Laurent?

MICHAUD. Why, yes! What a splendid pair they'd make.

My dear old friend, this is my advice. Get them married.

MME. RAQUIN. Laurent and Thérèse.

MICHAUD. I knew I was going to surprise you! I've been cherishing the plan for some time now. Think it over and trust my long experience. If you decide to see Thérèse marry again—and don't forget it will bring you some happiness in your old age and it will cure her of this sickness that is killing her—well, where could you find a better husband for her than Laurent?

MME. RAQUIN. I looked on them as brother and sister.

MICHAUD. But think of yourself. I want you all to be happy. I want the old days back again. You will have two children to close your eyes.

MME. RAQUIN. You know, you're almost persuading me. You're right, I do need a little comfort. But I am afraid we'd be doing wrong. No, no. Camille would punish us for forgetting him so soon.

MICHAUD. Who said anything about forgetting? Laurent is always talking about him. Dash it all, it will still be a family affair.

MME. RAQUIN. I am old . . . I even find it difficult to move about now. I only ask to die in peace.

MICHAUD. That's right now. I've persuaded you. It's the only way to avoid bringing a stranger into the home. And I hope it won't be long before you're dandling your grandchildren on your knee. Ah, you're smiling. I knew I should make you smile.

MME. RAQUIN. Oh, it's wrong . . . wrong of me to smile. I'm still very troubled about it. But they'll never agree. They've never thought of such a thing.

MICHAUD. Rubbish! We're going to manage this properly. They're too sensible not to see that their marriage is necessary for this household's happiness. That's the line to take . . . the household's happiness. I'll settle with Laurent while we're shutting up the

shop together . . . and I'll call Thérèse up to you.
We'll announce the engagement this evening.

[THÉRÈSE *enters looking utterly dejected.*]

MME. RAQUIN. What's the matter, my child? You have
not spoken a word the whole evening. Do—do try
not to be so unhappy—for the sake of our friends.
[THÉRÈSE *gives a vague gesture.*] I know we can't always control our grief . . . Are you feeling ill?

THÉRÈSE. No, I'm just very tired.

MME. RAQUIN. You must tell me if you're not well. If
you're ill we must look after you. Is it your heart perhaps—or your chest?

THÉRÈSE. No . . . I don't know . . . there's nothing the
matter. It's just that everything in me seems—seems
numb.

MME. RAQUIN. My dear, dear, child. It hurts me so much
that you're so silent . . . so alone. You are all I have.

THÉRÈSE. You . . . you tell me to forget?

MME. RAQUIN. No, I didn't say that. I couldn't say that.
But I've a right to ask these questions. I must not
force my grief on you. And it's my duty to try and
find out how to console you. Now, answer me frankly.

THÉRÈSE. I'm very tired.

MME. RAQUIN. I want you to answer me. You live too
much alone . . . you're moping. It's not natural to
grieve forever at your age.

THÉRÈSE. What are you trying to tell me?

MME. RAQUIN. Nothing, dear. I'm only trying to find out
what's wrong. I know that it can't be very cheerful,
living with a sad old woman. And then this house . . .
so dismal and dark. Perhaps you would like. . . .

THÉRÈSE. I don't want anything.

MME. RAQUIN. Now listen, dear. Don't be cross with me,
but we've had a sort of idea . . . perhaps it's stupid
. . . but we thought of getting you married again.

THÉRÈSE. Married? Me? Oh, never, never. Don't you
trust me?

MME. RAQUIN [*very moved*]. That's what I told them. I

said that you had never fogotten my boy . . . that he was always in your heart. They made me do it. Yes, you know, they're right, my child. The house is too sad. No one comes here. Now, now. It would do no harm to think over what they say.

THÉRÈSE. No.

MME. RAQUIN. Yes, yes. You should marry again. I can't remember what Michaud said to convince me . . . but I agreed with him . . . and I said I would try and persuade you. Now, if you like, I'll call him. He'll know what to say better than I do.

THÉRÈSE. Can't you leave me in peace! No, my heart is dead to all that. Me marry! Heavens above! And who is the man?

MME. RAQUIN. Well, they had a splendid idea—they thought of someone. Michaud is downstairs now—talking to Laurent. . . .

THÉRÈSE. Laurent—so you thought of Laurent! But I don't love him—I don't want to love him!

MME. RAQUIN. But they're right—really they are. I quite agree with them. Laurent is like one of the family . . . you know how kind he is . . . what a help he has been to us. I felt the same as you did when they first suggested it. It didn't seem right somehow. But when I thought it over it seemed to me that you'd be less unfaithful to our beloved's memory if you married his friend . . . the friend who saved your life.

THÉRÈSE. But . . . I'm still mourning for him. I want to go on mourning for him.

MME. RAQUIN. I know, but you must stop. I will and so must you. You see, they want us to be happy. They said it would give me two children—that it would give me comfort and happiness in my last days. I'm being selfish, you see. I want to see you smile. Say you will, dear . . . do it for me.

THÉRÈSE. My only wish has been to please you—you know that.

MME. RAQUIN. Yes, you are a good girl. [*Trying to*

smile.] It will make my last years happy. We will make a new warm life for ourselves. Laurent will love us both. I will share him with you. You will lend him to me sometimes to help a stupid old woman.

THÉRÈSE. My dear, dear Aunt. But all the same, I wish you had left me alone with my heartache.

MME. RAQUIN. That means you will do it?

THÉRÈSE. Yes.

MME. RAQUIN [*very moved*]. Thank you, my child. You have made me so happy. [*Falls into armchair by table.*] Oh, my son, my poor son and I was the first to betray you!

MICHAUD [*enters*]. Well, I've persuaded him, but my word! I had a bit of difficulty. He's doing it for your sake. I begged him to do it for you. He's just coming up. He's putting the screws in the shutters. And Thérèse?

MME. RAQUIN. Yes, she agrees.

[MICHAUD *goes to* THÉRÈSE *and talks quietly to her.*]

SUZANNE [*enters, followed by* GRIVET]. No, no, Monsieur Grivet, you're a conceited man. I won't dance with you at the wedding. Now then, tell me the truth. You've never got married in case it interferes with your little ways, eh?

GRIVET. You've hit the nail on the head, my dear.

SUZANNE. What a dreadful man! Now, you understand, not one step do I dance with you at the wedding. [*Goes to join* THÉRÈSE *and* MICHAUD.]

GRIVET. All these young girls think it's fun to get married. I've tried to do it five times . . . [*To* MME. RAQUIN.] . . . the last time to a schoolteacher. The banns were published and everything went well until she told me she liked coffee in the mornings. [*Disgusted.*] Coffee! I can't bear coffee. For thirty years I have had chocolate. It would have ruined my whole life. So I broke it off. I was right . . . don't you think so?

MME. RAQUIN [*smiling*]. Most certainly.

GRIVET. It's a good thing when people get on together. And Michaud saw at once that Thérèse and Laurent were made for one another.

MME. RAQUIN [*seriously*]. You're right, my friend.

GRIVET. You remember the old song—
"When a well-matched pair is wed
 Happy is the marriage bed."
[*Looks at watch.*] Good gracious! A quarter to eleven! [*Sits down, puts on his galoshes and takes his umbrella.*]

LAURENT [*having just come up from the shop, goes to* MME. RAQUIN]. Monsieur Michaud and I have just been talking about your happiness. Your children are longing to make you happy—dear Mother.

MME. RAQUIN [*very moved*]. Yes, Laurent dear, call me your Mother.

LAURENT. Thérèse, are you willing to make our Mother happy?

THÉRÈSE. Yes. It is our duty.

MME. RAQUIN. My children. [*Takes the hands of both in her own.*] Marry her, Laurent. Make her less unhappy and Camille will thank you. You have made me very happy. All that I ask is that Heaven will not punish us for it.

ACT THREE.

The time is 3 o'clock in the morning. The fire is glowing and the lamp is lit. The room is decked in white—white bed curtains, and lace-trimmed bedspread, lace antimacassars on the chairbacks. There are flowers everywhere—on the sideboard, on the mantelpiece and on the table.

As the curtain rises THÉRÈSE, MME. RAQUIN *and* SUZANNE *come in through the door at the back. They are dressed in their wedding clothes.* MME. RAQUIN *and* SUZANNE *are not wearing their hats or shawls.* THÉRÈSE *is in grey silk. She goes wearily to sit* L. SUZANNE *remains for a moment at the door for a little tussle with* GRIVET *and* MICHAUD *who are attempting to follow the ladies.*

SUZANNE. No, no, Uncle! Monsieur Grivet—no! You are not coming into the bride's room. It's not proper. [MICHAUD *and* GRIVET *ignore her protests and enter.*]

MICHAUD [*in an undertone to* SUZANNE]. Keep quiet, it's a joke [*To* GRIVET.] Have you got the nettles?

GRIVET. Yes, of course. I've had them all day long—in my jacket pocket. It was beastly uncomfortable in church and in the restaurant. [*He goes furtively to the bed.*]

MME. RAQUIN. Now then, gentlemen, you can't stay in here, while we are undressing the bride.

MICHAUD. Undressing the bride! What a delightful idea! If you need any help I daresay we could be of use. [*Joins* GRIVET.]

SUZANNE. I've never seen Uncle so jolly. He was as red as a beetroot by the end of dinner.

MME. RAQUIN. Let them have their little joke; we can

forgive it on a wedding night. There was always plenty of fun at Vernon. They couldn't get a wink of sleep all night, the poor bridal couples.

GRIVET [*by the bed*]. My word, this bed is comfortable. Monsieur Michaud, just feel it.

MICHAUD. By Jove, there must be three mattresses on it, at least. [*In an undertone.*] Have you put the nettles in?

GRIVET. Right in the middle.

MICHAUD [*roaring with laughter*]. You're a real old comic and no mistake!

GRIVET [*laughing*]. We managed it well, didn't we!

MME. RAQUIN [*smiling*]. You are keeping the bride waiting, gentlemen.

SUZANNE. Aren't you two ever going—making a nuisance of yourselves!

MICHAUD. All right, all right, we're going.

GRIVET [*to* THÉRÈSE]. Good night, Madame—and our congratulations.

THÉRÈSE [*rising and then sitting again*]. Thank you both.

GRIVET [*shaking* MME. RAQUIN's *hand as he leaves*]. You're not angry with us, are you?

MME. RAQUIN. How could I be angry with old friends and on a wedding night?

[*Exeunt* MICHAUD *and* GRIVET.]

SUZANNE [*calling after them*]. Now, don't come back. The bridegroom is the only one who has the right to come in—and then only when we let him.

MME. RAQUIN [*to* THÉRÈSE]. You must get undressed, Thérèse. It's nearly three o'clock.

[THÉRÈSE *is in chair below fireplace,* MME. RAQUIN *on sofa facing fire and* SUZANNE *on hearthrug.*]

THÉRÈSE. I'm worn out. The ceremony, then the drive and then that never-ending dinner. Let me be—just for a little, please.

SUZANNE. Yes, it was hot in that restaurant. It gave me a headache, but I felt better when I was in the cab.

[*To* MME. RAQUIN.] But it's you who ought to feel tired—with your poor legs. You know the doctor said you are not to do too much.

MME. RAQUIN. He said a severe shock might be fatal, that's all. But today I have been calm and happy. Everything went off very well, I think—don't you? Just right.

SUZANNE. The mayor was most mayor-like. When he started to read from his little red book, the bridegroom hung his head. Monsieur Grivet's signature on the register was magnificent.

MME. RAQUIN. The priest was very moving in church.

SUZANNE. Oh, everyone was crying. I kept my eye on Thérèse. She didn't look much like laughing either. But what heaps of people there were on the boulevards in the afternoon. We went from the Madeleine to the Bastille twice. The people were quite amused at us. Half of the wedding party were asleep by the time we got to that Batignolles restaurant. [*Laughs.*]

MME. RAQUIN. Thérèse, you ought to get undressed, my child.

THÉRÈSE. In a minute. Go on talking.

SUZANNE. I know—shall I be your lady's maid? Do let me—then you won't tire yourself.

MME. RAQUIN. Give me her hat. [*Takes it and puts it in wardrobe.*]

SUZANNE. There, you see, there's no need for you to move. Oh, but you'll have to stand up for me to take off your dress.

THÉRÈSE [*standing*]. You do bully me, don't you?

MME. RAQUIN. It's late, my child.

SUZANNE [*unhooking dress*]. A husband—oh, it must be awful. A friend of mine who got married simply cried and cried—you hardly pull yourself in at all and your waist is quite small. You're right to wear your bodices rather long. Oh dear, that was a pin. It's very firmly fixed. I ought to go and get Monsieur Grivet to help. [*Giggles.*]

THÉRÈSE. I'm shivering. Hurry up, dear.

SUZANNE. We'll go over by the fire. [*They both cross to fire.*] Oh, look, there's a stain on the flounce. It's simply lovely, this silk. It would stand alone. But how nervous you are, darling. I can feel you trembling when I touch you—like Thisbe when I tickle her. Thisbe's the cat Uncle gave me. But I'll be careful. I won't tickle you.

THÉRÈSE. I think I—I think it's a cold coming.

SUZANNE. There now—the last hook—I've finished. [*Takes off dress and hands it to* MME. RAQUIN.] Now I'll do your hair for the night, shall I?

MME. RAQUIN. Yes, that's right. [*Goes out with dress through door at back.*]

SUZANNE [*after seating* THÉRÈSE *by the fire*]. There, now you have a nice rosy face. You were as pale as a ghost.

THÉRÈSE. It's the firelight.

SUZANNE [*behind her, taking down her hair*]. Put your head down a bit. What lovely hair you have. Tell me—I want to ask you a question—I'm afraid I'm very inquisitive—You are trembling and it is because your heart is beating so hard—that's it, isn't it?

THÉRÈSE. My heart isn't seventeen years old, like yours, my dear.

SUZANNE. I'm not being a nuisance, am I? All day long I've been thinking that if I were in your place I should be such a silly little stupid. So I decided that I'd watch you and see how you got ready for your wedding night. Then perhaps I wouldn't seem so stupid when my turn comes. You are a little sad—but you are not afraid. I'm so frightened that I should sob my heart out.

THÉRÈSE. Is the Blue Prince so terrible then?

SUZANNE. Oh, don't laugh at me! It suits you to have your hair down. You look like a queen in a picture book—I don't think plaits, do you? I'll just roll it up in your neck.

THÉRÈSE. Just tie it back.

[MME. RAQUIN *returns and takes a white dressing gown from the wardrobe.*]

SUZANNE. If you promise not to laugh at me, I'll tell you what I should be feeling in your place. I should be happy—oh, happier than I have ever been in my life. And yet, at the same time, I should be terribly frightened. It would be like walking above the clouds—in Heaven—and coming to a strange place—a beautiful place, but terrifying—with the loveliest music and the most exquisite flowers. And in that dazzling light I should go forward, drawn on in spite of myself, by a joy so thrilling that it would seem as if I must die of it. Is that how you feel?

THÉRÈSE [*almost whispering*]. Yes. Music—flowers—a great light—all the springtime of youth and love.

SUZANNE. You're still shivering.

THÉRÈSE. I have caught cold. I can't get warm.

MME. RAQUIN [*goes to sit by fire*]. I'm going to warm your dressing gown. [*Holds the dressing gown to the fire.*]

SUZANNE. And while the Blue Prince was waiting—just as Monsieur Laurent is waiting now—I should take a wicked delight in making him impatient. Then, when he was at the door, I shouldn't be able to think any more. I'd want to run away so that he couldn't find me. And then—I don't know—I'm dizzy when I think of it.

MME. RAQUIN [*smiling as she turns the dressing gown*]. Then don't think of it. Children think of nothing but dolls, flowers, and husbands.

THÉRÈSE. Life is harsher than that.

SUZANNE [*to* THÉRÈSE]. But isn't that how you feel?

THÉRÈSE. Yes. [*Quietly.*] I could have wished that it was not in winter—and in this room. In Vernon, in May, the acacias are in bloom, and the nights are warm.

SUZANNE. Now your hair is done—Now put on your nice warm dressing gown.

[THÉRÈSE *and* MME. RAQUIN *rise.*]

MME. RAQUIN [*helping* THÉRÈSE *to put on dressing gown*]. It is burning my hands.

SUZANNE. I do hope you're not cold any longer.

THÉRÈSE. No, thank you.

SUZANNE. Oh, how nice you look. You're like a real bride now—all that lace!

MME. RAQUIN. Now we're going to leave you alone, my child.

THÉRÈSE. No, not alone! Wait a moment. I think there's something else . . .

MME. RAQUIN. No, don't say anything. I haven't let myself speak. You must have noticed. I didn't want to upset you. If you knew what an effort it has been! All day my heart has been full and yet I'm happy in spite of it. We must put away the past. You saw how cheerful Michaud was. We must be cheerful too.

THÉRÈSE. Yes. You are right. I'm being stupid. Good night.

MME. RAQUIN. Good night. [*Turning back.*] Tell me— are you troubled about anything? Is there anything distressing you that you're keeping from me? It's the thought that we've been working for your happiness that has helped me to bear this. Love your husband. He deserves nothing but love and affection from both of us. Love him as you loved . . . No, I won't say that. I don't want to say that. We have done our best and I wish you great happiness, my child, in return for all the comfort you are to me.

SUZANNE. Poor Thérèse—Anyone would think you were leaving her with a pack of wolves in a nasty dark cave. Well, the cave smells very nice. Roses everywhere. Just a lovely nest.

THÉRÈSE. The flowers must have cost a lot. It was very naughty of you.

MME. RAQUIN. I know how much you love the spring. I wanted you to have a bit of it in your room on your wedding night. You can imagine you are in Suzanne's dream—in the clouds—in Heaven. There now, you are smiling. Be happy among your flowers. Good night, my child. [*Kisses her.*]

SUZANNE. Aren't you going to kiss me too, darling? [THÉRÈSE *kisses her.*]

There now you are quite pale again. [*Looks round the room as she goes out.*] A room like this—all flowers—it's thrilling.

[THÉRÈSE *is left alone and she goes slowly back to sit by the fire.* LAURENT, *still in his wedding suit, comes quietly into the room, closes the door and walks with an uneasy air.*]

LAURENT. Thérèse, my darling . . .

THÉRÈSE [*pushing him away*]. No, not yet—I'm cold.

LAURENT [*after a pause*]. At last we're alone, Thérèse, my Thérèse. They've all gone and we're free to love each other. Our life is our own, this is our room and you are mine—my dear wife,—because I've won you —and you wanted me to win you. [*Tries to kiss her.*]

THÉRÈSE [*pushing him away*]. No—presently—I'm shivering with cold.

LAURENT. My poor darling! Give me your feet. I'll warm them in my hands. [*Kneels before her and tries to take her feet, but she draws them away.*] The time has come at last—do you realize? Think of it! We have been waiting a whole year for today—working for it for a whole year. We have earned it, haven't we? It's worth all we have suffered. We have had to be so careful but now we have got our reward for it all.

THÉRÈSE. Yes, I've thought of it. Don't stay down there. Sit down for a while. Let's just talk for a bit.

LAURENT [*getting up*]. Why are you trembling? The door is shut and I am your husband. You didn't tremble when I used to come in the old days—you laughed and you used to talk so loudly that people might have heard us. Now you are talking so quietly, just as if someone is listening on the other side of the wall. Why, now we can talk as loudly as we like, and laugh and make love. No one is going to disturb us, this is our wedding night.

THÉRÈSE [*in terror*]. Don't say that—don't say it. You are pale too, Laurent, paler than I am. You are just talking for the sake of saying something. Don't pretend to be brave. Why, we haven't the courage to kiss yet. You're afraid you would look a fool if you didn't kiss me, aren't you! So silly! We're not ordinary married people . . . Sit down . . . let's talk about something. [*He goes behind her and leans against the mantelpiece. She changes her tone, speaking in a domestic, detached tone.*] The wind has been very high today.

LAURENT. Yes, and very cold too. It went down a bit this afternoon.

THÉRÈSE. Some of the women's dresses on the boulevards . . . oh well . . . It is to be hoped that the apricot trees will be late in flowering this year—

LAURENT. Frost in March is bad for the fruit trees. You remember—in Vernon . . . [*He stops and both are silent in thought.*]

THÉRÈSE [*quietly*]. Vernon . . . I was a little girl . . . [*Resumes her domestic, detached tone.*] Put a log on the fire. It's quite nice here now. Is it four o'clock yet, do you think?

LAURENT [*looking at clock*]. No, not yet. [*Goes and sits at other end of room.*]

THÉRÈSE. It's extraordinary how long the night is! Are you the same as I am? I don't like being in a cab very much. Driving about for hours is the stupidest thing. It makes me sleepy. And I hate meals in restaurants too.

LAURENT. There's nothing like home cooking.

THÉRÈSE. I wouldn't say that in the country.

LAURENT. No. But there are very good things to eat in the country. Do you remember . . . the little inns by the river . . . ?

THÉRÈSE. Be quiet; Why do you wake those memories? I hear them hammering in your head—I hear them hammering in my own—and then we begin to go over the whole ghastly story again. Don't let's talk any more. We mustn't think any more. Behind all your words I hear other words. While you're talking, I hear what you're thinking. You'd got as far as the accident, hadn't you? Don't talk any more. [*Pause.*]

LAURENT. Thérèse, say something—please. I can't bear this silence. Talk to me.

THÉRÈSE [*sitting down, her hands pressed to her head*]. Shut your eyes. Try to think of nothing.

LAURENT. No. I want to hear the sound of your voice. Say something to me—anything—as you did before—that the weather is bad, the night is long . . .

THÉRÈSE. Even then I think. I can't *not* think. But you're right. Silence is not good and I feel I must go on talking. [*Tries to smile and speaks in a gay manner.*] The Mairie was freezing this morning. My feet were like ice. But I warmed them over the grating in church. Did you see the grating? It was close to where we knelt down.

LAURENT. Yes. Grivet planted himself on top of it the whole of the service. He looked triumphant, the old devil—He was very funny, wasn't he?

[*They both try to laugh.*]

THÉRÈSE. The church was rather dark; it was the weather. Did you notice the lace on the altar cloth? It must have cost ten francs a meter at least. There's nothing so good in the shop. The smell of the incense made me feel ill—so sweet. At first I thought we were the only people there in that great empty church and I was glad. [*Her voice becomes more serious.*] Then I heard chanting . . . You must have seen—in a chapel on the other side of the nave . . . ?

LAURENT [*reluctantly*]. I thought I saw people with tapers.

THÉRÈSE [*in growing terror*]. It was a funeral. When I

raised my eyes I saw the black pall with a great white cross. [*Rises and recoils.*] The coffin passed quite close to us. I saw it. A little narrow shabby coffin, so sordid and miserable. Some poor creature. [*She has reached* LAURENT *and falls on his shoulder. They are both trembling. Then pulling herself together she speaks in a low and urgent voice.*] When you went to the Morgue, you saw him?

LAURENT. Yes.

THÉRÈSE. Did he look as if he had suffered much?

LAURENT. Horribly.

THÉRÈSE. His eyes were open and he was looking at you, wasn't he?

LAURENT. Yes. He was dreadful—blue and bloated with the water. And he was grinning—the corner of his mouth was twisted.

THÉRÈSE. Grinning, was he? Tell me . . . tell me everything . . . tell me how he. . . . On the nights when I couldn't sleep I could never see him clearly and I must. I must see him.

LAURENT [*loudly and shaking* THÉRÈSE]. Be quiet. Wake up, I tell you, wake up. We're both asleep. What was it you were saying to me? If I answered you, I was lying. I saw nothing—nothing—nothing. What fool of a game are we playing, the two of us!

THÉRÈSE. I knew the words would break out of us, in spite of ourselves. Everything has been leading us to it—the apricot trees in flower—the little inns by the river—the miserable coffin. We shall never be able to talk of ordinary things again. He is there, behind all our thoughts.

LAURENT. Kiss me . . .

THÉRÈSE. All the time I knew perfectly well that you were only talking about him—that I was only talking about him. We can't help it. The frightful thing has been going round and round in our minds and now it's out.

LAURENT [*trying to take her in his arms*]. Thérèse, kiss

me. It will make us sane again. That's why we're
married—so that we can find peace in each other's
arms. Kiss me and let us forget, my dear, dear wife.

THÉRÈSE [*pushing him away*]. Please—no—not yet. Comfort me. Be kind to me. Be as you used to be.

[*A pause, and then* LAURENT, *as if struck by a sudden
idea, goes out through door at back.*]

THÉRÈSE [*alone*]. He has gone—I'm alone—Laurent,
don't leave me. I belong to you. He has gone and now
I am alone. I think the lamp is going out—If it goes
out—if I am left in the dark—I don't want to be
alone—I don't want to be in the dark—Why wouldn't
I let him kiss me? I don't know what was the matter
with me—my lips were like ice—I felt that if he
kissed me I should die. Where can he have gone?
[*There is a knock on the little door.*] Oh God—he's
come back—the other—he's come back for my wedding night. Can't you hear him! He's knocking on
the bed—he's calling from my pillow—Go away—I'm
afraid. [*She is trembling, her hands over her eyes,
then slowly she becomes calmer and smiles.*] No, it
is not that one, it is my own dear love, my love of
the old days. It was a beautiful thought, Laurent
darling. Thank you. I remember your signal. [*She
opens the door to* LAURENT. *They repeat their actions
in the corresponding scene in Act I.*] You, my dear
one. I knew you would come. I was sure of it. I was
thinking of you. It is so long since I had you alone—
to myself, like this.

LAURENT. Do you remember—I couldn't sleep because
of you. And I used to dream when we should be together for always. Tonight, beloved, that dream has
come true—You are here—in my arms—for ever.

THÉRÈSE. The sun will always shine for us—

LAURENT. Kiss me, my wife.

THÉRÈSE [*breaking away*]. No, no. What's the use of
pretending? We're not in love any longer. We have
killed love. Don't you know that I can feel you are

frozen even in my arms? Let us talk calmly now. We can't go on like this—it wouldn't be decent.

LAURENT. You belong to me and I will keep you. And I'll get rid of those fears of yours. It would be cruel if we didn't love one another any longer—if the happiness we dreamed of were a nightmare. My darling . . . put your arms round me.

THÉRÈSE. No, that's asking for sorrow.

LAURENT. Can't you see how absurd it is—to spend the night like this after all those times when we risked so much. No one will come in.

THÉRÈSE [in terror]. You have said that before—don't say it again. I beg of you. Perhaps he might come. [Struggling.] Our kisses would draw him here. I'm afraid, I tell you, afraid.

[LAURENT goes to take her in his arms when he catches sight of Camille's portrait which hangs over the sideboard.]

LAURENT [recoiling in terror and pointing to portrait]. There—there—Camille—

THÉRÈSE [quickly placing herself behind him]. I told you—I felt something cold behind me—Where can you see him?

LAURENT. There—in the shadows.

THÉRÈSE. Behind the bed?

LAURENT. No—to the right. He's not moving. He's looking at us—all the time looking at us. He's just the same as when I saw him—pale, all covered with mud —and with that crooked smile.

THÉRÈSE [watching]. But it is his portrait you are looking at.

LAURENT. His portrait?

THÉRÈSE. Yes, the one you painted, don't you remember?

LAURENT. No—I don't know—it is his portrait, you think? I saw the eyes move—wait a minute—they're moving again. His portrait? All right—take it down.

He is annoying me, staring at us like that.

THÉRÈSE. No, I dare not.

LAURENT. Please—take it down.

THÉRÈSE. No.

LAURENT. We'll put it face to the wall then we won't be afraid any more and perhaps we will be able to love each other.

THÉRÈSE. Why don't you take it down?

LAURENT. Because his eyes never leave me. I tell you, his eyes are moving—They are following me about—they won't leave me alone . . . [*Slowly going nearer.*] I shall keep my head down and if I can't see him any longer . . . [*He takes down the picture with a gesture of fury.*]

[*The door opens and* MME. RAQUIN *appears on the threshold.*]

MME. RAQUIN. What is the matter? I heard someone call out.

LAURENT [*unable to take his eyes from the portrait which he is still holding*]. It is horrible—There he is —just as when we threw him into the river.

MME. RAQUIN. Oh, my God—they killed my child.

[THÉRÈSE *in despair gives a scream of terror.* LAURENT *throws the portrait on the bed in fright and recoils before* MME. RAQUIN.]

MME. RAQUIN [*muttering*]. Murderers—Murderers!

[*She staggers to the bed and on trying to hold on to the bed curtains she tears them down. A terrifying figure, she leans against the wall, breathing deeply. Her eyes never leave* LAURENT *who crosses and stands by* THÉRÈSE.]

LAURENT. The doctor warned her—a sudden shock—

MME. RAQUIN [*making a supreme effort she goes towards them*]. My boy—my poor child—wretches—wretches!

THÉRÈSE. It's horrible! She is all crooked . . . I'm afraid . . . I don't dare to go and help her . . .

MME. RAQUIN [*overcome, she falls into a chair*]. Oh, it's horrible . . . I can't . . . I can't . . .

[*She loses her power of speech and stiff in her chair she fixes* LAURENT *and* THÉRÈSE *with her eyes.*]

THÉRÈSE. She is dying.

LAURENT. No, her eyes are alive . . . they are threatening us . . . May God turn her lips and her arms to stone.

ACT FOUR.

It is 5 o'clock in the afternoon. Once more the room has taken on its atmosphere of darkness and damp. The curtains are dirty and the whole appearance is one of neglect. There is dust everywhere; dish cloths lie forgotten on chairs and piles of dirty crockery clutter up the furniture. A mattress has been rolled up and thrown behind one of the bed curtains. When the curtain rises THÉRÈSE *and* SUZANNE *are sewing at the work-table.*

THÉRÈSE. You have found out where the Blue Prince lives, at last, then! So it's not true, what people say, that love begets fools.

SUZANNE. I don't know about that but I'm quite bright at times. After a while, you know, it wasn't much fun seeing my Prince from a mile away and looking all the time so—so well-behaved. Between you and me, he was far too well-behaved.

THÉRÈSE. So you like bold, bad lovers!

SUZANNE. I'm not sure. It seems to me that a lover you're not afraid of isn't a proper lover at all. When I saw my Prince over there, against the sky, in the midst of the chimney-pots, I thought I was looking at one of those angels in my prayer-book, with clouds all round their feet. Pretty—but after a time, boring, you know. So, on my birthday I got Uncle to give me a map of Paris.

THÉRÈSE. A map of Paris?

SUZANNE. Yes. Uncle was rather surprised. As soon as I had the map I set very seriously to work. I drew lines with a ruler, then I measured with my compasses, and I added and multiplied. When I thought I had found the Prince's roof, I marked it with a pin. The next day I made Uncle go along the street where the house ought to be.

THÉRÈSE [*laughing*]. Dear Suzanne! What a nice little story. [*Looks at clock and in a sudden change of tone.*] Five o'clock already! Laurent will soon be home.

SUZANNE. Why, what's the matter? You were so happy a second ago.

THÉRÈSE [*recovering herself*]. And so you discovered the Blue Prince's house with your map?

SUZANNE. No—I did not. [*Sits on table.*] If you only knew where my map led me! One day it took me to a huge place that made floor polish—another day to a photographer's studio—and another to a school—or a prison, I don't know which. You're not laughing! And yet it's very funny. Aren't you well?

THÉRÈSE. Yes . . . yes . . . I was thinking that my husband would be coming. When you are married you must have this lucky map framed.

SUZANNE [*rising, passing behind* THÉRÈSE]. But I told you—it was no use. Weren't you listening? One afternoon I went to the Saint Sulpice flower market. I wanted some nasturtiums for the roof. Whom do you think I saw there? The Blue Prince! . . . loaded with flowers. Pots in his pockets, pots under his arms and pots in his hands. He looked so embarrassed when he caught sight of me. Then he followed me. He didn't know what to do with his pots. He told me they were for his roof. After that he became friendly with Uncle and asked for my hand and now I'm marrying him . . . So there you are! I made paper birds with the map and now I only look at the moon through the telescope. Have you been listening, darling?

THÉRÈSE. Yes, and it's a lovely fairy story. So now you

will live happily ever after, surrounded by everything that's gay and beautiful. Dear child, with
your bluebird—if you only knew ... [*Looks at clock.*]
Five o'clock. It is five o'clock, isn't it? I must lay the
table.

SUZANNE. I'll help you, I'll just move these things.
[THÉRÈSE *rises and* SUZANNE *helps her to lay the table
for three people.*] It is heartless of me, I know, to be
so cheerful when your happiness has been so spoiled.
How is poor Madame Raquin today?

THÉRÈSE. She still can't speak or move but I don't think
she suffers at all.

SUZANNE. The doctor did warn her that if she got over-
tired ... Oh, it's a cruel thing, paralysis. It's just as
if the poor old darling had been suddenly turned
into stone. When she's sitting in her chair, so rigid,
her white head so erect and her hands so pale, in her
lap, she makes me think of those terrifying statues
of mourning on the tombs in churches. I don't know
why, but it terrifies me. She can't raise her hands,
can she?

THÉRÈSE. Her hands and her legs are dead.

SUZANNE. How dreadful! Uncle says that she can't even
hear or understand. He thinks it would be a good
thing if her mind goes entirely.

THÉRÈSE. He's wrong. She can hear and understand
everything. Her mind is quite clear and her eyes are
alive.

SUZANNE. Yes, they seem to have got bigger; they are
enormous now. They are black now and terrible in
that dead-looking face. You know, I'm not a nervous
person and yet when I think about her in the night,
it makes me shudder. You know those stories about
people who have been buried alive? I can see her
there—in a grave—still alive and not able to call out
because of the great weight of earth pressing on her.
What does she think about all day long? It's terrible

to be like that—to be doing nothing but think and think . . . But you are both so good to her.

THÉRÈSE. We are only doing our duty.

SUZANNE. And you two are the only ones who understand what she is saying with her eyes, aren't you? I can't understand her at all. Monsieur Grivet pretends to know her slightest wishes but his answers are all at cross-purposes. It's a mercy that she has you both with her. She has everything possible done for her. Uncle often says that this is a God-fearing house. There'll be happier days to come, you'll see. Does the doctor give any hope?

THÉRÈSE. Very little.

SUZANNE. I was here when he came the last time and he said that the poor darling might recover the use of her limbs and her tongue.

THÉRÈSE. We can't count on it. We dare not count on it.

SUZANNE. You must go on hoping.

[*They have finished laying the table and come downstage.*]

SUZANNE. We never see Monsieur Laurent here these days.

THÉRÈSE. Now that he's left the office and started painting again, he leaves in the morning and often doesn't come back until the evening. He is working hard and wants to send a large picture to the next Salon.

SUZANNE. He has become very dignified. His laugh is quieter and he looks so distinguished. You won't be angry with me if I tell you something, will you? Well, I shouldn't have wanted him as a husband as he used to be, but now I think he's most attractive. I'll tell you something else if you promise to keep it secret.

THÉRÈSE. I don't gossip.

SUZANNE. No, you don't. You keep everything to yourself. Well then, yesterday when we were going past your husband's studio in the rue Mazarin, Uncle suddenly thought we would go up. You know how Monsieur Laurent hates being disturbed at his work but all the same he didn't receive us too badly. You'd never guess what he's working at.

THÉRÈSE. A big picture.

SUZANNE. No, the canvas for the big picture is still quite blank. We found him surrounded by small canvases —sketches of faces. There were children's faces and women's faces and old men's faces. Uncle, who is quite a critic, was very taken with them. He says that your husband has become a great painter. It wasn't flattery because he didn't think much of him before. But what surprised me was that all the faces resembled someone. They were like. . . .

THÉRÈSE. Like whom?

SUZANNE. I don't want to hurt you . . . but they were all like poor Monsieur Camille.

THÉRÈSE [*trembling*]. No—no—you imagined it.

SUZANNE. But they were. The children's faces, the women's faces, the old men's faces . . . they all had something which reminded me of him—Uncle would have liked them to have more color. They are rather pale and they all had a crooked little smile . . .

[LAURENT *is heard at the door.*]

SUZANNE. Ah, there's your husband. Don't say anything about it. I expect he's going to give you a surprise with all those heads.

LAURENT. Good evening, Suzanne. Have you both been working hard?

THÉRÈSE. Yes.

LAURENT. I'm worn out. [*Falls into chair.*]

SUZANNE. Painting must be very tiring—all that standing.

LAURENT. I haven't been painting today. I walked to Saint Cloud and back. It did me good. Is dinner ready, Thérèse?

THÉRÈSE. Yes.

SUZANNE. I'm just going.

THÉRÈSE. Your uncle promised to come and fetch you. You must wait for him. You won't worry us.

SUZANNE. All right. I want some crewel needles—I'll go down to the shop and steal some. [*As she starts to go down the shop bell rings.*] Ah, a customer! I'll see what she wants. [*She goes down.*]

LAURENT [*pointing to mattress*]. Why didn't you put that mattress away? There's no need for people to know that we use two beds.

THÉRÈSE. You could quite well have put it away yourself this morning. I do as I please.

LAURENT [*roughly*]. Now don't start a quarrel. It isn't night yet.

THÉRÈSE. Well, if you amuse yourself away from home and take walks all day long, it's all the same to me. It's peaceful when you're not here but as soon as you come in, all hell opens. Let me at least have my sleep during the day. You know what the nights are like.

LAURENT [*more gently*]. Your tongue is even sharper than mine, Thérèse.

THÉRÈSE [*after a pause*]. Are you going to fetch her in for her dinner? Michaud is coming. I am always terrified when she is here with them. I have seen a look in her eyes for some time now. You see—she'll find a way to talk. We had better wait until he and Suzanne have gone.

LAURENT. Rubbish. Michaud would like to see his old friend, although I'm not so happy when he goes into her room. But what can she tell him? Why, she can't lift her little finger.

[*Exit* LAURENT *through door at back. Enter* MICHAUD *and* SUZANNE.]

MICHAUD. Ah, the table's laid.

THÉRÈSE. That's right, Monsieur Michaud. [*She goes to the sideboard from which she takes a cloth, lettuce and a salad bowl. She sits and during the following scene she prepares the lettuce.*]

MICHAUD. You people do yourselves pretty well, don't

you? These lovers have a devilish good appetite. Put on your hat, Suzanne. [*Looks around.*] And how is my dear Madame Raquin? [*Enter* LAURENT *pushing* MME. RAQUIN *in her armchair. Her hair is white; dressed in black she sits stiff and mute.* LAURENT *places her by table.*] Ah, here is the dear lady herself.

SUZANNE [*kissing* MME. RAQUIN]. We all love you very much. You must be brave.

MICHAUD. How her eyes shine! She's pleased to see us. [*To* MME. RAQUIN.] We're old friends, you and I, aren't we? Do you remember, when I was superintendent of police? It was at the time of the Gorge aux Loups murder, I think, when we first met. You must remember—that woman and that man who murdered a van driver. I arrested them myself—in their filthy cottage. They were guillotined at Rouen.

GRIVET [*enters during this speech and catches the end of it*]. Ah, that story of the van driver. I know it. You told me—very interesting, I thought. Monsieur Michaud has a nose for crime. Good evening, everybody.

MICHAUD. And what are you doing here at this hour of the day?

GRIVET. I happened to be passing and I thought I'd give myself a treat. I've come to have a little chat with Madame Raquin. But you were just going to have a meal, I see. Am I disturbing you?

LAURENT. Not at all.

GRIVET. Madame Raquin and I get on so well together. Just one look and I know what she wants.

MICHAUD. Well, perhaps you can tell me what she's trying to say to me. She's staring so hard at me.

GRIVET. Just a minute—I can read her eyes like a book. [*Sits beside* MME. RAQUIN, *touches her arm and waits for her to turn her head slowly to him.*] There, now —let's have a nice friendly little chat. Is there anything you want to ask Monsieur Michaud? Is there? No, nothing at all—that's just as I thought. [*To* MI-

CHAUD.] You were flattering yourself! It's me she wants, not you at all. [*Turns back to* MME. RAQUIN.] Now then, what is it? Ah yes, I understand—you are hungry.

SUZANNE [*leaning over back of armchair*]. Would you like us to go, dear?

GRIVET. Yes, of course, she's hungry. And she's asked me to stay for a little game of dominoes, this evening. I'm so sorry, Madame Raquin, but I shan't be able to accept your invitation—you know my little ways. But I promise you I'll come on Thursday.

MICHAUD. She didn't say anything at all to you. You made it up. Now let me try.

LAURENT [*to* THÉRÈSE, *who rises*]. You're right. Keep an eye on her. There's a terrible look in her eyes.

[*He takes the cloth and salad bowl from* THÉRÈSE *and puts them on the sideboard.*]

MICHAUD. Now, Madame, I'm entirely at your disposal, as always. Why are you looking at me like that? If you could only find some way of letting me know what it is you want.

SUZANNE. You hear what Uncle says. We would do any mortal thing you want.

GRIVET. I've told you what she wants. It's quite plain.

MICHAUD [*insistently*]. Can't you make us understand? Look, Laurent. She keeps staring at me so strangely.

LAURENT. I don't see anything strange about her.

SUZANNE. Thérèse, you can always understand her, can't you?

MICHAUD. Yes, you help her—please.

THÉRÈSE. You're making a mistake. She doesn't want anything. She's just the same as usual. [*She goes to face* MME. RAQUIN, *but cannot meet her eyes.*] That's right, isn't it? You don't want anything, do you? [*Recoils at what she sees in* MME. RAQUIN's *eyes.*]

MICHAUD. Ah well! Perhaps Monsieur Grivet is right.

GRIVET. Of course I am. She's hungry and she has invited me for a game of dominoes.

LAURENT. Why don't you stay, Monsieur Grivet? And you too, Monsieur Michaud. We should be pleased.

MICHAUD. No thanks. I'm busy this evening.

THÉRÈSE [to LAURENT]. For pity's sake . . . don't let them stay—

MICHAUD. Good night to you all. [Starts to go.]

GRIVET. Good night—good night. [Following MICHAUD.]

SUZANNE [still by MME. RAQUIN's chair]. Look—look—her fingers are moving!

[MICHAUD and GRIVET crowd round the chair, giving cries of astonishment.]

THÉRÈSE [in an undertone to LAURENT]. What an effort she's making—we can't escape now—it's our punishment. [They huddle together.]

MICHAUD [to MME. RAQUIN]. What's this? Why, you are your old self again. Look at your fingers—they are dancing a jig. [There is a pause while MME. RAQUIN fixes her glittering eyes on THÉRÈSE and LAURENT.] Look—she has managed to lift her hand and put it on the table.

GRIVET. Oho—we are a real little gadabout, we are. Our hands are going for a long walk.

THÉRÈSE. She's coming back to life—a statue coming to life!

LAURENT. Don't be afraid—hands don't speak.

SUZANNE. It looks as if she is making signs with her fingers.

GRIVET. Yes, what is she doing there on the oilcloth?

MICHAUD. She's writing, can't you see—She has just made a capital T.

THÉRÈSE [faintly]. Hands do speak, Laurent.

GRIVET. Good Heavens! She's writing. [To MME. RAQUIN.] Now, not too fast—not too fast. I'll try and read. No, no, I didn't get that. Begin again. [Pause]. It's amazing. T. . . . Tea—that's it—She wants some tea.

SUZANNE. No, no. She wrote Thérèse's name.

MICHAUD. Why, Monsieur Grivet, you don't know how

to read. [*Reading.*] "Thérèse and . . ." Go on, Madame Raquin.

LAURENT [*to* THÉRÈSE]. A hand from the grave. She shan't finish. I'll nail her hand there before I'll let her finish. [*Makes as if to take knife from pocket.*]

THÉRÈSE [*holding him back*]. Stop—you will ruin everything.

MICHAUD. Why, it's perfectly clear. "Thérèse and Laurent . . ." She's writing your names.

GRIVET. Yes, upon my word, your two names. It's wonderful.

MICHAUD [*watching fingers*]. "Thérèse and Laurent have . . ." Well, what have they? Bless their hearts.

GRIVET. Oh, she's stopped. Oh dear, dear, dear!

MICHAUD [*to* MME. RAQUIN]. Now finish the sentence—just one more try. [MME. RAQUIN *looks long at* THÉRÈSE *and* LAURENT, *then she slowly turns her head.*] You are looking at each one of us,—yes, we want to know the end of the sentence. [*She stays motionless for a moment, savoring the terror of the two murderers, then lets her hand fall into her lap.*]

MICHAUD. Ah, now your hand has fallen.

SUZANNE [*touching the hand*]. It is like a stone in her lap.

[*The three of them talk excitedly in a group behind the chair.*]

THÉRÈSE [*in an undertone*]. I thought it was the end for us—we're safe now, aren't we? Her hand is not moving.

LAURENT. Pull yourself together—lean on me—I felt I was choking.

GRIVET. I wish she had finished the sentence; it was a pity she didn't.

MICHAUD. Yes, I could follow her easily. I wonder what she wanted to say.

SUZANNE. That Thérèse and Laurant have made her so happy with all their kindness.

MICHAUD. Why, of course! You're much quicker than

we are, my dear. "Thérèse and Laurent have made me very happy . . . Thérèse and Laurent have my blessing." That's how the sentence goes, isn't it, Madame? You want to see that justice is done to them, don't you? [*To* THÉRÈSE *and* LAURENT.] You are two such dear souls. You certainly deserve a fine reward . . . here or hereafter.

LAURENT. You would have done the same.

GRIVET. They have had their reward. Do you know what the people round here call them? They call them a pair of turtledoves.

MICHAUD. And *we* arranged the marriage. Come along now, Monsieur Grivet. We must let them have their dinner now. [*To* MME. RAQUIN.] These little hands will soon wake up again, and so will the legs. It's a good sign to have been able to move your fingers. You'll soon be well now. Good night, dear Madame.

SUZANNE [*to* MME. RAQUIN]. Till tomorrow, darling.

GRIVET [*to* MME. RAQUIN]. There now, I said we always get on so well and we're going to play dominoes together on Thursdays, aren't we? And we'll beat Monsieur Michaud, you'll see, we'll beat him. [*To* THÉRÈSE *and* LAURENT.] Good night, my turtledoves. You know, you are a couple of turtledoves . . .

[*While* MICHAUD, GRIVET *and* SUZANNE *are going down the stairs*, THÉRÈSE *goes out through door at back and returns with a soup tureen.*]

[*During this scene* MME. RAQUIN'S *face reflects all she is thinking, for she registers anger, horror, cruel gloating, implacable vengeance, and with burning eyes she follows the murderers through all their wrangling and their distress.*]

LAURENT. She would have given us away.

THÉRÈSE [*serves* LAURENT *and herself with soup*]. Be quiet. Leave her alone.

LAURENT [*sitting back of table*]. Do you think she would spare us if she could speak? Michaud and Grivet were smiling rather queerly when they talked about our happiness. They'll find out in the end, you'll see. Grivet went out with his hat on the side of his head, didn't he?

THÉRÈSE [*puts soup tureen before the fire*]. Yes, I think so.

LAURENT. And when he went he buttoned up his overcoat and put his hands in his pockets. He used to button up his overcoat like that at the office when he wanted to look important. And the way he said "Good night, my turtledoves!" There's something frightening—sinister—about the idiot.

THÉRÈSE. Be quiet. Don't exaggerate things. Don't drag him into our nightmare.

LAURENT. When he screws up his mouth—you know—in that way that makes him look so stupid, I feel he's laughing at us. I never trust people who pretend to be fools. I tell you, he knows everything.

THÉRÈSE. They're far too simple. Yet it would put an end to it all if they did hand us over. But they'll see nothing. They will go on treading their humdrum, peaceful, self-satisfied way through the horrors of our life. [*Sits at table.*] Let's talk of something else. What madness is it that makes you always come back to this when she's here with us?

LAURENT. I have no spoon. [THÉRÈSE *fetches one from the sideboard, gives it to him and sits.*] Aren't you going to give her anything to eat?

THÉRÈSE. Yes, when I have finished my soup.

LAURENT [*tasting soup*]. It's beastly—you have made it too salt. [*Pushes it away.*] It is just sheer spite. You know I hate salt.

THÉRÈSE. Laurent—please don't start to pick a quarrel. Can't you see I'm tired out? I've had as much as I can bear.

LAURENT. That's right. Make a martyr of yourself. You make my life a torment with your everlasting nagging.

THÉRÈSE. You want us to quarrel, don't you?

LAURENT. I want you to stop talking to me like that.

THÉRÈSE. Oh, do you? [*Pushing away her plate.*] All right. Just as you like. We won't have any dinner tonight again. We'll tear each other to pieces and she shall hear us. It's our daily treat these days.

LAURENT [*with quiet force*]. And who starts it? You watch me—you whip me on the raw and you're not happy until the pain drives me mad.

THÉRÈSE. Well, I didn't say the soup was salt, did I? Any excuse does. You magnify the smallest trifle and fly into a fury. Now, tell me the truth. Be honest. It makes you happy to wrangle the whole evening, doesn't it? To exhaust yourself so that at night you can get a little sleep when you go to bed.

LAURENT. You don't sleep any more than I do.

THÉRÈSE. Oh, you have made life hideous. I dread the night and its terrors. He is there—between us. This room is full of death.

LAURENT. It's your fault.

THÉRÈSE. My fault did you say? Is it my fault that instead of the comfortable life you dreamed of, you've made everything impossible—full of fear and hate?

LAURENT. Yes, it's your fault.

THÉRÈSE. Stop it. I'm not a fool. Do you think I don't know you? You've always been on the lookout for the main chance. When you took me as your mistress it was because it cost you nothing. You dare not deny it. I hate you. Can't you see I hate you?

LAURENT. Which of us is trying to pick the quarrel now?

THÉRÈSE. I hate you. You killed Camille.

LAURENT. Shut your mouth. [*Pointing to* MME. RAQUIN.] Just now you told me to hold my tongue in front of her. Don't force me to remind you of the facts, to go over the whole story again in front of her.

THÉRÈSE. Let her hear. Let her suffer. Haven't I suffered? The truth is that you killed Camille.

LAURENT. It's a lie. You know it. It's a lie. I may have

been the one to throw him into the river but it was you who drove me to murder him.

THÉRÈSE. I?

LAURENT. Yes, you! Don't pretend you don't know. Don't make me drag it from you by force. I want you to confess your guilt, to accept your share. That at least, might be some comfort to me.

THÉRÈSE. But it wasn't I who killed Camille.

LAURENT. But it was you—it was. You were on the bank and I whispered to you "I'm going to throw him in the river." You agreed and got into the boat. You must see that you killed him too.

THÉRÈSE. It isn't true. I was mad. I didn't know what I was doing. I didn't want you to kill him.

LAURENT. Then when I upset the boat in the middle of the river, didn't I warn you? You clung to my neck and let him drown like a dog.

THÉRÈSE. It isn't true. It was you who killed him.

LAURENT. And then in the cab, on the way back, you put your hand in mine . . . I was burning for you . . .

THÉRÈSE. It was you who killed him.

LAURENT. You don't remember—you don't intend to remember. You drove me mad with love here, in this room. You put me against your husband. You wanted to get rid of him. You didn't care for him. He was always ill, you said. Was I like this three years ago? Was I? Was I evil? I was decent. I wouldn't have harmed anyone. I wouldn't have killed a fly.

THÉRÈSE. It was you who killed him.

LAURENT. Twice you've made me act like a wild beast. I was sane and contented—and now see what you have done to me. I tremble at every shadow like a frightened child. My nerves are as bad as yours. I'm not the stuff that murderers are made of. From adultery you led me to murder before I realized what was happening and now, when I look back at what I've done, I'm terrified. I can see, as if in a dream, the arrest, the trial, the guillotine. [*Rises.*] And you—you shake with terror in the night—you can't help it. You know that if his ghost came, he would strangle you first.

THÉRÈSE. No, no, don't say it. It was you who killed him.

LAURENT. Listen to me. It is cowardly to deny your share in what we did. You want to make my burden heavier, don't you? Well, you have driven me to the end of my tether. I'd sooner make an end of things. I am quite calm, you see. [*Takes his hat.*] I am going to tell the whole story to the police.

THÉRÈSE [*scornfully*]. That's a good idea!

LAURENT. They will arrest both of us. We'll see what the judge thinks about your innocence.

THÉRÈSE. Do you think I'm afraid? I'm more sick and tired of it than you are. If you don't go to the police, I shall.

LAURENT. I don't need you to come with me. I can tell them everything.

THÉRÈSE. No. Whenever we quarrel, as soon as you have run through all your arguments, you make this same threat. Today you're going to mean it. Well, I'm not a coward like you. I'm quite ready to follow you to the scaffold. Let's go. I'm coming too. [*Goes with him to the stairs.*]

LAURENT. Just as you like. We'll go and see the Inspector together.

[*He goes downstairs.* THÉRÈSE *clings to handrail, motionless, and listening. She begins to tremble with fear.* MADAME RAQUIN *turns her head, a grim smile on her face.*]

THÉRÈSE. He has gone down. He's at the bottom now. Will he have the courage to give us up? I don't want it—I'll run after him—I'll take hold of him and bring him back—suppose he shouts it out in the street— suppose he tells the people he meets—Oh God—it was wrong of me to drive him so far. I should have had more sense. [*Listening.*] He's still in the shop—the bell hasn't rung. What can he be doing? He's coming up—yes, now I can hear him—he's coming up. I knew he was too much of a coward. [*Shouting.*] Coward! Coward!

[LAURENT *returns, sits R. by the worktable, collapsing with his head in his hands.*]

LAURENT. I can't. I can't.

THÉRÈSE [*jeering as she goes to him*]. Well, you're soon back. What did they say to you? Haven't you any blood in your veins? I'm sorry for you.

[*Passes between* LAURENT *and fire, faces him, her fists planted on the worktable.*]

LAURENT [*sitting, speaking almost inaudibly*]. I can't . . .

THÉRÈSE. You are weaker than I. You should be supporting me. How do you think we can make ourselves forget?

LAURENT. So you admit you had a share in it?

THÉRÈSE. Oh yes. I'm guilty. More guilty than you, if you like. I ought to have stopped you . . . Camille was a good man.

LAURENT. Don't let's start it all over again—please, I implore you. When you have driven me frantic then you are happy. Don't look at me—don't smile at me. I shall escape when the time comes. [*Takes small bottle from his pocket.*] This is dreamless sleep—the remission of my sentence. Two drops of prussic acid —and I have no more to worry about.

THÉRÈSE. Poison! I dare you to drink it—you're too much of a coward! Go on, Laurent, drink it—drink a drop of it—just to see—

LAURENT. Be quiet—stop nagging me.

THÉRÈSE. I'm not worried—you won't drink it.

LAURENT. Be quiet!

THÉRÈSE. You don't understand how women feel. Don't you realize that I hate you now that I see your hands are stained with my husband's blood?

LAURENT [*pacing up and down in a frenzy of hallucination*]. Will you be quiet! There's a hammering in my head—it is splitting my brain—What devil has got hold of you—talking now of remorse and of your grief for him? I can't get away from him. He did this—he did that—he was good—he was noble. I'm going mad. He is living with us—he sits on my chair—he is next to me at the table—he makes himself at home with us. He has eaten from the plate that I use—he still eats from it. I'm not myself any more—I am Camille. I have his wife and his place at table—I have his bed—I am Camille—Camille—Camille—

THÉRÈSE. That's a nice thing you're doing, painting him in all your pictures.

LAURENT. Ah, so you know that, do you? [*Lowering his voice.*] It's terrible. My hands don't belong to me any more. I can't paint any more. He is always there—in my hands. These hands, these two hands are not mine. If I don't cut them off, they will betray me. They are his—his. He has robbed me of them.

THÉRÈSE. This is retribution.

LAURENT. Tell me, haven't I got Camille's mouth? Oh, did you hear? That's just how Camille would have said that. Listen. "I have his mouth. I have his mouth." That's it exactly. I speak like him. I laugh like him. He is there all the time, inside my head, hammering at it with his fists.

THÉRÈSE. Retribution.

LAURENT. Go away, woman. You are driving me mad. Go away, or I'll . . . [*Forces her to her knees and raises his hand as if to strike.*]

THÉRÈSE [*on her knees*]. Go on—finish it—kill me as you killed him! Camille never struck me. You are a monster! Go on—kill me as you killed him.

[LAURENT, *demented, crosses, and sits by the alcove, his head in his hands. During all this* MME. RAQUIN *has succeeded in pushing a knife off the table and it falls by* THÉRÈSE. *The noise of its falling takes* THÉRÈSE'S *attention from* LAURENT *whom she has been watching. Slowly turning her head she lets her eyes travel from the knife to* MME. RAQUIN.]

THÉRÈSE. You made it fall. There is a devil from hell in your eyes!—what is it you want to say—you are right—that creature has made my life intolerable. If he were not there all the time to remind me of what I want to forget I'd have nothing to worry about—I could live my life in peace. [*Looking at* MME. RAQUIN *as she picks up the knife.*] You are looking at the knife, aren't you? Well, I've got it and he shan't torment me any longer. He killed Camille because he was in the way. All right then—he's in my way! [*Rises, with the knife in her hand.*]

LAURENT [*the bottle of poison in his hand*]. Let's forget all this and finish supper, shall we?

THÉRÈSE. Just as you like. [*To herself.*] I can't wait for the night—This knife burns me—

LAURENT. What's in your mind? Come and sit down—Wait a minute—I'll give you something to drink. [*Pours out a glass of water.*]

THÉRÈSE [*to herself*]. Better to end it all now. [*Goes towards him with the knife raised; she sees* LAURENT *put poison in the glass and seizes his arm.*] Laurent, what are you putting in that?

LAURENT [*catching sight of the knife*]. Why are you holding up your arm? [*Pause.*] Put down that knife.

THÉRÈSE. After you have put down that bottle. [*Looking at each other with hate and dropping the knife and the bottle.*]

LAURENT [*collapsing into a chair*]. Both of us—both of us—the same thought—the same horrible thought . . .

THÉRÈSE [*falling into a chair*]. Oh, Laurent, we loved each other so much—and now we have come to this—poison and a knife! [*She catches sight of* MME.

RAQUIN *and then rises with a sudden cry.*] Laurent—look!

LAURENT [*rising and staring in terror at* MME. RAQUIN]. She was there—all the time—to watch us die!

THÉRÈSE. But don't you see her lips are moving! She is smiling—oh, it's a horrible smile!

LAURENT. Now she's beginning to tremble.

THÉRÈSE. She's going to speak—I tell you, she's going to speak.

LAURENT. I know how to stop her.

[*Is about to hurl himself on* MME. RAQUIN *when she slowly gets to her feet. He recoils, walks away and then turns.*]

MME. RAQUIN [*standing and speaking in a deep hollow voice*]. You murdered the child, now you dare to strike the mother.

THÉRÈSE. Have mercy on us. Don't hand us over to the law.

MME. RAQUIN. Hand you over! No! I thought of it at first when my strength began to come back. I began to write your name on that table. But I stopped. Human justice would be too swift, I thought. I want to watch you pay for your crime, here, in this room where you robbed me of my happiness.

THÉRÈSE [*sobbing and falling at* MME. RAQUIN'S *feet*]. Forgive me—my remorse is choking me—I am a wicked woman. See, I am on my knees to you—I am at your mercy—I beg you to have pity.

MME. RAQUIN [*supporting herself on the table as her voice gradually gains strength*]. Pity! Did you have pity on my poor child—the child I worshipped? Don't ask for pity. I have no more pity—you have robbed me of pity.

[LAURENT *falls on his knees.*]

MME. RAQUIN. No, I shall not save you from yourselves. I am going to watch remorse tearing you like savage beasts. Hand you over? No, I shall not hand you over. You're mine, mine alone, and I'm going to keep you mine.

THÉRÈSE. No, no, it would be intolerable. We will be our own judges and the verdict is "Guilty."

[*She picks up the bottle, drinks eagerly and falls crashing at* MME. RAQUIN's *feet.* LAURENT *snatches the bottle from her and drinks. He falls R. behind the worktable and chairs.*]

MME. RAQUIN [*slowly sitting*]. Dead! dead!

HENRIK IBSEN

James Huneker, one of the most distinguished American critics of music and drama of the last generation, once remarked that Henrik Ibsen was probably "the best hated artist of the nineteenth century." It may seem odd today that the bewhiskered old Norwegian could have evoked that kind of violent antipathy from his contemporaries, but I suspect Huneker was very nearly right. For Ibsen shook and shattered staid Victorian sensibilities by bringing up in public subjects that were utterly taboo there, by championing a multitude of unpopular attitudes toward the society of his time, by challenging, indeed, many of the very bases of complacent middle-class morality. When he was through, little was left of the fragile "doll's houses" in which nineteenth-century families had been cozily living. And, as for the stages of the Western world, they too would never be the same.

This "mover and shaker" was born in 1828 in an obscure little Norwegian seaport called Skien. His youth was almost as dull as his environment, but the latter provided young Henrik with a chance to observe in his formative years the small-town small-mindedness of his neighbors, which he would return to castigate in play after play in his later life. With his teens behind him, Ibsen got a job from Ole Bull, the progressive manager of a small theatre in Bergen, and soon became its official playwright; thence he moved on to Christiania, the Norwegian capital which we now call Oslo. The chance to travel presented itself; he went first to Denmark and Germany, a few years later to Vienna, Switzerland and Italy. Up to this point he had written principally historical dramas: *Catiline, Lady Inger of Östrat, The Vikings of Helgeland,* and *The Pretenders.* Now he was ready to tackle the present day man and his problems.

One of the major preoccupations of our own best contemporary dramatists is the problem of compromise. Play after play has been written since the Second World War on this theme. I think offhand of Lindsay and Crouse's *State of the Union,* of Robert E. Sherwood's last play, *The Rugged Path,* of J. P. Marquand's *Point of No Return,* of Maxwell Anderson's *Joan of Lorraine* and *Barefoot in Athens,* of Chapman and Coxe's adaptation of Melville's *Billy Budd,* of Arthur Miller's *The Crucible,* of Gore Vidal's *The Best Man.* Whether comic or serious, all of these plays reflect in one way or another their authors' concern for the way a man allows himself to adjust his way of life to the exigencies of his time, for the point at which he stands fast for what he believes, for the price he must pay for adherence to the dictates of his personal conscience.

Ibsen was there more than a century before them with two plays: *Brand* and *Peer Gynt.* Each is concerned with the broad questions of conscience and of compromise. They are early plays and he was only laying the groundwork for his own attitude. This comes more clearly into focus when we move on to the plays of his maturer days. There were thirteen of them in the thirty years that followed, the years between 1869 when *The League of Youth* appeared and 1899 when his last mysterious symbolic piece, *When We Dead Awaken,* was completed. During those intervening three decades came *Pillars of Society, A Doll's House, Ghosts, An Enemy of the People, The Wild Duck, Rosmersholm, The Lady from the Sea, Hedda Gabler, The Master*

Builder, Little Eyolf and *John Gabriel Borkman.*

The play by which Ibsen is represented in this collection, *An Enemy of the People,* comes chronologically after *Ghosts,* the play which had probably shocked the Victorian world more than any other of his works. In *A Doll's House* Ibsen had exposed the inequities of a society which placed women in spiritual and economic bondage to their husbands. In *Ghosts* he showed what can happen when a wife does *not* leave her husband (as Nora *had* done in the earlier play); again he seemed to be demanding freedom of action, to be attacking social pressures, lies and illusions.

As I have said, *Ghosts,* which dared to present hereditary venereal disease as a theme on the stage, made for Ibsen many shocked enemies. He replied to them with the play in this volume which seemed almost a dramatization of his own situation as he saw it: the one man of truth opposed and defeated by a self-centered, blind, conscienceless majority. "The majority is always wrong," cries Dr. Stockmann, as he is driven out of town for trying to help his fellow citizens. Certainly there is more than a trace of the subjective in Ibsen's writing here, and nowhere in his works do those twin themes of conscience and compromise come more fully into focus.

Ibsen, however, was not really a revolutionary. He was not proposing any overthrow of his wrong-headed majority. He believed that it merely needed to clean house. Society was not to be destroyed; it simply had to be purified; and in one play after another he sought to show how this was to be accomplished: not through the new sciences, but by a review of family and personal relations, by destroying false moral values, by exposing cant and hypocrisy. In other words, his attack was on ethical rather than social or political grounds. His fight, as John Howard Lawson has pointed out, was against conventions, not against the conditions out of which the conventions were derived. (This is why to the true revolutionist of our day Ibsen has nothing significant to offer.)

It is understandable that our contemporary American playwright who has evidenced more strongly than any of his fellows a social conscience and who like Ibsen before him has been castigated by representatives of the majority, should have been attracted to *An Enemy of the People* and have made the version of it which I include in this anthology. Arthur Miller has unquestionably been profoundly influenced by Ibsen in both his style and his outlook. In this play they clasp hands across the century that divides them.

An Enemy of the People

by HENRIK IBSEN

Adapted by Arthur Miller

CHARACTERS

Morten Kiil
Billing
Mrs. Stockmann
Peter Stockmann
Hovstad
Dr. Stockmann
Morten
Ejlif
Captain Horster
Petra
Aslaksen
The Drunk
Townspeople

SYNOPSIS OF SCENES
The action takes place in a Norwegian town

ACT ONE.
Scene 1: Dr. Stockmann's living room.
Scene 2: The same, the following morning.

ACT TWO.
Scene 1: Editorial office of the *People's Daily Messenger.*
Scene 2: A room in Captain Horster's house.

ACT THREE.
Scene: Dr. Stockmann's living room the following morning.

Throughout, in the stage directions, right and left mean stage right and stage left.

ACT ONE.

Scene 1.

It is evening. DR. STOCKMANN'S *living room is simply but cheerfully furnished. A doorway, upstage right, leads into the entrance hall, which extends from the front door to the dining room, running unseen behind the living room. At the left is another door, which leads to the* DOCTOR'S *study and other rooms. In the upstage left corner is a stove. Toward the left foreground is a sofa with a table behind it. In the right foreground are two chairs, a small table between them, on which stand a lamp and a bowl of apples. At the back, to the left, an open doorway leads to the dining room, part of which is seen. The windows are in the right wall, a bench in front of them.*

As the curtain rises, BILLING *and* MORTEN KIIL *are eating in the dining room.* BILLING *is junior editor of the* People's Daily Messenger. KIIL *is a slovenly old man who is feeding himself in a great hurry. He gulps his last bite and comes into the living room, where he puts on his coat and ratty fur hat.* BILLING *comes in to help him.*

BILLING. You sure eat fast, Mr. Kiil. [*Billing is an enthusiast to the point of foolishness*].
KIIL. Eating don't get you anywhere, boy. Tell my daughter I went home.
[KIIL *starts across to the front door.* BILLING *returns to his food in the dining room.* KIIL *halts at the bowl*

*of apples; he takes one, tastes it, likes it, takes an-
other and puts it in his pocket, then continues on
toward the door. Again he stops, returns, and takes
another apple for his pocket. Then he sees a tobacco can on the table. He covers his action from*
BILLING'S *possible glance, opens the can, smells it,
pours some into his side pocket. He is just closing the
can when* CATHERINE STOCKMANN *enters from the
dining room.]*

MRS. STOCKMANN. Father! You're not going, are you?

KIIL. Got business to tend to.

MRS. STOCKMANN. Oh, you're only going back to your
room and you know it. Stay! Mr. Billing's here, and
Hovstad's coming. It'll be interesting for you.

KIIL. Got all kinds of business. The only reason I came
over was the butcher told me you bought roast beef
today. Very tasty, dear.

MRS. STOCKMANN. Why don't you wait for Tom? He
only went for a little walk.

KIIL [*taking out his pipe*]. You think he'd mind if I
filled my pipe?

MRS. STOCKMANN. No, go ahead. And here—take some
apples. You should always have some fruit in your
room.

KIIL. No, no, wouldn't think of it.

[*The doorbell rings.*]

MRS. STOCKMANN. That must be Hovstad. [*She goes to
the door and opens it.*]

[PETER STOCKMANN, *the Mayor, enters. He is a bachelor,
nearing sixty. He has always been one of those men
who make it their life work to stand in the center
of the ship to keep it from overturning. He probably
envies the family life and warmth of this house, but
when he comes he never wants to admit he came
and often sits with his coat on.*]

MRS. STOCKMANN. Peter! Well, this is a surprise!

PETER STOCKMANN. I was just passing by . . . [*He sees*
KIIL *and smiles, amused.*] Mr. Kiil!

KIIL [*sarcastically*]. Your Honor! [*He bites into his apple and exits.*]

MRS. STOCKMANN. You mustn't mind him, Peter, he's getting terribly old. Would you like a bite to eat?

PETER STOCKMANN. No, no thanks. [*He sees* BILLING *now, and* BILLING *nods to him from the dining room.*]

MRS. STOCKMANN [*embarrassed*]. He just happened to drop in.

PETER STOCKMANN. That's all right. I can't take hot food in the evening. Not with my stomach.

MRS. STOCKMANN. Can't I ever get you to eat anything in this house?

PETER STOCKMANN. Bless you, I stick to my tea and toast. Much healthier and more economical.

MRS. STOCKMANN [*smiling*]. You sound as though Tom and I throw money out the window.

PETER STOCKMANN. Not you, Catherine. He wouldn't be home, would he?

MRS. STOCKMANN. He went for a little walk with the boys.

PETER STOCKMANN. You don't think that's dangerous, right after dinner? [*There is a loud knocking on the front door.*] *That* sounds like my brother.

MRS. STOCKMANN. I doubt it, so soon. Come in, please. [HOVSTAD *enters. He is in his early thirties, a graduate of the peasantry struggling with a terrible conflict. For while he hates authority and wealth, he cannot bring himself to cast off a certain desire to partake of them. Perhaps he is dangerous because he wants more than anything to belong, and in a radical that is a withering wish, not easily to be borne.*]

MRS. STOCKMANN. Mr. Hovstad—

HOVSTAD. Sorry I'm late. I was held up at the printing shop. [*Surprised.*] Good evening, Your Honor.

PETER STOCKMANN [*rather stiffly*]. Hovstad. On business, no doubt.

HOVSTAD. Partly. It's about an article for the paper—

PETER STOCKMANN [*sarcastically*]. Ha! I don't doubt it.

I understand my brother has become a prolific contributor to—what do you call it?—the *People's Daily Liberator?*

HOVSTAD [*laughing, but holding his ground*]. The *People's Daily Messenger,* sir. The Doctor sometimes honors the *Messenger* when he wants to uncover the real truth of some subject.

PETER STOCKMANN. The truth! Oh, yes, I see.

MRS. STOCKMANN [*nervously to* HOVSTAD]. Would you like to . . . [*She points to dining room.*]

PETER STOCKMANN. I don't want you to think I blame the Doctor for using your paper. After all, every performer goes for the audience that applauds him most. It's really not your paper I have anything against, Mr. Hovstad.

HOVSTAD. I really didn't think so, Your Honor.

PETER STOCKMANN. As a matter of fact, I happen to admire the spirit of tolerance in our town. It's magnificent. Just don't forget that we have it because we all believe in the same thing; it brings us together.

HOVSTAD. Kirsten Springs, you mean.

PETER STOCKMANN. The springs, Mr. Hovstad, our wonderful new springs. They've changed the soul of this town. Mark my words, Kirsten Springs are going to put us on the map, and there is no question about it.

MRS. STOCKMANN. That's what Tom says too.

PETER STOCKMANN. Everything is shooting ahead—real estate going up, money changing hands every hour, business humming—

HOVSTAD. And no more unemployment.

PETER STOCKMANN. Right. Give us a really good summer, and sick people will be coming here in carloads. The springs will turn into a regular fad, a new Carlsbad. And for once the well-to-do people won't be the only ones paying taxes in this town.

HOVSTAD. I hear reservations are really starting to come in?

PETER STOCKMANN. Coming in every day. Looks very promising, very promising.

HOVSTAD. That's fine. [*To* MRS. STOCKMANN.] Then the Doctor's article will come in handy.

PETER STOCKMANN. He's written something again?

HOVSTAD. No, it's a piece he wrote at the beginning of the winter, recommending the water. But at the time I let the article lie.

PETER STOCKMANN. Why, some hitch in it?

HOVSTAD. Oh, no, I just thought it would have a bigger effect in the spring, when people start planning for the summer.

PETER STOCKMANN. That's smart, Mr. Hovstad, very smart.

MRS. STOCKMANN. Tom is always so full of ideas about the springs; every day he—

PETER STOCKMANN. Well, he ought to be, he gets his salary from the springs, my dear.

HOVSTAD. Oh, I think it's more than that, don't you? After all, Doctor Stockmann *created* Kirsten Springs.

PETER STOCKMANN. You don't say! I've been hearing that lately, but I did think I had a certain modest part—

MRS. STOCKMANN. Oh, Tom always says—

HOVSTAD. I only meant the original idea was—

PETER STOCKMANN. My good brother is never at a loss for ideas. All sorts of ideas. But when it comes to putting them into action you need another kind of man, and I did think that at least people in this house would—

MRS. STOCKMANN. But Peter, dear—we didn't mean to— Go get yourself a bite, Mr. Hovstad, my husband will be here any minute.

HOVSTAD. Thank you, maybe just a little something. [*He goes into the dining room and joins* BILLING *at the table.*]

PETER STOCKMANN [*lowering his voice*]. Isn't it remarkable? Why is it that people without background can never learn tact?

MRS. STOCKMANN. Why let it bother you? Can't you and Thomas share the honor like good brothers?

PETER STOCKMANN. The trouble is that certain men are never satisfied to share, Catherine.

MRS. STOCKMANN. Nonsense. You've always gotten along beautifully with Tom— That must be him now.

[*She goes to the front door, opens it.* DR. STOCKMANN *is laughing and talking outside. He is in the prime of his life. He might be called the eternal amateur— a lover of things, of people, of sheer living, a man for whom the days are too short, and the future fabulous with discoverable joys. And for all this most people will not like him—he will not compromise for less than God's own share of the world while they have settled for less than Man's.*]

DR. STOCKMANN [*in the entrance hall*]. Hey, Catherine! Here's another guest for you! Here's a hanger for your coat, Captain. Oh, that's right, you don't wear overcoats! Go on in, boys. You kids must be hungry all over again. Come here, Captain Horster, I want you to get a look at this roast. [*He pushes* CAPTAIN HORSTER *along the hallway to the dining room.* EJLIF *and* MORTEN *also go to the dining room.*]

MRS. STOCKMANN. Tom, dear . . . [*She motions toward* PETER *in the living room.*]

DR. STOCKMANN. [*turns around in the doorway to the living room and sees* PETER]. Oh, Peter . . . [*He walks across and stretches out his hand.*] Say now, this is really nice.

PETER STOCKMANN. I'll have to go in a minute.

DR. STOCKMANN. Oh, nonsense, not with the toddy on the table. You haven't forgotten the toddy, have you, Catherine?

MRS. STOCKMANN. Of course not, I've got the water boiling. [*She goes into the dining room.*]

PETER STOCKMANN. Toddy too?

DR. STOCKMANN. Sure, just sit down and make yourself at home.

PETER STOCKMANN. No, thanks, I don't go in for drinking parties.

DR. STOCKMANN. But this is no party.

PETER STOCKMANN. What else do you call it? [*He looks toward the dining room.*] It's extraordinary how you people can consume all this food and live.

DR. STOCKMANN [*rubbing his hands*]. Why? What's finer than to watch young people eat? Peter, those are the fellows who are going to stir up the whole future.

PETER STOCKMANN [*a little alarmed*]. Is that so! What's there to stir up? [*He sits in a chair to the left.*]

DR. STOCKMANN [*walking around*]. Don't worry, they'll let us know when the time comes. Old idiots like you and me, we'll be left behind like—

PETER STOCKMANN. I've never been called *that* before.

DR. STOCKMANN. Oh, Peter, don't jump on me every minute! You know your trouble, Peter? Your impressions are blunted. You ought to sit up there in that crooked corner of the north for five years, the way I did, and then come back here. It's like watching the first seven days of creation!

PETER STOCKMANN. Here!

DR. STOCKMANN. Things to work and fight for, Peter! Without that you're dead. Catherine, you sure the mailman came today?

MRS. STOCKMANN [*from the dining room*]. There wasn't any mail today.

DR. STOCKMANN. And another thing, Peter—a good income; *that's* something you learn to value after you've lived on a starvation diet.

PETER STOCKMANN. When did you starve?

DR. STOCKMANN. Damned near! It was pretty tough going a lot of the time up there. And now, to be able to live like a prince! Tonight, for instance, we had roast beef for dinner, and, by God, there was enough left for supper too. Please have a piece— come here.

PETER STOCKMANN. Oh, no, no—please, certainly not.

DR. STOCKMANN. At least let me show it to you! Come in here—we even have a tablecloth. [*He pulls his brother toward the dining room.*]

PETER STOCKMANN. I saw it.

DR. STOCKMANN. Live to the hilt! that's my motto. Anyway, Catherine says I'm earning almost as much as we spend.

PETER STOCKMANN [*refusing an apple*]. Well, you are improving.

DR. STOCKMANN. Peter, that was a joke! You're supposed to laugh! [*He sits in the other chair to the left.*]

PETER STOCKMANN. Roast beef twice a day is no joke.

DR. STOCKMANN. Why can't I give myself the pleasure of having people around me? It's a necessity for me to to see young, lively, happy people, free people burning with a desire to do something. You'll see. When Hovstad comes in we'll talk and—

PETER STOCKMANN. Oh, yes, Hovstad. That reminds me. He told me he was going to print one of your articles.

DR. STOCKMANN. One of my articles?

PETER STOCKMANN. Yes, about the springs—an article you wrote during the winter?

DR. STOCKMANN. Oh, that one! In the first place, I don't want that one printed right now.

PETER STOCKMANN. No? It sounded to me like it would be very timely.

DR. STOCKMANN. Under normal conditions, maybe so. [*He gets up and walks across the floor.*]

PETER STOCKMANN [*looking after him*]. Well, What is abnormal about the conditions now?

DR. STOCKMANN [*stopping*]. I can't say for the moment, Peter—at least not tonight. There could be a great deal abnormal about conditions; then again, there could be nothing at all.

PETER STOCKMANN. Well, you've managed to sound mysterious. Is there anything wrong? Something you're keeping from me? Because I wish once in a while you'd remind yourself that I am chairman of the board for the springs.

DR. STOCKMANN. And I would like *you* to remember that, Peter. Look, let's not get into each other's hair.

PETER STOCKMANN. I don't make a habit of getting into people's hair! But I'd like to underline that everything concerning Kirsten Springs must be treated in a businesslike manner, through the proper channels, and dealt with by the legally constituted authorities. I can't allow anything done behind my back in a roundabout way.

DR. STOCKMANN. When did I ever go behind your back, Peter?

PETER STOCKMANN. You have an ingrained tendency to go your own way, Thomas, and that simply can't go on in a well-organized society. The individual really must subordinate himself to the over-all, or—[*groping for words, he points to himself*]—to the authorities who are in charge of the general welfare. [*He gets up.*]

DR. STOCKMANN. Well, that's probably so. But how the hell does that concern me, Peter?

PETER STOCKMANN. My dear Thomas, this is exactly what you will never learn. But you had better watch out because someday you might pay dearly for it. Now I've said it. Good-bye.

DR. STOCKMANN. Are you out of your mind? You're absolutely on the wrong track.

PETER STOCKMANN. I am usually not. Anyway, may I be excused? [*He nods toward the dining room.*] Good-bye, Catherine. Good evening, gentlemen. [*He leaves.*]

MRS. STOCKMANN [*entering the living room*]. He left?

DR. STOCKMANN. And burned up!

MRS. STOCKMANN. What did you do to him now?

DR. STOCKMANN. What does he want from me? He can't expect me to give him an accounting of every move I make, every thought I think, until I am ready to do it.

MRS. STOCKMANN. Why? What should you give him an accounting of?

DR. STOCKMANN [*hesitantly*]. Just leave that to me, Catherine. Peculiar the mailman didn't come today.

[HOVSTAD, BILLING, *and* CAPTAIN HORSTER *have gotten up from the dining-room table and enter the living room.* EJLIF *and* MORTEN *come in a little later.* CATHERINE *exits.*]

BILLING [*stretching out his arms*]. After a meal like that, by God, I feel like a new man. This house is so—

HOVSTAD [*cutting him off*]. The Mayor certainly wasn't in a glowing mood tonight.

DR. STOCKMANN. It's his stomach. He has a lousy digestion.

HOVSTAD. I think two editors from the *People's Daily Messenger* didn't help either.

DR. STOCKMANN. No, it's just that Peter is a lonely man. Poor fellow, all he knows is official business and duties, and then all that damn weak tea that he pours into himself. Catherine, may we have the toddy?

MRS. STOCKMANN [*calling from the dining room*]. I'm just getting it.

DR. STOCKMANN. Sit down here on the couch with me, Captain Horster—a rare guest like you—sit here. Sit down, friends.

HORSTER. This used to be such an ugly house. Suddenly it's beautiful!

[BILLING *and* HOVSTAD *sit down at the right.* MRS. STOCKMANN *brings a tray with pot, glasses, bottles, etc. on it, and puts it on the table behind the couch.*]

BILLING [*to* HORSTER, *intimately, indicating* STOCKMANN]. Great man!

MRS. STOCKMANN. Here you are. Help yourselves.

DR. STOCKMANN [*taking a glass*]. We sure will. [*He mixes the toddy.*] And the cigars, Ejlif—you know where the box is. And Morten, get my pipe. [*The boys go out to the left.*] I have a sneaking suspicion that Ejlif is snitching a cigar now and then, but I don't pay any attention. Catherine, you know where I put it? Oh, he's got it. Good boys! [*The boys bring the various things in.*] Help yourselves, fellows. I'll stick to the pipe. This one's gone through plenty of blizzards with me up in the north. Skol! [*He looks around.*] Home! What an invention, heh?

[*The boys sit down on the bench near the windows.*]

MRS. STOCKMANN [*who has sat down and is now knitting*]. Are you sailing soon, Captain Horster?

HORSTER. I expect to be ready next week.

MRS. STOCKMANN. And then to America, Captain?

HORSTER. Yes, that's the plan.

BILLING. Oh, then you won't be home for the new election?

HORSTER. Is there going to be another election?

BILLING. Didn't you know?

HORSTER. No, I don't get mixed up in those things.

BILLING. But you are interested in public affairs, aren't you?

HORSTER. Frankly, I don't understand a thing about it. [*He does, really, although not very much.* CAPTAIN HORSTER *is one of the longest silent roles in dramatic literature, but he is not to be thought of as characterless therefor. It is not a bad thing to have a courageous, quiet man for a friend, even if it has gone out of fashion.*]

MRS. STOCKMANN [*sympathetically*]. Neither do I, Captain. Maybe that's why I'm always so glad to see you.

BILLING. Just the same, you ought to vote, Captain.

HORSTER. Even if I don't understand anything about it?

BILLING. Understand! What do you mean by that? Society, Captain, is like a ship—every man should do something to help navigate the ship.

HORSTER. That may be all right on shore, but on board a ship it doesn't work out so well.

[PETRA *in hat and coat and with textbooks and notebooks under her arm comes into the entrance hall. She is Ibsen's clear-eyed hope for the future—and probably ours. She is forthright, determined, and knows the meaning of work, which to her is the creation of good on the earth.*]

PETRA [*from the hall*]. Good evening.

DR. STOCKMANN [*warmly*]. Good evening, Petra!

BILLING [*to* HORSTER]. Great young woman!

[*There are mutual greetings.* PETRA *removes her coat and hat and places the books on a chair in the entrance hall.*]

PETRA [*entering the living room*]. And here you are, lying around like lizards while I'm out slaving.

DR. STOCKMANN. Well, you come and be a lizard too. Come here, Petra, sit with me. I look at her and say to myself, "How did I do it?"

[PETRA *goes over to her father and kisses him.*]

BILLING. Shall I mix a toddy for you?

PETRA [*coming up to the table*]. No, thanks, I had better do it myself—you always mix it too strong. Oh, Father, I forgot—I have a letter for you. [*She goes to the chair where her books are.*]

DR. STOCKMANN [*alerted*]. Who's it from?

PETRA. I met the mailman on the way to school this morning and he gave me your mail too, and I just didn't have time to run back.

DR. STOCKMANN [*getting up and walking toward her*]. And you don't give it to me until now!

PETRA. I really didn't have time to run back, Father.

MRS. STOCKMANN. If she didn't have time . . .

DR. STOCKMANN. Let's see it—come on, child! [*He takes the letter and looks at the envelope.*] Yes, indeed.

MRS. STOCKMANN. Is that the one you've been waiting for?

DR. STOCKMANN. I'll be right back. There wouldn't be a light on in my room, would there?

MRS. STOCKMANN. The lamp is on the desk, burning away.

DR. STOCKMANN. Please excuse me for a moment. [*He goes into his study and quickly returns.* MRS. STOCKMANN *hands him his glasses. He goes out again.*]

PETRA. What is that, Mother?

MRS. STOCKMANN. I don't know. The last couple of days he's been asking again and again about the mailman.

BILLING. Probably an out-of-town patient of his.

PETRA. Poor Father, he's got much too much to do. [*She mixes her drink.*] This ought to taste good.

HOVSTAD. By the way, what happened to that English novel you were going to translate for us?

PETRA. I started it, but I've gotten so busy—

HOVSTAD. Oh, teaching evening school again?

PETRA. Two hours a night.

BILLING. Plus the high school every day?

PETRA [*sitting down on the couch*]. Yes, five hours, and every night a pile of lessons to correct!

MRS. STOCKMANN. She never stops going.

HOVSTAD. Maybe that's why I always think of you as kind of breathless and—well, breathless.

PETRA. I love it. I get so wonderfully tired.

BILLING [*to* HORSTER]. She looks tired.

MORTEN. You must be a wicked woman, Petra.

PETRA [*laughing*]. Wicked?

MORTEN. You work so much. My teacher says that work is a punishment for our sins.

EJLIF. And you believe that?

MRS. STOCKMANN. Ejlif! Of course he believes his teacher!

BILLING [*smiling*]. Don't stop him . . .

HOVSTAD. Don't you like to work, Morten?

MORTEN. Work? No.

HOVSTAD. Then what will you ever amount to in this world?

MORTEN. Me? I'm going to be a Viking.

EJLIF. You can't! You'd have to be a heathen!

MORTEN. So I'll be a heathen.

MRS. STOCKMANN. I think it's getting late, boys.

BILLING. I agree with you, Morten. I think—

MRS. STOCKMANN [*making signs to* BILLING]. You certainly don't, Mr. Billing.

BILLING. Yes, by God, I do. I am a real heathen and proud of it. You'll see, pretty soon we're all going to be heathens!

MORTEN. And then we can do anything we want!

BILLING. Right! You see, Morten—

MRS. STOCKMANN [*interrupting*]. Don't you have any homework for tomorrow, boys? Better go in and do it.

EJLIF. Oh, can't we stay in here a while?

MRS. STOCKMANN. No, neither of you. Now run along.

[*The boys say good night and go off at the left.*]

HOVSTAD. You really think it hurts them to listen to such talk?

MRS. STOCKMANN. I don't know, but I don't like it.

[DR. STOCKMANN *enters from his study, an open letter in his hand. He is like a sleepwalker, astonished, engrossed. He walks toward the front door.*]

MRS. STOCKMANN. Tom!

[*He turns, suddenly aware of them.*]

DR. STOCKMANN. Boys, there is going to be news in this town!

BILLING. News?

MRS. STOCKMANN. What kind of news?

DR. STOCKMANN. A terrific discovery, Catherine.

HOVSTAD. Really?

MRS. STOCKMANN. That you made?

DR. STOCKMANN. That I made. [*He walks back and forth.*] Now let the baboons running this town call me a lunatic! Now they'd better watch out. Oh, how the mighty have fallen!

PETRA. What is it, Father?

DR. STOCKMANN. Oh, if Peter were only here! Now you'll see how human beings can walk around and make judgments like blind rats.

HOVSTAD. What in the world's happened, Doctor?

DR. STOCKMANN [*stopping at the table*]. It's the general opinion, isn't it, that our town is a sound and healthy spot?

HOVSTAD. Of course.

MRS. STOCKMANN. What happened?

DR. STOCKMANN. Even a rather unusually healthy spot! Oh, God, a place that can be recommended not only to all people but to sick people!

MRS. STOCKMANN. But, Tom, what are you—

DR. STOCKMANN. And we certainly have recommended it. I myself have written and written, in the *People's Messenger*, pamphlets—

HOVSTAD. Yes, yes, but—

DR. STOCKMANN. The miraculous springs that cost such a fortune to build, the whole Health Institute, is a pesthole!

PETRA. Father! The springs?

MRS. STOCKMANN [*simultaneously*]. Our springs?

BILLING. That's unbelievable!

DR. STOCKMANN. You know the filth up in Windmill Valley? That stuff that has such a stinking smell? It comes down from the tannery up there, and the same damn poisonous mess comes right out into the blessed, miraculous water we're supposed to *cure* people with!

HORSTER. You mean actually where our beaches are?

DR. STOCKMANN. Exactly.

HOVSTAD. How are you so sure about this, Doctor?

DR. STOCKMANN. I had a suspicion about it a long time ago—last year there were too many sick cases among the visitors, typhoid and gastric disturbances.

MRS. STOCKMANN. That did happen. I remember Mrs. Svensen's niece—

DR. STOCKMANN. Yes, dear. At the time we thought that

the visitors brought the bug, but later this winter I got a new idea and I started investigating the water.

MRS. STOCKMANN. So that's what you've been working on!

DR. STOCKMANN. I sent samples of the water to the University for an exact chemical analysis.

HOVSTAD. And that's what you have just received?

DR. STOCKMANN [*waving the letter again*]. This is it. It proves the existence of infectious organic matter in the water.

MRS. STOCKMANN. Well, thank God you discovered it in time.

DR. STOCKMANN. I think we can say that, Catherine.

MRS. STOCKMANN. Isn't it wonderful!

HOVSTAD. And what do you intend to do now, Doctor?

DR. STOCKMANN. Put the thing right, of course.

HOVSTAD. Do you think that can be done?

DR. STOCKMANN. Maybe. If not, the whole Institute is useless. But there's nothing to worry about—I am quite clear on what has to be done.

MRS. STOCKMANN. But, Tom, why did you keep it so secret?

DR. STOCKMANN. What did you want me to do? Go out and shoot my mouth off before I really knew? [*He walks around, rubbing his hands.*] You don't realize what this means, Catherine—the whole water system has got to be changed.

MRS. STOCKMANN. The *whole* water system?

DR. STOCKMANN. The whole water system. The intake is too low, it's got to be raised to a much higher spot. The whole construction's got to be ripped out!

PETRA. Well, Father, at last you can prove they should have listened to you!

DR. STOCKMANN. Ha, she remembers!

MRS. STOCKMANN. That's right, you did warn them—

DR. STOCKMANN. Of course I warned them. When they started the damned thing I told them not to build it down there! But who am I, a mere scientist, to tell politicians where to build a health institute! Well, now they're going to get it, both barrels!

BILLING. This is tremendous! [*To* HORSTER.] He's a great man!

DR. STOCKMANN. It's bigger than tremendous. [*He starts toward his study.*] Wait'll they see this! [*He stops.*] Petra, my report is on my desk . . . [PETRA *goes into his study.*] An envelope, Catherine! [*She goes for it.*] Gentlemen, this final proof from the University—[PETRA *comes out with the report, which he takes*]—and my report—[*He flicks the pages.*]—five solid, explosive pages . . .

MRS. STOCKMANN [*handing him an envelope*]. Is this big enough?

DR. STOCKMANN. Fine. Right to the Board of Directors! [*He inserts the report, seals the envelope, and hands it to* CATHERINE.] Will you give this to the maid—what's her name again?

MRS. STOCKMANN. Randine, dear, Randine.

DR. STOCKMANN. Tell our darling Randine to wipe her nose and run over to the Mayor right now.

[MRS. STOCKMANN *just stands there looking at him.*]

DR. STOCKMANN. What's the matter, dear?

MRS. STOCKMANN. I don't know . . .

PETRA. What's Uncle Peter going to say about this?

MRS. STOCKMANN. That's what I'm wondering.

DR. STOCKMANN. What can he say! He ought to be damn glad that such an important fact is brought out before we start an epidemic! Hurry, dear!

[CATHERINE *exits at the left.*]

HOVSTAD. I would like to put a brief item about this discovery in the *Messenger*.

DR. STOCKMANN. Go ahead. I'd really be grateful for that now.

HOVSTAD. Because the public ought to know soon.

DR. STOCKMANN. Right away.

BILLING. By God, you'll be the leading man in this town, Doctor.

DR. STOCKMANN [*walking around with an air of satisfaction*]. Oh, there was nothing to it. Every detective gets a lucky break once in his life. But just the same I—

BILLING. Hovstad, don't you think the town ought to pay Dr. Stockmann some tribute?

DR. STOCKMANN. Oh, no, no . . .

HOVSTAD. Sure, let's all put in a word for—

BILLING. I'll talk to Aslaksen about it!

[CATHERINE *enters*.]

DR. STOCKMANN. No, no, fellows, no fooling around! I won't put up with any commotion. Even if the Board of Directors wants to give me an increase I won't take it—I just won't take it, Catherine.

MRS. STOCKMANN [*dutifully*]. That's right, Tom.

PETRA [*lifting her glass*]. Skol, Father!

EVERYBODY. Skol, Doctor!

HORSTER. Doctor, I hope this will bring you great honor and pleasure.

DR. STOCKMANN. Thanks, friends, thanks. There's one blessing above all others. To have earned the respect of one's neighbors is—is— Catherine, I'm going to dance!

[*He grabs his wife and whirls her around. There are shouts and struggles, general commotion. The boys in nightgowns stick their heads through the doorway at the right, wondering what is going on.* MRS. STOCKMANN, *seeing them, breaks away and chases them upstairs as the curtain falls.*]

Scene 2.

DR. STOCKMANN'S *living room the following morning. As the curtain rises,* MRS. STOCKMANN *comes in from the*

*dining room, a sealed letter in her hand. She goes to
the study door and peeks in.*

MRS. STOCKMANN. Are you there, Tom?

DR. STOCKMANN [*from within*]. I just got in. [*He enters
the living room.*] What's up?

MRS. STOCKMANN. From Peter. It just came. [*She hands
him the envelope.*]

DR. STOCKMANN. Oh, let's see. [*He opens the letter and
reads.*] "I am returning herewith the report you sub-
mitted . . ." [*He continues to read, mumbling to himself.*]

MRS. STOCKMANN. Well, what does he say? Don't stand
there!

DR. STOCKMANN [*putting the letter in his pocket*]. He
just says he'll come around this afternoon.

MRS. STOCKMANN. Oh. Well, maybe you ought to try to
remember to be home then.

DR. STOCKMANN. Oh, I sure will. I'm through with my
morning visits anyway.

MRS. STOCKMANN. I'm dying to see how he's going to
take it.

DR. STOCKMANN. Why, is there any doubt? He'll probably make it look like he made the discovery, not I.

MRS. STOCKMANN. But aren't you a little bit afraid of
that?

DR. STOCKMANN. Oh, underneath he'll be happy, Catherine. It's just that Peter is so afraid that somebody
else is going to do something good for this town.

MRS. STOCKMANN. I wish you'd go out of your way and
share the honors with him. Couldn't we say that he
put you on the right track or something?

DR. STOCKMANN. Oh, I don't mind—as long as it makes
everybody happy.

[MORTEN KIIL *sticks his head through the doorway. He
looks around searchingly and chuckles. He will continue chuckling until he leaves the house. He is the
archetype of the little twinkle-eyed man who sneaks*

into so much of Ibsen's work. He will chuckle you
right over the precipice. He is the dealer, the man
with the rat's finely tuned brain. But he is sometimes
likable because he is without morals and announces
the fact by laughing.]

KIIL [slyly]. Is it really true?

MRS. STOCKMANN [walking toward him]. Father!

DR. STOCKMANN. Well, good morning!

MRS. STOCKMANN. Come on in.

KIIL. It better be true or I'm going.

DR. STOCKMANN. What had better be true?

KIIL. This crazy story about the water system. Is it
true?

MRS. STOCKMANN. Of course it's true! How did you find
out about it?

KIIL. Petra came flying by on her way to school this
morning.

DR. STOCKMANN. Oh, she did?

KIIL. Ya. I thought she was trying to make a fool out of
me—

MRS. STOCKMANN. Now why would she do that?

KIIL. Nothing gives more pleasure to young people
than to make fools out of old people. But this is
true, eh?

DR. STOCKMANN. Of course it's true. Sit down here. It's
pretty lucky for the town, eh?

KIIL [fighting his laughter]. Lucky for the town!

DR. STOCKMANN. I mean, that I made the discovery before it was too late.

KIIL. Tom, I never thought you had the imagination to
pull your own brother's leg like this.

DR. STOCKMANN. Pull his leg?

MRS. STOCKMANN. But, Father, he's not—

KIIL. How does it go now, let me get it straight. There's
some kind of—like cockroaches in the waterpipes—

DR. STOCKMANN [laughing]. No, not cockroaches.

KIIL. Well, some kind of little animals.

MRS. STOCKMANN. Bacteria, Father.

KIIL [*who can barely speak through his laughter*]. Ah, but a whole mess of them, eh?

DR. STOCKMANN. Oh, there'd be millions and millions.

KIIL. And nobody can see them but you, is that it?

DR. STOCKMANN. Yes, that's—well, of course anybody with a micro— [*He breaks off.*] What are you laughing at?

MRS. STOCKMANN [*smiling at* KIIL]. You don't understand, Father. Nobody can actually see bacteria, but that doesn't mean they're not there.

KIIL. Good girl, you stick with him! By God, this is the best thing I ever heard in my life!

DR. STOCKMANN [*smiling*]. What do you mean?

KIIL. But tell me, you think you are actually going to get your brother to believe this?

DR. STOCKMANN. Well, we'll see soon enough!

KIIL. You really think he's that crazy?

DR. STOCKMANN. I hope the whole town will be that crazy, Morten.

KIIL. Ya, they probably are, and it'll serve them right too—they think they're so much smarter than us old-timers. Your good brother ordered them to bounce me out of the council, so they chased me out like a dog! Make jackasses out of all of them, Stockmann!

DR. STOCKMANN. Yes, but, Morten—

KIIL. Long-eared, short-tailed jackasses! [*He gets up.*] Stockmann, if you can make the Mayor and his elegant friends grab at this bait, I will give a couple of hundred crowns to charity, and right now, right on the spot.

DR. STOCKMANN. Well, that would be very kind of you, but I'm—

KIIL. I haven't got much to play around with, but if you can pull the rug out from under him with this cockroach business, I'll give at least fifty crowns to some poor people on Christmas Eve. Maybe this'll teach them to put some brains back in Town Hall!

[HOVSTAD *enters from the hall.*]

HOVSTAD. Good morning! Oh, pardon me . . .

KIIL [*enjoying this proof immensely*]. Oh, this one is in on it, too?

HOVSTAD. What's that, sir?

DR. STOCKMANN. Of course he's in on it.

KIIL. Couldn't I have guessed that! And it's going to be in the papers, I suppose. You're sure tying down the corners, aren't you? Well, lay it on thick. I've got to go.

DR. STOCKMANN. Oh, no, stay a while, let me explain it to you!

KIIL. Oh, I get it, don't worry! Only you can see them, heh? That's the best idea I've ever—damn it, you shouldn't do this for nothing! [*He goes toward the hall.*]

MRS. STOCKMANN [*following him out, laughing*]. But, Father, you don't understand about bacteria.

DR. STOCKMANN [*laughing*]. The old badger doesn't believe a word of it.

HOVSTAD. What does he think you're doing?

DR. STOCKMANN. Making an idiot out of my brother—imagine that?

HOVSTAD. You got a few minutes?

DR. STOCKMANN. Sure, as long as you like.

HOVSTAD. Have you heard from the Mayor?

DR. STOCKMANN. Only that he's coming over later.

HOVSTAD. I've been thinking about this since last night—

DR. STOCKMANN. Don't say?

HOVSTAD. For you as a medical man, a scientist, this is a really rare opportunity. But I've been wondering if you realize that it ties in with a lot of other things.

DR. STOCKMANN. How do you mean? Sit down. [*They sit at the right.*] What are you driving at?

HOVSTAD. You said last night that the pollution comes from impurities in the ground—

DR. STOCKMANN. It comes from the poisonous dump up in Windmill Valley.

HOVSTAD. Doctor, I think it comes from an entirely different dump.

DR. STOCKMANN. What do you mean?

HOVSTAD [*with growing zeal*]. The same dump that is poisoning and polluting our whole social life in this town.

DR. STOCKMANN. For God's sake, Hovstad, what are you babbling about?

HOVSTAD. Everything that matters in this town has fallen into the hands of a few bureaucrats.

DR. STOCKMANN. Well, they're not all bureaucrats—

HOVSTAD. They're all rich, all with old reputable names, and they've got everything in the palm of their hands.

DR. STOCKMANN. Yes, but they happen to have ability and knowledge.

HOVSTAD. Did they show ability and knowledge when they built the water system where they did?

DR. STOCKMANN. No, of coure not, but that happened to be a blunder, and we'll clear it up now.

HOVSTAD. You really imagine it's going to be as easy as all that?

DR. STOCKMANN. Easy or not easy, it's got to be done.

HOVSTAD. Doctor, I've made up my mind to give this whole scandal very special treatment.

DR. STOCKMANN. Now wait. You can't call it a scandal yet.

HOVSTAD. Doctor, when I took over the *People's Messenger* I swore I'd blow that smug cabal of old, stubborn, self-satisfied fogies to bits. This is the story that can do it.

DR. STOCKMANN. But I still think we owe them a deep debt of gratitude for building the springs.

HOVSTAD. The Mayor being your brother, I wouldn't ordinarily want to touch it, but I know you'd never let that kind of thing obstruct the truth.

DR. STOCKMANN. Of course not, but . . .

HOVSTAD. I want you to understand me. I don't have to

tell you I come from a simple family. I know in my bones what the underdog needs—he's got to have a say in the government of society. That's what brings about ability, intelligence, and self-respect in people.

DR. STOCKMANN. I understand that, but . . .

HOVSTAD. I think a newspaperman who turns down any chance to give the underdog a lift is taking on a responsibility that I don't want. I know perfectly well that in fancy circles they call it agitation, and they can call it anything they like if it makes them happy, but I have my own conscience—

DR. STOCKMANN [interrupting]. I agree with you, Hovstad, but this is just the water supply and— [There is a knock on the door.] Damn it! Come in!

[MR. ASLAKSEN, the publisher, enters from the hall. He is simply but neatly dressed. He wears gloves and carries a hat and an umbrella in his hand. He is so utterly drawn it is unnecessary to say anything at all about him.]

ASLAKSEN. I beg your pardon, Doctor, if I intrude . . .

HOVSTAD [standing up]. Are you looking for me, Aslaksen?

ASLAKSEN. No, I didn't know you were here. I want to see the Doctor.

DR. STOCKMANN. What can I do for you?

ASLAKSEN. Is it true, Doctor, what I hear from Mr. Billing, that you intend to campaign for a better water system?

DR. STOCKMANN. Yes, for the Institute. But it's not a campaign.

ASLAKSEN. I just wanted to call and tell you that we are behind you a hundred per cent.

HOVSTAD [to DR. STOCKMANN]. There, you see!

DR. STOCKMANN. Mr. Aslaksen, I thank you with all my heart. But you see—

ASLAKSEN. We can be important, Doctor. When the

little businessman wants to push something through, he turns out to be the majority, you know, and it's always good to have the majority on your side.

DR. STOCKMANN. That's certainly true, but I don't understand what this is all about. It seems to me it's a simple, straightforward business. The water—

ASLAKSEN. Of course we intend to behave with moderation, Doctor. I always try to be a moderate and careful man.

DR. STOCKMANN. You are known for that, Mr. Aslaksen, but—

ASLAKSEN. The water system is very important to us little businessmen, Doctor. Kirsten Springs are becoming a gold mine for this town, especially for the property owners, and that is why, in my capacity as chairman of the Property Owners Association—

DR. STOCKMANN. Yes.

ASLAKSEN. And furthermore, as a representative of the Temperance Society— You probably know, Doctor, that I am active for prohibition.

DR. STOCKMANN. So I have heard.

ASLAKSEN. As a result, I come into contact with all kinds of people, and since I am known to be a law-abiding and solid citizen, I have a certain influence in this town—you might even call it a little power.

DR. STOCKMANN. I know that very well, Mr. Aslaksen.

ASLAKSEN. That's why you can see that it would be practically nothing for me to arrange a demonstration.

DR. STOCKMANN. Demonstration! What are you going to demonstrate about?

ASLAKSEN. The citizens of the town complimenting you for bringing this important matter to everybody's attention. Obviously it would have to be done with the utmost moderation so as not to hurt the authorities.

HOVSTAD. This could knock the big-bellies right into the garbage can!

ASLAKSEN. No indiscretion or extreme aggressiveness toward the authorities, Mr. Hovstad! I don't want any wild-eyed radicalism on this thing. I've had enough of that in my time, and no good ever comes of it. But for a good solid citizen to express his calm, frank, and free opinion is something nobody can deny.

DR. STOCKMANN [*shaking the publisher's hand*]. My dear Aslaksen, I can't tell you how it heartens me to hear this kind of support. I am happy—I really am—I'm happy. Listen! Wouldn't you like a glass of sherry?

ASLAKSEN. I am a member of the Temperance Society. I—

DR. STOCKMANN. Well, how about a glass of beer?

ASLAKSEN [*considers, then*]. I don't think I can go quite that far, Doctor. I never take anything. Well, good day, and I want you to remember that the little man is behind you like a wall.

DR. STOCKMANN. Thank you.

ASLAKSEN. You have the solid majority on your side, because when the little—

DR. STOCKMANN [*trying to stop* ASLAKSEN's *talk*]. Thanks for that, Mr. Aslaksen, and good day.

ASLAKSEN. Are you going back to the printing shop, Mr. Hovstad?

HOVSTAD. I just have a thing or two to attend to here.

ASLAKSEN. Very well. [*He leaves.*]

HOVSTAD. Well, what do you say to a little hypodermic for these fence-sitting deadheads?

DR. STOCKMANN [*surprised*]. Why? I think Aslaksen is a very sincere man.

HOVSTAD. Isn't it time we pumped some guts into these well-intentioned men of good will? Under all their liberal talk they still idolize authority, and that's got to be rooted out of this town. This blunder of the water system has to be made clear to every voter. Let me print your report.

DR. STOCKMANN. Not until I talk to my brother.

HOVSTAD. I'll write an editorial in the meantime, and if the Mayor won't go along with us—

DR. STOCKMANN. I don't see how you can imagine such a thing!

HOVSTAD. Believe me, Doctor, it's possible, and then—

DR. STOCKMANN. Listen, I promise you: he will go along, and then you can print my report, every word of it.

HOVSTAD. On your word of honor?

DR. STOCKMANN [*giving* HOVSTAD *the manuscript*]. Here it is. Take it. It can't do any harm for you to read it. Return it to me later.

HOVSTAD. Good day, Doctor.

DR. STOCKMANN. Good day. You'll see, it's going to be easier than you think, Hovstad!

HOVSTAD. I hope so, Doctor. Sincerely. Let me know as soon as you hear from His Honor. [*He leaves.*]

DR. STOCKMANN [*goes to dining room and looks in*]. Catherine! Oh, you're home already, Petra!

PETRA [*coming in*]. I just got back from school.

MRS. STOCKMANN [*entering*]. Hasn't he been here yet?

DR. STOCKMANN. Peter? No, but I just had a long chat with Hovstad. He's really fascinated with my discovery, and you know, it has more implications that I thought at first. Do you know what I have backing me up?

MRS. STOCKMANN. What in heaven's name have you got backing you up?

DR. STOCKMANN. The solid majority.

MRS. STOCKMANN. Is that good?

DR. STOCKMANN. Good? It's wonderful. You can't imagine the feeling, Catherine, to know that your own town feels like a brother to you. I have never felt so at home in this town since I was a boy. [*A noise is heard.*]

MRS. STOCKMANN. That must be the front door.

DR. STOCKMANN. Oh, it's Peter then. Come in.

PETER STOCKMANN [*entering from the hall*]. Good morning!

DR. STOCKMANN. It's nice to see you, Peter.

MRS. STOCKMANN. Good morning. How are you today?

PETER STOCKMANN. Well, so so. [*To* DR. STOCKMANN.] I received your thesis about the condition of the springs yesterday.

DR. STOCKMANN. I got your note. Did you read it?

PETER STOCKMANN. I read it.

DR. STOCKMANN. Well, what do you have to say?

[PETER STOCKMANN *clears his throat and glances at the women.*]

MRS. STOCKMANN. Come on, Petra. [*She and* PETRA *leave the room at the left.*]

PETER STOCKMANN [*after a moment*]. Thomas, was it really necessary to go into this investigation behind my back?

DR. STOCKMANN. Yes. Until I was convinced myself, there was no point in—

PETER STOCKMANN. And now you are convinced?

DR. STOCKMANN. Well, certainly. Aren't you too, Peter? [*Pause.*] The University chemists corroborated . . .

PETER STOCKMANN. You intend to present this document to the Board of Directors, officially, as the medical officer of the springs?

DR. STOCKMANN. Of course, something's got to be done, and quick.

PETER STOCKMANN. You always use such strong expressions, Thomas. Among other things, in your report you say that we *guarantee* our guests and visitors a permanent case of poisoning.

DR. STOCKMANN. But, Peter, how can you describe it any other way? Imagine! Poisoned internally and externally!

PETER STOCKMANN. So you merrily conclude that we must build a waste-disposal plant—and reconstruct a brand-new water system from the bottom up!

DR. STOCKMANN. Well, do you know some other way out? I don't.

PETER STOCKMANN. I took a little walk over to the city engineer this morning and in the course of conversation I sort of jokingly mentioned these changes—as something we might consider for the future, you know.

DR. STOCKMANN. The future won't be soon enough, Peter.

PETER STOCKMANN. The engineer kind of smiled at my extravagance and gave me a few facts. I don't suppose you have taken the trouble to consider what your proposed changes would cost?

DR. STOCKMANN. No, I never thought of that.

PETER STOCKMANN. Naturally. Your little project would come to at least three hundred thousand crowns.

DR. STOCKMANN [*astonished*]. That expensive!

PETER STOCKMANN. Oh, don't look so upset—it's only money. The worst thing is that it would take some two years.

DR. STOCKMANN. Two years?

PETER STOCKMANN. At the least. And what do you propose we do about the springs in the meantime? Shut them up, no doubt! Because we would have to, you know. As soon as the rumor gets around that the water is dangerous, we won't have a visitor left. So that's the picture, Thomas. You have it in your power literally to ruin your own town.

DR. STOCKMANN. Now look, Peter! I don't want to ruin anything.

PETER STOCKMANN. Kirsten Springs are the blood supply of this town, Thomas—the only future we've got here. Now will you stop and think?

DR. STOCKMANN. Good God! Well, what do you think we ought to do?

PETER STOCKMANN. Your report has not convinced me that the conditions are as dangerous as you try to make them.

DR. STOCKMANN. Now listen; they are even worse than the report makes them out to be. Remember, summer is coming, and the warm weather!

PETER STOCKMANN. I think you're exaggerating. A capable physician ought to know what precautions to take.

DR. STOCKMANN. And what then?

PETER STOCKMANN. The existing water supply for the springs is a fact, Thomas, and has got to be treated as a fact. If you are reasonable and act with discretion, the directors of the Institute will be inclined to take under consideration any means to make possible improvements, reasonably and without financial sacrifices.

DR. STOCKMANN. Peter, do you imagine that I would ever agree to such trickery?

PETER STOCKMANN. Trickery?

DR. STOCKMANN. Yes, a trick, a fraud, a lie! A treachery, a downright crime, against the public and against the whole community!

PETER STOCKMAN. I said before that I am not convinced that there is any actual danger.

DR. STOCKMANN. Oh, you aren't? Anything else is impossible! My report is an absolute fact. The only trouble is that you and your administration were the ones who insisted that the water supply be built where it is, and now you're afraid to admit the blunder you committed. Damn it! Don't you think I can see through it all?

PETER STOCKMANN. All right, let's suppose that's true. Maybe I do care a little about my reputation. I still say I do it for the good of the town—without moral authority there can be no government. And that is why, Thomas, it is my duty to prevent your report from reaching the Board. Some time later I will bring up the matter for discussion. In the meantime, not a single word is to reach the public.

DR. STOCKMANN. Oh, my dear Peter, do you imagine you can prevent that!

PETER STOCKMANN. It will be prevented.

DR. STOCKMANN. It can't be. There are too many people who already know about it.

PETER STOCKMANN [*angered*]. Who? It can't possibly be those people from the *Daily Messenger* who—

DR. STOCKMANN. Exactly. The liberal, free, and independent press will stand up and do its duty!

PETER STOCKMANN. You are an unbelievably irresponsible man, Thomas! Can't you imagine what consequences that is going to have for you?

DR. STOCKMANN. For me?

PETER STOCKMANN. Yes, for you and your family.

DR. STOCKMANN. What the hell are you saying now!

PETER STOCKMANN. I believe I have the right to think of myself as a helpful brother, Thomas.

DR. STOCKMANN. You have been, and I thank you deeply for it.

PETER STOCKMANN. Don't mention it. I often couldn't help myself. I had hoped that by improving your finances I would be able to keep you from running completely hog wild.

DR. STOCKMANN. You mean it was only for your own sake?

PETER STOCKMANN. Partly, yes. What do you imagine people think of an official whose closest relatives get themselves into trouble time and time again?

DR. STOCKMANN. And that's what I have done?

PETER STOCKMANN. You do it without knowing it. You're like a man with an automatic brain—as soon as an idea breaks into your head, no matter how idiotic it may be, you get up like a sleepwalker and start writing a pamphlet about it.

DR. STOCKMANN. Peter, don't you think it's a citizen's duty to share a new idea with the public?

PETER STOCKMANN. The public doesn't need new ideas— the public is much better off with old ideas.

DR. STOCKMANN. You're not even embarrassed to say that?

PETER STOCKMANN. Now look, I'm going to lay this out once and for all. You're always barking about authority. If a man gives you an order he's persecuting you. Nothing is important enough to respect once you decide to revolt against your superiors. All right then, I give up. I'm not going to try to change you any more. I told you the stakes you are playing for here, and now I am going to give you an order. And I warn you, you had better obey it if you value your career.

DR. STOCKMANN. What kind of an order?

PETER STOCKMANN. You are going to deny these rumors officially.

DR. STOCKMANN. How?

PETER STOCKMANN. You simply say that you went into the examination of the water more thoroughly and you find that you overestimated the danger.

DR. STOCKMANN. I see.

PETER STOCKMANN. And that you have complete confidence that whatever improvements are needed, the management will certainly take care of them.

DR. STOCKMANN [*after a pause*]. My convictions come from the condition of the water. My convictions will change when the water changes, and for no other reason.

PETER STOCKMANN. What are you talking about convictions? You're an official, you keep your convictions to yourself!

DR. STOCKMANN. To myself?

PETER STOCKMANN. As an official, I said. God knows, as a private person that's something else, but as a subordinate employee of the Institute, you have no right to express any convictions or personal opinions about anything connected with policy.

DR. STOCKMANN. Now you listen to me. I am a doctor and a scientist—

PETER STOCKMANN. This has nothing to do with science!

DR. STOCKMANN. Peter, I have the right to express my opinion on anything in the world!

PETER STOCKMANN. Not about the Institute—that I forbid.

DR. STOCKMANN. You forbid!

PETER STOCKMANN. I forbid you as your superior, and when I give orders you obey.

DR. STOCKMANN. Peter, if you weren't my brother—

PETRA [*throwing the door at the left open*]. Father! You aren't going to stand for this! [*She enters.*]

MRS. STOCKMANN [*coming in after her*]. Petra, Petra!

PETER STOCKMANN. What have you two been doing, eavesdropping?

MRS. STOCKMANN. You were talking so loud we couldn't help . . .

PETRA. Yes, I was eavesdropping!

PETER STOCKMANN. That makes me very happy.

DR. STOCKMANN [*approaching his brother*]. You said something to me about forbidding—

PETER STOCKMANN. You forced me to.

DR. STOCKMANN. So you want me to spit in my own face officially—is that it?

PETER STOCKMANN. Why must you always be so colorful?

DR. STOCKMANN. And if I don't obey?

PETER STOCKMANN. Then we will publish our own statement, to calm the public.

DR. STOCKMANN. Good enough! And I will write against you. I will stick to what I said, and I will prove that I am right and that you are wrong, and what will you do then?

PETER STOCKMANN. Then I simply won't be able to prevent your dismissal.

DR. STOCKMANN. What!

PETRA. Father!

PETER STOCKMANN. Dismissed from the Institute is what I said. If you want to make war on Kirsten Springs, you have no right to be on the Board of Directors.

DR. STOCKMANN [*after a pause*]. You'd dare to do that?

PETER STOCKMANN. Oh, no, you're the daring man.

PETRA. Uncle, this is a rotten way to treat a man like Father!

MRS. STOCKMANN. Will you be quiet, Petra!

PETER STOCKMANN. So young and you've got opinions already—but that's natural. [*To* MRS. STOCKMANN.] Catherine dear, you're probably the only sane person in this house. Knock some sense into his head, will you? Make him realize what he's driving his whole family into.

DR. STOCKMANN. My family concerns nobody but myself.

PETER STOCKMANN. His family and his own town.

DR. STOCKMANN. I'm going to show you who loves his town. The people are going to get the full stink of this corruption, Peter, and then we will see who loves his town!

PETER STOCKMANN. You love your town when you blindly, spitefully, stubbornly go ahead trying to cut off our most important industry?

DR. STOCKMANN. That source is poisoned, man. We are getting fat by peddling filth and corruption to innocent people!

PETER STOCKMANN. I think this has gone beyond opinions and convictions, Thomas. A man who can throw that kind of insinuation around is nothing but a traitor to society!

DR. STOCKMANN [*starting toward his brother in a fury*]. How dare you to—

MRS. STOCKMANN [*stepping between them*]. Tom!

PETRA [*grabbing her father's arm*]. Be careful, Father!

PETER STOCKMANN [*with dignity*]. I won't expose myself to violence. You have been warned. Consider what you owe yourself and your family! Good day! [*He exits.*]

DR. STOCKMANN [*walking up and down*]. He's insulted. *He's* insulted!

MRS. STOCKMANN. It's shameful, Tom.

PETRA. Oh, I would love to give him a piece of my mind!

DR. STOCKMANN. It was my own fault! I should have shown my teeth right from the beginning. He called me a traitor to society. Me! Damn it all, that's not going to stick!

MRS. STOCKMANN. Please, think! He's got all the power on his side.

DR. STOCKMANN. Yes, but I have the truth on mine.

MRS. STOCKMANN. Without power, what good is the truth?

PETRA. Mother, how can you say such a thing?

DR. STOCKMANN. That's ridiculous, Catherine. I have the liberal press with me, and the majority. If that isn't power, what is?

MRS. STOCKMANN. But, for heaven's sake, Tom, you aren't going to—

DR. STOCKMANN. What am I not going to do?

MRS. STOCKMANN. You aren't going to fight it out in public with your brother!

DR. STOCKMANN. What the hell else do you want me to do?

MRS. STOCKMANN. But it won't do you any earthly good. If they won't do it, they won't. All you'll get out of it is a notice that you're fired.

DR. STOCKMANN. I am going to do my duty, Catherine. Me, the man he calls a traitor to society!

MRS. STOCKMANN. And how about your duty toward your family—the people you're supposed to provide for?

PETRA. Don't always think of us first, Mother.

MRS. STOCKMANN [*to* PETRA]. You can talk. If worst comes to worst, you can manage for yourself. But what about the boys, Tom, and you and me?

DR. STOCKMANN. What about you? You want me to be the miserable animal who'd crawl up the boots of that damn gang? Will you be happy if I can't face myself the rest of my life?

MRS. STOCKMANN. Tom, Tom, there's so much injustice in the world! You've simply got to learn to live with it. If you go on this way, God help us, we'll have no money again. Is it so long since the north that you've forgotten what it was to live like we lived? Haven't we had enough of that for one lifetime? [*The boys enter.*] What will happen to them? We've got nothing if you're fired!

DR. STOCKMANN. Stop it! [*He looks at the boys.*] Well, boys, did you learn anything in school today?

MORTEN [*looking at them, puzzled*]. We learned what an insect is.

DR. STOCKMANN. You don't say!

MORTEN. What happened here? Why is everybody—

DR. STOCKMANN. Nothing, nothing. You know what I'm going to do, boys? From now on I'm going to teach you what a man is. [*He looks at* MRS. STOCK-MANN. *She cries as the curtain falls.*]

ACT TWO.

Scene 1.

The editorial office of the People's Daily Messenger. *At the back of the room, to the left, is a door leading to the printing room. Near it, in the left wall, is another door. At the right of the stage is the entrance door. In the middle of the room there is a large table covered with papers, newspapers, and books. Around it are a few chairs. A writing desk stands against the right wall. The room is dingy and cheerless, the furniture shabby.*

As the curtain rises, BILLING *is sitting at the desk, reading the manuscript.* HOVSTAD *comes in after a moment from the printing room.* BILLING *looks up.*

BILLING. The Doctor not come yet?

HOVSTAD. No, not yet. You finish it?

[BILLING *holds up a hand to signal "just a moment." He reads on, the last paragraph of the manuscript.* HOVSTAD *comes and stands over him, reading with him. Now* BILLING *closes the manuscript, glances up at* HOVSTAD *with some trepidation, then looks off.* HOVSTAD, *looking at* BILLING, *walks a few steps away.*]

HOVSTAD. Well? What do you think of it?

BILLING [*with some hesitation*]. It's devastating. The Doctor is a brilliant man. I swear, I myself never really understood how incompetent those fat fellows are, on top. [*He picks up the manuscript and waves it a little.*] I hear the rumble of revolution in this.

HOVSTAD [*looking toward the door*]. Sssh! Aslaksen's inside.

BILLING. Aslaksen's a coward. With all that moderation talk, all he's saying is, he's yellow. You're going to print this, aren't you?

HOVSTAD. Sure, I'm just waiting for the Doctor to give the word. If his brother hasn't given in, we put it on the press anyway.

BILLING. Yes, but if the Mayor's against this it's going to get pretty rough. You know that, don't you?

HOVSTAD. Just let him try to block the reconstruction —the little businessmen and the whole town'll be screaming for his head. Aslaksen'll see to that.

BILLING [*ecstatically*]. The stockholders'll have to lay out a fortune of money if this goes through!

HOVSTAD. My boy, I think it's going to bust them. And when the springs go busted, the people are finally going to understand the level of genius that's been running this town. Those five sheets of paper are going to put in a liberal administration once and for all.

BILLING. It's a revolution. You know that? [*With hope and fear.*] I mean it, we're on the edge of a real revolution!

DR. STOCKMANN [*entering*]. Put it on the press!

HOVSTAD [*excited*]. Wonderful! What did the Mayor say?

DR. STOCKMANN. The Mayor has declared war, so war is what it's going to be! [*He takes the manuscript from* BILLING.] And this is only the beginning! You know what he tried to do?

BILLING [*calling into the printing room*]. Mr. Aslaksen, the Doctor's here!

DR. STOCKMANN [*continuing*]. He actually tried to blackmail me! He's got the nerve to tell me that I'm not allowed to speak my mind without his permission! Imagine the shameless effrontery!

HOVSTAD. He actually said it right out?

DR. STOCKMANN. Right to my face! The trouble with me was I kept giving them credit for being our kind of people, but they're dictators! They're people who'll try to hold power even if they have to poison the town to do it.

[*Toward the last part of* DR. STOCKMANN'S *speech* ASLAKSEN *enters.*]

ASLAKSEN. Now take it easy, Doctor, you—you mustn't always be throwing accusations. I'm with you, you understand, but moderation—

DR. STOCKMANN [*cutting him off*]. What'd you think of the article, Hovstad?

HOVSTAD. It's a masterpiece. In one blow you've managed to prove beyond any doubt what kind of men are running us.

ASLAKSEN. May we print it now, then?

DR. STOCKMANN. I should say *so!*

HOVSTAD. We'll have it ready for tomorrow's paper.

DR. STOCKMANN. And listen, Mr. Aslaksen, do me a favor; will you? You run a fine paper, but supervise the printing personally, eh? I'd hate to see the weather report stuck into the middle of my article.

ASLAKSEN [*laughing*]. Don't worry, that won't happen this time!

DR. STOCKMANN. Make it perfect, eh? Like you were printing money. You can't imagine how I'm dying to see it in print. After all the lies in the papers, the half-lies, the quarter-lies—to finally see the absolute, unvarnished truth about something important. And this is only the beginning. We'll go on to other subjects and blow up every lie we live by! What do you say, Aslaksen?

ASLAKSEN [*nodding in agreement*]. But just remember . . .

[BILLING *and* HOVSTAD *together with* ASLAKSEN.] Moderation!

ASLAKSEN [*to* BILLING *and* HOVSTAD]. I don't know what's so funny about that!

BILLING [*enthralled*]. Doctor Stockmann, I feel as though I were standing in some historic painting. Goddammit, this is a historic day! Someday this scene'll be in a museum, entitled, "The Day the Truth Was Born."

DR. STOCKMANN [*suddenly*]. Oh! I've got a patient half-bandaged down the street. [*He leaves.*]

HOVSTAD [*to* ASLAKSEN]. I hope you realize how useful he could be to us.

ASLAKSEN. I don't like that business about "this is only the beginning." Let him stick to the springs.

BILLING. What makes you so scared all the time?

ASLAKSEN. I have to live here. It'd be different if he were attacking the national government or something, but if he thinks I'm going to start going after the whole town administration—

BILLING. What's the difference? Bad is bad!

ASLAKSEN. Yes, but there is a difference. You attack the national government, what's going to happen? Nothing. They go right on. But a town administration—they're liable to be overthrown or something! I represent the small property owners in this town—

BILLING. Ha! It's always the same. Give a man a little property and the truth can go to hell!

ASLAKSEN. Mr. Billing, I'm older than you are. I've seen fire-eaters before. You know who used to work at that desk before you? Councilman Stensford—*councilman!*

BILLING. Just because I work at a renegade's desk, does that mean—

ASLAKSEN. You're a politician. A politician never knows where he's going to end up. And besides you applied for a job as secretary to the Magistrate, didn't you?

HOVSTAD [*surprised, laughs*]. Billing!

BILLING [*to* HOVSTAD]. Well, why not? If I get it I'll have a chance to put across some good things. I could put plenty of big boys on the spot with a job like that!

ASLAKSEN. All right, I'm just saying. [*He goes to the printing-room door.*] People change. Just remember when you call me a coward—I may not have made the hot speeches, but I never went back on my beliefs either. Unlike some of the big radicals around here, I didn't change. Of course, I *am* a little more moderate, but moderation is—

HOVSTAD. Oh, God!

ASLAKSEN. I don't see what's so funny about that! [*He glares at* HOVSTAD *and goes out.*]

BILLING. If we could get rid of him we—

HOVSTAD. Take it easy—he pays the printing bill, he's not that bad. [*He picks up the manuscript.*] I'll get the printer on this. [*He starts out.*]

BILLING. Say, Hovstad, how about asking Stockmann to back us? Then we could really put out a paper!

HOVSTAD. What would he do for money?

BILLING. His father-in-law.

HOVSTAD. Kiil? Since when has he got money?

BILLING. I think he's loaded with it.

HOVSTAD. No! Why, as long as I've known him he's worn the same overcoat, the same suit—

BILLING. Yeah, and the same ring on his right hand. You ever get a look at that boulder? [*He points to his finger.*]

HOVSTAD. No, I never—

BILLING. All year he wears the diamond inside, but on New Year's Eve he turns it around. Figure it out—when a man has no visible means of support, what is he living on? Money, right?

[PETRA *enters, carrying a book.*]

PETRA. Hello.

HOVSTAD. Well, fancy seeing you here. Sit down. What—

PETRA [*walking slowly up to* HOVSTAD]. I want to ask you a question. [*She starts to open the book.*]

BILLING. What's that?

PETRA. The English novel you wanted translated.

HOVSTAD. Aren't you going to do it?

PETRA [*with deadly seriousness and curiosity*]. I don't get this.

HOVSTAD. You don't get what?

PETRA. This book is absolutely against everything you people believe.

HOVSTAD. Oh, it isn't that bad.

PETRA. But, Mr. Hovstad, it says if you're good there's a supernatural force that'll fix it so you end up happy. And if you're bad you'll be punished. Since when does the world work that way?

HOVSTAD. Yes, Petra, but this is a newspaper, people like to read that kind of thing. They buy the paper for that and then we slip in our political stuff. A newspaper can't buck the public—

PETRA [*astonished, beginning to be angry*]. You don't say! [*She starts to go.*]

HOVSTAD [*hurrying after her*]. Now, wait a minute, I don't want you to go feeling that way. [*He holds the manuscript out to* BILLING.] Here, take this to the printer, will you?

BILLING [*taking the manuscript*]. Sure. [*He goes.*]

HOVSTAD. I just want you to understand something. I never even read that book. It was Billing's idea.

PETRA [*trying to penetrate his eyes*]. I thought he was a radical.

HOVSTAD. He is. But he's also a—

PETRA [*testily*]. A newspaperman.

HOVSTAD. Well, that too, but I was going to say that Billing is trying to get the job as secretary to the Magistrate.

PETRA. What?

HOVSTAD. People are—people, Miss Stockmann.

PETRA. But the Magistrate! He's been fighting everything progressive in this town for thirty years.

HOVSTAD. Let's not argue about it, I just didn't want you to go out of here with a wrong idea of me. I guess you know that I—I happen to admire women like you. I've never had a chance to tell you, but I—

well, I want you to know it. Do you mind? [*He smiles.*]

PETRA. No, I don't mind, but—reading that book upset me. I really don't understand. Will you tell me why you're supporting my father?

HOVSTAD. What's the mystery? It's a matter of principle.

PETRA. But a paper that'll print a book like this has no principle.

HOVSTAD. Why do you jump to such extremes? You're just like . . .

PETRA. Like what?

HOVSTAD. I simply mean that . . .

PETRA [*moving away from him*]. Like my father, you mean. You really have no use for him, do you?

HOVSTAD. Now wait a minute!

PETRA. What's behind this? Are you just trying to hold my hand or something?

HOVSTAD. I happen to agree with your father, and that's why I'm printing his stuff.

PETRA. You're trying to put something over, I think. Why are you in this?

HOVSTAD. Who're you accusing? Billing gave you that book, not me!

PETRA. But you don't mind printing it, do you? What are you trying to do with my father? You have no principles—what are you up to here?

[ASLAKSEN *hurriedly enters from the printing shop,* STOCKMANN'S *manuscript in his hand.*]

ASLAKSEN. My God! Hovstad! [*He sees* PETRA.] Miss Stockmann.

PETRA [*looking at* HOVSTAD]. I don't think I've been so frightened in my life. [*She goes out.*]

HOVSTAD [*starting after her*]. Please, you mustn't think I—

ASLAKSEN [*stopping him*]. Where are you going? The Mayor's out there.

HOVSTAD. The Mayor!

ASLAKSEN. He wants to speak to you. He came in the back door. He doesn't want to be seen.

HOVSTAD. What does he want? [*He goes to the printing-room door, opens it, calls out with a certain edge of servility.*] Come in, Your Honor!

PETER STOCKMANN [*entering*]. Thank you.

[HOVSTAD *carefully closes the door.*]

PETER STOCKMANN [*walking around*]. It's clean! I always imagined this place would look dirty. But it's clean. [*Commendingly.*] Very nice, Mr. Aslaksen. [*He puts his hat on the desk.*]

ASLAKSEN. Not at all, Your Honor—I mean to say, I always . . .

HOVSTAD. What can I do for you, Your Honor? Sit down?

PETER STOCKMANN [*sits, placing his cane on the table*]. I had a very annoying thing happen today, Mr. Hovstad.

HOVSTAD. That so?

PETER STOCKMANN. It seems my brother has written some sort of—memorandum. About the springs.

HOVSTAD. You don't say.

PETER STOCKMANN [*looking at HOVSTAD now*]. He mentioned it . . . to you?

HOVSTAD. Yes. I think he said something about it.

ASLAKSEN [*nervously starts to go out, attempting to hide the manuscript*]. Will you excuse me, gentlemen . . .

PETER STOCKMANN [*pointing to the manuscript*]. That's it, isn't it?

ASLAKSEN. This? I don't know, I haven't had a chance to look at it, the printer just handed it to me . . .

HOVSTAD. Isn't that the thing the printer wanted the spelling checked?

ASLAKSEN. That's it, it's only a question of spelling. I'll be right back.

PETER STOCKMANN. I'm very good at spelling. [*He holds out his hand.*] Maybe I can help you.

HOVSTAD. No, Your Honor, there's some Latin in it. You wouldn't know Latin, would you?

PETER STOCKMANN. Oh, yes. I used to help my brother with his Latin all the time. Let me have it.

[ASLAKSEN *gives him the manuscript.* PETER STOCKMANN *looks at the title on the first page, then glances up sarcastically at* HOVSTAD, *who avoids his eyes.*]

PETER STOCKMANN. You're going to print this?

HOVSTAD. I can't very well refuse a signed article. A signed article is the author's responsibility.

PETER STOCKMANN. Mr. Aslaksen, you're going to allow this?

ASLAKSEN. I'm the publisher, not the editor, Your Honor. My policy is freedom for the editor.

PETER STOCKMANN. You have a point—I can see that.

ASLAKSEN [*reaching for the manuscript*]. So if you don't mind . . .

PETER STOCKMANN. Not at all. [*But he holds on to the manuscript. After a pause.*] This reconstruction of the springs—

ASLAKSEN. I realize, Your Honor—it does mean tremendous sacrifices for the stockholders.

PETER STOCKMANN. Don't upset yourself. The first thing a Mayor learns is that the less wealthy can always be prevailed upon to demand a spirit of sacrifice for the public good.

ASLAKSEN. I'm glad you see that.

PETER STOCKMANN. Oh, yes. Especially when it's the wealthy who are going to do the sacrificing. What you don't seem to understand, Mr. Aslaksen, is that so long as I am Mayor, any changes in those springs are going to be paid for by a municipal loan.

ASLAKSEN. A municipal—you mean you're going to tax the people for this?

PETER STOCKMANN. Exactly.

HOVSTAD. But the springs are a private corporation!

PETER STOCKMANN. The corporation built Kirsten Springs out of its own money. If the people want them changed, the people naturally must pay the bill. The corporation is in no position to put out any more money. It simply can't do it.

ASLAKSEN [*to* HOVSTAD]. That's impossible! People will never stand for a new tax. [*To the* MAYOR.] Is this a fact or your opinion?

PETER STOCKMANN. It happens to be a fact. Plus another fact—you'll forgive me for talking about facts in a newspaper office—but don't forget that the springs will take two years to make over. Two years without income for your small businessmen, Mr. Aslaksen, and a heavy new tax besides. And all because— [*his private emotion comes to the surface; he throttles the manuscript in his hand*]—because of this dream, this hallucination, that we live in a pesthole!

HOVSTAD. That's based on science.

PETER STOCKMANN [*raising the manuscript and throwing it down on the table*]. This is based on vindictiveness, on his hatred of authority and nothing else. [*He pounds on the manuscript.*] This is the mad dream of a man who is trying to blow up our way of life! It has nothing to do with reform or science or anything else, but pure and simple destruction! And I intend to see to it that the people understand it exactly so!

ASLAKSEN [*hit by this*]. My God! [*To* HOVSTAD.] Maybe . . . You sure you want to support this thing, Hovstad?

HOVSTAD [*nervously*]. Frankly I'd never thought of it in quite that way. I mean . . . [*To the* MAYOR.] When you think of it psychologically it's completely possible, of course, that the man is simply out to—I don't know what to say, Your Honor. I'd hate to hurt the town in any way. I never imagined we'd have to have a new tax.

PETER STOCKMANN. You should have imagined it because you're going to have to advocate it. Unless, of course, liberal and radical newspaper readers enjoy high taxes. But you'd know that better than I. I happen to have here a brief story of the actual facts. It proves that, with a little care, nobody need be harmed at all by the water. [*He takes out a long envelope.*] Of course, in time we'd have to make a few minor structural changes and we'd pay for those.

HOVSTAD. May I see that?

PETER STOCKMANN. I want you to *study* it, Mr. Hovstad, and see if you don't agree that—

BILLING [*entering quickly*]. Are you expecting the Doctor?

PETER STOCKMANN [*alarmed*]. He's here?

BILLING. Just coming across the street.

PETER STOCKMANN. I'd rather not run into him here. How can I . . .

BILLING. Right this way, sir, hurry up!

ASLAKSEN [*at the entrance door, peeking*]. Hurry up!

PETER STOCKMANN [*going with* BILLING *through the door at the left*]. Get him out of here right away! [*They exit.*]

HOVSTAD. Do something, do something!

[ASLAKSEN *pokes among some papers on the table.* HOVSTAD *sits at the desk, starts to* "*write.*" DR. STOCKMANN *enters.*]

DR. STOCKMANN. Any proofs yet? [*He sees they hardly turn to him.*] I guess not, eh?

ASLAKSEN [*without turning*]. No, you can't expect them for some time.

DR. STOCKMANN. You mind if I wait?

HOVSTAD. No sense in that, Doctor, it'll be quite a while yet.

DR. STOCKMANN [*laughing, places his hand on* HOVSTAD'S *back*]. Bear with me, Hovstad, I just can't wait to see it in print.

HOVSTAD. We're pretty busy, Doctor, so . . .

DR. STOCKMANN [*starting toward the door*]. Don't let me hold you up. That's the way to be, busy, busy. We'll make this town shine like a jewel! [*He has opened the door, now he comes back.*] Just one thing. I—

HOVSTAD. Couldn't we talk some other time? We're very—

DR. STOCKMANN. Two words. Just walking down the street now, I looked at the people, in the stores, driving the wagons, and suddenly I was—well, touched, you know? By their innocence, I mean. What I'm driving at is, when this exposé breaks they're liable to start making a saint out of me or something, and I—Aslaksen, I want you to promise me that you're not going to try to get up any dinner for me or—

ASLAKSEN [*turning toward the* DOCTOR]. Doctor, there's no use concealing—

DR. STOCKMANN. I knew it. Now look, I will simply not attend a dinner in my honor.

HOVSTAD [*getting up*]. Doctor, I think it's time we—

[MRS. STOCKMANN *enters.*]

MRS. STOCKMANN. I thought so. Thomas, I want you home. Now come. I want you to talk to Petra.

DR. STOCKMANN. What happened? What are you doing here?

HOVSTAD. Something wrong, Mrs. Stockmann?

MRS. STOCKMANN [*leveling a look of accusation at* HOVSTAD]. Doctor Stockmann is the father of three children, Mr. Hovstad.

DR. STOCKMANN. Now look, dear, everybody knows that. What's the—

MRS STOCKMANN [*restraining an outburst at her husband*]. Nobody would *believe* it from the way you're dragging us into this disaster!

DR. STOCKMANN. What disaster?

MRS. STOCKMANN [*to* HOVSTAD]. He treated you like a son, now you make a fool of him?

HOVSTAD. *I'm* not making a—

DR. STOCKMANN. Catherine! [*He indicates* HOVSTAD.] How can you accuse—

MRS. STOCKMANN [*to* HOVSTAD]. He'll lose his job at the

springs, do you realize that? You print the article, and they'll grind him up like a piece of flesh!

DR. STOCKMANN. Catherine, you're embarrassing me! I beg your pardon, gentlemen . . .

MRS. STOCKMANN. Mr. Hovstad, what are you up to?

DR. STOCKMANN. I won't have you jumping at Hovstad, Catherine!

MRS. STOCKMANN. I want you home! This man is not your friend!

DR. STOCKMANN. He is my friend! Any man who shares my risk is my friend! You simply don't understand that as soon as this breaks everybody in this town is going to come out in the streets and drive that gang of— [*He picks up the* MAYOR'S *cane from the table, notices what it is, and stops. He looks from it to* HOVSTAD *and* ASLAKSEN.] What's this? [*They don't reply. Now he notices the hat on the desk and picks it up with the tip of the cane. He looks at them again. He is angry, incredulous.*] What the hell is he doing here?

ASLAKSEN. All right, Doctor, now let's be calm and—

DR. STOCKMANN [*starting to move*]. Where is he? What'd he do, talk you out of it? Hovstad! [HOVSTAD *remains immobile.*] He won't get away with it! Where'd you hide him? [*He opens the door at the left.*]

ASLAKSEN. Be careful, Doctor!

[PETER STOCKMANN *enters with* BILLING *through the door* DR. STOCKMANN *opened.* PETER STOCKMANN *tries to hide his embarrassment.*]

DR. STOCKMANN. Well, Peter, poisoning the water was not enough! You're working on the press now, eh? [*He crosses to the entrance door.*]

PETER STOCKMANN. My hat, please. And my stick. [DR. STOCKMANN *puts on the* MAYOR'S *hat.*] Now what's *this* nonsense! Take that off, that's official insignia!

DR. STOCKMANN. I just wanted you to realize, Peter— [*He takes off the hat and looks at it.*]—that anyone may wear this hat in a democracy, and that a free citizen is not afraid to touch it. [*He hands him the hat.*] And as for the baton of command, Your Honor, it can pass from hand to hand. [*He hands the cane to* PETER STOCKMANN.] So don't gloat yet. The people haven't spoken. [*He turns to* HOVSTAD *and* ASLAKSEN.] And I have the people because I have the truth, my friends!

ASLAKSEN. Doctor, we're not scientists. We can't judge whether your article is really true.

DR. STOCKMANN. Then print it under my name. Let *me* defend it!

HOVSTAD. I'm not printing it. I'm not going to sacrifice this newspaper. When the whole story gets out the public is not going to stand for any changes in the springs.

ASLAKSEN. His Honor just told us, Doctor—you see, there will have to be a new tax—

DR. STOCKMANN. Ahhhhh! Yes. I see. That's why you're not scientists suddenly and can't decide if I'm telling the truth. Well. So!

HOVSTAD. Don't take that attitude. The point is—

DR. STOCKMANN. The point, the point, oh, the point is going to fly through this town like an arrow, and I am going to fire it! [*To* ASLAKSEN.] Will you print this article as a pamphlet? I'll pay for it.

ASLAKSEN. I'm not going to ruin this paper and this town. Doctor, for the sake of your family—

MRS. STOCKMANN. You can leave his family out of this, Mr. Aslaksen. God help me, I think you people are horrible!

DR. STOCKMANN. My article, if you don't mind.

ASLAKSEN [*giving it to him*]. Doctor, you won't get it printed in this town.

PETER STOCKMANN. Can't you forget it? [*He indicates* HOVSTAD *and* ASLAKSEN.] Can't you see now that everybody—

DR. STOCKMANN. Your Honor, I can't forget it, and you

will never forget it as long as you live. I am going to call a mass meeting, and I—

PETER STOCKMANN. And who is going to rent you a hall?

DR. STOCKMANN. Then I will take a drum and go from street to street, proclaiming that the springs are befouled and poison is rotting the body politic! [*He starts for the door.*]

PETER STOCKMANN. And I believe you really are that mad!

DR. STOCKMANN. Mad? Oh, my brother, you haven't even heard me raise my voice yet. Catherine? [*He holds out his hand, she gives him her elbow. They go stiffly out.*]

[PETER STOCKMANN *looks regretfully toward the exit, then takes out his manuscript and hands it to* HOVSTAD, *who in turn gives it to* BILLING, *who hands it to* ASLAKSEN, *who takes it and exits.* PETER STOCKMANN *puts his hat on and moves toward the door. Blackout.*]

The Curtain Falls

Scene 2

A room in CAPTAIN HORSTER'S *house. The room is bare, as though unused for a long time. A large doorway is at the left, two shuttered windows at the back, and another door at the right. Upstage right, packing cases have been set together, forming a platform, on which are a chair and a small table. There are two chairs next to the platform at the right. One chair stands downstage left.*

The room is angled, thus making possible the illusion of a large crowd off in the wing to the left. The platform faces the audience at an angle, thus giving the speakers the chance to speak straight out front and creating the illusion of a large crowd by addressing "people" in the audience.

As the curtain rises the room is empty. CAPTAIN HORSTER *enters, carrying a pitcher of water, a glass, and a bell. He is putting these on the table when* BILLING *enters. A crowd is heard talking outside in the street.*

BILLING. Captain Horster?

HORSTER [*turning*]. Oh, come in. I don't have enough chairs for a lot of people so I decided not to have chairs at all.

BILLING. My name is Billing. Don't you remember, at the Doctor's house?

HORSTER [*a little coldly*]. Oh, yes, sure. I've been so busy I didn't recognize you. [*He goes to a window and looks out.*] Why don't those people come inside?

BILLING. I don't know, I guess they're waiting for the Mayor or somebody important so they can be sure it's respectable in here. I wanted to ask you a question before it begins, Captain. Why are you lending your house for this? I never heard of you connected with anything political.

HORSTER [*standing still*]. I'll answer that. I travel most of the year and—did you ever travel?

BILLING. Not abroad, no.

HORSTER. Well, I've been in a lot of places where people aren't allowed to say unpopular things. Did you know that?

BILLING. Sure, I've read about it.

HORSTER [*simply*]. Well, I don't like it. [*He starts to go out.*]

BILLING. One more question. What's your opinion about the Doctor's proposition to rebuild the springs?

HORSTER [*turning, thinks, then*]. Don't understand a thing about it.

[*Three citizens enter.*]

HORSTER. Come in, come in. I don't have enough chairs so you'll just have to stand. [*He goes out.*]

FIRST CITIZEN. Try the horn.

SECOND CITIZEN. No, let him start to talk first.

THIRD CITIZEN [*a big beef of a man, takes out a horn*]. Wait'll they hear this! I could blow your mustache off with this!

[HORSTER *returns. He sees the horn and stops abruptly.*]

HORSTER. I don't want any roughhouse, you hear me?

[MRS. STOCKMANN *and* PETRA *enter.*]

HORSTER. Come in. I've got chairs just for you.

MRS. STOCKMANN [*nervously*]. There's quite a crowd on the sidewalk. Why don't they come in?

HORSTER. I suppose they're waiting for the Mayor.

PETRA. Are all those people on his side?

HORSTER. Who knows? People are bashful, and it's so unusual to come to a meeting like this, I suppose they—

BILLING [*going over to this group*]. Good evening, ladies. [*They simply look at him.*] I don't blame you for not speaking. I just wanted to say I don't think this is going to be a place for ladies tonight.

MRS. STOCKMANN. I don't remember asking your advice, Mr. Billing.

BILLING. I'm not as bad as you think, Mrs. Stockmann.

MRS. STOCKMANN. Then why did you print the Mayor's statement and not a word about my husband's report? Nobody's had a chance to find out what he really stands for. Why, everybody on the street there is against him already!

BILLING. If we printed his report it only would have hurt your husband.

MRS. STOCKMANN. Mr. Billing, I've never said this to anyone in my life, but I think you're a liar.

[*Suddenly the* THIRD CITIZEN *lets out a blast on his horn. The women jump,* BILLING *and* HORSTER *turn around quickly.*]

HORSTER. You do that once more and I'll throw you out of here!

[PETER STOCKMANN *enters. Behind him comes the crowd. He pretends to be unconnected with them. He goes straight to* MRS. STOCKMANN, *bows.*]

PETER STOCKMANN. Catherine? Petra?

PETRA. Good evening.

PETER STOCKMANN. Why so coldly? He wanted a meeting and he's got it. [*To* HORSTER.] Isn't he here?

HORSTER. The Doctor is going around town to be sure there's a good attendance.

PETER STOCKMANN. Fair enough. By the way, Petra, did you paint that poster? The one somebody stuck on the Town Hall?

PETRA. If you can call it painting, yes.

PETER STOCKMANN. You know I could arrest you? It's against the law to deface the Town Hall.

PETRA. Well, here I am. [*She holds out her hands for the handcuffs.*]

MRS. STOCKMANN [*taking it seriously*]. If you arrest her, Peter, I'll never speak to you!

PETER STOCKMANN [*laughing*]. Catherine, you have no sense of humor!

[*He crosses and sits down at the left. They sit right. A* DRUNK *comes out of the crowd.*]

DRUNK. Say, Billy, who's runnin'? Who's the candidate?

HORSTER. You're drunk, Mister, now get out of here!

DRUNK. There's no law says a man who's drunk can't vote!

HORSTER [*pushing the* DRUNK *toward the door as the crowd laughs*]. Get out of here! Get out!

DRUNK. I wanna vote! I got a right to vote!

[ASLAKSEN *enters hurriedly, sees* PETER STOCKMANN, *and rushes to him.*]

ASLAKSEN. Your Honor . . . [*He points to the door.*] He's . . .

DR. STOCKMANN [*offstage*]. Right this way, gentlemen! In you go, come on, fellows!

[HOVSTAD *enters, glances at* PETER STOCKMANN *and* ASLAKSEN, *then at* DR. STOCKMANN *and another crowd behind him, who enter.*]

DR. STOCKMANN. Sorry, no chairs, gentlemen, but we couldn't get a hall, y'know, so just relax. It won't take long anyway. [*He goes to the platform, sees* PETER STOCKMANN.] Glad you're here, Peter!

PETER STOCKMANN. Wouldn't miss it for the world.

DR. STOCKMANN. How do you feel, Catherine?

MRS. STOCKMANN [*nervously*]. Just promise me, don't lose your temper . . .

HORSTER [*seeing the* DRUNK *pop in through the door*]. Did I tell you to get out of here!

DRUNK. Look, if you ain't votin', what the hell's going on here? [HORSTER *starts after him.*] Don't push!

PETER STOCKMANN [*to the* DRUNK]. I order you to get out of here and stay out!

DRUNK. I don't like the tone of your voice! And if you don't watch your step I'm gonna tell the Mayor right now, and he'll throw yiz all in the jug! [*To all.*] What're you, a revolution here?

[*The crowd bursts out laughing; the* DRUNK *laughs with them, and they push him out.* DR. STOCKMANN *mounts the platform.*]

DR. STOCKMANN [*quieting the crowd*]. All right, gentlemen, we might as well begin. Quiet down, please. [*He clears his throat.*] The issue is very simple—

ASLAKSEN. We haven't elected a chairman, Doctor.

DR. STOCKMANN. I'm sorry, Mr. Aslaksen, this isn't a meeting. I advertised a lecture and I—

A CITIZEN. I came to a meeting, Doctor. There's got to be some kind of control here.

DR. STOCKMANN. What do you mean, control? What is there to control?

SECOND CITIZEN. Sure, let him speak, this is no meeting!

THIRD CITIZEN. Your Honor, why don't you take charge of this—

DR. STOCKMANN. Just a minute now!

THIRD CITIZEN. Somebody responsible has got to take charge. There's a big difference of opinion here—

DR. STOCKMANN. What makes you so sure? You don't even know yet what I'm going to say.

THIRD CITIZEN. I've got a pretty good idea what you're

going to say, and I don't like it! If a man doesn't like it here, let him go where it suits him better. We don't want any troublemakers here!

[*There is assent from much of the crowd.* DR. STOCK-MANN *looks at them with new surprise.*]

DR. STOCKMANN. Now look, friend, you don't know anything about me—

FOURTH CITIZEN. We know plenty about you, Stockmann!

DR. STOCKMANN. From what? From the newspapers? How do you know I don't like this town? [*He picks up his manuscript.*] I'm here to save the life of this town!

PETER STOCKMANN [*quickly*]. Now just a minute, Doctor, I think the democratic thing to do is to elect a chairman.

FIFTH CITIZEN. I nominate the Mayor!

[*Seconds are heard.*]

PETER STOCKMANN. No, no, no! That wouldn't be fair. We want a neutral person. I suggest Mr. Aslaksen—

SECOND CITIZEN. I came to a lecture, I didn't—

THIRD CITIZEN [*to* SECOND CITIZEN]. What're you afraid of, a fair fight? [*To the* MAYOR.] Second Mr. Aslaksen!

[*The crowd assents.*]

DR. STOCKMANN. All right, if that's your pleasure. I just want to remind you that the reason I called this meeting was that I have a very important message for you people and I couldn't get it into the press, and nobody would rent me a hall. [*To* PETER STOCK-MANN.] I just hope I'll be given time to speak here. Mr. Aslaksen?

[*As* ASLAKSEN *mounts the platform and* DR. STOCKMANN *steps down*, KIIL *enters, looks shrewdly around.*]

ASLAKSEN. I just have one word before we start. Whatever is said tonight, please remember, the highest civic virtue is moderation. [*He can't help turning to* DR. STOCKMANN, *then back to the crowd.*] Now if anybody wants to speak—

[*The* DRUNK *enters suddenly.*]

DRUNK [*pointing at* ASLAKSEN]. I heard that! Since when you allowed to electioneer at the poles? [CITIZENS *push him toward the door amid laughter.*] I'm gonna report this to the Mayor, goddammit! [*They push him out and close the door.*]

ASLAKSEN. Quiet, please, quiet. Does anybody want the floor?

[DR. STOCKMANN *starts to come forward, raising his hand, but* PETER STOCKMANN *also has his hand raised.*]

PETER STOCKMANN. Mr. Chairman!

ASLAKSEN [*quickly recognizing* PETER STOCKMANN]. His Honor the Mayor will address the meeting.

[DR. STOCKMANN *stops, looks at* PETER STOCKMANN, *and, suppressing a remark, returns to his place. The* MAYOR *mounts the platform.*]

PETER STOCKMANN. Gentlemen, there's no reason to take very long to settle this tonight and return to our ordinary, calm, and peaceful life. Here's the issue: Doctor Stockmann, my brother—and believe me, it is not easy to say this—has decided to destroy Kirsten Springs, our Health Institute—

DR. STOCKMANN. Peter!

ASLAKSEN [*ringing his bell*]. Let the Mayor continue, please. There mustn't be any interruptions.

PETER STOCKMANN. He has a long and very involved way of going about it, but that's the brunt of it, believe me.

THIRD CITIZEN. Then what're we wasting time for? Run him out of town!

[*Others join in the cry.*]

PETER STOCKMANN. Now wait a minute. I want no violence here. I want you to understand his motives. He is a man, always has been, who is never happy unless he is badgering authority, ridiculing authority, destroying authority. He wants to attack the springs so he can prove that the administration blundered in the construction.

DR. STOCKMANN [*to* ASLAKSEN]. May I speak? I—

ASLAKSEN. The Mayor's not finished.

PETER STOCKMANN. Thank you. Now there are a number of people here who seem to feel that the Doctor has a right to say anything he pleases. After all, we are a democratic country. Now, God knows, in ordinary times I'd agree a hundred per cent with anybody's right to say anything. But these are not ordinary times. Nations have crises, and so do towns. There are ruins of nations, and there are ruins of towns all over the world, and they were wrecked by people who, in the guise of reform, and pleading for justice, and so on, broke down all authority and left only revolution and chaos.

DR. STOCKMANN. What the hell are you talking about!

ASLAKSEN. I'll have to insist, Doctor—

DR. STOCKMANN. I called a lecture! I didn't invite him to attack me. He's got the press and every hall in town to attack me, and I've got nothing but this room tonight!

ASLAKSEN. I don't think you're making a very good impression, Doctor.

[*Assenting laughter and catcalls. Again* DR. STOCKMANN *is taken aback by this reaction.*]

ASLAKSEN. Please continue, Your Honor.

PETER STOCKMANN. Now this is our crisis. We know what this town was without our Institute. We could barely afford to keep the streets in condition. It was a dead, third-rate hamlet. Today we're just on the verge of becoming internationally known as a resort. I predict that within five years the income of every man in this room will be immensely greater. I predict that our schools will be bigger and better. And in time this town will be crowded with fine carriages; great homes will be built here; first-class stores will open all along Main Street. I predict that if we are not defamed and maliciously attacked we will someday be one of the richest and most beautiful resort towns in the world. There are your choices. Now all you've got to do is ask yourselves a simple question: Has any one of us the right, the "democratic right," as they like to call it, to pick at minor flaws in the springs, to exaggerate the most picayune faults? [*Cries of No, No!*] And to attempt to publish these defamations for the whole world to see? We live or die on what the outside world thinks of us. I believe there is a line that must be drawn, and if a man decides to cross that line, we the people must finally take him by the collar and declare, "You cannot say that!"

[*There is an uproar of assent.* ASLAKSEN *rings the bell.*]

PETER STOCKMANN [*continuing*]. All right then. I think we all understand each other. Mr. Aslaksen, I move that Doctor Stockmann be prohibited from reading his report at this meeting! [*He goes back to his chair, which meanwhile* KIIL *has occupied.*]

[ASLAKSEN *rings the bell to quiet the enthusiasm.* DR. STOCKMANN *is jumping to get up on the platform, the report in his hand.*]

ASLAKSEN. Quiet, please. Please now. I think we can proceed to the vote.

DR. STOCKMANN. Well, aren't you going to let me speak at all?

ASLAKSEN. Doctor, we are just about to vote on that question.

DR. STOCKMANN. But damn it, man. I've got a right to—

PETRA [*standing up*]. Point of order, Father!

DR. STOCKMANN [*picking up the cue*]. Yes, point of order!

ASLAKSEN [*turning to him now*]. Yes, Doctor.

[DR. STOCKMANN, *at a loss, turns to* PETRA *for further instructions.*]

PETRA. You want to discuss the motion.

DR. STOCKMANN. That's right, damn it, I want to discuss the motion!

ASLAKSEN. Ah . . . [*He glances at* PETER STOCKMANN.] All right, go ahead.

DR. STOCKMANN [*to the crowd*]. Now, listen. [*He points at* PETER STOCKMANN.] He talks and he talks and he talks, but not a word about the facts! [*He holds up the manuscript.*]

THIRD CITIZEN. We don't want to hear any more about the water!

FOURTH CITIZEN. You're just trying to blow up everything!

DR. STOCKMANN. Well, judge for yourselves, let me read—

[*Cries of No, No, No! The man with the horn blows it.* ASLAKSEN *rings the bell.* DR. STOCKMANN *is utterly shaken. Astonished, he looks at the maddened faces. He lowers the hand holding the manuscript and steps back, defeated.*]

ASLAKSEN. Please, please now, quiet. We can't have this uproar! [*Quiet returns.*] I think, Doctor, that the majority wants to take the vote before you start to speak. If they so will, you can speak. Otherwise, majority rules. You won't deny that.

DR. STOCKMANN [*turns, tosses the manuscript on the floor, turns back to* ASLAKSEN]. Don't bother voting. I understand everything now. Can I have a few minutes—

PETER STOCKMANN. Mr. Chairman!

DR. STOCKMANN [*to his brother*]. I won't mention the Institute. I have a new discovery that's a thousand times more important than all the Institutes in the world. [*To* ASLAKSEN.] May I have the platform.

ASLAKSEN [*to the crowd*]. I don't see how we can deny him that, as long as he confines himself to—

DR. STOCKMANN. The springs are not the subject. [*He mounts the platform, looks at the crowd.*] Before I go into my subject I want to congratulate the liber-als and radicals among us, like Mr. Hovstad—

HOVSTAD. What do you mean, radical! Where's your evidence to call me a radical!

DR. STOCKMANN. You've got me there. There isn't any evidence. I guess there never really was. I just wanted to congratulate you on your self-control tonight—you who have fought in every parlor for the principle of free speech these many years.

HOVSTAD. I believe in democracy. When my readers are overwhelmingly against something, I'm not going to impose my will on the majority.

DR. STOCKMANN. You have begun my remarks, Mr. Hovstad. [*He turns to the crowd.*] Gentlemen, Mrs. Stockmann, Miss Stockmann. Tonight I was struck by a sudden flash of light, a discovery second to none. But before I tell it to you—a little story. I put in a good many years in the north of our country. Up there the rulers of the world are the great seal and the gigantic squadrons of duck. Man lives on ice, huddled together in little piles of stones. His whole life consists of grubbing for food. Nothing more. He can barely speak his own language. And it came to me one day that it was romantic and sentimental for a man of my education to be tending these people. They had not yet reached the stage where they needed a doctor. If the truth were to be told, a vet-erinary would be more in order.

BILLING. Is that the way you refer to decent hard-work-ing people!

DR. STOCKMANN. I expected that, my friend, but don't think you can fog up my brain with that magic word—the People! Not any more! Just because there is a mass of organisms with the human shape, they do not automatically become a People. That honor has to be earned! Nor does one automatically be-come a Man by having human shape, and living in a house, and feeding one's face—and agreeing with one's neighbors. That name *also* has to be earned. Now, when I came to my conclusions about the springs—

PETER STOCKMANN. You have no right to—

DR. STOCKMANN. That's a picayune thing, to catch me on a word, Peter. I am not going into the springs. [*To the crowd.*] When I became convinced of my theory about the water, the authorities moved in at once, and I said to myself, I will fight them to the death, because—

THIRD CITIZEN. What're you trying to do, make a revolution here? He's a revolutionist!

DR. STOCKMANN. Let me finish. I thought to myself: The majority, I have the majority! And let me tell you friends, it was a grand feeling. Because that's the reason I came back to this place of my birth. I wanted to give my education to this town. I loved it so, I spent months without pay or encouragement and dreamed up the whole project of the springs. And why? Not as my brother says, so that fine carriages could crowd our streets, but so that we might cure the sick, so that we might meet people from all over the world and learn from them, and become broader and more civilized. In other words, more like Men, more like A People.

A CITIZEN. You don't like anything about this town, do you?

ANOTHER CITIZEN. Admit it, you're a revolutionist, aren't you? Admit it!

DR. STOCKMANN. I don't admit it! I proclaim it now! I am a revolutionist! I am in revolt against the age-old lie that the majority is always right!

HOVSTAD. He's an aristocrat all of a sudden!

DR. STOCKMANN. And more! I tell you now that the majority is always wrong, and in this way!

PETER STOCKMANN. Have you lost your mind! Stop talking before—

DR. STOCKMANN. Was the majority right when they stood

by while Jesus was crucified? [*Silence.*] Was the majority right when they refused to believe that the earth moved around the sun and let Galileo be driven to his knees like a dog? It takes fifty years for the majority to be right. The majority is never right until it *does* right.

HOVSTAD. I want to state right now, that although I've been this man's friend, and I've eaten at his table many times, I now cut myself off from him absolutely.

DR. STOCKMANN. Answer me this! Please, one more moment! A platoon of soldiers is walking down a road toward the enemy. Every one of them is convinced he is on the right road, the safe road. But two miles ahead stands one lonely man, the outpost. He sees that this road is dangerous, that his comrades are walking into a trap. He runs back, he finds the platoon. Isn't it clear that this man must have the right to warn the majority, to argue with the majority, to fight with the majority if he believes he has the truth? Before many can know something, *one* must know it! [*His passion has silenced the crowd.*] It's always the same. Rights are sacred until it hurts for somebody to use them. I beg you now—I realize the cost is great, the inconvenience is great, the risk is great that other towns will get the jump on us while we're rebuilding—

PETER STOCKMANN. Aslaksen, he's not allowed to—

DR. STOCKMANN. Let me prove it to you! The water is poisoned!

THIRD CITIZEN [*steps up on the platform, waves his fist in* DR. STOCKMANN's *face*]. One more word about poison and I'm gonna take you outside!

[*The crowd is roaring; some try to charge the platform. The horn is blowing.* ASLAKSEN *rings his bell.* PETER STOCKMANN *steps forward, raising his hands.* KIIL *quietly exits.*]

PETER STOCKMANN. That's enough. Now stop it! Quiet!

There is not going to be any violence here! [*There is silence. He turns to* DR. STOCKMANN.] Doctor, come down and give Mr. Aslaksen the platform.

DR. STOCKMANN [*staring down at the crowd with new eyes*]. I'm not through yet.

PETER STOCKMANN. Come down or I will not be responsible for what happens.

MRS. STOCKMANN. I'd like to go home. Come on, Tom.

PETER STOCKMANN. I move the chairman order the speaker to leave the platform.

VOICES. Sit down! Get off that platform!

DR. STOCKMANN. All right. Then I'll take this to out-of-town newspapers until the whole country is warned!

PETER STOCKMANN. You wouldn't dare!

HOVSTAD. You're trying to ruin this town—that's all; trying to ruin it.

DR. STOCKMANN. You're trying to build a town on a morality so rotten that it will infect the country and the world! If the only way you can prosper is this murder of freedom and truth, then I say with all my heart, "Let it be destroyed! Let the people perish!"

[*He leaves the platform.*]

FIRST CITIZEN [*to the* MAYOR]. Arrest him! Arrest him!

SECOND CITIZEN. He's a traitor!

[*Cries of "Enemy! Traitor! Revolution!"*]

ASLAKSEN [*ringing for quiet*]. I would like to submit the following resolution: The people assembled here tonight, decent and patriotic citizens, in defense of their town and their country, declare that Doctor Stockmann, medical officer of Kirsten Springs, is an enemy of the people and of his community.

[*An uproar of assent starts.*]

MRS. STOCKMANN [*getting up*]. That's not true! He loves this town!

DR. STOCKMANN. You damned fools, you fools!

[*The* DOCTOR *and his family are all standing together, at the right, in a close group.*]

ASLAKSEN [*shouting over the din*]. Is there anyone

against this motion! Anyone against!

HORSTER [*raising his hand*]. I am.

ASLAKSEN. One? [*He looks around.*]

DRUNK [*who has returned, raising his hand*]. Me too! You can't do without a doctor! Anybody'll . . . tell you . . .

ASLAKSEN. Anyone else? With all votes against two, this assembly formally declares Doctor Thomas Stockmann to be the people's enemy. In the future, all dealings with him by decent, patriotic citizens will be on that basis. The meeting is adjourned.

[*Shouts and applause. People start leaving.* DR. STOCK-MANN *goes over to* HORSTER.]

DR. STOCKMANN. Captain, do you have room for us on your ship to America?

HORSTER. Any time you say, Doctor.

DR. STOCKMANN. Catherine? Petra?

[*The three start for the door, but a gantlet has formed, dangerous and silent, except for:*]

THIRD CITIZEN. You'd better get aboard soon, Doctor!

MRS. STOCKMANN. Let's go out the back door.

HORSTER. Right this way.

DR. STOCKMANN. No, no. No back doors. [*To the crowd.*] I don't want to mislead anybody—the enemy of the people is not finished in this town—not quite yet. And if anybody thinks—

[*The horn blasts, cutting him off. The crowd starts yelling hysterically:* "Enemy! Traitor! Throw him in the river! Come on, throw him in the river! Enemy! Enemy! Enemy!" *The* STOCKMANNS, *erect, move out through the crowd, with* HORSTER. *Some of the crowd follow them out, yelling.*]

[*Downstage, watching, are* PETER STOCKMANN, BILLING, ASLAKSEN, *and* HOVSTAD. *The stage is throbbing with the chant,* "Enemy, Enemy, Enemy!" *as the curtain falls.*]

ACT THREE.

DR. STOCKMANN's *living room the following morning. The windows are broken. There is great disorder. As the curtain rises,* DR. STOCKMANN *enters, a robe over shirt and trousers—it's cold in the house. He picks up a stone from the floor, lays it on the table.*

DR. STOCKMANN. Catherine! Tell what's-her-name there are still some rocks to pick up in here.

MRS. STOCKMANN [*from inside*]. She's not finished sweeping up the glass.

[*As* DR. STOCKMANN *bends down to get at another stone under a chair a rock comes through one of the last remaining panes. He rushes to the window, looks out.* MRS. STOCKMANN *rushes in.*]

MRS. STOCKMANN [*frightened*]. You all right?

DR. STOCKMANN [*looking out*]. A little boy. Look at him run! [*He picks up the stone.*] How fast the poison spreads—even to the children!

MRS. STOCKMANN [*looking out the window*]. It's hard to believe this is the same town.

DR. STOCKMANN [*adding this rock to the pile on the table*]. I'm going to keep these like sacred relics. I'll put them in my will. I want the boys to have them in their homes to look at every day. [*He shudders.*] Cold in here. Why hasn't what's-her-name got the glazier here?

MRS. STOCKMANN. She's getting him . . .

DR. STOCKMANN. She's been getting him for two hours! We'll freeze to death in here.

MRS. STOCKMANN [*unwillingly*]. He won't come here, Tom.

DR. STOCKMANN [*stops moving*]. No! The glazier's afraid to fix my windows?

MRS. STOCKMANN. You don't realize—people don't like to be pointed out. He's got neighbors, I suppose, and— [*She hears something.*] Is that someone at the door, Randine?

[*She goes to front door. He continues picking up stones. She comes back.*]

MRS. STOCKMANN. Letter for you.

DR. STOCKMANN [*taking and opening it*]. What's this now?

MRS. STOCKMANN [*continuing his pick-up for him*]. I don't know how we're going to do any shopping with everybody ready to bite my head off and—

DR. STOCKMANN. Well, what do you know? We're evicted.

MRS. STOCKMANN. Oh, no!

DR. STOCKMANN. He hates to do it, but with public opinion what it is . . .

MRS. STOCKMANN [*frightened*]. Maybe we shouldn't have let the boys go to school today.

DR. STOCKMANN. Now don't get all frazzled again.

MRS. STOCKMANN. But the landlord is such a nice man. If he's got to throw us out, the town must be ready to murder us!

DR. STOCKMANN. Just calm down, will you? We'll go to America, and the whole thing'll be like a dream.

MRS. STOCKMANN. But I don't want to go to America— [*She notices his pants.*] When did this get torn?

DR. STOCKMANN [*examining the tear*]. Must've been last night.

MRS. STOCKMANN. Your best pants!

DR. STOCKMANN. Well, it just shows you, that's all—when a man goes out to fight for the truth he should never wear his best pants. [*He calms her.*] Stop worrying, will you? You'll sew them up, and in no time at all we'll be three thousand miles away.

MRS. STOCKMANN. But how do you know it'll be any different there?

DR. STOCKMANN. I don't know. It just seems to me, in a big country like that, the spirit must be bigger. Still, I suppose they must have the solid majority there too. I don't know, at least there must be more room to hide there.

MRS. STOCKMANN. Think about it more, will you? I'd hate to go half around the world and find out we're in the same place.

DR. STOCKMANN. You know, Catherine, I don't think I'm ever going to forget the face of that crowd last night.

MRS. STOCKMANN. Don't think about it.

DR. STOCKMANN. Some of them had their teeth bared, like animals in a pack. And who leads them? Men who call themselves liberals! Radicals! [*She starts looking around at the furniture, figuring.*] The crowd lets out one roar, and where are they, my liberal friends? I bet if I walked down the street now not one of them would admit he ever met me! Are you listening to me?

MRS. STOCKMANN. I was just wondering what we'll ever do with this furniture if we go to America.

DR. STOCKMANN. Don't you ever listen when I talk, dear?

MRS. STOCKMANN. Why must I listen? I know you're right.

[PETRA *enters.*]

MRS. STOCKMANN. Petra! Why aren't you in school?

DR. STOCKMANN. What's the matter?

PETRA [*with deep emotion, looks at* DR. STOCKMANN, *goes up and kisses him*]. I'm fired.

MRS. STOCKMANN. They wouldn't!

PETRA. As of two weeks from now. But I couldn't bear to stay there.

DR. STOCKMANN [*shocked*]. Mrs. Busk fired you?

MRS. STOCKMANN. Who'd ever imagine she could do such a thing!

PETRA. It hurt her. I could see it, because we've always agreed so about things. But she didn't dare do anything else.

DR. STOCKMANN. The glazier doesn't dare fix the windows, the landlord doesn't dare let us stay on—

PETRA. The landlord!

DR. STOCKMANN. Evicted, darling! Oh, God, on the wreckage of all the civilizations in the world there ought to be a big sign: "They Didn't Dare!"

PETRA. I really can't blame her, Father. She showed me three letters she got this morning—

DR. STOCKMANN. From whom?

PETRA. They weren't signed.

DR. STOCKMANN. Oh, naturally. The big patriots with their anonymous indignation, scrawling out the darkness of their minds onto dirty little slips of paper—that's morality, and *I'm* the traitor! What did the letters say?

PETRA. Well, one of them was from somebody who said that he'd heard at the club that somebody who visits this house said that I had radical opinions about certain things.

DR. STOCKMANN. Oh, wonderful! Somebody heard that somebody heard that she heard, that he heard . . . ! Catherine, pack as soon as you can. I feel as though vermin were crawling all over me.

[HORSTER *enters*.]

HORSTER. Good morning.

DR. STOCKMANN. Captain! You're just the man I want to see.

HORSTER. I thought I'd see how you all were.

MRS. STOCKMANN. That's awfully nice of you, Captain, and I want to thank you for seeing us through the crowd last night.

PETRA. Did you get home all right? We hated to leave you alone with that mob.

HORSTER. Oh, nothing to it. In a storm there's just one thing to remember: it will pass.

DR. STOCKMANN. Unless it kills you.

HORSTER. You mustn't let yourself get too bitter.

DR. STOCKMANN. I'm trying, I'm trying. But I don't guarantee how I'll feel when I try to walk down the street with "Traitor" branded on my forehead.

MRS. STOCKMANN. Don't think about it.

HORSTER. Ah, what's a word?

DR. STOCKMANN. A word can be like a needle sticking in your heart, Captain. It can dig and corrode like an acid, until you become what they want you to be— really an enemy of the people.

HORSTER. You mustn't ever let that happen, Doctor.

DR. STOCKMANN. Frankly, I don't give a damn any more. Let summer come, let an epidemic break out, then they'll know whom they drove into exile. When are you sailing?

PETRA. You really decided to go, Father?

DR. STOCKMANN. Absolutely. When do you sail, Captain?

HORSTER. That's what I really came to talk to you about.

DR. STOCKMANN. Why? Something happen to the ship?

MRS. STOCKMANN [*happily, to* DR. STOCKMANN]. You see! We can't go!

HORSTER. No, the ship will sail. But I won't be aboard.

DR. STOCKMANN. No!

PETRA. You fired too? 'Cause I was this morning.

MRS. STOCKMANN. Oh, Captain, you shouldn't have given us your house.

HORSTER. Oh, I'll get another ship. It's just that the owner, Mr. Vik, happens to belong to the same party as the Mayor, and I suppose when you belong to a party, and the party takes a certain position . . . Because Mr. Vik himself is a very decent man.

DR. STOCKMANN. Oh, they're all decent men!

HORSTER. No, really, he's not like the others.

DR. STOCKMANN. He doesn't have to be. A party is like a

sausage grinder: it mashes up clearheads, longheads, fatheads, blockheads—and what comes out? Meatheads!

[*There is a knock on the hall door.* PETRA *goes to answer.*]

MRS. STOCKMANN. Maybe that's the glazier!

DR. STOCKMANN. Imagine, Captain! [*He points to the window.*] Refused to come all morning!

[PETER STOCKMANN *enters, his hat in his hand. Silence.*]

PETER STOCKMANN. If you're busy . . .

DR. STOCKMANN. Just picking up broken glass. Come in, Peter. What can I do for you this fine, brisk morning? [*He demonstratively pulls his robe tighter around his throat.*]

MRS. STOCKMANN. Come inside, won't you, Captain?

HORSTER. Yes, I'd like to finish our talk, Doctor.

DR. STOCKMANN. Be with you in a minute, Captain.

[HORSTER *follows* PETRA *and* CATHERINE *out through the dining-room doorway.* PETER STOCKMANN *says nothing, looking at the damage.*]

DR. STOCKMANN. Keep your hat on if you like, it's a little drafty in here today.

PETER STOCKMANN. Thanks, I believe I will. [*He puts his hat on.*] I think I caught cold last night—that house was freezing.

DR. STOCKMANN. I thought it was kind of warm—suffocating, as a matter of fact. What do you want?

PETER STOCKMANN. May I sit down? [*He indicates a chair near the window.*]

DR. STOCKMANN. Not there. A piece of the solid majority is liable to open your skull. Here.

[*They sit on the couch.* PETER STOCKMANN *takes out a large envelope.*]

DR. STOCKMANN. Now don't tell me.

PETER STOCKMANN. Yes. [*He hands the* DOCTOR *the envelope.*]

DR. STOCKMANN. I'm fired.

PETER STOCKMANN. The Board met this morning. There was nothing else to do, considering the state of public opinion.

DR. STOCKMANN [*after a pause*]. You look scared, Peter.

PETER STOCKMANN. I—I haven't completely forgotten that you're still my brother.

DR. STOCKMANN. I doubt that.

PETER STOCKMANN. You have no practice left in this town, Thomas.

DR. STOCKMANN. Oh, people always need a doctor.

PETER STOCKMANN. A petition is going from house to house. Everybody is signing it. A pledge not to call you any more. I don't think a single family will dare refuse to sign it.

DR. STOCKMANN. You started that, didn't you?

PETER STOCKMANN. No. As a matter of fact, I think it's all gone a little too far. I never wanted to see you ruined, Thomas. This will ruin you.

DR. STOCKMANN. No, it won't.

PETER STOCKMANN. For once in your life, will you act like a responsible man?

DR. STOCKMANN. Why don't you say it, Peter? You're afraid I'm going out of town to start publishing about the springs, aren't you?

PETER STOCKMANN. I don't deny that. Thomas, if you really have the good of the town at heart, you can accomplish everything without damaging anybody, including yourself.

DR. STOCKMANN. What's this now?

PETER STOCKMANN. Let me have a signed statement saying that in your zeal to help the town you went overboard and exaggerated. Put it any way you like, just so you calm anybody who might feel nervous about the water. If you'll give me that, you've got your job. And I give you my word, you can gradually make all the improvements you feel are necessary. Now, that gives you what you want . . .

DR. STOCKMANN. You're nervous, Peter.

PETER STOCKMANN [*nervously*]. I am not nervous!

DR. STOCKMANN. You expect me to remain in charge while people are being poisoned? [*He gets up.*]

PETER STOCKMANN. In time you can make your changes.

DR. STOCKMANN. When, five years, ten years? You know your trouble, Peter? You just don't grasp—even now —that there are certain men you can't buy.

PETER STOCKMANN. I'm quite capable of understanding that. But you don't happen to be one of those men.

DR. STOCKMANN [*after a slight pause*]. What do you mean by that now?

PETER STOCKMANN. You know damned well what I mean by that. Morten Kiil is what I mean by that.

DR. STOCKMANN. Morten Kiil?

PETER STOCKMANN. Your father-in-law, Morten Kiil.

DR. STOCKMANN. I swear, Peter, one of us is out of his mind! What are you talking about?

PETER STOCKMANN. Now don't try to charm me with that professional innocence!

DR. STOCKMANN. What are you talking about?

PETER STOCKMANN. You don't know that your father-in-law has been running around all morning buying up stock in Kirsten Springs?

DR. STOCKMANN [*perplexed*]. Buying up stock?

PETER STOCKMANN. Buying up stock, every share he can lay his hands on!

DR. STOCKMANN. Well, I don't understand, Peter. What's that got to do with—

PETER STOCKMANN [*walking around agitatedly*]. Oh, come now, come now, come now!

DR. STOCKMANN. I hate you when you do that! Don't just walk around gabbling "Come now, come now!" What the hell are you talking about?

PETER STOCKMANN. Very well, if you insist on being dense. A man wages a relentless campaign to destroy confidence in a corporation. He even goes so far as to call a mass meeting against it. The very next morning, when people are still in a state of shock about it all, his father-in-law runs all over town, picking up shares at half their value.

DR. STOCKMANN [*realizing, turns away*]. My God!

PETER STOCKMANN. And you have the nerve to speak to me about principles!

DR. STOCKMANN. You mean you actually believe that I . . . ?

PETER STOCKMANN. I'm not interested in psychology! I believe what I see! And what I see is nothing but a man doing a dirty, filthy job for Morten Kiil. And let me tell you—by tonight every man in this town'll see the same thing!

DR. STOCKMANN. Peter, you, you . . .

PETER STOCKMANN. Now go to your desk and write me a statement denying everything you've been saying, or . . .

DR. STOCKMANN. Peter, you're a low creature!

PETER STOCKMANN. All right then, you'd better get this one straight, Thomas. If you're figuring on opening another attack from out of town, keep this in mind: the morning it's published I'll send out a subpoena for you and begin a prosecution for conspiracy. I've been trying to make you respectable all my life; now if you want to make the big jump there'll be nobody there to hold you back. Now do we understand each other?

DR. STOCKMANN. Oh, we do, Peter! [PETER STOCKMANN *starts for the door.*] Get the girl—what the hell is her name—scrub the floors, wash down the walls, a pestilence has been here!

[KIIL *enters.* PETER STOCKMANN *almost runs into him.* PETER *turns to his brother.*]

PETER STOCKMANN [*pointing to* KIIL]. Ha! [*He turns and goes out.*]

[KIIL, *humming quietly, goes to a chair.*]

DR. STOCKMANN. Morten! What have you done? What's the matter with you? Do you realize what this makes me look like?

[KIIL *has started taking some papers out of his pocket.* DR. STOCKMANN *breaks off on seeing them.* KIIL *places them on the table.*]

DR. STOCKMANN. Is that—them?

KIIL. That's them, yes. Kirsten Springs shares. And very easy to get this morning.

DR. STOCKMANN. Morten, don't play with me—what is this all about?

KIIL. What are you so nervous about? Can't a man buy some stock without . . . ?

DR. STOCKMANN. I want an explanation, Morten.

KIIL [*nodding*]. Thomas, they hated you last night—

DR. STOCKMANN. You don't have to tell me that.

KIIL. But they also believed you. They'd love to murder you, but they believe you. [*Slight pause.*] The way they say it, the pollution is coming down the river from Windmill Valley.

DR. STOCKMANN. That's exactly where it's coming from.

KIIL. Yes. And that's exactly where my tannery is.

[*Pause.* DR. STOCKMANN *sits down slowly*].

DR. STOCKMANN. Well, Morten, I never made a secret to you that the pollution was tannery waste.

KIIL. I'm not blaming you. It's my fault. I didn't take you seriously. But it's very serious now. Thomas, I got that tannery from my father; he got it from his father; and his father got it from my great-grandfather. I do not intend to allow my family's name to stand for the three generations of murdering angels who poisoned this town.

DR. STOCKMANN. I've waited a long time for this talk, Morten. I don't think you can stop that from happening.

KIIL. No, but you can.

DR. STOCKMANN. I?

KIIL [*nudging the shares*]. I've bought these shares because—

DR. STOCKMANN. Morten, you've thrown your money away. The springs are doomed.

KIIL. I never throw my money away, Thomas. These were bought with your money.

DR. STOCKMANN. My money? What . . . ?

KIIL. You've probably suspected that I might leave a little something for Catherine and the boys?

DR. STOCKMANN. Well, naturally, I'd hoped you'd . . .

KIIL [touching the shares]. I decided this morning to invest that money in some stock.

DR. STOCKMANN [slowly getting up]. You bought that junk with Catherine's money!

KIIL. People call me "badger," and that's an animal that roots out things, but it's also some kind of a pig, I understand. I've lived a clean man and I'm going to die clean. You're going to clean my name for me.

DR. STOCKMANN. Morten . . .

KIIL. Now I want to see if you really belong in a strait jacket.

DR. STOCKMANN. How could you do such a thing? What's the matter with you!

KIIL. Now don't get excited, it's very simple. If you should make another investigation of the water—

DR. STOCKMANN. I don't *need* another investigation, I—

KIIL. If you think it over and decide that you ought to change your opinion about the water—

DR. STOCKMANN. But the water is poisoned! It is poisoned!

KIIL. If you simply go on insisting the water is poisoned—[he holds up the shares]—with these in your house, then there's only one explanation for you—you're absolutely crazy. [He puts the shares down on the table again.]

DR. STOCKMANN. You're right! I'm mad! I'm insane!

KIIL [with more force]. You're stripping the skin off your family's back! Only a madman would do a thing like that!

DR. STOCKMANN. Morten, Morten, I'm a penniless man! Why didn't you tell me before you bought this junk?

KIIL. Because you would understand it better if I told

you after. [*He goes up to* DR. STOCKMANN, *holds him by the lapels. With terrific force, and the twinkle still in his eye.*] And, goddammit, I think you do understand it now, don't you? Millions of tons of water come down that river. How do you know the day you made your tests there wasn't something unusual about the water?

DR. STOCKMANN [*not looking at* KIIL]. Yes, but I . . .

KIIL. How do you know? Why couldn't those little animals have clotted up only the patch of water you souped out of the river? How do you know the rest of it wasn't pure?

DR. STOCKMANN. It's not probable. People were getting sick last summer . . .

KIIL. They were sick when they came here or they wouldn't have come!

DR. STOCKMANN [*breaking away*]. Not intestinal diseases, skin diseases . . .

KIIL [*following him*]. The only place anybody gets a bellyache is here! There are no carbuncles in Norway? Maybe the food was bad. Did you ever think of the food?

DR. STOCKMANN [*with the desire to agree with him*]. No, I didn't look into the food . . .

KIIL. Then what makes you so sure it's the water?

DR. STOCKMANN. Because I tested the water and—

KIIL [*taking hold of him again*]. Admit it! We're all alone here. You have some doubt.

DR. STOCKMANN. Well, there's always a possible . . .

KIIL. Then part of it's imaginary.

DR. STOCKMANN. Well, nothing is a hundred per cent on this earth, but—

KIIL. Then you have a perfect right to doubt the other way! You have a scientific right! And did you ever think of some disinfectant? I bet you never even thought of that.

DR. STOCKMANN. Not for a mass of water like that, you can't . . .

KIIL. Everything can be killed. That's science! Thomas, I never liked your brother either, you have a perfect right to hate him.

DR. STOCKMANN. I didn't do it because I hate my brother.

KIIL. Part of it, part of it, don't deny it! You admit there's some doubt in your mind about the water, you admit there may be ways to disinfect it, and yet you went after your brother as though these doubts didn't exist; as though the only way to cure the thing was to blow up the whole Institute! There's hatred in that, boy, don't forget it. [*He points to the shares.*] These can belong to you now, so be sure, be sure! Tear the hatred out of your heart, stand naked in front of yourself—*are you sure?*

DR. STOCKMANN. What right have you to gamble my family's future on the strength of my convictions?

KIIL. Aha! Then the convictions are not really that strong!

DR. STOCKMANN. I am ready to hang for my convictions! But no man has a right to make martyrs of others; my family is innocent. Sell back those shares, give her what belongs to her. I'm a penniless man!

KIIL. Nobody is going to say Morten Kiil wrecked this town. [*He gathers up the shares.*] You retract your convictions—or these go to my charity.

DR. STOCKMANN. Everything?

KIIL. There'll be a little something for Catherine, but not much. I want my good name. It's exceedingly important to me.

DR. STOCKMANN [*bitterly*]. And charity . . .

KIIL. Charity will do it, or you will do it. It's a serious thing to destroy a town.

DR. STOCKMANN. Morten, when I look at you, I swear to God I see the devil!

[*The door opens, and before we see who is there . . .*]

DR. STOCKMANN. You!

[ASLAKSEN *enters, holding up his hand defensively.*]

ASLAKSEN. Now don't get excited! Please!

[HOVSTAD *enters. He and* ASLAKSEN *stop short and smile on seeing* KIIL.]

KIIL. Too many intellectuals here: I'd better go.

ASLAKSEN [*apologetically*]. Doctor, can we have five minutes of—

DR. STOCKMANN. I've got nothing to say to you.

KIIL [*going to the door*]. I want an answer right away. You hear? I'm waiting. [*He leaves.*]

DR. STOCKMANN. All right, say it quick, what do you want?

HOVSTAD. We don't expect you to forgive our attitude at the meeting, but . . .

DR. STOCKMANN [*groping for the word*]. Your attitude was prone . . . prostrated . . . prostituted!

HOVSTAD. All right, call it whatever you—

DR. STOCKMANN. I've got a lot on my mind, so get to the point. What do you want?

ASLAKSEN. Doctor, you should have told us what was in back of it all. You could have had the *Messenger* behind you all the way.

HOVSTAD. You'd have had public opinion with you now. Why didn't you tell us?

DR. STOCKMANN. Look, I'm very tired, let's not beat around the bush!

HOVSTAD [*gesturing toward the door where* KIIL *went out*]. He's been all over town buying up stock in the springs. It's no secret any more.

DR. STOCKMANN [*after a slight pause*]. Well, what about it?

HOVSTAD [*in a friendly way*]. You don't want me to spell it out, do you?

DR. STOCKMANN. I certainly wish you would. I—

HOVSTAD. All right, let's lay it on the table. Aslaksen, you want to . . . ?

ASLAKSEN. No, no, go ahead.

HOVSTAD. Doctor, in the beginning we supported you. But it quickly became clear that if we kept on supporting you in the face of public hysteria—

DR. STOCKMANN. Your paper created the hysteria.

HOVSTAD. One thing at a time, all right? [*Slowly, to drive it into* DR. STOCKMANN'S *head.*] We couldn't go on supporting you because, in simple language, we didn't have the money to withstand the loss in circulation. You're boycotted now? Well, the paper would have been boycotted too, if we'd stuck with you.

ASLAKSEN. You can see that, Doctor.

DR. STOCKMANN. Oh, yes. But what do you want?

HOVSTAD. *The People's Messenger* can put on such a campaign that in two months you will be hailed as a hero in this town.

ASLAKSEN. We're ready to go.

HOVSTAD. We will prove to the public that you had to buy up the stock because the management would not make the changes required for public health. In other words, you did it for absolutely scientific, public-spirited reasons. Now what do you say, Doctor?

DR. STOCKMANN. You want money from me, is that it?

ASLAKSEN. Well, now, Doctor . . .

HOVSTAD [*to* ASLAKSEN]. No, don't walk around it. [*To* DR. STOCKMANN.] If we started to support you again, Doctor, we'd lose circulation for a while. We'd like you—or Mr. Kiil rather—to make up the deficit. [*Quickly.*] Now that's open and aboveboard, and I don't see anything wrong with it. Do you?

[*Pause.* DR. STOCKMANN *looks at him, then turns and walks to the windows, deep in thought.*]

ASLAKSEN. Remember, Doctor, you need the paper, you need it desperately.

DR. STOCKMANN [*returning*]. No, there's nothing wrong with it at all. I—I'm not at all averse to cleaning up my name—although for myself it never was dirty. But I don't *enjoy* being hated, if you know what I mean.

ASLAKSEN. Exactly.

HOVSTAD. Aslaksen, will you show him the budget . . .

[ASLAKSEN *reaches into his pocket.*]

DR. STOCKMANN. Just a minute. There is one point. I hate to keep repeating the same thing, but the water is poisoned.

HOVSTAD. Now, Doctor . . .

DR. STOCKMANN. Just a minute. The Mayor says that he will levy a tax on everybody to pay for the reconstruction. I assume you are ready to support that tax at the same time you're supporting me.

ASLAKSEN. That tax would be extremely unpopular.

HOVSTAD. Doctor, with you back in charge of the baths, I have absolutely no fear that anything can go wrong.

DR. STOCKMANN. In other words, you will clean up my name—so that I can be in charge of the corruption.

HOVSTAD. But we can't tackle everything at once. A new tax—there'd be an uproar!

ASLAKSEN. It would ruin the paper!

DR. STOCKMANN. Then you don't intend to do anything about the water?

HOVSTAD. We have faith you won't let anyone get sick.

DR. STOCKMANN. In other words, gentlemen, you are looking for someone to blackmail into paying your printing bill.

HOVSTAD [*indignantly*]. We are trying to clear your name, Doctor Stockmann! And if you refuse to co-operate, if that's going to be your attitude . . .

DR. STOCKMANN. Yes? Go on. What will you do?

HOVSTAD [*to* ASLAKSEN]. I think we'd better go.

DR. STOCKMANN [*stepping in their way*]. What will you do? I would like you to tell me. Me, the man two minutes ago you were going to make into a hero— what will you do now that I won't pay you?

ASLAKSEN. Doctor, the public is almost hysterical . . .

DR. STOCKMANN. To my face, tell me what you are going to do!

HOVSTAD. The Mayor will prosecute you for conspiracy to destroy a corporation, and without a paper behind you, you will end up in prison.

DR. STOCKMANN. And you'll support him, won't you? I

want it from your mouth, Hovstad. This little victory you will not deny me. [HOVSTAD *starts for the door.* DR. STOCKMANN *steps into his way.*] Tell the hero, Hovstad. You're going to go on crucifying the hero, are you not? Say it to me! You will not leave here until I get this from your mouth!

HOVSTAD [*looking directly at* DR. STOCKMANN]. You are a madman. You are insane with egotism. And don't excuse it with humanitarian slogans, because a man who'll drag his family through a lifetime of disgrace is a demon in his heart! [*He advances on* DR. STOCKMANN.] You hear me? A demon who cares more for the purity of a public bath than the lives of his wife and children. Doctor Stockmann, you deserve everything you're going to get!

[DR. STOCKMANN *is struck by* HOVSTAD's *ferocious conviction.* ASLAKSEN *comes toward him, taking the budget out of his pocket.*]

ASLAKSEN [*nervously*]. Doctor, please consider it. It won't take much money, and in two months' time I promise you your whole life will change and . . .

[*Offstage* MRS. STOCKMANN *is heard calling in a frightened voice,* "What happened? My God, what's the matter?" *She runs to the front door.* DR. STOCKMANN, *alarmed, goes quickly to the hallway.* EJLIF *and* MORTEN *enter.* MORTEN's *head is bruised.* PETRA *and* CAPTAIN HORSTER *enter from the left.*]

MRS. STOCKMANN. Something happened! Look at him!

MORTEN. I'm all right, they just . . .

DR. STOCKMANN [*looking at the bruise*]. What happened here?

MORTEN. Nothing, Papa, I swear . . .

DR. STOCKMANN [*to* EJLIF]. What happened? Why aren't you in school?

EJLIF. The teacher said we better stay home the rest of the week.

DR. STOCKMANN. The boys hit him?

EJLIF. They started calling you names, so he got sore

and began to fight with one kid, and all of a sudden the whole bunch of them . . .

MRS. STOCKMANN [*to* MORTEN]. Why did you answer!

MORTEN [*indignantly*]. They called him a traitor! My father is no traitor!

EJLIF. But you didn't have to answer!

MRS. STOCKMANN. You should've known they'd all jump on you! They could have killed you!

MORTEN. I don't care!

DR. STOCKMANN [*to quiet him—and his own heart*]. Morten . . .

MORTEN [*pulling away from his father*]. I'll kill them! I'll take a rock and the next time I see one of them I'll kill him!

[DR. STOCKMANN *reaches for* MORTEN, *who, thinking his father will chastise him, starts to run.* DR. STOCKMANN *catches him and grips him by the arm.*]

MORTEN. Let me go! Let me . . . !

DR. STOCKMANN. Morten . . . Morten . . .

MORTEN [*crying in his father's arms*]. They called you traitor, an enemy . . . [*He sobs.*]

DR. STOCKMANN. Ssh. That's all. Wash your face.

[MRS. STOCKMANN *takes* MORTEN. DR. STOCKMANN *stands erect, faces* ASLAKSEN *and* HOVSTAD.]

DR. STOCKMANN. Good day, gentlemen.

HOVSTAD. Let us know what you decide and we'll—

DR. STOCKMANN. I've decided. I am an enemy of the people.

MRS. STOCKMANN. Tom, what are you . . . ?

DR. STOCKMANN. To such people, who teach their own children to think with their fists—to them I'm an enemy! And my boy . . . my boys . . . my family . . . I think you can count us all enemies.

ASLAKSEN. Doctor, you could have everything you want!

DR. STOCKMANN. Except the truth. I could have everything but that—that the water is poisoned!

HOVSTAD. But you'll be in charge.

DR. STOCKMANN. But the children are poisoned, the peo-

ple are poisoned! If the only way I can be a friend of
the people is to take charge of that corruption, then
I am an enemy! The water is poisoned, poisoned, poisoned! That's the beginning of it and that's the end
of it! Now get out of here!

HOVSTAD. You know where you're going to end?

DR. STOCKMANN. I said get out of here! [*He grabs* ASLAK-
SEN'S *umbrella out of his hand.*]

MRS. STOCKMANN. What are you doing?

[ASLAKSEN *and* HOVSTAD *back toward the door as* DR.
STOCKMANN *starts to swing.*]

ASLAKSEN. You're a fanatic, you're out of your mind!

MRS. STOCKMANN [*grabbing* DR. STOCKMANN *to take the
umbrella*]. What are you doing?

DR. STOCKMANN. They want me to buy the paper, the
public, the pollution of the springs, buy the whole
pollution of this town! They'll make a hero out of
me for that! [*Furiously, to* ASLAKSEN *and* HOVSTAD.]
But I'm not a hero, I'm the enemy—and now you're
first going to find out what kind of enemy I am!
I will sharpen my pen like a dagger—you, all you
friends of the people, are going to bleed before I'm
done! Go, tell them to sign the petitions! Warn them
not to call me when they're sick! Beat up my children! And never let her—[*he points to* PETRA]—in the
school again or she'll destroy the immaculate purity
of the vacuum there! See to all the barricades—the
truth is coming! Ring the bells, sound the alarm!
The truth, the truth is out, and soon it will be prowl-
ing like a lion in the streets!

HOVSTAD. Doctor, you're out of your mind.

[*He and* ASLAKSEN *turn to go. They are in the doorway.*]

EJLIF [*rushing at them*]. Don't you say that to him!

DR. STOCKMANN [*as* MRS. STOCKMANN *cries out, rushes
them with the umbrella*]. Out of here!

[*They rush out.* DR. STOCKMANN *throws the umbrella
after them, then slams the door. Silence. He has his
back pressed against the door, facing his family.*]

DR. STOCKMANN. I've had all the ambassadors of hell today, but there'll be no more. Now, now listen, Catherine! Children, listen. Now we're besieged. They'll call for blood now, they'll whip the people like oxen— [*A rock comes through a remaining pane. The boys start for the window.*] Stay away from there!

MRS. STOCKMANN. The Captain knows where we can get a ship.

DR. STOCKMANN. No ships.

PETRA. We're staying?

MRS. STOCKMANN. But they can't go back to school! I won't let them out of the house!

DR. STOCKMANN. We're staying.

PETRA. Good!

DR. STOCKMANN. We must be careful now. We must live through this. Boys, no more school. I'm going to teach you, and Petra will. Do you know any kids, street louts, hookey-players—

EJLIF. Oh, sure, we—

DR. STOCKMANN. We'll want about twelve of them to start. But I want them good and ignorant, absolutely uncivilized. Can we use your house, Captain?

HORSTER. Sure, I'm never there.

DR. STOCKMANN. Fine. We'll begin, Petra, and we'll turn out not taxpayers and newspaper subscribers, but free and independent people, hungry for the truth. Oh, I forgot! Petra, run to Grandpa and tell him—tell him as follows: NO!

MRS. STOCKMANN [*puzzled*]. What do you mean?

DR. STOCKMANN [*going over to* MRS. STOCKMANN]. It means, my dear, that we are all alone. And there'll be a long night before it's day—

[*A rock comes through a paneless window.* HORSTER *goes to the window. A crowd is heard approaching.*]

HORSTER. Half the town is out!

MRS. STOCKMANN. What's going to happen? Tom! What's going to happen?

DR. STOCKMANN [*holding his hands up to quiet her,*

and with a trembling mixture of trepidation and courageous insistence]. I don't know. But remember now, everybody. You are fighting for the truth, and that's why you're alone. And that makes you strong. We're the strongest people in the world . . .

[*The crowd is heard angrily calling outside. Another rock comes through a window.*]

DR. STOCKMANN. . . . and the strong must learn to be lonely!

[*The crowd noise gets louder. He walks upstage toward the windows as a wind rises and the curtains start to billow out toward him.*]

The Curtain Falls

AUGUST STRINDBERG

The battle between the sexes has always been and still remains the most entertaining and absorbing of all literary and artistic subjects. From the temptation of Adam by the first woman in the Book of Genesis to the cartoons of the late James Thurber in *The New Yorker*, the battle has raged. We have laughed about it with Aristophanes, Molière and Shaw. We have wept over the tragedy of it with Euripides, Shakespeare and Flaubert. But nowhere in the history of the literature of the stage have we seen it more violently presented than in the dramas of August Strindberg.

Love on the stage is frequently viewed with the confidence of St. Paul: it conquereth all. Certainly that—vulgarized—is the romantic approach. Occasionally, however, as in *Othello* or *Medea* or *Phèdre*, its consequences are revealed as destructive and consequently tragic. Sometimes, again, it is dissected out of existence or mud-bespattered beyond recognition. In the plays of Strindberg the emotional and sexual relationship between men and women is presented as one long primordial fight to the death. With him love and hate become so inextricably intertwined that one cannot find the true and shining face of love at all.

Although Strindberg, the greatest Swedish playwright of all time, was born in 1849, only twenty-one years after Ibsen and nine years after Zola, he seems infinitely more modern than either of them. True, his early romantic dramas, *The Outlaw* and *Master Olaf*, have no contemporaneous feeling; but from the time he came into his true power, first with *The Father* in 1887, then a year later with *Comrades,* and thereafter with *Creditors, The Dance of Death, Miss Julie,* and *There Are Crimes and Crimes,* he revealed a comprehension of psychological motivation that is altogether astounding in its modernity. These plays, except for minor details of environment and custom, might have been written last year and by a man who was a practicing psychiatrist! No wonder Eugene O'Neill acknowledged Strindberg as one of the greatest influences on his life and work.

The Father depicts the destruction of a man's brain through the machinations of a vindictive and malevolent wife. Both are bound irremediably by the laws of their own natures. However desirous of happiness they may be, they are helpless—especially so is the woman—against their own destructive·impulses. In both *Comrades* and *Creditors* we are treated to the same macabre spectacle of a woman in the process of devouring her husband.

In *The Dance of Death* the couple is equally balanced in guilt. In *Miss Julie,* the play I have included in this collection, the man is victorious—if one may say it is a victory for a man to force his mistress to commit suicide. As James Huneker, referring to *Miss Julie,* has written in *Iconoclasts* (and if anyone deserves to be treated in a book by that name it is Strindberg): "It is a tiny epic of hatred. . . . In comparison, the coda of Ibsen's *Ghosts* is a mild exercise in emotional arpeggios!"

In his Foreword to this play, which I wish space permitted me to include in its entirety, Strindberg analyzes his creation with almost scientific detachment. "I see Miss Julie's tragic fate," he says, "to be the result of many circumstances: the mother's character, the father's mistaken upbringing of the girl, her own nature, and the influence of her fiancé on a weak, degenerate mind.

Also, more directly, the festive mood of Midsummer Eve, her father's absence, her monthly indisposition, her preoccupation with animals, the excitation of the dance, the magic of dusk, the strongly aphrodisiac influence of flowers, and finally the chance that drives the couple into a room alone—to which must be added the urgency of the excited man. My treatment of the theme, moreover, is neither exclusively physiological nor psychological. I have not put the blame wholly on the inheritance from her mother, nor on her physical condition at the time, nor on immorality. I have not even preached a moral sermon; in the absence of a priest I leave this to the cook. I congratulate myself on this multiplicity of motives as being up-to-date. . . ."

Summing it up, later in the Foreword, he concludes: "My souls (characters) are conglomerations of past and present stages of civilization, bits from books and newspapers, scraps of humanity, rags and tatters of fine clothing, patched together as is the human soul." This is no nineteenth-century Victorian speaking; this is a modern man.

The author of this violence lived a violent life. The offspring of a misalliance, cradled in poverty and brought up in a household of ten which for a time was forced to share a meager three rooms, young August grew into a suspicious, sensitive, irritable youth, who quarreled with his professors at the University and lost the scholarship the King had awarded him after *The Outlaw*. His several marriages all ended unsatisfactorily. His mental state was far from stable. The violence finally came to an end on May 14th, 1912, and the old Swedish titan found peace at last.

During his sixty-three years he created a body of dramatic work that only now are we coming properly to appreciate. I have emphasized, as is proper, I feel, in a volume concerned with realism, those plays which were written in that manner. But it must be added that there is another Strindberg: the mystic and the symbolist, the artist who seems even more modern than the psychological naturalist represented here. This is the Strindberg who concluded that there is more to life than meets the eye, who cast away the camera for the x-ray, so to speak, in order to discover what lay beneath the surface image; the Strindberg who wrote *The Dream Play, The Spook Sonata, To Damascus* and *Easter*. For these dramas prepared the way for the expressionism of our own time: for the Germans Kaiser and Toller, for the Elmer Rice of *Th⸱ Adding Machine* and the O'Neill of *The Great God Brown*, even for Genêt, Beckett and Ionesco. Before all of them Strindberg marched in advance.

Miss Julie

by AUGUST STRINDBERG

Translated by E. M. Sprinchorn

Application for permission for any such use of this version should be made to the University of Minnesota Press, 2037 University Avenue S.E., Minneapolis, MN 55414.

Reprinted by permission from the University of Minnesota Press.

CHARACTERS

Miss Julie, twenty-five years old.
Jean, valet, thirty years old.
Christine, the cook, thirty-five years old.

The action of the play takes place in the kitchen of the Count's manor house on Midsummer Eve in Sweden in the 1880's.

The scene is a large kitchen. The walls and ceiling are covered with draperies and hangings. The rear wall runs obliquely upstage from the left. On this wall to the left are two shelves with pots and pans of copper, iron, and pewter. The shelves are decorated with goffered paper. A little to the right can be seen three-fourths of a deep arched doorway with two glass doors, and through them can be seen a fountain with a statue of Cupid, lilac bushes in bloom, and the tops of some Lombardy poplars. From the left of the stage the corner of a large, Dutch-tile kitchen stove protrudes with part of the hood showing. Projecting from the right side of the stage is one end of the servants' dining table of white pine, with a few chairs around it. The stove is decorated with branches of birch leaves; the floor is strewn with juniper twigs. On the end of the table is a large Japanese spice jar filled with lilacs. An icebox, a sink, a wash basin. Over the door a big, old-fashioned bell; and to the left of the door the gaping mouth of a speaking tube.

CHRISTINE *is standing at the stove, frying something. She is wearing a light-colored cotton dress and an apron.* JEAN *enters, dressed in livery and carrying a pair of high-top boots with spurs. He sets them where they are clearly visible.*

JEAN. Tonight she's wild again. Miss Julie's absolutely wild!

CHRISTINE. You took your time getting back!

JEAN. I took the Count down to the station, and on my

way back as I passed the barn I went in for a dance.
And there was Miss Julie leading the dance with the
game warden. But then she noticed me. And she
came right up and chose me for the ladies' waltz.
And she's been dancing ever since like—like I don't
know what. She's absolutely wild!

CHRISTINE. That's nothing new. But she's been worse
than ever during the last two weeks, ever since her
engagement was broken off.

JEAN. Yes, I never did hear all there was to that. He
was a good man, too, even if he wasn't rich. Well,
that's a woman for you. [*He sits down at the end of
the table.*] But, tell me, isn't it strange that a young
girl like her—all right, young woman—prefers to
stay home here with the servants rather than go with
her father to visit her relatives?

CHRISTINE. I suppose she's ashamed to face them after
that fiasco with her young man.

JEAN. No doubt. He wouldn't take any nonsense from
her. Do you know what happened, Christine? I do. I
saw the whole thing, even though I didn't let on.

CHRISTINE. Don't tell me you were there?

JEAN. Well, I was. They were in the barnyard one evening—and she was training him, as she called it. Do
you know what she was doing? She was making him
jump over her riding whip—training him like a dog.
He jumped over twice, and she whipped him both
times. But the third time, he grabbed the whip from
her, broke it in a thousand pieces—and walked off.

CHRISTINE. So that's what happened. Well, what do you
know.

JEAN. Yes, that put an end to that affair.—Now have
you got something good for me, Christine?

CHRISTINE [*serving him from the frying pan*]. Just a
little bit of kidney. I cut it especially for you.

JEAN [*smelling it*]. Wonderful! My special *délice!*
[*Feeling the plate.*] Hey, you didn't warm the plate!

CHRISTINE. You're more fussy than the Count himself when you set your mind to it. [*She rumples his hair gently.*]

JEAN [*irritated*]. Cut it out! Don't muss up my hair. You know I don't like that!

CHRISTINE. Oh, now don't get mad. Can I help it if I like you?

[*Jean eats.* CHRISTINE *gets out a bottle of beer.*]

JEAN. Beer on Midsummer Eve! No thank you! I've got something much better than that. [*He opens a drawer in the table and takes out a bottle of red wine with a gold seal.*] Do you see that? Gold Seal. Now give me a glass.—No, a wine glass of course. I'm drinking it straight.

CHRISTINE [*goes back to the stove and puts on a small saucepan*]. Lord help the woman who gets you for a husband. You're an old fussbudget!

JEAN. Talk, talk! You'd consider yourself lucky if you got yourself a man as good as me. It hasn't done you any harm to have people think I'm your fiancé. [*He tastes the wine.*] Very good. Excellent. But warmed just a little too little. [*Warming the glass in his hands.*] We bought this in Dijon. Four francs a liter, unbottled—and the tax on top of that. . . . What on earth are you cooking? It smells awful!

CHRISTINE. Some damn mess that Miss Julie wants for her dog.

JEAN. You should watch your language, Christine. . . . Why do you have to stand in front of the stove on a holiday, cooking for that mutt? Is it sick?

CHRISTINE. Oh, she's sick, all right! She sneaked out to the gatekeeper's mongrel and—got herself in a fix. And Miss Julie, you know, can't stand anything like that.

JEAN. She's too stuck-up in some ways and not proud enough in others. Just like her mother. The Countess felt right at home in the kitchen or down in the barn with the cows, but when she went driving, *one* horse wasn't enough for her; she had to have a pair. Her sleeves were always dirty, but her buttons had the royal crown on them. As for Miss Julie, she doesn't seem to care how she looks and acts. I mean, she's not really refined. Just now, down at the barn, she grabbed the game warden away from Anna and asked him to dance. You wouldn't see anybody in our class doing a thing like that. But that's what happens when the gentry try to act like the common people —they become common! . . . But she *is* beautiful! Magnificent! Ah, those shoulders—those—and so forth, and so forth!

CHRISTINE. Oh, don't exaggerate. Clara tells me all about her, and Clara dresses her.

JEAN. Clara, pooh! You women are always jealous of each other. *I've* been out riding with her. . . . And how she can dance!

CHRISTINE. Listen, Jean, you *are* going to dance with me, aren't you, when I am finished here?

JEAN. Certainly! Of course I am.

CHRISTINE. Promise?

JEAN. Promise! Listen if I say I'm going to do a thing, I do it. . . . Christine, I thank you for a delicious meal. [*He shoves the cork back into the bottle.*]

[MISS JULIE *appears in the doorway, talking to someone outside.*]

MISS JULIE. I'll be right back. Don't wait for me.

[JEAN *slips the bottle into the table drawer quickly and rises respectfully.* MISS JULIE *comes in and crosses over to* CHRISTINE, *who is at the mirror.*]

MISS JULIE. Did you get it ready?

[CHRISTINE *signals that* JEAN *is present.*]

JEAN [*polite and charming*]. Are you ladies sharing secrets?

MISS JULIE [*flipping her handkerchief in his face*]. Don't be nosey!

JEAN. Oh, that smells good! Violets.

MISS JULIE [*flirting with him*]. Don't be impudent! And don't tell me you're an expert on perfumes, too. I know you're an expert dancer.—No, don't look! Go away!

JEAN [*inquisitive, but deferential*]. What are you cooking? A witch's brew for Midsummer Eve? Something that reveals what the stars have in store for you, so you can see the face of your future husband?

MISS JULIE [*curtly*]. You'd have to have good eyes to see that. [*To* CHRISTINE.] Pour it into a small bottle, and seal it tight. . . . Jean, come and dance a schottische with me.

JEAN [*hesitating*]. I hope you don't think I'm being rude, but I've already promised this dance to Christine.

MISS JULIE. She can always find someone else. Isn't that so, Christine? You don't mind if I borrow Jean for a minute, do you?

CHRISTINE. It isn't up to me. If Miss Julie is gracious enough to invite you, it isn't right for you to say no, Jean. You go on, and thank her for the honor.

JEAN. Frankly, Miss Julie, I don't want to hurt your feelings, but I wonder if it is wise—I mean for you to dance twice in a row with the same partner. Especially since the people around here are so quick to spread gossip.

MISS JULIE [*bridling*]. What do you mean? What kind of gossip? What are you trying to say?

JEAN [*retreating*]. If you insist on misunderstanding me, I'll have to speak more plainly. It just doesn't look right for you to prefer one of your servants to the others who are hoping for the same unusual honor.

MISS JULIE. Prefer! What an idea! I'm really surprised. I, the mistress of the house, am good enough to come to their dance, and when I feel like dancing, I want to dance with someone who knows how to lead. After all I don't want to look ridiculous.

JEAN. As you wish. I am at your orders.

MISS JULIE [*gently*]. Don't take it as an order. Tonight we're all just happy people at a party. There's no question of rank. Now give me your arm.—Don't worry, Christine. I won't run off with your boy friend.

[JEAN *gives her his arm and leads her out.*]

PANTOMIME SCENE. *This should be played as if the actress were actually alone. She turns her back on the audience when she feels like it; she does not look out into the auditorium; she does not hurry as if she were afraid the audience would grow impatient.*

CHRISTINE *alone. In the distance the sound of the violins playing the schottische.* CHRISTINE, *humming in time with the music, cleans up after* JEAN, *washes the dishes, dries them, and puts them away in a cupboard. Then she takes off her apron, takes a little mirror from one of the table drawers, and leans it against the jar of lilacs on the table. She lights a tallow candle, heats a curling iron, and curls the bangs on her forehead. Then she goes to the doorway and stands listening to the music. She comes back to the table and finds the handkerchief that* MISS JULIE *left behind. She smells it, spreads it out, and then, as if lost in thought, stretches it, smooths it out, folds it in four, and so on.*

[JEAN *enters alone.*]

JEAN. I told you she was wild! You should have seen the way she was dancing. They were peeking at her from behind the doors and laughing at her. Can you figure her out, Christine?

CHRISTINE. You might know it's her monthlies, Jean. She always acts peculiar then. . . . Well, are you going to dance with me?

JEAN. You're not mad at me because I broke my promise?

CHRISTINE. Of course not. Not for a little thing like that, you know that. And I know my place.

JEAN [*grabs her around the waist*]. You're a sensible girl, Christine. You're going to make somebody a good wife—

[MISS JULIE, *coming in, sees them together. She is unpleasantly surprised.*]

MISS JULIE [*with forced gaiety*]. Well, aren't you the gallant beau—running away from your partner!

JEAN. On the contrary, Miss Julie. As you can see, I've hurried back to the partner I deserted.

MISS JULIE [*changing tack*]. You know, you're the best dancer I've met.—But why are you wearing livery on a holiday. Take it off at once.

JEAN. I'd have to ask you to leave for a minute. My black coat is hanging right here—[*He moves to the right and points.*]

MISS JULIE. You're not embarrassed because I'm here, are you? Just to change your coat? Go in your room and come right back again. Or else you can stay here and I'll turn my back.

JEAN. If you'll excuse me, Miss Julie. [*He goes off to the right. His arm can be seen as he changes his coat.*]

MISS JULIE [*to* CHRISTINE]. Tell me something, Christine. Is Jean your fiancé? He seems so intimate with you.

CHRISTINE. Fiancé? I suppose so. At least that's what we say.

MISS JULIE. What do you mean?

CHRISTINE. Well, Miss Julie, you have had fiancés yourself, and you know—

MISS JULIE. But we were properly engaged—!

CHRISTINE. I know, but did anything come of it?

[JEAN *comes back, wearing a cutaway coat and derby.*]

MISS JULIE. *Très gentil, monsieur Jean! Très gentil!*

JEAN. *Vous voulez plaisanter, madame.*

MISS JULIE. *Et vous voulez parler français!* Where did you learn to speak French?

JEAN. In Switzerland. I was *sommelier* in one of the biggest hotels in Lucerne.

MISS JULIE. But you look quite the gentleman in that coat! *Charmant!* [*She sits down at the table.*]

JEAN. Flatterer!

MISS JULIE [*stiffening*]. Who said I was flattering you?

JEAN. My natural modesty would not allow me to presume that you were paying sincere compliments to someone like me, and therefore I assumed that you were exaggerating, or, in other words, flattering me.

MISS JULIE. Where on earth did you learn to talk like that? Do you go to the theatre often?

JEAN. And other places. I get around.

MISS JULIE. But weren't you born in this district?

JEAN. My father worked as a farm hand on the county attorney's estate, next door to yours. I used to see you when you were little. But of course you didn't notice me.

MISS JULIE. Did you really?

JEAN. Yes. I remember one time in particular—. But I can't tell you about that!

MISS JULIE. Of course you can. Oh, come on, tell me. Just this once—for me.

JEAN. No. No, I really couldn't. Not now. Some other time maybe.

MISS JULIE. Some other time? That means never. What's the harm in telling me now?

JEAN. There's no harm. I just don't feel like it.—Look at her. [*He nods at* CHRISTINE, *who has fallen asleep in a chair by the stove.*]

MISS JULIE. Won't she make somebody a pretty wife! I'll bet she snores, too.

JEAN. No, she doesn't. But she talks in her sleep.

MISS JULIE [*cynically*]. Now how would you know she talks in her sleep?

JEAN [*coolly*]. I've heard her. . . .

[*Pause. They look at each other.*]

MISS JULIE. Why don't you sit down?

JEAN. I wouldn't take the liberty in your presence.

MISS JULIE. But if I were to order you—?

JEAN. I'd obey.

MISS JULIE. Well then, sit down.—Wait a minute. Could you get me something to drink first?

JEAN. I don't know what there is in the icebox. Only beer, I suppose.

MISS JULIE. *Only* beer?! I have simple tastes. I prefer beer to wine.

[JEAN *takes a bottle of beer from the icebox and opens it. He looks in the cupboard for a glass and a saucer, and serves her.*]

JEAN. At your service.

MISS JULIE. Thank you. Don't you want to drink, too?

JEAN. I'm not much of a beer-drinker, but if it's your wish—

MISS JULIE. My wish! I should think a gentleman would want to keep his lady company.

JEAN. That's a point well taken! [*He opens another bottle and takes a glass.*]

MISS JULIE. Now drink a toast to me! [JEAN *hesitates.*] You're not shy, are you? A big, strong man like you? [*Playfully,* JEAN *kneels and raises his glass in mock gallantry.*]

JEAN. To my lady's health!

MISS JULIE. Bravo! Now if you would kiss my shoe, you will have hit it off perfectly. [JEAN *hesitates, then boldly grasps her foot and touches it lightly with his lips.*] Superb! You should have been an actor.

JEAN [*rising*]. This has got to stop, Miss Julie! Someone might come and see us.

MISS JULIE. What different would that make?

JEAN. People would talk, that's what! If you knew how their tongues were wagging out there just a few minutes ago, you wouldn't—

MISS JULIE. What sort of things did they say? Tell me. Sit down and tell me.

JEAN [*sitting down*]. I don't want to hurt your feelings, but they used expressions that—that hinted at certain —you know what I mean. After all, you're not a child. And when they see a woman drinking, alone with a man—and a servant at that—in the middle of the night—well . . .

MISS JULIE. Well what?! Besides, we're not alone. Christine is here.

JEAN. Yes, asleep!

MISS JULIE. I'll wake her up then. [*She goes over to* CHRISTINE.] Christine! Are you asleep? [CHRISTINE *babbles in her sleep.*] Christine!—How sound she sleeps!

CHRISTINE [*talking in her sleep*]. Count's boots are brushed . . . put on the coffee . . . right away, right away, . . . mm-mm . . . pooffff . . . right.

[MISS JULIE *grabs* CHRISTINE's *nose.*]

MISS JULIE. Wake up, will you!

JEAN [*sternly*]. Let her alone!

MISS JULIE [*sharply*]. What!

JEAN. She's been standing over the stove all day. She's worn out when evening comes. Anyone asleep is entitled to some respect.

MISS JULIE [*changing tack*]. That's a very kind thought. It does you credit. Thank you. [*She offers* JEAN *her hand.*] Now come on out and pick some lilacs for me.

[*During the following,* CHRISTINE *wakes up and, drunk with sleep, shuffles off to the right to go to bed.*]

JEAN. With you, Miss Julie?

MISS JULIE. Yes, with me.

JEAN. That's no good. Absolutely not.

MISS JULIE. I don't know what you're thinking. Maybe you're letting your imagination run away with you.

JEAN. I'm not. The other people are.

MISS JULIE. In what way? Imagining that I'm—*verliebt* in a servant?

JEAN. I'm not conceited, but it's been known to happen. And to these people nothing's sacred.

MISS JULIE. Why, I believe you're an aristocrat!

JEAN. Yes, I am.

MISS JULIE. I'm climbing down—

JÉAN. Don't climb down, Miss Julie! Take my advice. No one will ever believe that you climbed down deliberately. They'll say that you fell.

MISS JULIE. I think more highly of these people than you do. Let's see who's right! Come on! [*She looks him over, challenging him.*]

JEAN. You know, you're very strange.

MISS JULIE. Perhaps. But then so are you. . . . Besides, everything is strange. Life, people, everything. It's all scum, drifting and drifting on the water until it sinks—sinks. There's a dream I have every now and then. It's coming back to me now. I'm sitting on top of a pillar that I've climbed up somehow and I don't know how to get back down. When I look down I get dizzy. I have to get down but I don't have the courage to jump. I can't hold on much longer and I want to fall; but I don't fall. I know I won't have any peace until I get down; no rest until I get down, down on the ground. And if I ever get down on the ground, I'd want to go farther down, right down into the earth. . . . Have you ever felt anything like that?

JEAN. Never! I used to dream that I'm lying under a tall tree in a dark woods. I want to get up, up to the very top, to look out over the bright landscape with the sun shining on it, to rob the bird's nest up there with the golden eggs in it. I climb and I climb, but the trunk is so thick, and so smooth, and it's such a long way to that first branch. But I know that if I could just reach that first branch, I'd go right to the top as if on a ladder. I've never reached it yet, but some day I will—even if only in my dreams.

MISS JULIE. Here I am talking about dreams with you. Come out with me. Only into the park a way. [*She offers him her arm, and they start to go.*]

JEAN. Let's sleep on nine midsummer flowers, Miss Julie, and then our dreams will come true!

[MISS JULIE *and* JEAN *suddenly turn around in the doorway.* JEAN *is holding his hand over one eye.*]

MISS JULIE. You've caught something in your eye. Let me see.

JEAN. It's nothing. Just a bit of dust. It'll go away.

MISS JULIE. The sleeve of my dress must have grazed your eye. Sit down and I'll help you. [*She takes him by the arm and sits him down. She takes his head and leans it back. With the corner of her handkerchief she tries to get out the bit of dust.*] Now sit still, absolutely still. [*She slaps his hand.*] Do as you're told. Why, I believe you're trembling—a big, strong man like you. [*She feels his biceps.*] With such big arms!

JEAN [*warningly*]. Miss Julie!

MISS JULIE. Yes, *Monsieur Jean?*

JEAN. *Attention! Je ne suis qu'un homme!*

MISS JULIE. Sit still, I tell you! . . . There now! It's out. Kiss my hand and thank me!

JEAN [*rising to his feet*]. Listen to me, Miss Julie— Christine has gone to bed!—Listen to me, I tell you!

MISS JULIE. Kiss my hand first!

JEAN. Listen to me!

MISS JULIE. Kiss my hand first!

JEAN. All right. But you'll have no one to blame but yourself.

MISS JULIE. For what?

JEAN. For what! Are you twenty-five years old and still a child? Don't you know it's dangerous to play with fire?

MISS JULIE. Not for me. I'm insured!

JEAN [*boldly*]. Oh, no you're not! And even if you are, there's inflammable stuff next door.

MISS JULIE. Meaning you?

JEAN. Yes. Not just because it's me, but because I'm a young man—

MISS JULIE. And irresistibly handsome? What incredible conceit! A Don Juan, maybe! Or a Joseph! Yes, bless my soul, that's it: you're a Joseph!

JEAN. You think so?!

MISS JULIE. I'm almost afraid so! [JEAN *boldly steps up to her, grabs her around the waist, kisses her. She slaps his face.*] None of that!

JEAN. Are you still playing games or are you serious?

MISS JULIE. I'm serious.

JEAN. Then you must have been serious just a moment ago, too! You take your games too seriously and that's dangerous. Well, I'm tired of your games, and if you'll excuse me, I'll return to my work. The Count will be wanting his boots on time, and it's long past midnight.

MISS JULIE. Put those boots down.

JEAN. No! This is my job. It's what I'm here for. But I never undertook to be a playmate for you. That's something I could never be. I consider myself too good for that.

MISS JULIE. You are proud.

JEAN. In some ways. Not in others.

MISS JULIE. Have you ever been in love?

JEAN. We don't use that word around here. But I've been interested in a lot of girls, if that's what you mean. . . . I even got sick once because I couldn't have the one I wanted—really sick, like the princes in the Arabian Nights—who couldn't eat or drink for love.

MISS JULIE. Who was the girl? [JEAN *does not reply.*] Who was she?

JEAN. You can't make me tell you that.

MISS JULIE. Even if I ask you as an equal—ask you—as a friend? . . . Who was she?

JEAN. You.

MISS JULIE [*sitting down*]. How—amusing. . . .

JEAN. Yes, maybe so. Ridiculous. . . . That's why I didn't want to tell you about it before. But now I'll tell you the whole story. . . . Have you any idea what the world looks like from below? Of course you haven't. No more than a hawk or eagle has. You hardly ever see their backs because they're always soaring above us. I lived with seven brothers and sisters—and a pig—out on the waste land where there wasn't even a tree growing. But from my window I could see the wall of the Count's garden with the apple trees sticking up over it. That was the Garden of Eden for me, and there were many angry angels with flaming swords standing guard over it. But in spite of them, I and the other boys found a way to the Tree of Life. . . . I'll bet you despise me.

MISS JULIE. All boys steal apples.

JEAN. That's what you say now. But you still despise me. Never mind. One day I went with my mother into this paradise to weed the onion beds. Next to the vegetable garden stood a Turkish pavilion, shaded by jasmine and hung all over with honeysuckle. I couldn't imagine what it was used for. I only knew I had never seen such a beautiful building. People went in, and came out again. And one day the door was left open. I sneaked in. The walls were covered with portraits of kings and emperors, and the windows had red curtains with tassels on them.—You do know what kind of place I'm talking about, don't you? . . . I— [*He breaks off a lilac and holds it under* MISS JULIE'S *nose*.] I had never been inside a castle, never seen anything besides the church. But this was more beautiful. And no matter what I tried to think about, my thoughts always came back—to that little pavilion. And little by little there arose in me a desire to experience just for once the whole pleasure of . . . *Enfin,* I sneaked in, looked about, and marveled. Then I heard someone coming! There was only one way out—for the upper-class people. But for me there was one more—a lower one. And I had no other choice but to take it. [MISS JULIE, *who has taken the lilac from* JEAN, *lets it fall to the table.*] Then I began to run like mad, plunging through the raspberry bushes, ploughing through the strawberry patches, and came up on the rose terrace. And there I caught sight of a pink dress and a pair of white stockings. That was you. I crawled under a pile of weeds, under—well, you can imagine what it was like—under thistles that pricked me and wet dirt that stank to high heaven. And all the while I could see you walking among the roses. I said to myself, "If it's true that a thief can enter heaven and be with the angels, isn't it strange that a poor man's child here on God's green earth can't enter the Count's park and play with the Count's daughter."

MISS JULIE [*sentimentally*]. Do you think all poor children have felt that way?

JEAN [*hesitatingly at first, then with mounting conviction*]. If all poor ch—? Yes—yes, naturally. Of course!

MISS JULIE. It must be terrible to be poor.

JEAN [*with exaggerated pain and poignancy*]. Oh, Miss Julie! You don't know! A dog can lie on the sofa with its mistress; a horse can have its nose stroked by the hand of a countess; but a servant—! [*Changing his tone.*] Of course, now and then you meet somebody with guts enough to work his way up in the world, but how often?—Anyway, you know what I did afterwards? I threw myself into the millstream with all my clothes on. Got fished out and spanked. But the following Sunday, when Pa and everybody else in the house went to visit Grandma, I arranged things so I'd be left behind. Then I washed myself all over with soap and warm water, put on my best clothes, and went off to church—just to see you there once more. I saw you, and then I went home determined to die. But I wanted to die beautifully and comfortably, without pain. I remembered that it was fatal to sleep under an alder bush. And we had a big one that had just blossomed out. I stripped it of every leaf and blossom it had and made a bed of them in a bin of oats. Have you ever noticed how smooth oats are? As smooth to the touch as human skin. . . . So I pulled the lid of the bin shut and closed my eyes—fell asleep. And when they woke me I was really very sick. But I didn't die, as you can see.—What was I trying to prove? I don't know. There was no hope of winning you. But you were a symbol of the absolute hopelessness of my ever getting out of the circle I was born in.

MISS JULIE. You know, you have a real gift for telling stories. Did you go to school?

JEAN. A little. But I've read a lot of novels and gone to the theatre. And I've also listened to educated people talk. That's how I've learned the most.

MISS JULIE. You mean to tell me you stand around listening to what we're saying!

JEAN. Certainly! And I've heard an awful lot, I can tell you—sitting on the coachman's seat or rowing the boat. One time I heard you and a girl friend talking—

MISS JULIE. Really? . . . And just what did you hear?

JEAN. Well, now, I don't know if I could repeat it. I can tell you I was a little amazed. I couldn't imagine where you had learned such words. Maybe at bottom there isn't such a big difference as you might think, between people and people.

MISS JULIE. How vulgar! At least people in my class don't behave like you when we're engaged.

JEAN [looking her in the eye]. Are you sure?—Come on now, it's no use playing the innocent with me.

MISS JULIE. He was a beast. The man I offered my love was a beast.

JEAN. That's what you all say—afterwards.

MISS JULIE. All?

JEAN. I'd say so, since I've heard the same expression used several times before in similar circumstances.

MISS JULIE. What kind of circumstances?

JEAN. The kind we're talking about. I remember the last time I—

MISS JULIE [*rising*]. That's enough! I don't want to hear any more.

JEAN. How strange! Neither did she! . . . Well, now if you'll excuse me, I'll go to bed.

MISS JULIE [*softly*]. Go to bed on Midsummer Eve?

JEAN. That's right. Dancing with that crowd up there really doesn't amuse me.

MISS JULIE. Jean, get the key to the boathouse and row me out on the lake. I want to see the sun come up.

JEAN. Do you think that's wise?

MISS JULIE. You sound as if you were worried about your reputation.

JEAN. Why not? I don't particularly care to be made ridiculous, or to be kicked out without a recommendation just when I'm trying to establish myself. Besides, I have a certain obligation to Christine.

MISS JULIE. Oh, I see. It's Christine now.

JEAN. Yes, but I'm thinking of you, too. Take my advice, Miss Julie, and go up to your room.

MISS JULIE. When did you start giving me orders?

JEAN. Just this once. For your own sake! Please! It's very late. You're so tired, you're drunk. You don't know what you're doing. Go to bed, Miss Julie.—Besides, if my ears aren't deceiving me, they're coming this way, looking for me. If they find us here together, you're done for!

THE CHORUS [*is heard coming nearer, singing*].

> Two ladies came from out the clover,
> Tri-di-ri-di-ralla, tri-di-ri-di-ra.
> And one of them was green all over,
> Tri-di-ri-di-ralla-la.
> They told us they had gold aplenty,
> Tri-di-ri-di-ralla, tri-di-ri-di-ra.
> But neither of them owned a penny.

Tri-di-ri-di-ralla-la.
This wreath for you I may be plaiting,
Tri-di-ri-di-ralla, tri-di-ri-di-ra.
But it's for another I am waiting,
Tri-di-ri-ralla-la!

MISS JULIE. I know these people. I love them just as they love me. Let them come. You'll find out.

JEAN. No, Miss Julie, they don't love you! They take the food you give them, but they spit on it as soon as your back is turned. Believe me! Just listen to them. Listen to what they're singing.—No, you'd better not listen.

MISS JULIE [*listening*]. What are they singing?

JEAN. A dirty song—about you and me!

MISS JULIE. How disgusting! Oh, what cowardly, sneaking—

JEAN. That's what the mob always is—cowards! You can't fight them; you can only run away.

MISS JULIE. Run away? Where? There's no way out of here. And we can't go in to Christine.

JEAN. What about my room? What do you say? The rules don't count in a situation like this. You can trust me. I'm your friend, remember? Your true, devoted, and respectful friend.

MISS JULIE. But suppose—suppose they looked for you there?

JEAN. I'll bolt the door. If they try to break it down, I'll shoot. Come, Miss Julie! [*On his knees.*] Please, Miss Julie!

MISS JULIE [*meaningfully*]. You promise me that you—?

JEAN. I swear to you!

[MISS JULIE *goes out quickly to the right.* JEAN *follows her impetuously.*]

[THE BALLET. *The country people enter in festive costumes, with flowers in their hats. The fiddler is in the lead. A keg of small beer and a little keg of liquor, decorated with greenery, are set up on the table. Glasses are brought out. They all drink, after which they form a circle and sing and dance the round dance, "Two ladies came from out the clover." At the end of the dance they all leave singing.]*

[MISS JULIE *comes in alone; looks at the devastated kitchen; clasps her hands together; then takes out a powder puff and powders her face.* JEAN *enters. He is in high spirits.]*

JEAN. You see! You heard them, didn't you? You've got to admit it's impossible to stay here.

MISS JULIE. No, I don't. But even if I did, what could we do?

JEAN. Go away, travel, get away from here!

MISS JULIE. Travel? Yes—but where?

JEAN. Switzerland, the Italian lakes. You've never been there?

MISS JULIE. No. Is it beautiful?

JEAN. Eternal summer, oranges, laurel trees, ah . . . !

MISS JULIE. But what are we going to do there?

JEAN. I'll set up a hotel—a first-class hotel with a first-class clientele.

MISS JULIE. Hotel?

JEAN. I tell you that's the life! Always new faces, new languages. Not a minute to think about yourself or worry about your nerves. No looking for something to do. The work keeps you busy. Day and night the bells ring, the trains whistle, the busses come and go. And all the while the money comes rolling in. I tell you it's the life!

MISS JULIE. Yes, that's the life. But what about me?

JEAN. The mistress of the whole place, the star of the establishment! With your looks—and your personality—it can't fail. It's perfect! You'll sit in the office like a queen, setting your slaves in motion by pressing an electric button. The guests will file before your throne and timidly lay their treasures on your table. You can't imagine how people tremble when you shove a bill in their face! I'll salt the bills and you'll sugar them with your prettiest smile. Come on, let's get away from here—[*He takes a timetable from his pocket.*]—right away—the next train! We'll be in Malmo at 6:30; Hamburg 8:40 in the morning; Frankfurt to Basle in one day; and to Como by way of the Gotthard tunnel in—let me see—three days! Three days!

MISS JULIE. You make it sound so wonderful. But, Jean, you have to give me strength. Tell me you love me. Come and put your arms around me.

JEAN [*hesitates*]. I want to . . . but I don't dare. Not any more, not in this house. I do love you—without a shadow of a doubt. How can you doubt that, Miss Julie?

MISS JULIE [*shyly, very becomingly*]. You don't have to be formal with me, Jean. You can call me Julie. There aren't any barriers between us now. Call me Julie.

JEAN [*agonized*]. I can't! There are still barriers between us, Miss Julie, as long as we stay in this house! There's the past, there's the Count. I've never met anyone I feel so much respect for. I've only got to see his gloves lying on a table and I shrivel up. I only have to hear that bell ring and I shy like a frightened horse. I only have to look at his boots standing there so stiff and proud and I feel my spine bending. [*He kicks the boots.*] Superstitions, prejudices that they've drilled into us since we were children! But they can be forgotten just as easily! Just we get to another country where they have a republic! They'll crawl on their hands and knees when they see my uniform. On their hands and knees, I tell you! But not me! Oh, no. I'm not made for crawling. I've got guts, backbone. And once I grab that first branch, you just watch me climb. I may be a valet now, but next year I'll be owning property; in ten years, I'll be living off my investments. Then I'll go to Rumania, get myself some decorations, and maybe—

notice I only say maybe—end up as a count!

MISS JULIE. How wonderful, wonderful.

JEAN. Listen, in Rumania you can buy titles. You'll be a countess after all. *My* countess.

MISS JULIE. But I'm not interested in that. I'm leaving all that behind. Tell me you love me, Jean, or else— or else what difference does it make what I am?

JEAN. I'll tell you a thousand times—but later! Not now. And not here. Above all, let's keep our feelings out of this or we'll make a mess of everything. We have to look at this thing calmly and coolly, like sensible people. [*He takes out a cigar, clips the end, and lights it.*] Now you sit there and I'll sit here, and we'll talk as if nothing had happened.

MISS JULIE [*in anguish*]. My God, what are you? Don't you have any feelings?

JEAN. Feelings? Nobody's got more feelings than I have. But I've learned how to control them.

MISS JULIE. A few minutes ago you were kissing my shoe—and now—!

JEAN [*harshly*]. That was a few minutes ago. We've got other things to think about now!

MISS JULIE. Don't speak to me like that, Jean!

JEAN. I'm just trying to be sensible. We've been stupid once; let's not be stupid again. Your father might be back at any moment, and we've got to decide our future before then.—Now what do you think about my plans? Do you approve or don't you?

MISS JULIE. I don't see anything wrong with them. Except one thing. For a big undertaking like that, you'd need a lot of capital. Have you got it?

JEAN [*chewing on his cigar*]. Have I got it? Of course I have. I've got my knowledge of the business, my vast experience, my familiarity with languages. That's capital that counts for something, let me tell you.

MISS JULIE. You can't even buy the railway tickets with it.

JEAN. That's true. That's why I need a backer—someone to put up the money.

MISS JULIE. Where can you find him on a moment's notice?

JEAN. You'll find him—if you want to be my partner.

MISS JULIE. I can't. And I don't have a penny to my name.

[*Pause.*]

JEAN. Then you can forget the whole thing.

MISS JULIE. Forget—?

JEAN. And things will stay just the way they are.

MISS JULIE. Do you think I'm going to live under the same roof with you as your mistress? Do you think I'm going to have people sneering at me behind my back? How do you think I'll ever be able to look my father in the face after this? No, no! Take me away from here, Jean—the shame, the humiliation. . . . What have I done? Oh, my God, my God! What have I done? [*She bursts into tears.*]

JEAN. Now don't start singing that tune. It won't work. What have you done that's so awful? You're not the first.

MISS JULIE [*crying hysterically*]. Now you despise me!— I'm falling, I'm falling!

JEAN. Fall down to me, and I'll lift you up again!

MISS JULIE. What awful hold did you have over me? What drove me to you? The weak to the strong? The falling to the rising! Or maybe it was love? Love? This? You don't know what love is!

JEAN. Want to bet? Did you think I was a virgin?

MISS JULIE. You're vulgar! The things you say, the things you think!

JEAN. That's the way I was brought up and that's the way I am! Now don't get hysterical and don't play the fine lady with me. We're eating off the same platter now. . . . That's better. Come over here and be a good girl and I'll treat you to something special.

[*He opens the table drawer and takes out the wine bottle. He pours the wine into two used glasses.*]

MISS JULIE. Where did you get that wine?

JEAN. From the wine cellar.

MISS JULIE. My father's burgundy!

JEAN. Should be good enough for his son-in-law.

MISS JULIE. I was drinking beer and you—!

JEAN. That shows that I have better taste than you.

MISS JULIE. Thief!

JEAN. You going to squeal on me?

MISS JULIE. Oh, God! Partner in crime with a petty house thief! I must have been drunk; I must have been walking in my sleep. Midsummer Night! Night of innocent games—

JEAN. Yes, very innocent!

MISS JULIE [*pacing up and down*]. Is there anyone here on earth as miserable as I am?

JEAN. Why be miserable? After such a conquest! Think of poor Christine in there. Don't you think she's got any feelings?

MISS JULIE. I thought so a while ago, but I don't now. A servant's a servant—

JEAN. And a whore's a whore!

MISS JULIE [*falls to her knees and clasps her hands together*]. Oh, God in heaven, put an end to my worthless life! Lift me out of this awful filth I'm sinking in! Save me! Save me!

JEAN. I feel sorry for you, I have to admit it. When I was lying in the onion beds, looking up at you on the rose terrace, I—I'm telling you the truth now—I had the same dirty thoughts that all boys have.

MISS JULIE. And you said you wanted to die for me!

JEAN. In the oat bin? That was only a story.

MISS JULIE. A lie, you mean.

JEAN [*beginning to get sleepy*]. Practically. I think I read it in a paper about a chimney sweep who curled up in a wood-bin with some lilacs because they were going to arrest him for nonsupport of his child.

MISS JULIE. Now I see you for what you are.

JEAN. What did you expect me to do? It's always the fancy talk that gets the women.

MISS JULIE. You dog!

JEAN. You bitch!

MISS JULIE. Well, now you've seen the eagle's back—

JEAN. Wasn't exactly its back—!

MISS JULIE. I was going to be your first branch—!

JEAN. A rotten branch—

MISS JULIE. I was going to be the window dressing for your hotel—!

JEAN. And I the hotel—!

MISS JULIE. Sitting at the desk, attracting your customers, padding your bills—!

JEAN. I could manage that myself—!

MISS JULIE. How can a human soul be so dirty and filthy?

JEAN. Then why don't you clean it up?

MISS JULIE. You lackey! You shoeshine boy! Stand up when I talk to you!

JEAN. You lackey lover! You bootblack's tramp! Shut your mouth and get out of here! Who do you think you are telling me I'm coarse? I've never seen anybody in my class behave as crudely as you did tonight. Have you ever seen any of the girls around here grab at a man like you did? Do you think any of the girls of my class would throw themselves at a man like that? I've never seen the like of it except in animals and prostitutes!

MISS JULIE [crushed]. That's right! Hit me! Walk all over me! It's all I deserve. I'm rotten. But help me! Help me to get out of this—if there is any way out for me!

JEAN [less harsh]. I'd be doing myself an injustice if I didn't admit that part of the credit for this seduction belongs to me. But do you think a person in my position would have dared to look twice at you if you hadn't asked for it? I'm still amazed—

MISS JULIE. And still proud.

JEAN. Why not? But I've got to confess the victory was a little too easy to give me any real thrill.

MISS JULIE. Go on, hit me more!

JEAN [standing up]. No. . . . I'm sorry for what I said. I never hit a person who's down, especially a woman. I can't deny that, in one way, it was good to find out that what I saw glittering up above was only fool's gold, to have seen that the eagle's back was as gray as its belly, that the smooth cheek was just powder, and that there could be dirt under the manicured nails, that the handkerchief was soiled even though it smelled of perfume. But, in another way, it hurt me to find that everything I was striving for wasn't very high above me after all, wasn't even real. It hurts me to see you sink far lower than your own cook. Hurts, like seeing the last flowers cut to pieces by the autumn rains and turned to muck.

MISS JULIE. You talk as if you already stood high above me.

JEAN. Well, don't I? Don't forget I could make you a countess but you can never make me a count.

MISS JULIE. But I have a father for a count. You can never have that!

JEAN. True. But I might father my own counts—that is, if—

MISS JULIE. You're a thief! I'm not!

JEAN. There are worse things than being a thief. A lot worse. And besides, when I take a position in a house, I consider myself a member of the family—in a way, like a child in the house. It's no crime for a child to steal a few ripe cherries when they're falling off the trees, is it? [He begins to feel passionate again.] Miss Julie, you're a beautiful woman, much too good for the likes of me. You got carried away by your emotions and now you want to cover up your mistake by telling yourself that you love me. You don't love me. You might possibly have been attracted by my looks—in which case your kind of love is no better than mine. But I could never be satisfied to be just an animal for you, and I could never make you love me.

MISS JULIE. Are you so sure of that?

JEAN. You mean there's a chance? I could love you, there's no doubt about that. You're beautiful, you're refined—[*He goes up to her and takes her hand.*]—educated, lovable when you want to be, and once you set a man's heart on fire, I'll bet it burns forever. [*He puts his arm around her waist.*] You're like hot wine with strong spices. One of your kisses is enough to—[*He attempts to lead her out, but she rather reluctantly breaks away from him.*]

MISS JULIE. Let me go. You don't get me that way.

JEAN. Then how? Not by petting you and not with pretty words, not by planning for the future, not by saving you from humiliation! Then how, tell me how?

MISS JULIE. How? How? I don't know how! I don't know at all!—I hate you like I hate rats, but I can't get away from you.

JEAN. Then come away *with* me!

MISS JULIE [*pulling herself together*]. Away? Yes, we'll go away!—But I'm so tired. Pour me a glass of wine, will you? [JEAN *pours the wine.* MISS JULIE *looks at her watch.*] Let's talk first. We still have a little time. [*She empties the glass of wine and holds it out for more.*]

JEAN. Don't overdo it. You'll get drunk.

MISS JULIE. What difference does it make?

JEAN. What difference? It looks cheap.—What did you want to say to me?

MISS JULIE. We're going to run away together, right? But we'll talk first—that is, I'll talk. So far you've done all the talking. You've told me your life, now I'll tell you mine. That way we'll know each other through and through before we become traveling companions.

JEAN. Wait a minute. Excuse me, but are you sure you won't regret this afterwards, when you've surrendered your secrets?

MISS JULIE. I thought you were my friend.

JEAN. I am—sometimes. But don't count on me.

MISS JULIE. You don't mean that. Anyway, everybody knows my secrets.—My mother's parents were very ordinary people, just commoners. She was brought up, according to the theories of her time, to believe in equality, the independence of women, and all that. And she had a strong aversion to marriage. When my father proposed to her, she swore she would never become his wife. . . . But she did anyway. I was born —against my mother's wishes, as far as I can make out. My mother decided to bring me up as a nature child. And on top of that I had to learn everything a boy learns, so I could be living proof that women were just as good as men. I had to wear boy's clothes, learn to handle horses—but not to milk the cows. I was made to groom the horses and handle them, and go out hunting—and even had to try and learn farming! And on the estate all the men were set to doing the work of women, and the women to doing men's work—with the result that the whole place threatened to fall to pieces, and we became the local laughing-stock. Finally my father must have come out of his trance. He rebelled, and everything was changed according to his wishes. Then my mother got sick. I don't know what kind of sickness it was, but she often had convulsions, and she would hide herself in the attic or in the garden, and sometimes she would stay out all night. Then there occurred that big fire you've heard about. The house, the stables, the cowsheds, all burned down—and under very peculiar circumstances that led one to suspect arson. You see, the accident occurred the day after the insurance expired, and the premiums on the new policy, which my father had sent in, were delayed through the messenger's carelessness, and didn't arrive on time. [*She refills her glass and drinks.*]

JEAN. You've had enough.

MISS JULIE. Who cares!—We were left without a penny to our name. We had to sleep in the carriages. My father didn't know where to turn for money to rebuild the house. Then Mother suggested to him that he might try to borrow money from an old friend of hers, who owned a brick factory, not far from here. Father takes out a loan, but there's no interest charged, which surprises him. So the place was rebuilt. [*She drinks some more.*] Do you know who set fire to the place?

JEAN. Your honorable mother!

MISS JULIE. Do you know who the brick manufacturer was?

JEAN. Your mother's lover?

MISS JULIE. Do you know whose money it was?

JEAN. Let me think a minute. . . . No, I give up.

MISS JULIE. It was my mother's!

JEAN. The Count's, you mean. Or was there a marriage settlement?

MISS JULIE. There wasn't a settlement. My mother had a little money of her own which she didn't want under my father's control, so she invested it with her—friend.

JEAN. Who grabbed it!

MISS JULIE. Precisely. He appropriated it. Well, my father finds out what happened. But he can't go to court, can't pay his wife's lover, can't prove that it's his wife's money. That was how my mother got her revenge because he had taken control of the house. He was on the verge of shooting himself. There was even a rumor that he tried and failed. But he took a new lease on life and he forced my mother to pay for her mistakes. Can you imagine what those five years were like for me? I felt sorry for my father, but I took my mother's side because I didn't know the whole story. She had taught me to distrust and hate all men—you've heard how she hated men—and I swore to her that I'd never be slave to any man.

JEAN. But you got engaged to the attorney.

MISS JULIE. Only to make him slave to me.

JEAN. But he didn't want any of that?

MISS JULIE. Oh, he wanted to well enough, but I didn't give him the chance. I got bored with him.

JEAN. Yes, so I noticed—in the barnyard.

MISS JULIE. What did you notice?

JEAN. I saw what I saw. *He* broke off the engagement.

MISS JULIE. That's a lie! It was I who broke it off. Did he tell you that? He's beneath contempt!

JEAN. Come on now, he isn't as bad as that. So you hate men, Miss Julie?

MISS JULIE. Yes, I do. . . . Most of the time. But sometimes, when I can't help myself—oh. . . . [*She shudders in disgust.*]

JEAN. Then you hate me, too?

MISS JULIE. You have no idea how much! I'd like to see you killed like an animal—

JEAN. Like a mad dog, without a moment's hesitation, right?

MISS JULIE. Right!

JEAN. But we don't have anything to shoot him with— and no dog! What are we going to do?

MISS JULIE. Go away from here.

JEAN. To torture ourselves to death?

MISS JULIE. No. To enjoy ourselves for a day or two, or a week, for as long as we can—and then—to die—

JEAN. Die? How stupid! I've got a better idea: start a hotel!

MISS JULIE [*continuing without hearing* JEAN]. —on the shores of Lake Como, where the sun is always shining, where the laurels bloom at Christmas, and the golden oranges glow on the trees.

JEAN. Lake Como is a stinking wet hole, and the only oranges I saw there were on the fruit stands. But it's a good tourist spot with a lot of villas and cottages that are rented out to lovers. Now there's a profitable business. You know why? They rent the villa for the whole season, but they leave after three weeks.

MISS JULIE [*innocently*]. Why after only three weeks?

JEAN. Because they can't stand each other any longer. Why else? But they still have to pay the rent. Then you rent it out again to another couple, and so on. There's no shortage of love—even if it doesn't last very long.

MISS JULIE. Then you don't want to die with me?

JEAN. I don't want to die at all! I enjoy life too much. And moreover, I consider taking your own life a sin against the Providence that gave us life.

MISS JULIE. You believe in God? You?

JEAN. Yes, certainly I do! I go to church every other Sunday.—Honestly, I've had enough of this talk. I'm going to bed.

MISS JULIE. Really? You think you're going to get off that easy? Don't you know that a man owes something to the woman he's dishonored?

JEAN [*takes out his purse and throws a silver coin on the table*]. There you are. I don't want to owe anybody anything.

MISS JULIE [*ignoring the insult*]. Do you know what the law says—?

JEAN. Aren't you lucky the law says nothing about the women who seduce men!

MISS JULIE. What else can we do but go away from here, get married, and get divorced?

JEAN. Suppose I refuse to enter into this *mésalliance*?

MISS JULIE. *Mésalliance?*

JEAN. For me! I've got better ancestors than you. I don't have any female arsonist in my family.

MISS JULIE. How can you know?

JEAN. You can't prove the opposite because we don't have any family records—except in the police courts. But I've read the whole history of your family in that book on the drawing-room table. Do you know who the founder of your family line was? A miller —who let his wife sleep with the king one night during the Danish war. I don't have any ancestors like that. I don't have any ancestors at all! But I can become an ancestor myself.

MISS JULIE. This is what I get for baring my heart and soul to someone too low to understand, for sacrificing the honor of my family—

JEAN. Dishonor!—I warned you, remember? Drinking makes one talk, and talking's bad.

MISS JULIE. Oh, how sorry I am! . . . If only it had never happened! . . . If only you at least loved me!

JEAN. For the last time—What do you expect of me? Do you want me to cry? Jump over your whip? Kiss you? Do you want me to lure you to Lake Como for three weeks and then—? What am I supposed to do? What do you want? I've had more than I can take. This is what I get for involving myself with women. . . . Miss Julie, I can see that you're unhappy; I know that you're suffering; but I simply cannot understand you. My people don't behave like this. We don't hate each other. We make love for the fun of it, when we can get any time off from our work. But we don't have time for it all day and all night like you do. If you ask me, you're sick, Miss Julie. I'm sure that's it, Miss Julie.

MISS JULIE. You can be understanding, Jean. You're talking to me like a human being now.

JEAN. Well, be human yourself. You spit on me but you don't let me wipe it off—on you!

MISS JULIE. Help me, Jean. Help me. Tell me what I should do, that's all—which way to go.

JEAN. For Christ's sake, if only I knew myself!

MISS JULIE. I've been crazy—I've been out of my mind—but does that mean there's no way out for me?

JEAN. Stay here as if nothing had happened. Nobody knows anything.

MISS JULIE. Impossible! Everybody who works here knows. Christine knows.

JEAN. They don't know a thing. And anyhow they'd never believe it.

MISS JULIE [slowly, significantly]. But . . . it might happen again.

JEAN. That's true!

MISS JULIE. And there might be consequences.

JEAN [stunned]. Consequences! What on earth have I been thinking of! You're right. There's only one thing to do; get away from here! Immediately! I can't go with you—that would give the whole game away. You'll have to go by yourself. Somewhere—I don't care where!

MISS JULIE. By myself? Where?—Oh, no, Jean, I can't. I can't!

JEAN. You've got to! Before the Count comes back. You know as well as I do what will happen if you stay here. After one mistake, you figure you might as well go on, since the damage is already done. Then you get more and more careless until—finally you're exposed. I tell you, you've got to get out of the country. Afterwards you can write to the Count and tell him everything—leaving me out, of course. He'd never be able to guess it was me. Anyway, I don't think he'd exactly like to find that out.

MISS JULIE. I'll go—if you'll come with me!

JEAN. Lady, are you out of your mind!? "Miss Julie elopes with her footman." The day after tomorrow it would be in all the papers. The Count would never live it down.

MISS JULIE. I can't go away. I can't stay. Help me. I'm so tired, so awfully tired. . . . Tell me what to do.

Order me. Start me going. I can't think any more, can't move any more.

JEAN. Now do you realize how weak you all are? What gives you the right to go strutting around with your noses in the air as if you owned the world? All right, I'll give you your orders. Go up and get dressed. Get some traveling money. And come back down here.

MISS JULIE [*almost in a whisper*]. Come up with me!

JEAN. To your room? . . . You're going crazy again! [*He hesitates a moment.*] No! No! Go! Right now! [*He takes her hand and leads her out.*]

MISS JULIE [*as she is leaving*]. Don't be so harsh, Jean.

JEAN. Orders always sound harsh. You've never had to take them.

[JEAN, *left alone, heaves a sigh of relief and sits down at the table. He takes out a notebook and a pencil and begins to calculate, counting aloud now and then. The pantomime continues until* CHRISTINE *enters, dressed for church, and carrying* JEAN'S *white tie and shirt front in her hand.*]

CHRISTINE. Lord in Heaven, what a mess! What on earth have you been doing?

JEAN. It was Miss Julie. She dragged the whole crowd in here. You must have been sleeping awfully sound if you didn't hear anything.

CHRISTINE. I slept like a log.

JEAN. You already dressed for church?

CHRISTINE. Yes, indeed. Don't you remember you promised to go to Communion with me today?

JEAN. Oh, yes, of course. I remember. I see you've brought my things. All right. Come on, put it on me. [*He sits down, and* CHRISTINE *starts to put the white tie and shirt front on him. Pause.*]

JEAN [*yawning*]. What's the lesson for today?

CHRISTINE. The beheading of John the Baptist, I suppose.

JEAN. My God, that will go on forever.—Hey, you're choking me! . . . Oh, I'm so sleepy, so sleepy.

CHRISTINE. What were you doing up all night? You look green in the face.

JEAN. I've been sitting here talking with Miss Julie.

CHRISTINE. That girl! She doesn't know how to behave herself!

[*Pause.*]

JEAN. Tell me something, Christine. . . .

CHRISTINE. Well, what?

JEAN. Isn't it strange when you think about it? Her, I mean.

CHRISTINE. What's so strange?

JEAN. Everything!

[*Pause.* CHRISTINE *looks at the half-empty glasses on the table.*]

CHRISTINE. Have you been drinking with her?

JEAN. Yes!

CHRISTINE. Shame on you!—Look me in the eyes. You haven't . . . ?

JEAN. Yes!

CHRISTINE. Is it possible? Is it really possible?

JEAN [*after a moment's consideration*]. Yes. It is.

CHRISTINE. Oh, how disgusting! I could never have believed anything like this would happen! No. No. This is too much!

JEAN. Don't tell me you're jealous of her?

CHRISTINE. No, not of her. If it had been Clara—or Sophie—I would have scratched your eyes out! But her—? That's different. I don't know why. . . . But it's still disgusting!

JEAN. Then you're mad at her?

CHRISTINE. No. Mad at you. You were mean and cruel to do a thing like that, very mean. The poor girl! . . . But let me tell you, I'm not going to stay in this house a moment longer, not when I can't have any respect for my employers.

JEAN. Why do you want to respect them?

CHRISTINE. Don't try to be smart. You don't want to work for people who behave immorally, do you? Well, do you? If you ask me, you'd be lowering yourself by doing that.

JEAN. Oh, I don't know. I think it's rather comforting to find out that they're not one bit better than we are.

CHRISTINE. Well, I don't. If they're not any better, there's no point in us trying to be like them.—And think of the Count. Think of all the sorrows he's been through in his time. No, sir, I won't stay in this house any longer. . . . Imagine! You, of all people! If it had been the attorney fellow; if it had been somebody respectable—

JEAN. Now just a minute—!

CHRISTINE. Oh, you're all right in your own way. But there's a big difference between one class and another. You can't deny that. —No, this is something I can never get over. She was so proud, and so sarcastic about men, you'd never believe she'd go and throw herself at one. And at someone like you! And *she* was going to have Diana shot, because the poor thing ran after the gatekeeper's mongrel!—Well, I tell you, I've had enough! I'm not going to stay here any longer. On the twenty-fourth of October, I'm leaving.

JEAN. Then what'll you do?

CHRISTINE. Well, since you brought it up, it's about time that you got yourself a decent place, if we're going to get married.

JEAN. Why should I go looking for another place? I could never get a place like this if I'm married.

CHRISTINE. Well, of course not! But you could get a job as a doorkeeper, or maybe try to get a government job as a caretaker somewhere. The government don't pay much, but they pay regular. And there's a pension for the wife and children.

JEAN [*wryly*]. Fine, fine! But I'm not the kind of fellow

who thinks about dying for his wife and children this early in the game. I hate to say it, but I've got slightly bigger plans than that.

CHRISTINE Plans! Hah! What about your obligations? You'd better start giving them a little thought!

JEAN. Don't start nagging me about obligations! I know what I have to do without you telling me. [*He hears a sound upstairs.*] Anyhow, we'll have plenty of chance to talk about this later. You just go and get yourself ready, and we'll be off to church.

CHRISTINE. Who is that walking around up there?

JEAN. I don't know. Clara, I suppose. Who else?

CHRISTINE [*starting to leave*]. It can't be the Count, can it? Could he have come back without anybody hearing him?

JEAN [*frightened*]. The Count? No, it can't be. He would have rung.

CHRISTINE [*leaving*]. God help us! I've never heard of the like of this.

[*The sun has now risen and strikes the tops of the trees in the park. The light shifts gradually until it is shining very obliquely through the windows.* JEAN *goes to the door and signals.* MISS JULIE *enters, dressed for travel, and carrying a small bird cage, covered with a towel. She sets the cage down on a chair.*]

MISS JULIE. I'm ready now.

JEAN. Shh! Christine's awake.

MISS JULIE [*she is extremely tense and nervous during the following*]. Did she suspect anything?

JEAN. She doesn't know a thing.—My God, what happened to you?

MISS JULIE. What do you mean? Do I look so strange?

JEAN. You're white as a ghost, and you've—excuse me— but you've got dirt on your face.

MISS JULIE. Let me wash it off. [*She goes over to the wash basin and washes her face and hands.*] There!

Do you have a towel? . . . Oh, look, the sun's coming up!

JEAN. That breaks the magic spell!

MISS JULIE. Yes, we were spellbound last night, weren't we? Midsummer madness . . . Jean, listen to me! Come with me. I've got the money!

JEAN [*suspiciously*]. Enough?

MISS JULIE. Enough for a start. Come with me, Jean. I can't travel alone today. Midsummer Day on a stifling hot train, packed in with crowds of people, all staring at me—stopping at every station when I want to be flying. I can't, Jean, I can't! . . . And everything will remind me of the past. Midsummer Day when I was a child and the church was decorated with leaves—birch leaves and lilacs . . . the table spread for dinner with friends and relatives . . . and after dinner, dancing in the park, with flowers and games. Oh, no matter how far you travel, the memories tag right along in the baggage car . . . and the regrets and the remorse.

JEAN. All right, I'll go with you! But it's got to be now—before it's too late! This very instant!

MISS JULIE. Hurry and get dressed! [*She picks up the bird cage.*]

JEAN. But no baggage! It would give us away.

MISS JULIE. Nothing. Only what we can take to our seats.

JEAN [*as he gets his hat*]. What in the devil have you got there? What is that?

MISS JULIE. It's only my canary. I can't leave it behind.

JEAN. A canary! My God, do you expect us to carry a bird cage around with us? You're crazy. Put that cage down!

MISS JULIE. It's the only thing I'm taking with me from my home—the only living thing who loves me since Diana was unfaithful to me! Don't be cruel, Jean. Let me take it with me.

JEAN. I told you to put that cage down!—And don't

talk so loud. Christine can hear us.

MISS JULIE. No, I won't leave it with a stranger. I won't. I'd rather have you kill it.

JEAN. Let me have the little pest, and I'll wring its neck.

MISS JULIE. Yes, but don't hurt it. Don't—. No, I can't do it!

JEAN. Don't worry, I can. Give it here.

[MISS JULIE *takes the bird out of the cage and kisses it.*]

MISS JULIE. Oh, my little Serena, must you die and leave your mistress?

JEAN. You don't have to make a scene of it. It's a question of your whole life and future. You're wasting time! [JEAN *grabs the canary from her, carries it to the chopping block, and picks up a meat cleaver.* MISS JULIE *turns away.*] You should have learned how to kill chickens instead of shooting revolvers— [*He brings the cleaver down.*] —then a drop of blood wouldn't make you faint.

MISS JULIE [*screaming*]. Kill me too! Kill me! You can kill an innocent creature without turning a hair— then kill me. Oh, how I hate you! I loathe you! There's blood between us. I curse the moment I first laid eyes on you! I curse the moment I was conceived in my mother's womb.

JEAN. What good does your cursing do? Let's get out of here!

MISS JULIE [*approaches the chopping block as if drawn to it against her will*]. No, I don't want to go yet. I can't.—I have to see.—Shh! I hear a carriage coming! [*She listens but keeps her eyes fastened on the chopping block and cleaver.*] You don't think I can stand the sight of blood, do you? You think I'm so weak! Oh, I'd love to see your blood and your brains on that chopping block. I'd love to see the whole of your sex swimming in a sea of blood just like that. I think I could drink out of your skull. I'd like to bathe my feet in your ribs! I could eat your heart roasted whole!—You think I'm weak! You think I loved you because my womb hungered for your seed. You think I want to carry your brood under my heart and nourish it with my blood! Bear your child and take your name!—Come to think of it, what is your name anyway? I've never heard your last name. You probably don't even have one. I'd be Mrs. Door-keeper or Madame Floorsweeper. You dog with my name on your collar—you lackey with my initials on your buttons! Do you think I'm going to share you with my cook and fight over you with my maid?! Ohhh!—You think I'm a coward who wants to run away. No, I'm going to stay. Come hell or high water, I don't care! My father comes home—finds his bureau broken into—his money gone. Then he rings—on that bell—two rings for the valet. And then he sends for the sheriff—and I tell him everything. Everything! Oh, it'll be wonderful to have it all over . . . if only it will be over. . . . He'll have a stroke and die. Then there'll be an end to all of us. There'll be peace . . . and quiet . . . forever. . . . His coat of arms will be broken on the coffin; the Count's line dies out. But the valet's line will continue in an orphanage, win triumphs in the gutter, and end in jail!*

[CHRISTINE enters, dressed for church and with a hymn-book in her hand. MISS JULIE rushes over to her and throws herself into her arms as if seeking protection.]

MISS JULIE. Help me, Christine! Help me against this man!

CHRISTINE [cold and unmoved]. This is a fine way to behave on a holy day! [She sees the chopping block.] Just look at the mess you've made there! How do you explain that? And what's all this shouting and screaming about?

*Most editions of *Miss Julie* have a speech by Jean at this point: "Now there speaks the royal blood! Brava, Miss Julie. Only you mustn't let the cat out of the bag about the miller and his wife." Strindberg wanted this speech expunged as not in keeping with Jean's character.

MISS JULIE. Christine, you're a woman, you're my friend! I warn you, watch out for this—this monster!

JEAN [*ill at ease and a little embarrassed*]. If you ladies are going to talk, I think I'll go and shave. [*He slips out to the right.*]

MISS JULIE. You've got to understand, Christine! You've got to listen to me!

CHRISTINE. No, I don't. I don't understand this kind of shenanigans at all. Where do you think you're going dressed like that? And Jean with his hat on?— Well?—Well?

MISS JULIE. Listen to me, Christine! If you'll just listen to me, I'll tell you everything.

CHRISTINE. I don't want to know anything.

MISS JULIE. You've got to listen to me—!

CHRISTINE. What about? About your stupid behavior with Jean? I tell you that doesn't bother me at all, because it's none of my business. But if you have any silly idea about talking him into skipping out with you, I'll soon put a stop to that.

MISS JULIE [*extremely tense*]. Christine, please don't get upset. Listen to me. I can't stay here, and Jean can't stay here. So you see, we have to go away.

CHRISTINE. Hm, hm, hm.

MISS JULIE [*suddenly brightening up*]. Wait! I've got an idea! Why couldn't all three of us go away together? —out of the country—to Switzerland—and start a hotel. I've got the money, you see. Jean and I would be responsible for the whole affair—and Christine, you could run the kitchen, I thought. Doesn't that sound wonderful! Say yes! Say you'll come, Christine, then everything will be settled. Say you will! Please! [*She throws her arms around* CHRISTINE *and pats her.*]

CHRISTINE [*remaining aloof and unmoved*]. Hm. Hm.

MISS JULIE [*presto tempo*]. You've never been traveling, Christine. You have to get out and see the world. You can't imagine how wonderful it is to travel by train—constantly new faces—new countries. We'll go to Hamburg, and stop over to look at the zoo—you'll love that. And we'll go to the theatre and the opera. And then when we get to Munich, we'll go to the museums, Christine. They have Rubenses and Raphaels there—those great painters, you know. Of course you've heard about Munich where King Ludwig lived—you know, the king who went mad. And then we can go and see his castles—they're built just like the ones you read about in fairy tales. And from there it's just a short trip to Switzerland—with the Alps. Think of the Alps, Christine, covered with snow in the middle of summer. And oranges grow there, and laurel trees that are green the whole year round.—[JEAN *can be seen in the wings at the right, sharpening his straight razor on a strap held between his teeth and his left hand. He listens to* MISS JULIE *with a satisfied expression on his face, now and then nodding approvingly.* MISS JULIE *continues tempo prestissimo.*]—And that's where we'll get a hotel. I'll sit at the desk while Jean stands at the door and receives the guests, goes out shopping, writes the letters. What a life that will be! The train whistle blowing, then the bus arriving, then a bell ringing upstairs, then the bell in the restaurant rings—and I'll be making out the bills—and I know just how much to salt them—you can't imagine how timid tourists are when you shove a bill in their face!—And you, Christine, you'll run the whole kitchen—there'll be no standing at the stove for you—of course not. If you're going to talk to the people, you'll have to dress neatly and elegantly. And with your looks—I'm not trying to flatter you, Christine—you'll run off with some man one fine day—a rich Englishman, that's who it'll be, they're so easy to—[*Slowing down.*]—to catch.—Then we'll all be rich.—We'll build a villa on Lake Como. —Maybe it does rain there sometimes, but— [*More and more lifelessly.*] —the sun has to shine sometimes, too—even if it looks cloudy.—And—then . . . Or else we can always travel some more—and come back . . . [*Pause.*]—here . . . or somewhere else. . . .

CHRISTINE. Do you really believe a word of that yourself, Miss Julie?

MISS JULIE [*completely beaten*]. Do I believe a word of it myself?

CHRISTINE. Do you?

MISS JULIE [*exhausted*]. I don't know. I don't believe anything any more. [*She sinks down on the bench and lays her head between her arms on the table.*] Nothing. Nothing at all.

CHRISTINE [*turns to the right and faces* JEAN]. So! You were planning to run away, were you?

JEAN [*nonplused, lays his razor down on the table*]. We weren't exactly going to run away! Don't exaggerate. You heard Miss Julie's plans. Even if she's tired now after being up all night, her plans are perfectly practical.

CHRISTINE. Well, just listen to you! Did you really think you could get me to cook for that little—

JEAN [*sharply*]. You keep a respectful tongue in your mouth when you talk to your mistress! Understand?

CHRISTINE. Mistress!

JEAN. Yes, mistress!

CHRISTINE. Well of all the—! I don't have to listen—

JEAN. Yes, you do! You need to listen more and talk less. Miss Julie is your mistress. Don't forget that! And if you're going to despise her for what she did, you ought to despise yourself for the same reason.

CHRISTINE. I've always held myself high enough to—

JEAN. High enough to make you look down on others!

CHRISTINE. —enough to keep from lowering myself beneath my position. No one can say that the Count's cook has ever had anything to do with the stable groom or the swineherd. No one can say that!

JEAN. Yes, aren't you lucky you got involved with a decent man!

CHRISTINE. What kind of a decent man is it who sells the oats from the Count's stables?

JEAN. Listen to who's talking! You get a commission on the groceries and take bribes from the butcher!

CHRISTINE. How can you say a thing like that!

JEAN. And you tell me you can't respect your employers any more! You! You!

CHRISTINE. Are you going to church or aren't you? I should think you'd need a good sermon after your exploits.

JEAN. No, I'm not going to church! You can go alone and confess your own sins.

CHRISTINE. Yes, I'll do just that. And I'll come back with enough forgiveness to cover yours, too. Our Redeemer suffered and died on the cross for all our sins, and if we come to Him in faith and with a penitent heart, He will take all our sins upon Himself.

JEAN. Grocery sins included?

MISS JULIE. Do you really believe that, Christine?

CHRISTINE. With all my heart, as sure as I'm standing here. It was the faith I was born into, and I've held on to it since I was a little girl, Miss Julie. Where sin aboundeth, there grace aboundeth also.

MISS JULIE. If I had your faith, Christine, if only—

CHRISTINE. But you see, that's something you can't have without God's special grace. And it is not granted to everyone to receive it.

MISS JULIE. Then who receives it?

CHRISTINE. That's the secret of the workings of grace, Miss Julie, and God is no respecter of persons. With him the last shall be the first—

MISS JULIE. In that case, he does have respect for the last, doesn't he?

CHRISTINE [continuing]. —and it is easier for a camel to go through the eye of a needle than for a rich man to enter the kingdom of God. That's how things are, Miss Julie. I'm going to leave now—alone. And on my way out I'm going to tell the stable boy not to let any horses out, in case anyone has any ideas about leaving before the Count comes home. Goodbye. [*She leaves.*]

JEAN. She's a devil in skirts!—And all because of a canary!

MISS JULIE [*listlessly*]. Never mind the canary. . . . Do you see any way out of this, any end to it?

JEAN [*after thinking for a moment*]. No.

MISS JULIE. What would you do if you were in my place?

JEAN. In your place? Let me think. . . . An aristocrat, a woman, and—fallen. . . . I don't know.—Or maybe I do.

MISS JULIE [*picks up the razor and makes a gesture with it*]. Like this?

JEAN. Yes. But *I* wouldn't do it, you understand. That's the difference between us.

MISS JULIE. Because you're a man and I'm a woman? What difference does that make?

JEAN. Just the difference that there is—between a man and a woman.

MISS JULIE [*holding the razor in her hand*]. I want to! But I can't do it. My father couldn't do it either, that time he should have done it.

JEAN. No, he was right not to do it. He had to get his revenge first.

MISS JULIE. And now my mother is getting her revenge again through me.

JEAN. Haven't you ever loved your father, Miss Julie?

MISS JULIE. Yes, enormously. But I must have hated him too. I must have hated him without knowing it. It was he who brought me up to despise my own sex, to be half woman and half man. Who's to blame for what has happened? My father, my mother, myself? Myself? I don't have a self that's my own. I don't have a single thought I didn't get from my father, not an emotion I didn't get from my mother. And that last idea—about all people being equal—I got that from him, my betrothed. That's why I say he's beneath contempt. How can it be my own fault? Put the blame on Jesus, like Christine does? I'm too proud to do that—and too intelligent, thanks to what my father taught me. . . . A rich man can't get into heaven? That's a lie. But at least Christine, who's got money in the savings bank, won't get in. . . . Who's to blame? What difference does it make who's to blame? I'm still the one who has to bear the guilt, suffer the consequences—

JEAN. Yes, but—

[*The bell rings sharply twice.* MISS JULIE *jumps up.* JEAN *changes his coat.*]

JEAN. The Count's back! What if Christine—? [*He goes to the speaking tube, taps on it, and listens.*]

MISS JULIE. Has he looked in his bureau yet?

JEAN. This is Jean, sir! [*Listens. The audience cannot hear what the* COUNT *says.*] Yes, sir! [*Listens.*] Yes, sir! Yes, as soon as I can. [*Listens.*] Yes, at once, sir! [*Listens.*] Very good, sir! In half an hour.

MISS JULIE [*trembling with anxiety*]. What did he say? For God's sake, what did he say?

JEAN. He ordered his boots and his coffee in half an hour.

MISS JULIE. Half an hour then! . . . Oh, I'm so tired. I can't bring myself to do anything. Can't repent, can't run away, can't stay, can't live . . . can't die. Help me, Jean. Command me, and I'll obey like a dog. Do me this last favor. Save my honor, save his name. You know what I ought to do but can't force myself to do. Let me use your will power. You command me and I'll obey.

JEAN. I don't know—I can't either, not now. I don't know why. It's as if this coat made me—. I can't give you orders in this. And now, after the Count has spoken to me, I—I can't really explain it—but—I've got the backbone of a damned lackey! If the Count came down here now and ordered me to cut my throat, I'd do it on the spot.

MISS JULIE. Pretend that you're him, and that I'm you. You were such a good actor just a while ago, when you were kneeling before me. You were the aristocrat then. Or else—have you ever been to the theatre and seen a hypnotist? [JEAN *nods*.] He says to his subject, "Take this broom!" and he takes it. He says, "Now sweep!" and he sweeps.

JEAN. But the person has to be asleep!

MISS JULIE [*ecstatic*]. I'm already asleep. The whole room has turned to smoke. You seem like an iron stove, a stove that looks like a man in black with a high hat. Your eyes are glowing like coals when the fire dies out. Your face is a white smudge, like ashes. [*The sun is now shining in on the floor and falls on* JEAN.] It's so good and warm— [*She rubs her hands together as if warming them at a fire.*] —and so bright—and so peaceful.

JEAN [*takes the razor and puts it in her hand*]. There's the broom. Go now, when the sun is up—out into the barn—and— [*He whispers in her ear.*]

MISS JULIE [*waking up*]. Thanks! I'm going to get my rest. But tell me one thing. Tell me that the first can also receive the gift of grace. Tell me that, even if you don't believe it.

JEAN. The first? I can't tell you that.—But wait a moment, Miss Julie. I know what I can tell you. You're no longer among the first. You're among—the last.

MISS JULIE. That's true! I'm among the very last. I am the last!—Oh!—Now I can't go! Tell me just once more, tell me to go!

JEAN. Now I can't either. I can't!

MISS JULIE. And the first shall be the last. . . .

JEAN. Don't think—don't think! You're taking all my strength away. You're making me a coward. . . . What! I thought I saw the bell move. No. . . . Let me stuff some paper in it.—Afraid of a bell! But it isn't just a bell. There's somebody behind it. A hand that makes it move. And there's something that makes the hand move.—Stop your ears, that's it, stop your ears! But it only rings louder. Rings louder and louder until you answer it. And then it's too late. Then the sheriff comes—and then— [*There are two sharp rings on the bell.* JEAN *gives a start, then straightens himself up.*] It's horrible! But there's no other way for it to end.—Go! [MISS JULIE *walks resolutely out through the door.*]

Curtain

GERHART HAUPTMANN

I used the theatrical season of 1892-93 as a springboard from which to dive into the bubbling theatrical waters of Europe's *fin-de-siècle*. Of the plays I have selected for this collection, only one, however, is listed among the premières of that amazing year. It was *The Weavers* by the German, Gerhart Hauptmann. That season it received its first production at the Freiebühne in Berlin under the direction of Otto Brahm.

While this book is concerned with plays and not with players, it is essential at some point to speak of the theatrical revolution that accompanied the revolt against the romantic past in playwriting. For the new scientific materialism that expressed itself on the stage as naturalism and realism required a new kind of mounting and of acting to bring it to proper life. No longer was the grand and operatic style of the cloak-and-sword drama viable. In portraying the kitchens of life a different kind of performance was necessary. A technique had to be developed that would reveal the intimate psychological relationships among the characters in these plays. And in dramas that tied man to his environment, that environment had to be depicted on the stage with freshly observed fact and detail.

The way was paved for this new kind of dramatic presentation by a theatre company that came into being in the last quarter of the nineteenth century in a small duchy in the center of Europe, Saxe-Meiningen. There the first of the modern "repertory theatres" was founded by the Duke himself who was a great theatre "buff." He engaged a man named Kroneyk to organize a company, evolve an artistic policy and direct the plays for him.

The Saxe-Meiningen troupe was not content, fortunately, to stay at home. Between 1874 and 1890 they toured most of Europe, giving some 2,500 performances in thirty-eight cities. In consequence they disseminated their ideas widely and became a major influence throughout the continent. Those who came to see their presentations discovered for the first time how superior a product a play can be that has been treated as an artistic dynamic whole; how visually effective it is to surround the three-dimensional actors with three-dimensional scenery instead of the old flat two-dimensional painted drops and wings; how persuasive it is to depict the characters onstage not as theatrical types but as individual, psychologically truthful, living people.

Stanislavski learned this lesson from the Meiningen Players and put it into practice when he founded the Moscow Art Theatre and developed his own "system." André Antoine was influenced by them when he founded his Théâtre Libre in Paris in 1887 in a tiny hall on a back street in Montmartre. Otto Brahm was responding in like fashion when he organized the Freiebühne two years later in Berlin. For the Meiningen style worked well for the new plays by Ibsen, Tolstoi, Strindberg, Becque, Chekhov, Hauptmann.

Gerhart Hauptmann's *Before Sunrise* had been the second production offered by that avant-garde experimental theatre, the Freiebühn. The author was then only twenty-seven. Born in Silesia, he had attended the Breslau Art Academy, had gone briefly to the University of Jena, had traveled abroad, had married a rich girl and now was settled comfortably in Berlin.

But *Before Sunrise* was not the product of a contented man's imagination. In this study of a degenerate family of Silesian farmers who have become enriched and corrupted by the discovery of coal on their land, Hauptmann revealed a deep concern for the sociological and moral influences that led to the deterioration and decay of his less fortunate fellows. In this same vein he continued his scientific probings of human behavior in *Lonely Lives, Rose Bernd, Teamster Henschel, Michael Kramer, The Beaver Coat* and—supremely—in *The Weavers.*

James Huneker, the American critic whom I have quoted frequently in these notes because he trod this particular critical path before me, called *The Weavers* "a quivering transcript of life . . . a mighty chorale of woe, malediction and want." It is a truly monumental work, resembling in a way a great symphony in five movements, each movement with its own theme and reaching its own climax, but each related to the whole, whose "leit-motif" may be summed up in one word—hunger.

This play is not the story of any one family but of a whole community. The mass is the hero. It is thus the precursor of all those social dramas of a later day which are concerned with the plight of the proletariat. But Hauptmann does not preach or propagandize as so many succeeding humanitarian dramatists have done. He simply paints the picture on his huge canvas and then allows his audience to make its own indictment. Because it is such a massive work—more than forty actors are required for its proper realization—it is seldom performed; and that is a pity, for *The Weavers* would be a powerfully moving drama on some great stage.

Hauptmann alone, of the five authors introduced in this anthology, lived well into this present century. He was awarded the Nobel Prize for Literature in 1932. He saw his native Germany defeated in two wars. He died in 1946 as the Russians were drawing his Silesian fields behind the border of Poland. He was eighty-four years old when his end came. He was the last of the great dramatists of that earlier time.

The Weavers

A Play of the Eighteen-Forties
by GERHART HAUPTMANN

Translated by Horst Frenz
and Miles Waggoner

Application for permission for any use of this play should be made to UNGAR Publishing, 36 Cooper Square, New York, NY 10003 from whom permission to reprint this play has been granted.

CHARACTERS

Dreissiger, a cotton manufacturer
Mrs. Dreissiger, his wife
Pfeifer, a manager
Neumann, a cashier
An Apprentice } at Dreissiger's
Johann, a coachman
A Young Girl
Weinhold, a tutor for Dreissiger's sons
Pastor Kittelhaus
Mrs. Kittelhaus, his wife
Heide, the Chief of Police
Kutsche, a policeman
Welzel, an innkeeper
Mrs. Welzel, his wife
Anna Welzel
Wiegand, a carpenter
A Traveling Salesman
A Farmer
A Forester
Schmidt, a physician
Hornig, a rag picker
Old Wittig, a smith
Weavers: Baecker—Moritz Jaeger—Old Baumert—Mother Baumert—Bertha Baumert—Emma Baumert—Fritz, Emma's son, four years old—August Baumert—Ansorge—Mrs. Heinrich—Old Hilse—Gottlieb Hilse—Luise, Gottlieb's wife—Mielchen, his daughter, six years old—Reimann—Heiber—A weaver woman—A boy, eight years old—A large crowd of young and old weavers and weaver women.

The action of the play takes place in the 1840's in Kasch-bach, Peterswaldau, and Langenbielau, cities at the foot of the mountains known as the Eulengebirge.

ACT ONE.

SCENE: *A spacious whitewashed room in Dreissiger's house at Peterswaldau, where the weavers must deliver their finished webs. At the left are uncurtained windows; in the back wall, a glass door. At the right is a similar door through which weavers, men, women, and children continuously come and go. Along the right wall, which, like the others, is almost entirely hidden by wooden stands for cotton, there is a bench on which the weavers, as they come in, spread out their finished webs to be examined. They step forward in the order of their arrival and offer their finished products.*
PFEIFER, *the manager, stands behind a large table on which the weavers lay their webs for inspection. He makes the inspection with the use of dividers and a magnifying glass. When he is finished, he lays the cotton on the scales, where an apprentice tests its weight. The same apprentice shoves the goods taken from the scales onto the stock shelves.* PFEIFER *calls out the amount to be paid to each weaver to* NEUMANN, *the cashier, who sits at a small table.*

It is a sultry day toward the end of May. The clock points to twelve. Most of the waiting weavers stand like men before the bar of justice where, tortured and anxious, they must await a life-and-death decision. They all give the impression of being crushed, like beggars. Passing from humiliation to humiliation and convinced that they are only tolerated, they are used to making themselves as inconspicuous as possible. Also, they have a stark, irresolute look—gnawing, brooding faces. Most of the men resemble each other, half-dwarf, half-school-master. They are flat-chested, coughing creatures with ashen gray faces: creatures of the looms, whose knees are bent with much sitting. At first glance, their women folk are less typical. They are broken, harried, worn out, while the men still have a certain look of pathetic gravity. The women's clothes are ragged, while those of the men are patched. Some of the young girls are not without charm—they have pale waxen complexions, delicate figures, large protruding melancholy eyes.

CASHIER NEUMANN [*counting out money*]. That leaves 16 silver groschen and 2 pfennigs.

FIRST WEAVER WOMAN [*in her thirties, very emaciated, puts the money away with trembling fingers*]. Thank ya, kindly, sir.

NEUMANN [*as the woman does not move on*]. Well, is something wrong again?

FIRST WEAVER WOMAN [*excitedly, in begging tone*]. I'd like a few pfennigs in advance. I need it awful bad.

NEUMANN. And I need a few hundred thalers. If it was just a matter of needing—! [*Already busy counting out money to another weaver, curtly*.] Mr. Dreissiger himself has to decide about advances.

FIRST WEAVER WOMAN. Then, maybe I could talk to Mr. Dreissiger hisself?

PFEIFER [*he was formerly a weaver. The type is un-mistakable; only he is well-groomed, well-fed, well-clothed, clean-shaven; also, a heavy user of snuff. He calls across brusquely*.] Mr. Dreissiger would have plenty to do, God knows, if he had to bother himself with every trifle. That's what we're here for. [*He measures and inspects a web with the magnifying glass.*] Damn it all! There's a draft! [*He wraps a heavy scarf around his neck.*] Shut the door when ya come in.

THE APPRENTICE [*in a loud voice to* PFEIFER]. It's just like talkin' to a block of wood.

PFEIFER. That's settled then! Weigh it! [*The weaver lays his web on the scales.*] If ya only understood your work better. It's got lumps in it again—I can tell without looking. A good weaver doesn't put off the winding who knows how long.

BAECKER [*enters. A young, exceptionally strong weaver whose behavior is free and easy, almost impertinent.* PFEIFER, NEUMANN, *and* THE APPRENTICE *glance at each other understandingly when he enters*]. Damn it, I'm sweatin' like a dog again.

FIRST WEAVER [*softly*]. Feels like rain.

OLD BAUMERT [*pushes through the glass door at the right. Behind the door, waiting weavers are seen jammed together, shoulder to shoulder.* OLD BAUMERT *has hobbled forward and has laid his bundle on a bench near* BAECKER'S. *He sits down next to it and wipes the sweat from his face*]. Ya sure earn a rest here.

BAECKER. Rest is better than money.

OLD BAUMERT. Ya need money too. Good day to ya, Baecker!

BAECKER. And good day to you, Father Baumert! Who knows how long we'll have to be waitin' around here again.

FIRST WEAVER. It don't matter whether a weaver has to wait an hour or a day. He just don't count.

PFEIFER. Be quiet, back there. I can't hear myself think.

BAECKER [*softly*]. Today's one of his bad days again.

PFEIFER [*to the weavers standing in front of him*]. How many times have I told you already. Ya ought to clean up the webs better. What sort of a mess is this? There are chunks of dirt in it, as long as my finger— and straw, and all kinds of rubbish.

WEAVER REIMANN. I guess I need a new pair of pincers.

THE APPRENTICE [*has weighed the web*]. And it's short weight, too.

PFEIFER. The kind of weavers ya have nowadays! You
hate to hand out the yarn. Oh, Lord, in my time! My
master would've made me pay for it. I tell you, weaving was a different thing in those days. Then, a man
had to understand his business. Today it's not necessary anymore. Reimann, 10 groschen.

WEAVER REIMANN. Yes, but one pound is allowed for
waste.

PFEIFER. I haven't time. That's settled. [*To the next
weaver.*] What have you got?

WEAVER HEIBER [*puts his web up on the counter. While
PFEIFER is inspecting it, HEIBER steps up to him and
speaks softly and eagerly*]. Please, forgive me, Mr.
Pfeifer, I would like to ask ya, sir, if perhaps ya
would be so kind as to do me a favor and not deduct
my advance this time.

PFEIFER [*measuring with the dividers and inspecting,
jeers*]. Well, now! That's just fine. It looks as if about
half the woof has been left on the spool again.

HEIBER [*continuing, as before*]. I'd be glad to make it
up next week for sure. Last week I had to put in two
days' work on the estate. And my wife's home, sick
in bed. . . .

PFEIFER [*putting the web on the scales*]. Here's another
piece of real sloppy work. [*Already taking a new web
for inspection.*] What a selvage—now it's broad, then
it's narrow. In one place the woof's all gathered together, who knows how much, then the reed has been
pulled apart. And scarcely seventy threads to the
inch. Whatever happened to the rest? Is that honest
work? I never saw such a thing!

HEIBER [*suppressing tears, stands humiliated and helpless*].

BAECKER [*low, to BAUMERT*]. I guess this riffraff would
like us to pay for the yarn, too.

FIRST WEAVER WOMAN [*who has withdrawn only a few
steps from the cashier's table, stares about from time
to time, seeking help, without moving from the spot.*

Then she takes heart and once more turns imploringly to the cashier]. I can hardly . . . I don't know . . . if ya don't give me an advance this time . . . O, Lord, Lord. . . .

PFEIFER [*calls across*]. All this calling on the Lord! Just leave the Lord in peace. You haven't been bothering much about the Lord up to now. It'd be better if you'd look after your husband instead, so he isn't seen sitting in the tavern window all day long. We can't give advances. We have to account for every cent. It's not our own money. Later they'd be asking us for it. People who are industrious and understand their business and do their work in fear of God don't ever need advances. So, that's settled.

NEUMANN. And if a Bielau weaver got four times as much pay, he'd squander four times as much and be in debt in the bargain.

FIRST WEAVER WOMAN [*in a loud voice, as if appealing to everyone's sense of justice*]. I'm certainly not lazy, but I just can't go on this way much longer. I've had two miscarriages, and my husband, he can't do no more than half the work neither; he went up to the shepherd at Zerlau, but he couldn't do nothin' for his trouble either . . . there's just so much a body can do. . . . We sure do work as much as we can. I ain't had much sleep for weeks, and everything'll be all right again if I can only get a bit of this weakness out of my bones. But ya got to have a little consideration. [*Beseeching him and fawning.*] Ya'll have to be good enough to let me have a few groschen, this time.

PFEIFER [*unperturbed*]. Fiedler, 11 groschen.

FIRST WEAVER WOMAN. Just a few groschen, so we can get some bread. The farmer won't give us no more credit. We got a house full of children. . . .

NEUMANN [*softly and with mock seriousness to* THE APPRENTICE]. Once a year the linen weaver has a brat, fa, la, la, la, la.

THE APPRENTICE [*chiming in*]. The first six weeks it's blind as a bat, fa, la, la, la, la.

REIMANN [*not touching the money that the cashier has counted out for him*]. We've always been gettin' 13½ groschen for a web.

PFEIFER [*calls across*]. If it doesn't suit you, Reimann, all you have to do is say the word. There are plenty of weavers. Especially weavers like you. For full weight, you'll get full pay.

REIMANN. That something should be wrong with the weight. . . .

PFEIFER. If there's nothing wrong with the cotton you bring, there'll be nothing wrong with your pay.

REIMANN. It really can't be that this web, here, should have too many flaws in it.

PFEIFER [*inspecting*]. He who weaves well, lives well.

HEIBER [*he has stayed close to* PFEIFER *waiting for a favorable opportunity. He smiled with the others at* PFEIFER's *remark; now he steps forward and speaks to him as he did before*]. I would like to ask ya, sir, if perhaps ya would be so kind and not deduct the 5 groschen advance this time. My wife's been sick in bed since before Ash Wednesday. She can't do a lick of work. And I have to pay a girl to tend the bobbin. And so—

PFEIFER [*takes a pinch of snuff*]. Heiber, you're not the only one I have to attend to. The others want their turn, too.

REIMANN. The way the warp was given to me—that's the way I wound it and that's the way I took it off again. I can't bring back better yarn than I take home.

PFEIFER. If ya don't like it, ya simply don't need to get any more warp here. There are plenty who'd run their feet off for it.

NEUMANN [*to* REIMANN]. Aren't you going to take the money?

REIMANN. I just can't take such pay.

NEUMANN [*without troubling himself further about* REIMANN]. Heiber, 10 groschen—take off the 5 groschen advance—leaves 5 groschen.

HEIBER [*steps up, looks at the money, stands there, shakes his head as if there were something he could not believe, and then quietly and carefully pockets the money*]. O my God—! [*Sighing.*] Ah, well!

OLD BAUMERT [*looking straight at* HEIBER]. Yes, yes, Franz! You've got cause for sighing there.

HEIBER [*speaking wearily*]. Ya see, I've got a sick girl layin' home. She needs a bottle of medicine.

OLD BAUMERT. What's wrong with her?

HEIBER. Ya see, she's been a sickly little thing from the time she was born. I really don't know . . . well, I can tell you: she brought it into the world with her. Such trouble's in the blood, and it keeps breakin' out over and over again.

OLD BAUMERT. There's something the matter everywhere. When you're poor, there's nothing but bad luck. There's no end to it and no salvation.

HEIBER. What have ya got in that bundle?

OLD BAUMERT. We haven't got a thing in the house. So I had our little dog killed. There ain't much to him, he was half-starved. He was a nice little dog. I couldn't kill him myself. I didn't have the heart.

PFEIFER [*has inspected* BAECKER'S *web, calls out*]. Baecker, 13½ groschen.

BAECKER. That's a measly hand-out for a beggar, not pay.

PFEIFER. Those who are done, have to get out. It's so crowded, we can't move around in here.

BAECKER [*to those standing about, without lowering his voice*]. That's a measly hand-out, that's all it is. And for that a man's to work the treadle from early morning till late at night. And after a man's been workin' behind a loom for eighteen days, evenin'

after evenin'—worn out, dizzy with the dust and terrible heat, then he's lucky if he gets 13½ groschen
for his drudgery.

PFEIFER. We'll have no back-talk here.

BAECKER. You can't make me hold my tongue.

PFEIFER [*jumps up, shouting*]. We'll see about that.
[*Walks toward the glass door and calls into the office.*] Mr. Dreissiger! Mr. Dreissiger, if you'll be so
kind!

DREISSIGER [*enters. He is about forty, fat, asthmatic.
With a severe look*]. What's—the matter, Pfeifer?

PFEIFER [*angrily*]. Baecker won't hold his tongue.

DREISSIGER [*draws himself up, throws his head back,
and stares at* BAECKER *with quivering nostrils*]. Oh,
yes—Baecker—[*To* PFEIFER.] Is that him—? [*The clerk
nods.*]

BAECKER [*impudently*]. Yes, indeed, Mr. Dreissiger!
[*Pointing to himself.*] That's him. [*Pointing to* DREIS-
SIGER.] And that's him.

DREISSIGER [*indignantly*]. How can he dare?

PFEIFER. He's too well off, that's what he is. He'll skate
on thin ice once too often.

BAECKER [*roughly*]. You shut up, you fool! Once, in
the new moon, your mother must have been ridin'
a broomstick with Satan to beget such a devil as
you for a son.

DREISSIGER [*in sudden anger, bellows*]. Shut up! Shut
up this minute, or else—[*He trembles, takes a few
steps forward.*]

BAECKER [*with determination, standing up to him*]. I'm
not deaf. I still hear good.

DREISSIGER [*controls himself, asks with apparent businesslike calm*]. Isn't he one of those—?

PFEIFER. He's a Bielau weaver. They can always be
found where trouble is brewing.

DREISSIGER [*trembling*]. Then I'm warning you: if it
happens once more, and if such a gang of half-
drunken young louts passes my house once again, as

they did last night, singing that vile song. . . .

BAECKER. I guess you mean "Bloody Justice"?

DREISSIGER. You know exactly what I mean. Let me tell you, if I hear that song once more, I'll get hold of one of you, and—on my honor, joking aside, I promise you I'll turn him over to the state's attorney. And if I find out who wrote this wretched song. . . .

BAECKER. That's a beautiful song—it is!

DREISSIGER. Another word and I'll send for the police—immediately. I won't lose any time! We know how to deal with young fellows like you. I've taken care of your kind before.

BAECKER. Well, now, that I can believe. A real manufacturer like you can gobble up two or three hundred weavers before a person has time to turn around . . . and not so much as a bone left over. Such a man's got four stomachs like a cow and teeth like a wolf. No, indeed—that's nothing at all to him!

DREISSIGER [*to the clerks*]. See to it that that fellow doesn't get another stick of work from us.

BAECKER. Oh, it's all the same to me whether I starve behind the loom or in a ditch by the side of the road.

DREISSIGER. Get out, this minute! Get out of here!

BAECKER [*firmly*]. I'll take my pay first.

DREISSIGER. How much has the man got coming, Neumann?

NEUMANN. Twelve groschen and five pfennigs.

DREISSIGER [*takes the money from the cashier in great haste and throws it down on the counter so that a few coins roll onto the floor*]. There you are—and now hurry—get out of my sight!

BAECKER. I'll take my pay first.

DREISSIGER. There's your pay; and if you don't hurry and get out. . . . It's exactly twelve . . . my dyers are taking off for lunch. . . .

BAECKER. My pay belongs in my hand. My pay belongs here. [*He points to the palm of his left hand.*]

DREISSIGER [*to the* APPRENTICE]. Pick it up, Tilgner.

[THE APPRENTICE *picks up the money and lays it in* BAECKER'S *hand.*]

BAECKER. Everything's got to be done right. [*He puts the money slowly in an old purse.*]

DREISSIGER. Well? [*As* BAECKER *still does not leave, impatiently.*] Shall I help you?

[*There is excited movement among the crowd of weavers. A long, deep sigh is heard, then a fall. Everyone's attention is turned to this new event.*]

DREISSIGER. What's happened there?

VARIOUS WEAVERS *and* WEAVER WOMEN. Someone's fainted. It's a sickly little boy. What's wrong? Is it consumption, maybe?

DREISSIGER. Why . . . what's that? Fainted? [*He goes up closer.*]

AN OLD WEAVER. He's layin' there.

[*They make room. A little* BOY, *about eight years old, is seen lying on the floor as if dead.*]

DREISSIGER. Does somebody know this boy?

OLD WEAVER. He's not from our village.

OLD BAUMERT. He looks like one of Heinrich's boys. [*He looks at him more closely.*] Yes, indeed! That is Heinrich's little Gustav.

DREISSIGER. Where do they live, these people?

OLD BAUMERT. Why, near us in Kaschbach, Mr. Dreissiger. He goes around playin' music, and in the daytime he works at the loom. They have nine children and the tenth's on the way.

VARIOUS WEAVERS *and* WEAVER WOMEN. They sure got a lot of trouble. Their roof leaks. The woman ain't got two shirts for the nine children.

OLD BAUMERT [*taking hold of the* BOY]. Why, my child, what's wrong with ya? Wake up, there now!

DREISSIGER. Take hold of him—here, help me—we'll pick him up. It's incomprehensible that anybody should let a weak child like that come such a long way. Bring some water, Pfeifer!

WEAVER WOMAN [*helps him sit up*]. Don't ya up and die on us, boy!

DREISSIGER. Or brandy, Pfeifer, brandy is better.

BAECKER [*forgotten by everybody has been watching. Now, with one hand on the doorknob, he calls across in a loud voice, mockingly*]. Give him something to eat, too, and he'll come to all right. [*Exit.*]

DREISSIGER. That fellow will come to no good. Take him under the arm, Neumann. Slowly—slowly . . . that's it . . . there, now . . . we'll take him into my room. Why, what is it?

NEUMANN. He's said something, Mr. Dreissiger! He's moving his lips.

DREISSIGER. What is it, little boy?

THE BOY [*whispers*]. I'm—hungry!

DREISSIGER [*turns pale*]. I can't understand him.

WEAVER WOMAN. I think he said. . . .

DREISSIGER. Well, we'll see. Let's not lose any time—he can lie on my sofa. We'll hear, then, what the doctor says.

[DREISSIGER, NEUMANN, *and the* WEAVER WOMAN *carry the* BOY *into the office. There is a commotion among the weavers, as among school children when the teacher leaves the classroom. They stretch, they whisper, they shift from one foot to the other. Soon there is a loud and general conversation among them.*]

OLD BAUMERT. I really do believe Baecker is right.

SEVERAL WEAVERS *and* WEAVER WOMEN. He said something like that, too. That's nothing new around here—people faintin' from hunger. Yes, and who knows what'll happen this winter if this cuttin' of wages keeps on—. And the potatoes bein' so bad this year—. It won't be no different here till we're all of us flat on our backs.

OLD BAUMERT. Ya might just as well put a rope 'round your neck and hang yourself on your loom like the Nentwich weaver did. Here, take a pinch of snuff —I was in Neurode, where my brother-in-law works in the snuff factory. He gave me a few grains. You carryin' anything nice in your kerchief?

AN OLD WEAVER. It's only a little bit of barley. The wagon from the Ullbrich miller was drivin' ahead of me, and there was a little slit in one of the sacks. That comes in handy, believe me.

OLD BAUMERT. There are twenty-two mills in Peterswaldau, and still there's nothin' left over for the likes of us.

AN OLD WEAVER. Ah, we mustn't get discouraged. Something always turns up and helps a little bit.

HEIBER. When we're hungry, we have to pray to the fourteen guardian angels, and if that don't fill ya up, then ya have to put a pebble in your mouth and suck on it. Right, Baumert?

[DREISSIGER *and* PFEIFER, *as well as the cashier, return.*]

DREISSIGER. It was nothing of any importance. The boy's quite all right again. [*Goes around excited and puffing.*] And yet it is a disgrace. A bit of wind would blow that wisp of a child away. It's really unbelievable how people—how parents can be so irresponsible. To load him down with two bundles of cotton and send him a good seven and a half miles on the road. It's really quite unbelievable. I will simply have to take steps to see to it that goods brought by children will not be accepted. [*He walks silently back and forth.*] In any case, I certainly hope that nothing of this sort happens again. On whose shoulders does the blame finally rest? The manufacturers, of course. We're blamed for everything. When a poor little fellow falls asleep in the snow in the wintertime, one of these reporter chaps comes running up, and in two days the gruesome story is in all the papers. The father, the parents, the ones who send the child out . . . oh, no . . . they aren't guilty, certainly not! It must be the manufacturer; the manufacturer is the goat. The weaver is always let off easy, the manufacturer is the one who catches it; he's a man without a heart, a dangerous fellow who can be bitten in the leg by every mad dog of a reporter. He lives in splendor and in comfort and pays the poor weavers starvation wages. These scribblers are absolutely silent about the fact that such a man has troubles, too, and sleepless nights; that he runs great risks such as the weaver never dreams of; that often he does nothing but calculate—dividing, adding, and multiplying, calculating and recalculating until he's nearly out of his mind; that he has to consider and weigh a hundred different kinds of things, and always has to fight and compete, you might say, as a matter of life and death; that not a single day goes by without annoyances and losses. All the people who're dependent on the manufacturer, who suck him dry and want to live off of him—think of that! No, no! You ought to be in my shoes for a while, then you'd get fed up with it soon enough, I tell you. [*After a little reflection.*] How that fellow, that scoundrel there, that Baecker, behaved! Now he'll go around and tell everybody how hard-hearted I am. That at the slightest opportunity I throw the weavers out. Is that true? Am I so hard-hearted?

MANY VOICES. No, Mr. Dreissiger!

DREISSIGER. Well, it doesn't look like that to me, either. And yet these rascals go around here and sing nasty songs about us manufacturers. They talk of hunger and yet they have so much money to spend that they can consume their liquor by the quart. They ought to look around in other places, and see how things are among the linen weavers. They can really talk of hard times. But you here, you cotton weavers, you can quietly thank God that things are as they are. And I ask the old, industrious, skilled weavers who are here: Tell me, can a worker, who does a good job, earn his living, working for me or can't he?

VERY MANY VOICES. Yes, Mr. Dreissiger!

DREISSIGER. There, you see! A fellow like Baecker can't,

of course. But I advise you, keep those fellows in check; if this goes too far, I'll just quit. Then I'll give up the whole business, and you'll see where you are. You'll see who'll give you work. Certainly not your fine Mr. Baecker.

FIRST WEAVER WOMAN [*has come up close to* DREISSIGER *and with fawning humility brushes some dust from his coat*]. You've gone and rubbed against something, Mr. Dreissiger, sir, you have.

DREISSIGER. Business is terrible, you know that yourselves. Instead of earning money, I'm actually losing it. If, in spite of this, I see to it that my weavers always have work, I expect them to appreciate it. The goods lie stocked up here in thousands of yards, and I don't know today if I'll ever sell them. Well, I've heard that a great number of weavers around here have no work at all, and so . . . well, Pfeifer can give you the details. The fact of the matter is this: so you'll see my good intentions—naturally, I can't just hand out charity. I'm not rich enough for that. But I can, up to a certain point, give the unemployed a chance to earn at least a little something. That I'm running a tremendous risk in doing that, well, that's my own affair. I think it's always better if a man can earn a piece of bread and cheese for himself every day rather than starve. Don't you think I'm right?

MANY VOICES. Yes, yes, Mr. Dreissiger.

DREISSIGER. I am therefore willing to put an additional two hundred weavers to work. Pfeifer will explain to you, under what conditions. [*He is about to leave.*]

FIRST WEAVER WOMAN [*steps in his path, speaks quickly, imploringly, urgently*]. Mr. Dreissiger, sir, I wanted to ask ya real kindly, if perhaps you . . . I've been laid up twice. . . .

DREISSIGER [*in haste*]. Speak to Pfeifer, my good woman, I'm late as it is. [*He turns away from her.*]

REIMANN [*stops him. In the tone of an injured and accusing man*]. Mr. Dreissiger, I really have a complaint to make. Mr. Pfeifer has . . . I always get 12½ groschen for a web, and. . . .

DREISSIGER [*interrupts him*]. There's the manager. Talk to him: he's the person to see.

HEIBER [*stops* DREISSIGER]. Mr. Dreissiger, sir, [*Stuttering, in confusion and haste.*] I wanted to ask ya if perhaps ya could . . . if maybe Mr. Pfeifer could . . . if he could. . . .

DREISSIGER. What is it you want?

HEIBER. The advance pay that I got last time. I mean that I. . . .

DREISSIGER. I really do not understand you.

HEIBER. I was pretty hard up, because. . . .

DREISSIGER. Pfeifer's business, that's Pfeifer's business. I really can't . . . take it up with Pfeifer. [*He escapes into the office.*]

[*The supplicants look helplessly at one another. One after the other, they step back, sighing.*]

PFEIFER [*starts the inspection again*]. Well, Annie, and what are you bringing us?

OLD BAUMERT. How much for a web, then, Mr. Pfeifer?

PFEIFER. Ten groschen for each web.

OLD BAUMERT. Ain't that something!

[*Excitement among the weavers, whispers and grumblings.*]

Curtain

ACT TWO.

SCENE: *A small room in the cottage of* WILHELM ANSORGE *in Kaschbach in the mountains called Eulengebirge.*

The narrow room measures less than six feet from the dilapidated floor to the smoke-blackened rafters. Two young girls, EMMA *and* BERTHA BAUMERT, *sit at looms.* MOTHER BAUMERT, *a crippled old woman, sits on a stool by the bed, at her spooling wheel. Her son,* AUGUST, *twenty years old, an idiot with small body and head and long spiderlike limbs, sits on a footstool, also reeling yarn.*

The weak, rosy light of the setting sun shines through two small window openings in the left wall. These are partly pasted over with paper and partly filled up with straw. The light falls on the pale, blond, loose hair of the girls, on their bare, bony shoulders and thin waxen necks, on the folds of their coarse chemises, which, with a short skirt of the roughest linen, constitute their entire clothing. The warm glow lights up the entire face, neck, and chest of the old woman. Her face is emaciated to a skeleton, with folds and wrinkles in the anemic skin. The sunken eyes are reddened and watery from the lint and smoke and from working by lamplight. She has a long goiter neck with sinews standing out. Her narrow chest is covered with faded shawls and rags. Part of the right wall, with the stove, stove bench, bedstead, and several gaudily tinted pictures of saints, is also lighted up. There are rags hanging on the bar of the stove to dry, and behind the stove, old worthless rubbish is piled up. On the bench are a few old pots and kitchen utensils; a heap of potato peelings is laid out to dry on a piece of paper. Skeins of yarn and reels hang from the rafters. Small baskets with bobbins stand beside the looms. In the back there is a low door without a lock; next to it, a bundle of willow switches leans against the wall. Several broken peck baskets lie about. The room is filled with the noise of the looms: the rhythmic movement of the lathe which shakes the walls and the floor, the shuffle and clicking of the shuttle moving rapidly back and forth. This blends with the low constant humming of the spooling wheels that sounds like the buzzing of bumble bees.

MOTHER BAUMERT [*in a pitiful, exhausted voice, as the girls stop their weaving and bend over their webs*]. Do ya have to make knots again?

EMMA [*the elder of the girls, twenty-two years old, is tying up the torn threads*]. This is the worst yarn!

BERTHA [*fifteen years old*]. The warp sure causes a lot of trouble.

EMMA. Where's he been so long? He's been gone since nine o'clock.

MOTHER BAUMERT. I should say so! Where can he be, girls?

BERTHA. Don't ya worry, mother!

MOTHER BAUMERT. I can't help it!

[*Emma continues weaving.*]

BERTHA. Wait a minute, Emma!

EMMA. What is it?

BERTHA. I thought I heard somebody comin'.

EMMA. That'll be Ansorge comin' home.

FRITZ [*a small four-year old boy, barefoot and dressed in rags, comes in crying*]. Mother, I'm hungry.

EMMA. Wait, Fritz, just you wait a bit. Grandfather's comin' soon. He's bringin' bread and grain.

FRITZ. But I'm so hungry, Mamma.

EMMA. I just told ya. Don't be so silly. He's comin' right away. He'll bring some nice bread and some coffee grain. When we stop workin', Mamma'll take the potato peelin's to the farmer, and he'll give her a bit of buttermilk for her boy.

FRITZ. But where's grandfather gone?

EMMA. He's at the manufacturer's, deliverin' a web.

FRITZ. At the manufacturer's?

EMMA. Yes, Fritz! Down at Dreissiger's in Peterswaldau.

FRITZ. Will he get some bread there?

EMMA. Yes, yes, they'll give him some money, and then he can buy some bread.

FRITZ. Will they give grandfather lots of money?

EMMA. Oh, stop talkin', boy. [*She continues weaving, as does* BERTHA. *Then both stop again.*]

BERTHA. August, go and ask Ansorge if he won't give us a light.

[AUGUST *leaves together with* FRITZ.]

MOTHER BAUMERT [*with ever-increasing childlike fear, almost whining*]. Children, children! Where can the man be?

BERTHA. Maybe he dropped in to see Hauffen.

MOTHER BAUMERT [*crying*]. If he just ain't gone to the tavern.

EMMA. I hope not, Mother! But our father ain't that kind.

MOTHER BAUMERT [*quite beside herself with a host of fears*]. Well . . . well . . . well, tell me what'll happen if he . . . if he comes home . . . if he drinks it all up and don't bring nothin' home? There ain't a handful of salt in the house, not a piece of bread . . . we need a shovelful of fuel. . . .

BERTHA. Don't ya worry, Mother! The moon's shining. We'll go to the woods. We'll take August along and bring back some firewood.

MOTHER BAUMERT. Sure, so the forester can catch ya?

ANSORGE [*an old weaver, with a gigantic frame, who has to bend low in order to enter the room, sticks his head and the upper part of his body through the door. His hair and beard are unkempt*]. Well, what do ya want?

BERTHA. Ya could give us a light!

ANSORGE [*muffled, as if speaking in the presence of a sick person*]. It's still light enough.

MOTHER BAUMERT. Now ya'll even make us sit in the dark.

ANSORGE. I've got to do the best I can. [*He goes out.*]

BERTHA. Now ya see how stingy he is.

EMMA. Yeah, we got to sit here till he gets good and ready.

MRS. HEINRICH [*enters. She is thirty years old, pregnant. Her face is worn from sorrow and anxious waiting*]. Good evenin' to ya all.

MOTHER BAUMERT. Well, Mother Heinrich, what's the news?

MRS. HEINRICH [*limping*]. I've stepped on a piece of glass.

BERTHA. Come over here and set down. I'll see if I can't get it out.

MRS. HEINRICH [*sits down;* BERTHA *kneels in front of her and busies herself with* MRS. HEINRICH's *foot.*]

MOTHER BAUMERT. How's things at home, Mother Heinrich?

MRS. HEINRICH [*breaks out in despair*]. Soon I won't be able to stand it no more. [*She fights in vain against a flood of tears. Then she weeps silently.*]

MOTHER BAUMERT. It'd be the best for the likes of us, Mother Heinrich, if the dear Lord would have pity on us and take us out of this world.

MRS. HEINRICH [*losing her self-control, weeps and cries out*]. My poor children are starvin'! [*She sobs and moans.*] I just don't know what to do. Ya try as hard as ya can, ya wear yourself out till ya drop. I'm more dead than alive, and still it ain't no different. Nine hungry mouths to feed and not enough to feed them. Where am I to get the food, huh? Last night I had a little bit of bread—it wasn't enough for the two littlest ones. Who was I supposed to give it to, huh? They all cried: Mama, me, Mama, me. . . . No, no! And all this while I'm still up and about. What'll it

be when I have to take to my bed? The few potatoes
we had was washed away. We ain't got a bite to eat.

BERTHA [*has removed the splinter and washed out the
wound*]. We'll put a piece of cloth around it. [*To
EMMA.*] Look and see if ya can find one.

MOTHER BAUMERT. We ain't no better off, Mother Heinrich.

MRS. HEINRICH. At least ya've still got your girls. Ya've
got a husband who can work for ya, but mine—he
fell down again this past week. He's had another
spell, and I was that scared to death—I didn't know
what to do. And after he's had one of them fits, he's
laid up for at least a week.

MOTHER BAUMERT. Mine ain't no better. He's ready to
collapse, too. He's got trouble with his chest and his
back. And there ain't a single pfennig in the house
either. If he don't bring some money home today, I
don't know what we're goin' to do either.

EMMA. That's so, Mother Heinrich. We're so bad off,
Father had to take little Ami with him . . . we had to
have him butchered so we can get something real in
our stomachs again.

MRS. HEINRICH. Ain't ya even got a handful of flour left
over?

MOTHER BAUMERT. Not even that much, Mother Heinrich; there ain't a pinch of salt left in the house.

MRS. HEINRICH. Well, then I don't know what to do!
[*Gets up, stands brooding.*] I really don't know what
to do! [*Crying out in anger and panic.*] I'd be satisfied if it was nothin' but pig swill!—but I just can't
go home empty-handed again. That just won't do.
God forgive me. I don't know nothin' else to do.
[*She limps out quickly, stepping only on the heel of
her left foot.*]

MOTHER BAUMERT [*calls after her, warning*]. Mother
Heinrich, don't ya go an' do nothin' foolish.

BERTHA. She won't do no harm to herself. Don't ya
worry.

EMMA. She always acts like that. [*She sits at the loom again and weaves for a few seconds.*]

[AUGUST *enters with a candle, lighting the way for his father,* OLD BAUMERT, *who drags in a bundle of yarn.*

MOTHER BAUMERT. My God, man, where in the world have ya been so long?

OLD BAUMERT. Ya don't have to snap at me like that, right away. Just let me catch my breath first. Better look an' see who's come in with me.

MORITZ JAEGER [*enters, stooping, through the door. He is a well-built, average-sized, red-cheeked soldier. His Hussar's cap sits jauntily on the side of his head; he wears good clothes and shoes and a clean shirt without a collar. He stands erect and gives a military salute. In a hearty voice*]. Good evening, Auntie Baumert.

MOTHER BAUMERT. Well, well, now! So you've come home again? And ya didn't forget us? Why, set down. Come here, set down.

EMMA [*with her skirt cleans off a wooden stool and shoves it toward* JAEGER]. Good evenin', Moritz! Did ya come back to have another look at how poor folks is living?

JAEGER. Well, now, say, Emma! I never really could believe it! Why, you've got a boy who'll soon be big enough to be a soldier. Where did ya get him?

BERTHA [*takes the small amount of food that her father brought in, puts the meat in a pan, and shoves it in the oven while* AUGUST *builds a fire*]. Ya know the Weaver Finger, don't ya?

MOTHER BAUMERT. He used to live here in the cottage with us. He would have married her, but his lungs was almost completely gone then. I warned the girl often enough. But would she listen to me? Now, he's dead and gone and forgotten a long time and she'll have to see how she can support the boy. But now, you tell me, Moritz, how's things been goin' with you?

OLD BAUMERT. You be quiet, Mother, can't ya see he's had plenty to eat; he's laughin' at all of us; he's got clothes like a prince and a silver pocket watch, and on top of all that, ten silver thalers in cash.

JAEGER [*stands with his legs apart, showing off, a boastful smile on his face*]. I can't complain. I didn't have a bad time in the army.

OLD BAUMERT. He was an orderly to a captain. Just listen to him—he talks like elegant folks.

JAEGER. I've got so used to fine talk that I can't help it.

MOTHER BAUMERT. No, no, well, I never! Such a good-for-nothin' as you was, and comin' into such money. You never was good for nothin' much; ya couldn't unwind two spools in a row. But you was always off and away, settin' wrenboxes and robin snares. You'd rather do that. Well, ain't that the truth?

JAEGER. It's true, Auntie Baumert. And I didn't catch just robins, I caught swallows, too.

EMMA. No matter how often we used to say swallows was poison.

JAEGER. It was all the same to me. But how have all of you been getting along, Auntie Baumert?

MOTHER BAUMERT. O dear Lord Jesus, it's been awful hard these last four years. I've been havin' bad pains. Just look at my fingers. I really don't know if it's the rheumatiz or what. I'm in such misery! I can hardly move a muscle. Nobody knows the kind of pain I have to put up with.

OLD BAUMERT. She really has it bad now. She won't be with us long.

BERTHA. In the mornin' we got to dress her, in the evenin' we got to undress her. We got to feed her like a little baby.

MOTHER BAUMERT [*continuing in a complaining, tearful voice*]. I got to be waited on, hand and foot. I ain't just sick. I'm also a burden. How often I've prayed to the good Lord if he'd only call me away. O Lord, O Lord, my life's too hard, it really is. I don't know . . . people might think . . . but I've been used to working hard from the time I was a child. I've always been able to do my share and now, all at once—[*She tries, in vain, to get up.*]—I just can't do nothin', no more! I've got a good husband and good children, but if I've got to sit by and see. . . . See how those girls look! They ain't got hardly no blood in 'em. They got as much color as a sheet. They keep workin' away at the treadle if they get anything for it or not. What kind of a life is that? They ain't been away from the treadle all year long. They ain't even earned enough so they could buy just a few clothes so they could be seen in public, or could step into church and get some comfort. They look like skeletons, they do, young girls of fifteen and twenty.

BERTHA [*at the stove*]. It's smokin' again.

OLD BAUMERT. Yeah, just look at that smoke. Do ya think something can be done about it? It'll damn soon collapse, that stove. We'll have to let it collapse, and we'll just have to swallow the soot. All of us cough, one worse than the other. Anyone as coughs, coughs, and if it chokes us, and if our lungs are coughed up with it, nobody cares a bit.

JAEGER. Why, that's Ansorge's business, he has to fix it, doesn't he?

BERTHA. A lot he cares. He does enough complainin'.

MOTHER BAUMERT. He thinks we're takin' up too much room, as it is.

OLD BAUMERT. And if we make a fuss, out we go. He ain't seen a bit of rent from us for almost half a year.

MOTHER BAUMERT. A man like that livin' alone could at least be civil.

OLD BAUMERT. He ain't got nothin' neither, Mother. Things is hard enough with him, too, even if he don't make a fuss about his troubles.

MOTHER BAUMERT. He's still got his house.

OLD BAUMERT. Oh, no, Mother, what are ya talkin'

about? There ain't hardly a stick of wood in this
house he can call his own.

JAEGER [*has sat down. He takes a short pipe with a
decorative tassel out of one coat pocket and a flask
of whiskey out of the other*]. This can't go on much
longer. I'm amazed at how things are with you people around here. Why, dogs in the city live better
than you live.

OLD BAUMERT [*eagerly*]. That's the truth, ain't it? You
know it, too? And if ya complain, they tell ya it's
just hard times.

ANSORGE [*enters with an earthen bowl full of soup in
one hand, a half-finished basket in the other*]. Welcome home, Moritz! So you're here again?

JAEGER. Thank you, Father Ansorge.

ANSORGE [*shoving his bowl into the oven*]. Say, if you
don't look like a count!

OLD BAUMERT. Show him your fine watch. He's brought
back a new suit, too, and ten silver thalers in cash.

ANSORGE [*shaking his head*]. Well, well! Well, well!

EMMA [*putting the potato peelings into a little sack*].
I'll take the peelin's over now. Maybe it'll be enough
for a little skimmed milk. [*She goes out.*]

JAEGER [*while all pay close and eager attention to him*].
Well, now, just think how often you've made it hot
as hell for me. They'll teach you manners, Moritz,
you always said, just you wait, when they take you
into the army. Well, now you see, it's gone pretty
well with me. In half a year, I had my stripes. You
have to be willing, that's the main thing. I polished
the sergeant's boots; I curried his horse, I brought
him his beer. I was as quick as a weasel. And I was
always on my toes; damn it, my gear was always clean
and sparkling. I was the first one in the stable, the
first one at roll call, the first one in the saddle; and
when it came to the attack—forward! Hell and
damnation! I was as keen as a hunting dog. I always
said to myself, nobody'll help you here, you can't get

out of this job; and I'd pull myself together and do it; and then, finally, the captain said about me, in front of the whole squadron: That's the way a Hussar ought to be. [*Silence. He lights his pipe.*]

ANSORGE [*shaking his head*]. My, and such luck you had! Well, well! Well, well! [*He sits down on the floor, with the willow switches beside him. Holding the basket between his legs, he continues mending it.*]

OLD BAUMERT. Let's just hope that ya brought us some of your good luck along with ya. Now maybe we could have a drink with ya, huh?

JAEGER. Why, sure, Father Baumert, and when this is gone, there'll be more. [*He throws a coin down on the table.*]

ANSORGE [*with foolish, grinning amazement*]. O Lord, such goin's on . . . over there, there's a roast sizzlin' and here's a quart of whiskey—[*He drinks from the bottle.*]—to your health, Moritz. Well, well! Well, well! [*From now on, the whiskey bottle is passed around.*]

OLD BAUMERT. If we could only have a little roast on holidays, instead of not seein' no meat at all, year in and year out. This way, ya've got to wait till a little dog crosses your path like this one did four weeks ago. And that don't happen often these days.

ANSORGE. Did ya have Ami killed?

OLD BAUMERT. He would've starved to death. . . .

ANSORGE. Well, well! Well, well!

MOTHER BAUMERT. And he was such a nice, friendly little dog.

JAEGER. Are you still so eager 'round here for roast dog?

OLD BAUMERT. O Lord, Lord, if we could only get our fill of it.

MOTHER BAUMERT. Yes, a piece of meat like that is sure rare around here.

OLD BAUMERT. Ain't ya got no appetite for such things

no more? Well, just stay here with us, Moritz, and ya'll soon get it back.

ANSORGE [*sniffing*]. Well, well! Well, well! That's something that tastes good, and it sure gives off a nice smell.

OLD BAUMERT [*sniffing*]. The real thing, ya might say.

ANSORGE. Now tell us what you think, Moritz. You know how things go, out there in the world. Will things ever be different here with us weavers, or what?

JAEGER. I should hope so.

ANSORGE. We can't live and we can't die up here. Things is really bad with us, believe me. We fight to the last, but in the end we have to give in. The wolf is always at the door. In the old days, when I could still work at the looms, I could half-way get along, in spite of hunger and hardship. It's been a long time since I've been able to get some real work. I can hardly make a livin' weavin' baskets. I work till late into the night and when I fall worn out into bed, I've slaved for just a few pfennigs. You got a' education, now you tell me—can anyone really make out in such hard times? I got to lay out three thalers for taxes on the house, one thaler for land taxes, three thalers for interest. I can figure on makin' fourteen thalers. That leaves me seven thalers to live on all year. Out of that, I have to buy food, firewood, clothes, shoes, and patches and thread for mendin', and ya have to have a place to live, and goodness knows what else. Is it any wonder a man can't pay the interest?

OLD BAUMERT. Somebody sure ought to go to Berlin and explain to the King how things is with us.

JAEGER. That won't do much good, either, Father Baumert. There's already been plenty said about it in the newspapers. But the rich, they turn and twist the whole thing so . . . they out-devil the very best Christians.

OLD BAUMERT [*shaking his head*]. To think that in Berlin they ain't got no more sense than that.

ANSORGE. Tell me, Moritz, do you think that can really be? Ain't there a law against it? When I go and pinch and scrape and work my fingers to the bone weaving baskets and still can't pay the interest, can the farmer take my cottage away from me? There ain't a farmer who don't want his money. I just don't know what's to become of me if I've got to get out of my cottage. . . . [*Speaking with a choked voice, through tears.*] Here I was born, here my father sat at his loom, for more than forty years. How often he said to Mother: Mother, he said, when my time comes, you hold on to the cottage. This cottage I've worked for, he told her. Here, every single nail stands for a night's work, every board, a year's dry bread. Ya'd really think. . . .

JAEGER. They'll take your last pfennig, they're capable of it.

ANSORGE. Well, well! Well, well! But if it comes to that, I'd rather they carried me out than have to walk out in my old age. Dyin' ain't nothin'! My father was glad enough to die—only at the end, the very end, he was a bit scared. But when I crawled into the bed with him, he quieted down again. When ya think about it, at the time I was a boy of thirteen. I was tired, and I fell asleep by the sick man. I didn't know no better—and when I woke up, he was stone cold.

MOTHER BAUMERT [*after a pause*]. Reach into the stove, Bertha, and hand Ansorge his soup.

BERTHA. Here it is, Father Ansorge.

ANSORGE [*weeping, while he eats*]. Well, well! Well, well!

[OLD BAUMERT *has begun to eat meat out of the pan.*]

MOTHER BAUMERT. Why, Father—Father, you wait. Let Bertha set it out on the table, proper.

OLD BAUMERT [*chewing*]. It was two years ago that I took the sacrament last. I sold my Sunday suit right afterward. We bought a little piece of pork with the money. I ain't had no meat to eat since then till this very evenin'.

JAEGER. We don't need meat; the manufacturers eat it for us. They wade around in fat way up to here. If anybody doesn't believe that, he only needs to go down to Bielau or Peterswaldau. They'd be amazed —one manufacturer's mansion right after the other— one palace right after the other. With plate glass windows and little towers and fine iron fences. No, no, that doesn't look anything like hard times. There's plenty there for roasts and pastries, for carriages and coaches, for governesses, and who knows what all. They're so puffed up they don't really know what to do with all their high and mighty riches.

ANSORGE. In the old days, it was all different. In those days the manufacturers gave the weavers enough to get along on. Today, they squander it all themselves. I say that's because them people in high places don't believe in God no more, or in the devil, neither. They don't know nothin' about commandments and punishment. So they steal our last bite of bread, and weaken and undermine us wherever they can. Them people are the ones that's causin' all the trouble. If our manufacturers was good men, there wouldn't be no hard times for us.

JAEGER. You listen here, and I'll read you something nice. [*He takes a few sheets of paper from his pocket.*] Come on, August, run to the tavern and get another bottle. Why, August, you're always laughing.

MOTHER BAUMERT. I don't know what's the matter with the boy, he's always happy. No matter what happens, he laughs till his sides are ready to split. Now, quick! [AUGUST *goes out with the empty whiskey flask.*] Huh, Father, you know what tastes good, don't ya?

OLD BAUMERT [*chewing, his spirits rising from the food and the whiskey*]. Moritz, you're our man. You can read and write. You know how things is with the weavers. You have a heart for us poor weaver folk. You ought to take up our cause around here.

JAEGER. If that's all. That'd be fine with me. I'd be glad to give those devils of manufacturers something to think about. I wouldn't mind a bit. I'm an easy-going fellow, but when I once get my dander up and get mad, I'd take Dreissiger in one hand and Dittrich in the other and I'd knock their heads together so hard sparks would shoot out of their eyes. If we could manage to stick together, we could start such an uproar against the manufacturers. . . . We wouldn't need the King for that, or the government, either; we could simply say, we want this and that, and we do not want this and that, and they'd soon whistle a different tune. If they once see we've got spunk, they'd soon pull in their horns. I know their kind! They're cowardly bastards.

MOTHER BAUMERT. And that's really the truth. I certainly ain't bad. I was always one to say, there has to be rich people, too. But when it comes to this. . . .

JAEGER. For my part, the devil can take them all. That's what the whole bunch deserves.

BERTHA. Where's father? [OLD BAUMERT *has quietly left.*]

MOTHER BAUMERT. I don't know where he could've gone.

BERTHA. Could it be he ain't used to meat no more?

MOTHER BAUMERT [*beside herself, crying*]. Now, ya see, now ya see! He can't even keep it down. He's had to throw it up, all that nice little bit of good food.

OLD BAUMERT [*re-enters, crying with rage*]. No, no! It'll soon be all over with me. I'm too far gone. Ya finally get ahold of something good, and ya can't even keep it down. [*He sits down on the stove bench, weeping*].

JAEGER [*in a sudden fanatic outburst*]. And, at the same time, there are people, judges, not far from here— pot-bellies—who haven't a thing to do all year long except idle away their time. And they'll say the weavers could get along fine, if only they weren't so lazy.

ANSORGE. They ain't men, they're monsters.

JAEGER. Never mind, he's got what's coming to him. Baecker and I, we've given him a piece of our mind, and before we left, we sang "Bloody Justice."

ANSORGE. O Lord, O Lord, is that the song?

JAEGER. Yes, yes, and I have it here.

ANSORGE. I think it's called "Dreissiger's Song," ain't it?

JAEGER. I'll read it to you.

MOTHER BAUMERT. Who made up the song?

JAEGER. That, nobody knows. Now listen.

[*He reads, spelling it out like a schoolboy, accenting it badly, but with unmistakably strong feeling. Despair, pain, courage, hate, thirst for revenge—are all expressed.*]

> Here a bloody justice thrives
> More terrible than lynching
> Here sentence isn't even passed
> To quickly end a poor man's life.
>
> Men are slowly tortured here,
> Here is the torture chamber,
> Here every heavy sigh that's heard
> Bears witness to man's misery.

OLD BAUMERT [*is deeply moved by the words of the song. He frequently has difficulty in resisting the temptation to interrupt* JAEGER. *Now he can no longer contain himself; stammering amid laughter and tears, to his wife*]. "Here is the torture chamber." Whoever wrote that, Mother, spoke the truth. You can bear witness to that . . . how does it go? "Here every sigh that's heard. . . ." What's the rest? . . . "bear witness . . ."

JAEGER. "Bears witness to man's misery."

OLD BAUMERT. Ya know, standin' or sittin', we sigh
with misery day after day.

[ANSORGE *has stopped working, his body bent over in
deep emotion.* MOTHER BAUMERT *and* BERTHA *are
continuously wiping their eyes.*]

JAEGER [*continues reading*].

The Dreissigers are hangmen all,
Their servants are the henchmen
All of them oppressing us
And never showing mercy.

You scoundrels all, you devil's brood

OLD BAUMERT [*trembling with rage, stamps the floor*].
Yes, devil's brood!!!

JAEGER [*reads*].

You demons from the pit of hell
Who steal the poor man's house and home
A curse will be your payment.

ANSORGE. Well, well, and that deserves a curse.

OLD BAUMERT [*doubling his fist, threatening*]. "Who
steal the poor man's house and home. . . !"

JAEGER [*reads*].

Begging, pleading doesn't help,
In vain is all complaining,
"If you don't like it you can go,
And starve until you're dead."

OLD BAUMERT. What does it say? "In vain is all complaining"? Every word, every single word. . . . It's
all as true as the Bible. "Begging, pleading doesn't
help."

ANSORGE. Well, well! Well, well! Then nothin' will
  help.

JAEGER [*reads*].

> Now think about the misery
> And pain of these poor wretches
> Without a bite of bread at home
> Are they not to be pitied?
>
> Pitied! Ha! Such human feeling
> Is unknown to you savages.
> Your goal is known to everyone,
> To bleed us poor men dry.

OLD BAUMERT [*springs up, in mad frenzy*]. "Bleed us
  poor men dry." That's right, bleed a poor man dry.
  Here I stand, Robert Baumert, master weaver from
  Kaschbach. Who can step up and say . . . I've been
  a good man all my life, and now look at me. What
  good's it done me? How do I look? What have they
  made of me? "Men are slowly tortured here." [*He
  stretches out his arms.*] Here, feel these, nothin' but
  skin and bones. "You scoundrels all, you devil's
  brood!!" [*He collapses onto a chair, weeping with
  anger and despair.*]

ANSORGE [*flings the basket into the corner, gets up, his
  entire body trembling with rage, stammers*]. There
  must be a change, I tell ya, here and now. We won't
  stand for it no more! We won't stand for it no more,
  come what may.

                                            Curtain

ACT THREE.

SCENE: *The tap room in the principal tavern in Peterswaldau. It is a large room, the raftered ceiling of which
is supported at the center by a wooden pillar, around
which there is a table. To the right of the pillar—one
of its jambs hidden by the pillar—is a door in the back
wall leading to another large room in which barrels
and brewing utensils can be seen. In the corner to the
right of the door is the bar—a high wooden counter
with shelves for mugs, glasses, and the like; behind the
bar is a cupboard with rows of liquor bottles; between
the counter and the liquor cabinet there is a narrow
space for the bartender. In front of the bar there is a
table covered with a brightly colored cloth. A decorative lamp hangs above the table, around which there
are a number of cane-chairs. Not far off in the right
wall, a door leads to a room used for special occasions.
Nearer the front, to the right, an old grandfather's
clock is ticking. To the left of the entrance, against the
rear wall, stands a table with bottles and glasses, and
beyond it, in the corner, a large tile stove. There are
three small windows in the left wall, under them a
bench. In front of each window there is a large wooden
table with its narrow end toward the wall. On the
broad side of the tables are benches with backs and at
the other narrow end, a single wooden chair. The walls
are painted blue and are hung with placards, posters,
and oil prints, among them the portrait of the King of
Prussia, William IV.*

Innkeeper WELZEL, *a good-natured giant of around
fifty, is drawing beer into a glass from a barrel behind
the counter.* MRS. WELZEL *is ironing at the stove. She is*

*a dignified-looking woman, neatly dressed, not quite
thirty-five years old.* ANNA WELZEL, *a well-dressed pretty
girl of seventeen with magnificent reddish-blonde hair,
sits behind the table, embroidering. For a moment she
looks up from her work and listens to the sounds of
children's voices singing a funeral hymn, off in the distance.* WIEGAND, *the carpenter, in his work clothes, sits
at the same table with a glass of Bavarian beer in front
of him. He gives the appearance of being the sort of
man who knows what is needed to get ahead in the
world: cunning, speed, and ruthless determination.* A
TRAVELING SALESMAN *sits at the pillar table, busily devouring a chopped steak. He is of medium height, well-
fed, rather puffy, disposed to heartiness, lively and impudent. He is dressed in the latest fashion. His baggage, consisting of traveling bag, sample case, umbrella,
overcoat, and steamer rug—lie on chairs beside him.*

WELZEL [*carrying a glass of beer to the* SALESMAN, *aside
to* WIEGAND]. The devil's loose in Peterswaldau today.

WIEGAND [*in a sharp, trumpeting voice*]. Well, of course,
it's delivery day up at Dreissiger's.

MRS WELZEL. Yes, but they weren't always so noisy.

WIEGAND. Well, it might be on account of the two hundred additional weavers that Dreissiger's gettin'
ready to take on.

MRS. WELZEL [*at her ironing*]. Yes, yes, that's it. If he
wanted two hundred, probably six hundred will
have showed up. We've got more'n enough of that
sort.

WIEGAND. Lord, yes, there's plenty of them. And no
matter how hard it goes with them, they don't die
out. They bring more children into the world than
we can ever use. [*For a moment, the hymn can be
more clearly heard.*] And to add to it, there's a
funeral today, too. Weaver Fabich died.

WELZEL. It took him long enough. He's been goin'
around for years lookin' like a ghost.

WIEGAND. I tell ya, Welzel, never in all my life have I glued together such a tiny, shabby coffin. It was such a measly little corpse, it didn't even weigh ninety pounds.

SALESMAN [*chewing*]. I really don't understand . . . wherever you look, in all the newspapers, you read the most horrible stories about conditions among the weavers, and you get the impression that all the people here are half-starved. And then you see such a funeral! Just as I came into the village, there were brass bands, schoolteachers, children, the Pastor, and a whole string of people; my God, you'd think the Emperor of China was being buried. If these people can pay for that. . . ! [*He drinks his beer. Then he puts the glass down and suddenly speaks in a frivolous tone.*] Isn't that so, Miss? Don't you agree with me?

[ANNA *smiles, embarrassed, and continues busily with her embroidery.*]

SALESMAN. Those must be slippers for Papa.

WELZEL. Oh, I don't like to wear them things.

SALESMAN. Just listen to that! I'd give half my fortune if those slippers were for me.

MRS. WELZEL. He just don't appreciate such things.

WIEGAND [*after he has coughed several times and moved his chair about, as if he wanted to speak*]. The gentleman has expressed himself mighty well about the funeral. Now tell us, young lady, isn't that just a small funeral?

SALESMAN. Yes, I must say. . . . That must cost a tremendous amount of money. Where do these people get the money for it?

WIEGAND. You'll forgive me for sayin' it, sir, there is so much folly among the poorer classes hereabouts. If you don't mind my sayin' so, they have such exaggerated ideas of the dutiful respect and the obligations that's due the deceased and the blessed dead. And when it's a matter of deceased parents, they are so superstitious that the descendants and the next of kin scrape together their last penny. And what the children can't raise, they borrow from the nearest money lender. And then they're in debts up to their necks; they'll be owing His Reverence the Pastor, the sexton, and everybody else in the neighborhood. And drinks and victuals and all the other necessary things. Oh yes, I approve of respectful duty on the part of children toward their parents, but not so that the mourners are burdened down the rest of their lives by such obligations.

SALESMAN. I beg your pardon, but I should think the Pastor would talk them out of it.

WIEGAND. Beggin' your pardon, sir, but here I would like to interpose that every little congregation has its ecclesiastical house of worship and must support its reverend pastor. The high clergy get a wonderful revenue and profit from such a big funeral. The more elaborate such a funeral can be arranged, the more profitable is the offertory that flows from it. Whoever knows the conditions of the workers hereabouts can, with unauthoritative certainty, affirm that the pastors only with reluctance tolerate small and quiet funerals.

HORNIG [*enters. A small, bow-legged old man with a strap over his shoulders and chest. He is a rag picker*]. Good mornin'. I'd like a drink. Well, young lady, any rags? Miss Anna, in my cart I've got beautiful hair ribbons, lingerie, ribbons, garters, pins and hairpins, hooks and eyes. I'll give them all to ya for a few rags [*Changing his tone.*] Then, out of the rags, they'll make fine white paper, and your sweetheart'll write ya a lovely letter on it.

ANNA. Oh no, thank you, I don't want a sweetheart.

MRS. WELZEL [*puts a hot bolt in the iron*]. That's the way the girl is. She don't want to think of gettin' married.

SALESMAN [*jumps up, apparently surprised and pleased,*

steps up to the table, and holds out his hand to ANNA]. That's sensible, Miss. You're just like me. O.K., let's shake on it! We'll both stay single.

ANNA [*blushing, gives him her hand*]. But surely you are married?

SALESMAN. God forbid, I just make believe I am. You think, perhaps, because I wear this ring? I just put it on my finger to prevent people from taking unfair advantage of my charming personality. Of you, I'm not afraid. [*He puts the ring in his pocket.*] Seriously, Miss, tell me, don't you ever want to get just the least bit married?

ANNA [*shaking her head*]. And why should I?

MRS. WELZEL. She'll stay single unless something very special turns up.

SALESMAN. Well, why not? One wealthy Silesian businessman married his mother's maid, and that rich manufacturer, Dreissiger, took an innkeeper's daughter, too. She isn't half as pretty as you, Miss, and now she rides in a carriage with liveried servants. Why not, indeed? [*He walks around, stretching his legs.*] I'll have a cup of coffee.

[ANSORGE *and* OLD BAUMERT *enter, each with a bundle, and quietly and humbly join* HORNIG *at the front table to the left.*]

WELZEL. Welcome, Father Ansorge. Is it you we're seein' again?

HORNIG. Did ya finally crawl out of your smoky nest?

ANSORGE [*awkwardly and visibly embarrassed*]. I went and got myself another web.

OLD BAUMERT. He's ready to work for 10 groschen.

ANSORGE. I never would've done it, but there's been an end to my basket weavin'.

WIEGAND. It's always better than nothin'. Ya know he's doin' it so ya'll have work. I'm very well acquainted with Dreissiger. A week ago I took out the storm windows for him. We were talkin' about it. He just does it out of pity.

ANSORGE. Well, well—well, well.

WELZEL [*setting a glass of whiskey in front of each of the weavers*]. Your health! Now tell me, Ansorge, how long has it been since ya stopped shavin'? The gentleman would like to know.

SALESMAN [*calls across*]. Now, Mr. Welzel, you know I didn't say that. I just noticed the master weaver because of his venerable appearance. One doesn't often run across such a powerful figure.

ANSORGE [*scratches his head, embarrassed*]. Well, well—well, well.

SALESMAN. Such extremely powerful, primitive men are seldom seen these days. We are so softened by civilization . . . but I find I still get pleasure out of such natural, unspoiled strength. What bushy eyebrows! Such a heavy beard. . . .

HORNIG. Well, look here, now I'll tell ya, sir—the people hereabouts are too poor to go to the barber, and they haven't been able to afford a razor in many a day. What grows, grows. They haven't anything to spend on the outer man.

SALESMAN. But I ask you, my good man, where would I. . . . [*Softly, to the tavern keeper.*] Would it be proper to offer the hairy one a glass of beer?

WELZEL. God forbid. He'll take nothin'. He's got queer notions.

SALESMAN. Well, then I won't. With your permission, Miss? [*He takes a seat at the table with her.*] I can assure you, from the time I came in, I've been so struck by your hair, such luster, such softness, such a mass of it! [*Delighted, he kisses his finger tips.*] And what color . . . like ripe wheat. What a furor you would cause if you came to Berlin with hair like that. *Parole d'honneur*, with such hair you could be presented at Court. [*Leaning back, looking at her hair.*] Exquisite, really exquisite.

WIEGAND. It's on account of her hair that she's got such a pretty nickname.

SALESMAN. What do they call her?

ANNA [*keeps on laughing to herself*]. Oh, don't you listen to them.

HORNIG. They call you Red Fox, don't they?

WELZEL. Now stop that! Stop turnin' the girl's head altogether. They've already put enough high and mighty ideas in her head. Today she wants a count, tomorrow it'll have to be a prince.

MRS. WELZEL. Don't ya run the girl down, man. It's no crime for a person to want to get ahead. Not everybody thinks the way you do. That wouldn't be good, either. Then nobody'd get ahead, then everybody'd always stay in the same old place. If Dreissiger's grandfather had thought the way you do, he'd still be a poor weaver. Now they're rich as can be. Old Tromtra, too, was no more than a poor weaver, now he owns twelve big estates and on top of that, he's got a title.

WIEGAND. You must admit, Welzel, on that score, your wife's right. I can vouch for that. If I'd thought like you, would I have seven journeymen today?

HORNIG. You sure know how to bide your time, we'll have to give ya credit for that. Even before the weaver's off his feet, you're already gettin' his coffin ready.

WIEGAND. You've got to tend to business if you want to get ahead.

HORNIG. Yes, you tend to yours, all right. You know better than the doctor does, when a weaver's child is goin' to die.

WIEGAND [*no longer smiling, suddenly furious*]. And you know better than the police does where the thieves sit among the weavers, the ones who hold out a few bobbins every week. Ya come after rags and ya get a bobbin of yarn, too, if there's a chance.

HORNIG. And your livin' lays in the graveyard. The more that go to rest on your wood shavings, the better it is for you. When ya look at all the children's graves, ya pat your belly and ya say, this year's been a good one again; the little rascals dropped like June bugs from the trees. So I can afford a bottle of whiskey again this week.

WIEGAND. Anyhow, at least I don't trade in stolen goods.

HORNIG. At the most, you bill some rich cotton manufacturer twice, or you take a few extra boards from Dreissiger's barn if the moon ain't shinin'.

WIEGAND [*turning his back on* HORNIG]. Oh, go on talkin' to anyone you please, but leave me alone. [*Suddenly.*] Hornig, the liar!

HORNIG. Coffin-maker!

WIEGAND [*to the others*]. He knows how to bewitch cattle.

HORNIG. Look out, let me tell ya, or I'll put the sign on you. [WIEGAND *turns pale.*]

MRS. WELZEL [*had gone out, and now sets a cup of coffee down in front of the* SALESMAN.] Would you perhaps rather have your coffee in the other room?

SALESMAN. Whatever put that idea in your head? [*With a longing look at* ANNA.] I'll stay here until I die.

[*A* YOUNG FORESTER *and a* FARMER *enter, the latter carrying a whip. Together*]. Good morning! [*They stop at the bar.*]

FARMER. We'll have two ginger beers.

WELZEL. Welcome to both of you! [*He pours the drinks; they both take their glasses, touch them to each other, take a sip, and place them back on the bar.*]

SALESMAN. Well, Forester, have you had a long trip?

FORESTER. Pretty far. I've come from Steinseiffersdorf.

[FIRST *and* SECOND OLD WEAVERS *enter and sit down next to* ANSORGE, BAUMERT, *and* HORNIG.]

SALESMAN. Pardon me, sir, are you one of Count Hochheim's foresters?

FORESTER. No, I'm one of Count Kailsch's.

SALESMAN. Oh, of course, of course—that's what I meant to say. It's most confusing here with all the counts and barons and other people of rank. You've got to have a good memory. What are you carrying the ax for?

FORESTER. I took it away from some thieves I caught stealing wood.

OLD BAUMERT. His Lordship is sure strict about a few sticks of firewood.

SALESMAN. I beg your pardon, it would scarcely do if everybody were to take. . . .

OLD BAUMERT. Beggin' your pardon, it's the same here as everywhere else with the big and the little thieves; there are those that carry on a wholesale lumber business and get rich from stolen wood, but if a poor weaver so much as. . . .

FIRST OLD WEAVER [interrupts BAUMERT]. We don't dare pick up a single twig, but the lords, they skin us alive. There's insurance money to pay, spinnin' money, payments in kind; then we have to run errands for nothin' and work on the estate, whether we want to or not.

ANSORGE. And that's the truth: what the manufacturers leave us, the noblemen take away.

SECOND OLD WEAVER [has taken a seat at the next table]. I've said it to the gentleman hisself. Beggin' your pardon, sir, I says to him, I can't do so many days' work on the estate this year. I just can't do it! And why not? Forgive me, but the water has ruined everything. My little bit of ground's been all washed away. I've got to slave night and day if I'm to keep alive. Such a flood . . . I tell ya, I just stood there and wrung my hands. That good soil washed right down the hill and straight into my cottage; and that fine, expensive seed. . . ! Oh my Lord, I just howled into the wind. I cried for a week, till I couldn't see no more. . . . And after that I wore myself out pushin' eighty wheelbarrows of dirt up the hill.

FARMER [roughly]. You do set up an awful howl, I must say. We all have to put up with what Heaven sends us. And if it don't go good in other ways with ya, who's to blame but yourselves? When times was good, what did ya do then? Ya gambled and drank it all up, that's what ya did. If ya had put something aside at that time, ya'd have had something saved for now, and ya wouldn't have had to steal wood and yarn.

FIRST YOUNG WEAVER [*standing with several friends in the other room, shouts through the door*]. A farmer's always a farmer, even if he sleeps till nine every mornin'.

FIRST OLD WEAVER. That's a fact; the farmer and the nobleman, they're two of a kind. If a weaver wants a place to live, the farmer says I'll give ya a little hole to live in. You pay me a nice rent, and help me bring in my hay and my grain, and if ya don't like it, ya'll see what happens. Every one of them's just like the next one.

OLD BAUMERT [*fiercely*]. We're just like an old apple that everybody takes a bite out of.

FARMER [*irritated*]. Oh, you starved wretches, what are you good for, anyway? Can ya handle a plow? Can ya even plow a straight furrow, or pitch fifteen shocks of oats onto a wagon? You're good for nothin' but loafin', and lyin' abed with your women. You're no good at all. You're no-account bums. No use at all. [*He pays and leaves. The* FORESTER *follows him, laughing.* WELZEL, *the* CARPENTER, *and* MRS. WELZEL *laugh out loud, the* SALESMAN *chuckles. Then the laughter quiets down, and there is silence.*]

HORNIG. A farmer like that's just like a bull. As if I didn't know how bad things was around here. All the things ya get to see up here in the villages. Four and five people layin' naked on a single straw ticking.

SALESMAN [*in a gently, rebuking tone*]. Permit me, my good man, to observe that there is a wide difference of opinion in regard to the distress in this region. If you can read. . . .

HORNIG. Oh, I read everything in the papers as well as
you do. No, no, I know these things from goin'
around and mixin' with the people. When a man's
lugged a pack around for forty years, he learns a
thing or two. What happened at the Fullers? The
children, they scratched around in the dung heap
with the neighbors' geese. Those people died there—
naked—on the cold stone floor. They had to eat
stinkin' weaver's glue, they was so hungry. Hunger
killed them off by the hundreds.

SALESMAN. If you can read, you must be aware that the
government has had a thorough investigation made
and that. . . .

HORNIG. We know all that. We know all that. The government sends a gentleman who before he sets out
knows everything better than if he'd seen it himself.
He walks around the village a little where the brook
widens and where the best houses are. He won't dirty
his good, shiny shoes goin' any farther. He thinks
everything is probably just as beautiful everywhere
else, and climbs into his carriage, and drives home
again. And then he writes to Berlin that he saw no
hardships at all. If he'd had a little bit of patience,
though, and had climbed around in the village up to
where the brook comes in and across it or, even better, off to the side where the little shacks are scattered, the old straw huts on the hills that are sometimes so black and broken-down they wouldn't be
worth the match it'd take to set 'em afire, then he'd
have made an altogether different report to Berlin.
Those gentlemen from the government ought to
have come to me, them that didn't want to believe
that there was no hardships here. I would've showed
them something, I would've opened their eyes to all
the hunger-holes around here.

[*The singing of the "Weavers' Song" is heard outside.*]

WELZEL. They're singin' that devil's song again.

WIEGAND. Yes, they're turnin' the whole village upside down.

MRS. WELZEL. It's like there's something in the air.

[JAEGER *and* BAECKER, *arm in arm, at the head of a band of young weavers, noisily enter the other room, and then come into the bar.*]

JAEGER. Squadron halt! Dismount!

[*The new arrivals seat themselves at the various tables at which weavers are already sitting, and start conversations with them.*]

HORNIG [*calling to* BAECKER]. Say, tell me, what's up that ya've got such a big crowd together?

BAECKER [*significantly*]. Maybe something's goin' to happen. Right, Moritz?

HORNIG. You don't say! Don't do nothin' foolish.

BAECKER. Blood's flowed already. Do ya want to see?

[*He pushes back his sleeve, stretches out his arm and shows him bleeding tattoo marks on his upper arm. Many of the young weavers at the other tables do the same.*]

BAECKER. We were at Barber Schmidt's havin' ourselves tattooed.

HORNIG. Well, now that's clear. No wonder there's so much noise in the streets, with such rascals tearin' around. . . !

JAEGER [*showing off, in a loud voice*]. Two quarts, right away, Welzel! I'll pay for it. Maybe you think I don't have the dough? Well, just you wait! If we wanted to, we could drink beer and lap up coffee till tomorrow morning as well as a traveling salesman. [*Laughter among the young weavers.*]

SALESMAN [*with comic surprise*]. Who or whom are you talking about—me?

[*The tavern keeper, his wife, their daughter,* WIEGAND, *and the* SALESMAN, *all laugh.*]

JAEGER. Always him who asks.

SALESMAN. Allow me to say, young man, that things seem to be going right well with you.

JAEGER. I can't complain, I'm a salesman for ready-made clothing. I go fifty-fifty with the manufacturers. The hungrier the weavers grow, the fatter I get. The greater their poverty, the fuller my cupboard.

BAECKER. Well done. Your health, Moritz!

WELZEL [*has brought the whiskey; on the way back to the bar, he stops and, in his usual phlegmatic and even manner, turns slowly to the weavers. Quietly and emphatically*]. You let the gentleman alone. He ain't done nothin' to you.

YOUNG WEAVERS' VOICES. We ain't done nothin' to him, either.

[MRS. WELZEL *has exchanged a few words with the* SALESMAN. *She takes the cup and the rest of the coffee into the next room. The* SALESMAN *follows her amidst the laughter of the weavers.*]

YOUNG WEAVERS' VOICES [*singing*]. The Dreissigers are hangmen all, Their servants are the henchmen. . . .

WELZEL. Sh, Sh! Sing that song wherever else ya want to, but I won't allow it here.

FIRST OLD WEAVER. He's quite right. Stop that singin'.

BAECKER [*shouts*]. But we've got to march past Dreissiger's again. He's got to hear our song once more.

WIEGAND. Don't go too far, or he might take it the wrong way.

[*Laughter and cries of "Ho-ho."*]

OLD WITTIG [*a gray-haired blacksmith, bareheaded, wearing a leather apron and wooden shoes, and covered with soot, as if he had just come from the smithy, enters and stands at the bar, waiting for a glass of brandy*]. Let 'em make a little noise. Barkin' dogs don't bite.

OLD WEAVERS' VOICES. Wittig, Wittig!

WITTIG. Here he is. What do ya want?

OLD WEAVERS' VOICES. Wittig is here.—Wittig, Wittig!—
Come here, Wittig, set with us!—Come over here,
Wittig!

WITTIG. I'm awful careful about settin' with such blockheads.

JAEGER. Come on, have a drink on me.

WITTIG. Oh, you keep your liquor. When I drink, I'll
pay for my own. [*He takes his glass of brandy and
sits down at the table with* BAUMERT *and* ANSORGE.
He pats the latter on the belly.] What do the weavers eat nowadays? Sauerkraut and plenty of lice.

OLD BAUMERT [*ecstatically*]. But what if they wasn't to
put up with it no more?

WITTIG [*with feigned surprise, staring stupidly at the
weaver*]. Well, well, well, Heinerle, tell me, is that
really you? [*Laughs without restraint.*] I laugh myself sick at you people. Old Baumert wants to start
a rebellion. Now we're in for it: now the tailors'll
start, too, then the baa-lambs'll be rising up, then
the mice and the rats. Good Lord, what a time that'll
be! [*He holds his sides with laughter.*]

OLD BAUMERT. Look here, Wittig, I'm the same man I
used to be. And I tell ya even now if things could
be settled peaceable, it'd be better.

WITTIG. Like hell it'll be settled peaceable. Where has
anything like this ever been settled peaceable?
Maybe things was settled peaceable in France?
Maybe Robespierre patted the hands of the rich?
There it was just "allay," go ahead! Always up to
the guillotine! Let's go. It had to be "along song-
fong." Roast geese just don't fly into your mouth.

OLD BAUMERT. If I could just halfway earn my
livin'. . . .

FIRST OLD WEAVER. We're fed up, up to here, Wittig.

SECOND OLD WEAVER. We don't even want to go home,
no more. . . . Whether we work or whether we lay
down and sleep, we starve either way.

FIRST OLD WEAVER. At home ya go completely crazy.

ANSORGE. It's all the same to me now, no matter what happens.

OLD WEAVERS' VOICES [*with mounting excitement*]. There's no peace left nowhere.—We ain't even got the spirit to work no more.—Up our way in Steinkunzendorf there's a man settin' by the brook all day long and washin' hisself, naked as God made him. . . . He's gone completely out of his head.

THIRD OLD WEAVER [*rises, moved by the spirit, and begins to "speak with tongues," raising his finger threateningly.*] Judgment Day is comin'! Don't join with the rich and the gentry. Judgment Day is comin'! Lord God of Sabaoth. . . .

[*Several laugh. He is pushed down into his chair.*]

WELZEL. All he has to do is drink just one glass of liquor and his head's in a whirl.

THIRD OLD WEAVER [*continues*]. Hearken, they don't believe in God nor hell nor Heaven. They just mock at religion.

FIRST OLD WEAVER. That's enough, now, that's enough.

BAECKER. You let the man say his prayers. Many a man could take it to heart.

MANY VOICES [*in a tumult*]. Let him talk—let him!

THIRD OLD WEAVER [*raising his voice*]. Hell has opened wide and its jaws are gaping open, wide open, crashing down all those who do harm to the poor and violence to the cause of the afflicted, saith the Lord. [*Tumult. Suddenly reciting like a schoolboy.*]

> And then how strange it is.
> If you will carefully observe
> How they the linen weavers' work despise.

BAECKER. But we're cotton weavers. [*Laughter.*]

HORNIG. The linen weavers are even worse off. They wander like ghosts around the mountains. Here you at least have the courage to rebel.

WITTIG. Do ya think, maybe, that here the worst is

over? That little bit of courage that they still have left in their bodies the manufacturers will knock right out of them.

BAECKER. Why, he said that the weavers will get so they'll work for just a slice of bread and cheese. [*Tumult.*]

VARIOUS OLD *and* YOUNG WEAVERS. Who said that?

BAECKER. That's what Dreissiger said about the weavers.

A YOUNG WEAVER. That son of a bitch ought to be strung up.

JAEGER. Listen to me, Wittig, you've always talked so much about the French Revolution. You always bragged so much. Now maybe the chance'll soon come for everybody to show how much of a man he is . . . whether he is a loud-mouth or a man of honor.

WITTIG [*starting up in a rage*]. Say one more word, boy! Did you ever hear the whistle of bullets? Did you ever stand at an outpost in enemy territory?

JAEGER. Now don't get mad. You know we're all comrades. I didn't mean any harm.

WITTIG. I don't give a rap for your comradeship. You puffed up fool!

[POLICEMAN KUTSCHE *enters.*]

SEVERAL VOICES. Sh! Sh! The Police!

[*There is a relatively long period of sh-ing before complete silence reigns.*]

KUTSCHE [*sits down by the center pillar amid the deep silence of all the others*]. I'd like a shot of whiskey, please. [*Again complete silence.*]

WITTIG. Well, Kutsche, you here to see that everything's all right with us?

KUTSCHE [*not listening to* WITTIG]. Good mornin', Mr. Wiegand.

WIEGAND [*still in the corner of the bar*]. Good mornin', Kutsche.

KUTSCHE. How's business?

WIEGAND. Fine, thanks for askin'.

BAECKER. The Chief of Police is afraid we might spoil our stomachs on all the wages we get. [*Laughter.*]

JAEGER. Isn't that so, Welzel, we've all had pork roast and gravy and dumplings and sauerkraut, and now we're getting ready to drink our champagne. [*Laughter.*]

WELZEL. Everything's the other way 'round.

KUTSCHE. And if ya did have champagne and roast, ya'd still not be satisfied. I don't have no champagne, neither, and I manage to get along.

BAECKER [*referring to* KUTSCHE'S *nose*]. He waters his red beet with brandy and beer. That's how it got so nice and ripe. [*Laughter.*]

WITTIG. A cop like him's got a hard life. Now, he's got to throw a starvin' little boy in jail for beggin', then he has to seduce a weaver's pretty daughter, then he has to get dead drunk and beat his wife so she goes runnin' to the neighbors for fear of her life. Ridin' about on his horse, lyin' in his featherbed . . . till nine, I tell ya, ain't that easy.

KUTSCHE. Always a'talkin'! You'll talk yourself into a big mess one of these days. It's been known for a long time what sort of a fellow you are. Even as high as the judge they've known about your rebellious tongue for a long time. I know someone who'll bring his wife and children to the poorhouse with his drinkin' and hangin' around taverns, and hisself into jail. He'll agitate and agitate until he comes to a terrible end.

WITTIG [*laughs bitterly*]. Who knows what's ahead? You might be right after all. [*Breaking out angrily.*] But if it comes to that, then I'll know who I can thank, who has blabbed to the manufacturers and to the nobles, and reviled and slandered me so I don't get a lick of work no more.—Who set the farmers and the millers against me so that, for a whole week, I haven't had a single horse to shoe or a wheel to put a rim on. I know who that is. I once yanked the damned scoun-

drel off his horse because he was thrashing a poor
little nitwit boy with a horsewhip for stealin' a few
green pears. I tell ya, and ya know me, put me in
jail, and ya'd better be makin' out your will at the
same time. If I get the slightest warnin', I'll take
whatever I can get my hands on, whether it's a horse-
shoe or a hammer, a wagon spoke or a bucket, and
I'll go lookin' for ya, and if I have to pull ya out of
bed, away from your woman, I'll do it and I'll cave
your skull in, as sure as my name is Wittig. [*He has
jumped up and is about to attack* KUTSCHE.]

OLD *and* YOUNG WEAVERS [*holding him back*]. Wittig,
Wittig, don't lose your head.

KUTSCHE [*has stood up involuntarily; his face is pale.
During what follows he keeps moving backward. The
nearer he gets to the door, the braver he becomes. He
speaks the last few words at the very threshold, and
then immediately disappears*]. What do ya want with
me? I've got nothin' to do with you. I've got to talk
to one of the weavers here. I've done nothin' to you
and I've got no business with you. But I'm to tell you
weavers this: the Chief of Police forbids ya to sing
that song—"Dreissiger's Song," or whatever it's called.
And if that singin' in the streets don't stop right
away, he'll see to it that you get plenty of time and
rest in jail. Then ya can sing on bread and water
as long as ya like. [*Leaves.*]

WITTIG [*shouts after him*]. He ain't got no right to forbid us anything, and if we roar till the windows rattle and they can hear us way off in Reichenbach, and
if we sing so the houses tumble down on all the
manufacturers and all the policemen's helmets dance
on their heads, it's nobody's business.

BAECKER [*in the meantime has stood up, and has given
the signal for the singing to begin. He begins to sing,
together with the others*].

> Here a bloody justice thrives
> More terrible than lynching

> Here sentence isn't even passed
> To quickly end a poor man's life.

[WELZEL *tries to quiet them, but no one listens to him.*
WIEGAND *holds his hands over his ears and runs away.
The weavers get up and, singing the following verses,
march after* WITTIG *and* BAECKER, *who, by nods, gestures, have signaled for everyone to leave.*]

> Men are slowly tortured here,
> Here is the torture chamber,
> Here every heavy sigh that's heard
> Bears witness to the misery.

[*Most of the weavers sing the following verse when they
are in the street; only a few young fellows are still
inside the taproom, paying for their drinks. At the
end of the next verse the room is empty except for*
WELZEL, *his wife, his daughter,* HORNIG, *and* OLD BAU-
MERT.]

> You scoundrels all, you devil's brood
> You demons from the pit of hell
> Who steal the poor man's house and home
> A curse will be your payment.

WELZEL [*calmly gathers up the glasses*]. Why, they're
completely out of their heads today.

[OLD BAUMERT *is about to leave.*]

HORNIG. Tell me, Baumert, what's afoot?

OLD BAUMERT. They'll be goin' to Dreissiger's to see if
he'll add to their wages.

WELZEL. Are you goin' to join up with such madness?

OLD BAUMERT. Well, you see, Welzel, it ain't up to me.
A young man sometimes may, and an old man must.
[*A trifle embarrassed, leaves.*]

HORNIG [*rises*]. It'll sure surprise me if things don't
come to a bad end here.

WELZEL. Who'd think the old fellows would completely
lose their heads?

HORNIG. Well, every man has his dream.

Curtain

ACT FOUR.

SCENE. *Peterswaldau—A living room in the house of the cotton manufacturer,* DREISSIGER. *It is luxuriously furnished in the cold style of the first half of the nineteenth century. The ceiling, stove, and doors are white; the wallpaper is a cold grayish blue, with straight lines and little flowers. The room is filled with red upholstered mahogany furniture, including chairs and cupboards, richly decorated and carved. The furniture is placed as follows: on the right, between two windows with cherry-red damask curtains, is a secretary with a drop leaf that folds down to form a desk; directly opposite it, the sofa, with an iron safe nearby; in front of the sofa a table, armchairs, and straight chairs; against the back wall, a gun case. Pictures reflecting poor taste hang in gilt frames on the walls. Above the sofa hangs a mirror with a heavily gilded rococo frame. A door on the left leads to the vestibule; an open double door in the back wall leads into the drawing room, also overloaded with uncomfortable, showy furnishings. In the drawing room,* MRS. DREISSIGER *and* MRS. KITTELHAUS, *the pastor's wife, can be seen looking at pictures while Pastor* KITTELHAUS *converses with the tutor,* WEINHOLD, *a student of theology.*

KITTELHAUS [*a small, friendly man, enters the front room, smoking and chatting amiably with the tutor, who is also smoking.* KITTELHAUS *looks around and, when he sees no one is in the room, shakes his head in amazement*]. Of course it is not at all surprising, Weinhold; you are young. At your age, we old fellows had—I won't say the same views—but yet, similar ones. Similar ones, at any rate. And there is, after all, something wonderful about youth—and all its beautiful ideals. Unfortunately, however, they are fleeting—fleeting as April sunshine. Just wait till you are my age. When once a man has said his say to the people from the pulpit for thirty years, fifty-two times a year, not counting holidays—then he, of necessity, becomes quieter. Think of me, Weinhold, when that time comes for you.

WEINHOLD [nineteen years old, pale, emaciated, tall and thin, with long, straight, blond hair. He is very restless and nervous in his movements]. With all respect, sir . . . I really don't know . . . there certainly is a great difference in temperaments.

KITTELHAUS. My dear Weinhold, you may be ever so restless a soul—[In a tone of reproof.] and that you are—you may be ever so violent—and rudely attack existing conditions, but that will subside. Yes, yes, I certainly do admit that we have colleagues who, though rather advanced in years, still play rather childish and foolish tricks. One preaches against drinking and founds temperance societies; another writes appeals which, undeniably, are most touching to read. But what does he accomplish with it? The distress among the weavers, where it exists, is not relieved thereby. And yet the peace of society is undermined by it. No, no, in such a case one might almost say, cobbler, stick to your last! A keeper of souls should not concern himself with bellies. Preach the pure word of God and, for the rest, let Him take care who provides shelter and food for the birds and sees that the lily in the field does not perish.—But now I would really like to know where our worthy host went so suddenly.

MRS. DREISSIGER [comes into the front room with the Pastor's wife. She is a pretty woman, thirty years old, a robust, healthy type. A certain discrepancy is noticeable between her manner of speaking or moving and her elegant attire]. You're quite right, Pastor.

Wilhelm's always that way. When something strikes him, he runs off and leaves me alone. I've talked to him about it plenty, but you can say what you will, that's the way it is.

KITTELHAUS. That's the way with businessmen, Madam.

WEINHOLD. If I'm not mistaken, something's been happening downstairs.

DREISSIGER [*enters, out of breath and excited*]. Well, Rosa, has the coffee been served?

MRS. DREISSIGER [*pouting*]. Oh, why do you always have to run away?

DREISSIGER [*lightly*]. Oh, what do you know about it?

KITTELHAUS. I beg your pardon! Have you had trouble, Mr. Dreissiger?

DREISSIGER. God knows, that I have every single day, my dear Pastor. I'm used to that. Well, Rosa? I guess you're taking care of it?

[MRS. DREISSIGER *in a bad temper pulls violently several times at the broad, embroidered bell pull.*]

DREISSIGER. Just now—[*After walking up and down a few times.*]—Mr. Weinhold, I would have liked you to have been there. You would have had an experience. At any rate . . . come, let's have a game of whist.

KITTELHAUS. Yes, yes, by all means. Shake the dust and trouble of the day from your shoulders, and come and be one of us.

DREISSIGER [*has stepped to the window, pushes the drapery aside, and looks out. Involuntarily*]. Rabble!—come here, Rosa! [*She comes.*] Tell me . . . that tall, red-headed fellow there. . . .

KITTELHAUS. That is the one they call Red Baecker.

DREISSIGER. Tell me, is he by any chance the one who insulted you, two days ago? You know, what you told me, when Johann helped you into the carriage.

MRS. DREISSIGER [*makes a wry face, drawls*]. I don't remember.

DREISSIGER. Now don't be that way. I've got to know.

I'm fed up with this impudence. If he's the one, I'll make him answer for it. [*The "Weavers' Song" is heard.*] Just listen to it! Just listen to it!

KITTELHAUS [*extremely indignant*]. Won't this nonsense ever come to an end? Now, really, I too must say, it's time the police took a hand. Permit me. [*He steps to the window.*] Look at that, Weinhold! Those aren't only young people; the old, steady weavers are running with the crowd. Men whom for years I have considered to be respectable and pious are in with them. They're taking part in this unheard-of nonsense. They are trampling God's law under their feet. Perhaps you would still like to defend these people, even now?

WEINHOLD. Certainly not, sir. That is, sir, *cum grano salis.* You must realize they are just hungry, ignorant men. They are expressing their dissatisfaction in the only way they know how. I don't expect such people. . . .

MRS. KITTELHAUS [*small, thin, faded, more like an old maid than a married woman*]. Mr. Weinhold, Mr. Weinhold! I must beg of you!

DREISSIGER. Mr. Weinhold, I regret very much. . . . I did not take you into my house so that you should give me lectures on humanitarianism. I must request that you restrict yourself to the education of my sons, and for the rest, leave my affairs to me—completely—to me alone! Do you understand?

WEINHOLD [*stands a moment, motionless and deathly pale, and then bows with a strange smile, softly*]. Of course, of course, I understand. I have seen it coming: that is why I wish to leave. [*Exit.*]

DREISSIGER [*brutally*]. Then, as soon as possible. We need the room.

MRS. DREISSIGER. Please, Wilhelm, Wilhelm!

DREISSIGER. Are you out of your mind? Are you defending a man that takes sides with such vulgarity and rowdyism as this insulting song?

MRS. DREISSIGER. But hubby, hubby, he really didn't. . . .

DREISSIGER. Reverend Kittelhaus, did he or did he not defend it?

KITTELHAUS. Mr. Dreissiger, one must ascribe it to his youth.

MRS. KITTELHAUS. I don't know—the young man comes from such a good and respectable family. His father was a civil servant for forty years and never allowed the slightest reproach to fall on himself. His mother was so overjoyed that he had found such an excellent position here. And now . . . now he shows so little appreciation of it.

PFEIFER [*tears open the vestibule door, shouts in*]. Mr. Dreissiger, Mr. Dreissiger! They've caught him. You ought to come. They've caught one of them.

DREISSIGER [*hastily*]. Has someone gone for the police?

PFEIFER. The Chief of Police is comin' up the stairs right now.

DREISSIGER [*at the door*]. Your humble servant, sir! I am very glad that you have come.

[KITTELHAUS *gestures to the ladies that it would be better if they withdrew. He, his wife, and* MRS. DREISSIGER *disappear into the drawing room.*]

DREISSIGER [*very excited, to the* CHIEF OF POLICE, *who has entered in the meantime*]. I have finally had my dyers catch one of the ringleaders. I couldn't put up with it any longer. This impudence simply goes beyond all bounds. It's shocking. I have guests, and these rascals dare . . . they insult my wife when she shows herself; my children aren't sure of their lives. Chances are my guests will be beaten up. I assure you—if blameless people—such as me and my family —in a law-abiding community—can be openly and continuously insulted . . . without proper punishment, really . . . then I regret that I have different ideas of law and order.

POLICE CHIEF [*a man of perhaps fifty, of medium height, fat, red-faced. He is wearing a cavalry uni-*

form, saber and spurs]. Certainly not . . . no . . . certainly not, Mr. Dreissiger!—I am at your service. Calm yourself, I am completely at your service. It is quite all right. . . . I am, in fact, very glad that you had one of the ringleaders caught. I am glad that this thing has finally come to a head. There are a few troublemakers around here that I've had it in for, for quite a long time.

DREISSIGER. You are right, a few young fellows, thoroughly shiftless rabble, lazy rascals, who lead a dissolute life, day after day, sitting around in the taverns till the last penny has trickled down their throats. But now I am determined, I will put an end to these professional slanderers, once and for all. It's in the common interest, not merely in my own.

POLICE CHIEF. By all means! Certainly—by all means, Mr. Dreissiger. Nobody could find fault with you there. And as far as it's within my power. . . .

DREISSIGER. The whip should be used on these ruffians.

POLICE CHIEF. Quite right, quite right. We must set an example.

KUTSCHE [*enters and salutes. As the vestibule door opens, the noise of heavy feet stumbling up the steps is heard*]. Chief, it's my duty to inform you that we have caught a man.

DREISSIGER. Would you like to see him, Chief?

POLICE CHIEF. Why, of course, of course. First of all, let's have a close look at him. Please do me the favor, Mr. Dreissiger, of not interfering. I'll see to it that you're given satisfaction, or my name isn't Heide.

DREISSIGER. I won't be satisfied—not until that man is brought before the state's attorney.

[JAEGER *is led in by five dyers. They have come directly from work. Their faces, hands, and clothes are stained with dye. The captured man has his cap cocked on the side of his head and displays a cheerful impudence. A few drinks of whiskey have put him*

in high spirits]. You miserable wretches, you! You
want to be workers, huh? You want to be comrades,
huh? Why, before I'd do a thing like this—before I'd
lay hands on a fellow worker of mine, I think I'd
let my hand rot off first.

[*At a signal from the* POLICE CHIEF, KUTSCHE *orders the
dyers to take their hands off the victim and to guard
the doors.* JAEGER, *now free, stands there impudently.*]

POLICE CHIEF [*shouts at* JAEGER]. Take your cap off, you!
[*Jaeger removes it, but very slowly. He continues to
smile ironically.*] What's your name?*

JAEGER [*simply and quietly*]. That's none of your business! [*The impact of the words creates a stir among
the others.*]

DREISSIGER. This is too much.

POLICE CHIEF [*changes color, is about to burst out, but
conquers his anger*]. We'll see about this later. I'm
asking you what your name is! [*When there is no reply, in rage.*] Speak up, you scoundrel, or I'll have
you whipped.

JAEGER [*perfectly cheerful and without batting an eye
at the furious outburst, calls over the heads of the
spectators to a pretty servant girl about to serve
coffee. She is perplexed at the unexpected sight and
stands still, open-mouthed*]. Why, tell me, Emily,
are you in service in high society now? Well, then,
see to it that you get out of here. The wind might
start blowing around here one of these days, and it'll
blow everything away—overnight.

[*The girl stares at* JAEGER. *When she realizes that the
speech is meant for her, she blushes with shame,
covers her eyes with her hands and runs out, leaving
the dishes in confusion on the table. Again there is
a commotion among the spectators.*]

---

*In the original, the chief of police uses the familiar "Du," whereupon
Jaeger makes the remark that the two had never gone "tending swine together," i.e., they had not been on familiar terms.

POLICE CHIEF [*almost losing control of himself, to* DREIS-SIGER]. As old as I am . . . I've never encountered such unheard-of impudence. . . .

[JAEGER *spits on the floor.*]

DREISSIGER. See here, you! You're not in a stable—understand?

POLICE CHIEF. Now, I'm at the end of my patience. For the last time—what is your name?

KITTELHAUS [*during this past scene has been peeking out from behind the partly open door of the drawing room and listening. Now, carried away by the incident and trembling with excitement, he comes forward to intervene*]. His name's Jaeger, Chief. Moritz . . . isn't it? Moritz Jaeger. [*To* JAEGER.] Why, Jaeger, don't you remember me?

JAEGER [*seriously*]. You are Reverend Kittelhaus.

KITTELHAUS. Yes, your pastor, Jaeger! If I'm the one who received you as an infant into the Communion of the Saints. The one—from whose hands you first received Holy Communion. Do you remember? There—I've worked and worked and brought the Word of God to your heart. Is this the thanks I get?

JAEGER [*gloomily, like a schoolboy who has been scolded*]. I've paid my thaler.

KITTELHAUS. Money, money—do you really believe that that vile, miserable money will. . . . Keep your money . . . I'd much rather you did. What nonsense that is! Behave yourself—be a good Christian! Think of what you've promised. Keep God's commandments—be good and pious. Money, money. . . .

JAEGER. I'm a Quaker now, Reverend. I don't believe in anything any more.

KITTELHAUS. What? A Quaker? Don't talk that way! Try to reform and leave words that you don't understand out of this! They're pious folk, not heathens like you. Quaker! What do you mean, Quaker?

POLICE CHIEF. With your permission, Reverend. [*He*

steps between him and JAEGER.] Kutsche! Tie his
hands!

[*Wild shouting outside: "Jaeger! Let Jaeger come on
out!"*]

DREISSIGER [*a little bit frightened, as are the others, has
stepped instinctively to the window*]. Now, what does
this mean?

POLICE CHIEF. I know. It means that they want this ruf-
fian back. But that favor we won't do them this time.
Understand, Kutsche? He goes to jail.

KUTSCHE [*the rope in his hand, hesitating*]. With all
respect, I'd like to say, Chief, we'll be havin' trouble.
That's a damn big crowd. A regular gang of cut-
throats, Chief. Baecker is among them, and the blacksmith. . . .

KITTELHAUS. With your kind permission—in order not
to create more ill-feeling, wouldn't it be more appropriate, Chief, if we tried to settle this peaceably?
Perhaps Jaeger will promise that he'll go along
quietly or. . . .

POLICE CHIEF. What are you thinking? This is my responsibility. I can't possibly agree to a thing like
that. Come on, Kutsche! Don't lose any time!

JAEGER [*putting his hands together and holding them
out, laughing*]. Tie them tight—as tight as you can.
It won't be for long.

[KUTSCHE, *with the help of the dyers, ties his hands.*]

POLICE CHIEF. Now, come on, march! [*To* DREISSIGER.] If
you're worried about this, have six of the dyers go
along. They can put him in the middle. I'll ride
ahead—Kutsche will follow. Whoever gets in our way
—will be cut down.

[*Cries from outside: "Cock-a-doodle-doo!! Woof, woof,
woof!"*]

POLICE CHIEF [*threatening, toward the window*]. Rabble! I'll cock-a-doodle-doo and woof-woof you. Get
going! Forward! March!

[*He marches out ahead, with drawn saber; the others follow with* JAEGER.]

JAEGER [*shouts as he leaves*]. And even if Milady Dreissiger acts so proud—she's no better than the likes of us. She's served my father his bit of whiskey a hundred times. Squadron, left wheel, ma-a-arch! [*Leaves, laughing.*]

DREISSIGER [*after a pause, apparently composed*]. What do you think, Pastor? Shall we begin our game of whist now? I don't think anything else will interfere now. [*He lights a cigar, gives several short. laughs. As soon as the cigar is lit, he laughs out loud.*] Now I'm beginning to find this business funny. That fellow! [*In a nervous burst of laughter.*] It really is indescribably funny. First the dispute at dinner with the tutor. Five minutes later, he leaves. Good riddance! Then this business. And now—let's get on with our whist.

KITTELHAUS. Yes, but. . . . [*Roars from downstairs.*] Yes, but . . . you know, those people are making a terrible row.

DREISSIGER. We'll simply retire to the other room. We'll be quite undisturbed there.

KITTELHAUS [*shaking his head*]. If I only knew what has happened to these people. I must admit that the tutor was right in this respect. At least—until a short time ago—I, too, was of the opinion that the weavers were humble, patient, compliant people. Don't you think so too, Mr. Dreissiger?

DREISSIGER. Certainly they used to be patient and easily managed—certainly they used to be a civilized and orderly people—as long as the so-called "humanitarians" kept their hands out of it. Then for the longest time the terrible misery of their lives was pointed out to them. Think of all the societies and committees for the relief of distress among the weavers. Finally the weaver himself believes it—and now he's all mixed up. Let some one come in and set him straight again. He won't be stopped now. Now he complains endlessly. This doesn't please him and that doesn't please him. Now, everything' has to be just so.

[*Suddenly a swelling roar of "Hurrah!" is heard from the crowd.*]

KITTELHAUS. So—with all their humanitarianism, they have accomplished nothing more than literally making wolves out of lambs, overnight.

DREISSIGER. No, Reverend, by the use of cool logic we might even be able to see the good side of this affair. Perhaps such happenings won't pass unnoticed in leading circles. Possibly at last they will come to the conclusion that such things can not go on any longer—that something must be done—if our home industries are not to collapse completely.

KITTELHAUS. Yes, but what would you say was the cause of this enormous falling off of trade?

DREISSIGER. Foreign countries have put up high tariff walls against our goods. Our best markets are thus cut off, and at home we've got to compete for our very lives. We have no protection—absolutely no protection.

PFEIFER [*staggers in, breathless and pale*]. Mr. Dreissiger! Oh, Mr. Dreissiger!

DREISSIGER [*standing in the doorway, about to enter the drawing room, turns, angrily*]. Well, Pfeifer, what is it this time?

PFEIFER. No . . . no. . . . This is the limit.

DREISSIGER. What's wrong now?

KITTELHAUS. You're alarming us—speak up!

PFEIFER [*hasn't recovered himself yet*]. This is the limit! I never saw anything like it! The authorities . . . they'll make them pay for it.

DREISSIGER. What the devil's got into you? Has anyone been—killed?

PFEIFER [*almost weeping with fear, cries out*]. They've

set Moritz Jaeger free, they've beaten up the Chief of Police, and chased him away, they've beaten up the policeman—and chased him away, too—without his helmet—his saber broken. . . . Oh, I never. . . .

DREISSIGER. Pfeifer, you've lost your mind.

KITTELHAUS. Why, that would be revolution.

PFEIFER [*sitting down in a chair, his whole body trembling, moaning*]. It's gettin' serious, Mr. Dreissiger! It's gettin' serious, Mr. Dreissiger.

DREISSIGER. Well, then, the entire police force isn't. . . .

PFEIFER. It's gettin' serious, Mr. Dreissiger!

DREISSIGER. Damn it all, Pfeifer, shut up!

MRS. DREISSIGER [*comes from the drawing room with* MRS. KITTELHAUS]. Oh, but this is really shocking, Wilhelm. Our lovely evening is being ruined. There you are, now Mrs. Kittelhaus wants to go home.

KITTELHAUS. My dear Mrs. Dreissiger, perhaps it would be best today. . . .

MRS. DREISSIGER. Wilhelm, you should put a stop to this.

DREISSIGER. You go and talk to them. You go! Go on! [*Stopping in front of the Pastor, bursts out.*] Am I really a tyrant? Am I really a slave-driver?

JOHANN, THE COACHMAN [*enters*]. If you please, 'ma'am, I've harnessed the horses. The tutor has already put Georgie and Carl in the carriage. If things get worse we'll drive off.

MRS. DREISSIGER. If what gets worse?

JOHANN. Well, I don't know, either. I'm just thinkin'— the crowds are gettin' bigger all the time. After all, they have chased off the Chief of Police along with Kutsche.

PFEIFER. I'm tellin' ya, it's gettin' serious, Mr. Dreissiger! It's gettin' serious!

MRS. DREISSIGER [*with mounting fear*]. What's going to happen? What do these people want? They couldn't attack us, Johann, could they?

JOHANN. There are some mangey dogs among them,

ma'am.

PFEIFER. It's gettin' serious—deadly serious.

DREISSIGER. Shut up, you ass! Are the doors barred?

KITTELHAUS. Do me a favor . . . do me a favor . . . I have
decided to . . . please do me a favor. . . . [*To*
JOHANN.] What is it that the people really want?

JOHANN [*embarrassed*]. The stupid good-for-nothin's,
they want more pay, that's what they want.

KITTELHAUS. Good, fine! I will go out and do my duty.
I will have a serious talk with them.

JOHANN. Reverend, don't do that. Words won't do no
good, here.

KITTELHAUS. My dear Mr. Dreissiger, just one word
more. I would like to ask you to post some men behind the door and lock it immediately after I've
gone.

MRS. KITTELHAUS. Oh, Joseph, are you really going to do
this?

KITTELHAUS. I'll do it, of course . . . I'll do it! I know
what I'm doing. Have no fear, the Lord will protect
me.

[MRS. KITTELHAUS *presses his hand, steps back, and wipes
tears from her eyes.*]

KITTELHAUS [*all the time the muffled noise of a large
crowd is heard from below*]. I'll act . . . I'll act as if
I were just quietly going home. I want to see
whether my holy office . . . whether I still command
the respect of these people . . . I want to see . . . [*He
takes his hat and stick.*] Forward then, in God's name.
[*Leaves, accompanied by* DREISSIGER, PFEIFER, *and*
JOHANN.]

MRS. KITTELHAUS. Dear Mrs. Dreissiger,—[*She bursts
into tears and puts her arms around* MRS. DREISSIGER'S
neck.]—if only nothing happens to him!

MRS. DREISSIGER [*absently*]. I really don't know, Mrs. Kittelhaus—I am so . . . I really don't know how I feel.
Such a thing can't hardly be humanly possible. If
that's how it is . . . then it's like it was a sin to be

rich. You know, if somebody had told me, I don't know but what, in the long run, I would rather have stayed in—in my humble circumstances.

MRS. KITTELHAUS. Dear Mrs. Dreissiger, believe me, there are disappointments and troubles enough in all walks of life.

MRS. DREISSIGER. Yes, of course—of course. I believe that, too. And if we've got more than other people . . . Lord knows, we certainly didn't steal it. Every single pfennig's been honestly earned. Surely it can't be that the people are going to attack us. Is it my husband's fault if business is bad?

[*From below comes tumultuous shouting. While the two women stare at each other, pale and terrified,* DREISSIGER *bursts in.*]

DREISSIGER. Rosa, throw on a coat and get into the carriage. I'll follow right after you!

[*He hurries to the safe, opens it, and takes out various valuables.*]

JOHANN [*enters*]. Everything's ready! But hurry, before they get to the back gate!

MRS. DREISSIGER [*panic-stricken, throws her arms around the coachman's neck*]. Johann, dear—good Johann! Save us, dearest Johann! Save my children, oh, oh. . . .

DREISSIGER. Be reasonable! Let go of Johann!

JOHANN. Madam, madam! Aw, don't be scared. Our horses are in good shape. Nobody can catch up with them. If they don't get out of the way, they'll get run over. [*Exit.*]

MRS. KITTELHAUS [*in helpless anxiety*]. But my husband? What about my husband. What will become of him, Mr. Dreissiger?

DREISSIGER. He is all right, Mrs. Kittelhaus. Just calm down, he is all right.

MRS. KITTELHAUS. I know something terrible's happened to him. You just won't tell me. You just won't say.

DREISSIGER. They'll be sorry for this, you mark my words. I know exactly who is responsible for it. Such

unheard of, shameless impudence will not go unpunished. A community that does harm to its pastor
—it's terrible! Mad dogs, that's what they are—beasts
gone mad. And they should be treated accordingly.
[*To* MRS. DREISSIGER, *who stands there, as if stunned.*]
Now go, and hurry up! [*Sounds of beating against
the entrance door are heard.*] Don't you hear me?
The mob's gone mad. [*The smashing of the downstairs windows is heard.*] They've gone absolutely
insane. There's nothing left to do but to get out.

[*A chorus of shouts is heard,* "We want Pfeifer!"
"Pfeifer come out!"]

MRS. DREISSIGER. Pfeifer, Pfeifer! They want Pfeifer outside.

PFEIFER [*rushes in*]. They're at the back gate, too. The
front door won't hold out another minute. Wittig is
beating it in with a stable bucket—like—like a mad
man.

[*From downstairs, the shouts become louder and
clearer,* "Pfeifer come out!" "Pfeifer come out!"]

[MRS. DREISSIGER *rushes off, as if pursued.* MRS. KITTEL-
HAUS *follows.*]

PFEIFER [*listens. His face changes color. Once he makes
out the cries, he is seized with an insane fear. He
speaks the following words frantically, crying, whim-
pering, pleading, whining all at the same time. He
overwhelms* DREISSIGER *with childish caresses, strokes
his cheeks and arms, kisses his hands, and, finally,
like a drowning man, puts his arms around him,
clutching him and not letting him go*]. Oh, good,
kind, merciful Mr. Dreissiger! Don't leave me behind. I have always served you loyally—I always
treated the people well. Wages were fixed—I couldn't
give them more. Don't leave me in the lurch. Don't! I
beg you. They'll kill me. If they find me—they'll
strike me dead. O, God in heaven, God in heaven,
my wife, my children. . . .

DREISSIGER [*as he leaves, vainly trying to free himself*

from PFEIFER]. Let go of me, man! We'll see, we'll see! [*Leaves with* PFEIFER.]

[*The room remains empty for a few seconds. In the drawing room, window panes are being smashed. A loud crash resounds through the house, followed by a roar of "Hurray," then silence. A few seconds pass, then soft and cautious footsteps of people coming upstairs to the second floor are heard; then, timid and shy cries: "To the left!—Get upstairs!—Sh!—Slow!—Don't shove!—Help push!—Smash!—Here we are!—Move on! We're goin' to a weddin'—You go in first! —No, you go!"*]

[*Young weavers and weaver girls appear in the vestibule door. They don't dare to enter, and each one tries to push the other one in. After a few moments, they overcome their timidity, and the poor, thin figures, some of them sickly, some ragged or patched, disperse throughout* DREISSIGER'S *room and the drawing room. At first they look around curiously and shyly, then they touch everything. The girls try out the sofas; they form groups that admire their reflections in the mirror. A few climb up on chairs to look at pictures and to take them down, and in the meantime a steady stream of wretched-looking figures moves in from the vestibule.*]

FIRST OLD WEAVER [*enters*]. No, no, this is goin' too far. Downstairs they're already startin' to break things up. It's crazy. There ain't no rhyme nor reason to it. In the end, that'll be a bad thing. Nobody with a clear head . . . would go along. I'll be careful and won't take part in such goin's on!

[JAEGER, BAECKER, WITTIG *with a wooden bucket,* BAUMERT *and a number of young and old weavers come storming in as if they were chasing something, yelling back and forth in hoarse voices.*]

JAEGER. Where is he?

BAECKER. Where is that dirty slave-driver?

OLD BAUMERT. If we're to eat grass, let him eat sawdust.

WITTIG. When we catch him, we'll string him up.

FIRST OLD WEAVER. We'll take him by the legs and throw him out of the window so he'll never get up again.

SECOND YOUNG WEAVER [*enters*]. He's flown the coop.

ALL. Who?

SECOND YOUNG WEAVER. Dreissiger.

BAECKER. Pfeifer, too?

VOICES. Let's look for Pfeifer! Look for Pfeifer!

OLD BAUMERT. Look for him, Little Pfeifer—there's a weaver for ya to starve! [*Laughter.*]

JAEGER. If we can't get this beast Dreissiger—we'll make him poor.

OLD BAUMERT. He'll be as poor as a churchmouse—just as poor.

[*All rush to the door of the drawing room, ready to destroy everything.*]

BAECKER [*runs ahead, turns around, and stops the others*]. Stop—listen to me! Once we're through here, we'll really get goin'. From here we'll go over to Bielau—to Dittrich's—he's the one who's got the steam power looms. . . . All the trouble comes from those factories.

ANSORGE [*comes in from the vestibule. After he has taken a few steps, he stands still, looks unbelievingly about, shakes his head, strikes his forehead, and says*]. Who am I? The Weaver Anton Ansorge? Has he gone crazy, Ansorge? It's true—things are buzzin' around in my head like a gadfly. What's he doin' here? He'll do whatever he wants to. Where is he, Ansorge? [*He strikes himself on the forehead.*] I ain't myself! I don't understand, I ain't quite right. Go away—you go away! Go away, you rebels! Heads off —legs off—hands off! You take my cottage, I'll take yours. Go to it!

[*With a yell, he goes into the drawing room. The rest follow him amid yells and laughter.*]

Curtain

ACT FIVE.

SCENE: *The tiny weaver's room at* OLD HILSE'S. *To the left is a small window, in front of it a loom; to the right, a bed with a table pushed up close to it. In the corner, to the right is the stove with a bench. Around the table, on the foot bench, on the edge of the bed, and on a wooden stool, the following persons are seated:* OLD HILSE; *his old, blind, and almost deaf wife; his son;* GOTTLIEB; *and* GOTTLIEB'S *wife,* LUISE. *They are at morning prayers. A winding wheel with bobbins stands between table and loom. On top of the smoky, brown rafters, all kinds of old spinning, winding, and weaving implements are stored. Long hanks of yarn hang down; all sorts of rubbish are strewn about the room. The very low, narrow room has a door leading to the hall in the back wall. Opposite it, another door in the entrance hall stands open and affords a view into a second weaver's room similar to the first. The hall is paved with stones, the plaster is crumbling, and a dilapidated wooden stair leads to the attic. A washtub on a wooden stool is partly visible; shabby bits of laundry and household goods of the poor are scattered about. The light falls from the left into all the rooms.*

OLD HILSE [*a bearded, heavy-boned man, now bent and worn with age, hard work, sickness, and exertion. An ex-soldier, he has lost one arm. He has a sharp nose, livid coloring. His hands tremble, and his body seems to be just skin, bones, and sinews. He has the deep-set, sore eyes characteristic of the weavers. He stands up, together with his son and daughter-in-law, and begins to pray*]. O Lord, we cannot be grateful enough that Thou this night, in Thy grace and goodness . . . hast taken pity upon us. That we have come to no harm this night. "Lord, Thy mercy reaches so far," and we are but poor, evil and sinful human beings not worthy to be trampled under Thy feet, so sinful and corrupted are we. But Thou, dear Father, willst look upon us and accept us for the sake of Thy beloved Son, our Lord and Savior, Jesus Christ. "Jesus' blood and righteousness, they are my jewels and my robe of glory. . . ." And if sometimes we despair under Thy scourge—when the fire of purification burns too raging hot, then do not count it too highly against us—forgive us our trespasses. Give us patience, O Heavenly Father, that after this suffering we may become part of Thy eternal blessedness. Amen.

MOTHER HILSE [*who has been bending forward in a great effort to hear, weeping*]. Father, you always say such a beautiful prayer.

[LUISE *goes to the washtub,* GOTTLIEB *into the room on the other side of the hall.*]

OLD HILSE. Wherever is the girl?

LUISE. She went over to Peterswaldau—to Dreissiger's. She finished windin' a few hanks of yarn again last night.

OLD HILSE [*speaking in a very loud voice*]. Well, Mother, now I'll bring ya the wheel.

MOTHER HILSE. Yes, bring it, bring it to me, Father.

OLD HILSE [*placing the wheel in front of her*]. I'd be glad to do it for ya. . . .

MOTHER HILSE. No . . . no. . . . What would I be doin' then with all that time?

OLD HILSE. I'll wipe your fingers off for ya a bit, so the yarn won't get greasy—do ya hear? [*He wipes her hands with a rag.*]

LUISE [*at the washtub*]. When did we have anything fat to eat?

OLD HILSE. If we don't have fat, we'll eat dry bread—
if we don't have bread, we'll eat potatoes—and if we
don't have potatoes neither, then we'll eat dry bran.

LUISE [*insolently*]. And if we ain't got rye flour, we'll do
like the Wenglers—we'll find out where the flayer
has buried an old dead horse. We'll dig it up and live
off the rotten beast—for a couple of weeks—that's
what we'll do, won't we?

GOTTLIEB [*from the back room*]. What kind of damn
nonsense are ya spoutin'?

OLD HILSE. Ya ought to be more careful with such god-
less talk! [*He goes to the loom, calls.*] Won't ya help
me, Gottlieb—there's a few threads to pull through.

LUISE [*from her work at the washtub*]. Gottlieb, you're
to lend a hand to your father.

[GOTTLIEB *enters. The old man and his son begin the
tiresome job of reeding. They have hardly begun
when* HORNIG *appears in the entrance hall.*]

HORNIG [*in the doorway*]. Good luck to your work!

OLD HILSE AND HIS SON. Thank ya, Hornig!

OLD HILSE. Tell me, when do ya sleep, anyhow? In the
daytime ya go about tradin'—in the night ya stand
watch.

HORNIG. Why, I don't get no sleep at all no more!

LUISE. Glad to see ya, Hornig!

OLD HILSE. Any good news?

HORNIG. A pretty piece of news. The people in Peterswaldau have risked their necks and have chased out
Dreissiger and his whole family.

LUISE [*with signs of excitement*]. Hornig's lyin' his head
off again.

HORNIG. Not this time, young woman! Not this time—I
have some pretty pinafores in the cart.—No, no, I'm
tellin' the honest-to-God truth. They've up and
chased him out. Yesterday evenin' he got to Reichenbach. By God! They didn't dare keep him there—
for fear of the weavers—so he had to hurry off to
Schweidnitz.

OLD HILSE [*picks up the thread of the warp carefully and pulls it close to the reed. His son catches the thread with a hook and pulls it through*]. Now, it's time for ya to stop, Hornig!

HORNIG. If I'm lyin', I don't want to leave this place alive, I swear. There ain't a child that don't know the story.

OLD HILSE. Now tell me, am I all mixed up, or are you?

HORNIG. Well, now. What I'm tellin' ya is as true as Amen in the church. I wouldn't of said nothin' if I hadn't been standin' right there, but that's the way I saw it. With my own eyes, just like I see you here, Gottlieb. They've smashed up the manufacturer's house, from cellar to attic. They threw the fine china from the attic window and smashed it—right down over the roof. Hundreds of pieces of cotton are layin' in the bottom of the brook! Believe me, the water can't even flow on no more; it swelled up over the banks; it turned real blue from all the indigo they poured out of the windows. The air itself was filled with all them blue clouds. No, no, they did a terrible job there. Not just in the house, mind you, . . . in the dye plant . . . in the warehouse. . . ! Banisters smashed, the floors torn up—mirrors broken—sofas, arm chairs—everything—torn and slashed—cut to pieces and smashed—trampled and hacked to pieces —damn it! believe me, it was worse than war!

OLD HILSE. And you say those were weavers from around here?

[*Slowly and incredulously, he shakes his head. A group of tenants of the house has gathered at the door, listening intently.*]

HORNIG. Well, who else? I could mention all of them by name. I led the Commissioner through the house. I talked with plenty of them. They were just as friendly as usual. They went about the whole business quietly—but they were thorough. The Commissioner talked with a lot of them. They were just as polite as usual. But they wouldn't stop. They hacked at the elegant furniture, just like they were workin' for wages.

OLD HILSE. You led the Commissioner through the house?.

HORNIG. Well, I sure wasn't afraid. The people all know me, always turnin' up like a bad penny. I never had trouble with nobody. I'm in good with all of them. As sure as my name is Hornig, I went through the house. Yes—and ya can really believe it—I was sore at heart—and I can tell ya about the Commissioner—he took it to heart, too. And why? Ya couldn't hear a single word the whole time, it was that quiet. It gave ya a real solemn feelin'—the way them poor hungry devils was takin' their revenge.

LUISE [*bursting out with excitement, trembling and wiping her eyes with her apron*]. That's only right—that had to happen!

VOICES OF THE TENANTS. There's enough slave-drivers 'round here. There's one livin' right over there.—He's got four horses and six coaches in his stable, and he lets his weavers starve!

OLD HILSE [*still incredulous*]. How could that have started over there?

HORNIG. Who knows? Who knows? One says this—another that.

OLD HILSE. What do they say?

HORNIG. By God, Dreissiger is supposed to have said the weavers could eat grass if they got hungry. I don't know no more.

[*Commotion among the tenants, who repeat it to each other with signs of indignation.*]

OLD HILSE. Now just listen to me, Hornig. For all I care, ya might say to me, Father Hilse, tomorrow you've got to die. That's likely, I'd answer, why not? —You might say, Father Hilse, tomorrow the King of Prussia will come to visit ya—but that weavers, men like me and my son—should be up to such things, never in the world, never, never will I believe that.

MIELCHEN [*a pretty girl of seven, with long, loose, flaxen hair. She runs in with a basket on her arm. She holds out a silver spoon to her mother*]. Mamma, Mamma, look what I've got! Ya can buy me a dress with it!

LUISE. Why are ya in such a hurry, child? [*With mounting excitement and curiosity.*] Tell me, what did ya come draggin' in this time? You're all out of breath. And the bobbins are still in the basket. What's the meanin' of all this, child?

OLD HILSE. Where did ya get the spoon?

LUISE. Could be she found it.

HORNIG. It's worth at least two or three thalers.

OLD HILSE [*beside himself*). Get out, girl! Hurry up and get out! Will ya do what I say, or do I have to get a stick to ya! And take the spoon back where ya got it. Out with you! Do ya want to make thieves out of all of us, huh? You—I'll knock the thievin' out of ya —[*He looks for something with which to hit her.*]

MIELCHEN [*clinging to her mother's skirt, cries*]. Grandpapa, don't hit me—we, we—really found it. The bob-bobbin girls—they all—got—one, too.

LUISE [*bursts out, torn between fear and anxiety*]. There now—ya see. She found it. That's what she did. Where did ya find it?

MIELCHEN [*sobbing*]. In Peters—waldau—we—found 'em —in front of—Dreissiger's house.

OLD HILSE. Well, now we're in a fine mess. Hurry up, now, or I'll help ya to get goin'.

MOTHER HILSE. What's goin' on?

HORNIG. I'll tell ya what, Father Hilse. Let Gottlieb put on his coat and take the spoon to the police.

OLD HILSE. Gottlieb, put your coat on.

GOTTLIEB [*already doing so, eagerly*]. And then I'll go on up to the office and I'll say, they shouldn't blame us, a child like that just don't understand such things. And so I'm bringin' the spoon back. Stop that cryin', girl!

[*The mother takes the crying child into the back room and shuts the door on her.* LUISE *returns.*]

HORNIG. That might well be worth all of three thalers.

GOTTLIEB. Come, give me a piece of cloth so it don't get hurt, Luise. My, my—what an expensive thing. [*He has tears in his eyes while he wraps up the spoon.*]

LUISE. If it was ours, we could live on it for weeks.

OLD HILSE. Hurry up! Get a move on. Go as fast as ya can. That would be something! That would just about finish me. Hurry up, so we get rid of that devil's spoon. [GOTTLIEB *leaves with the spoon.*]

HORNIG. Well, I'd better be goin'. [*He talks to some of the tenants for a few seconds on his way out, then leaves.*]

PHYSICIAN SCHMIDT [*a fidgety fat little man, with a cunning face, red from drinking, enters the house through the entrance hall*]. Good morning, people! Well, that's a fine business, that is. You can't fool me! [*Raising a warning finger.*] I know what you're up to. [*In the doorway, without coming into the room.*] Good morning, Father Hilse! [*To a woman in the hall.*] Well, Mother, how's the rheumatism? Better, eh? There you are! Now, let me see how things are with you, Father Hilse. What the devil's wrong with Mama Hilse?

LUISE. Doctor, the veins in her eyes are all dried up and she can't see at all no more.

SCHMIDT. That comes from the dust and the weaving by candlelight. Now tell me, do you know what it all means? All of Peterswaldau is on its feet, heading this way. I started out this morning in my buggy, thinking nothing was wrong, nothing at all. Then, I keep hearing the most amazing things. What in the devil's gotten into these people, Hilse? Raging like a pack of wolves. Starting a revolution, a rebellion; starting to riot; plundering and marauding. . . . Mielchen!

Why, where is Mielchen? [MIELCHEN, *her eyes still red from weeping, is pushed in by her mother.*] There, Mielchen, you just reach into my coat pocket. [MIELCHEN *does so.*] Those ginger snaps are for you. Well, well, not all at once, you rascal. First, a little song! "Fox, you stole the . . ." well? "Fox, you stole . . . the goose. . . ." Just you wait, what you did— you called the sparrows on the church fence dirty names. They reported you to the teacher. Now, what do you say to that! Close to fifteen hundred people are on the march. [*Ringing of bells in the distance.*] Listen—they're ringing the alarm bells in Reichenbach. Fifteen hundred people. It's really the end of the world. Uncanny!

OLD HILSE. Are they really comin' over here to Bielau?

SCHMIDT. Yes, of course, of course.—I drove right through. Right through the whole crowd. I wanted to get out and give each one of them a pill. They trudged along, one behind the other—like misery itself—and sang a song—it really turned your stomach—you actually began to gag. My driver, Friedrich, he trembled like an old woman. We had to have some strong bitters right afterwards. I wouldn't want to be a manufacturer—not even if I could afford to have fine rubber tires on my carriage. [*Distant singing.*] Just listen! As if you beat on an old cracked boiler with your knuckles. I tell you, they'll be here on top of us in less than five minutes. Goodbye, people. Don't do anything foolish. The soldiers'll be right behind them. Don't lose your heads. The people from Peterswaldau have lost theirs. [*Bells ring close by.*] Heavens, now our bells are beginning to ring, too. It'll drive the people completely crazy. [*Goes upstairs.*]

GOTTLIEB [*enters again. Still in the entrance hall, panting*]. I've seen them—I've seen them. [*To a woman in the hall.*] They're here, Auntie, they're here! [*In the doorway.*] They're here, Father, they're here!

They've got beanpoles and spikes and axes. They're stoppin' at Dittrich's and kickin' up a terrible row. I think he's given them money. Oh, my God, whatever is goin' to happen here? I won't look. So many people! So many people! If once they get goin' and make an attack—oh, damn it, damn it! Then our manufacturers'll have a bad time of it.

OLD HILSE. Why did you run so? You'll run like that till ya get your old trouble back, till you're flat on your back again, kickin' and hittin' all around ya.

GOTTLIEB [*with increasing excitement and joy*]. I had to run, or else they would've caught me and kept me there. They were all yellin' I should hold out my hand, too. Godfather Baumert was one of them. He said to me—Come and get your two bits, you're a poor starvin' creature too. He even said—Tell your Father . . . he said I should tell ya, Father, you should come and help make the manufacturers pay back for all the terrible drudgery. [*Passionately*.] Now times've changed, he said. Now it'd be different with us weavers. We should all of us come and help bring it about. Now we'd all have our half pound of meat on Sundays and blood sausage and cabbage on Holy Days. Now everything would be changed, he said to me.

OLD HILSE [*with repressed indignation*]. And he calls himself your godfather! And asked ya to take part in such criminal doin's? Don't ya have nothin' to do with such things, Gottlieb. The devil's got his hand in such carryin's on. That's Satan's work, what they're doin'.

LUISE [*overcome by passionate feeling, vehemently*]. Yes, yes, Gottlieb, just you hide behind the stove—crawl into the chimney corner—take a ladle in your hand and put a dish of buttermilk on your knee—put on a petticoat and say nice little prayers so you'll please Father!—And ya call that a man?

[*Laughter from the people in the entrance hall.*]

OLD HILSE [*trembling, with suppressed rage*]. And ya
call that a proper wife, huh? Let me tell ya straight
out—you call yourself a mother and have a vile
tongue like that? Ya think ya can tell your daughter
what she should do, and stir up your husband to
crime and wickedness?

LUISE [*completely uncontrolled*]. You with your big-
oted talk! It never filled one of my babies' bellies.
All four of 'em laid in filth and rags on account of it.
That didn't so much as dry one single diaper. I do
call myself a mother, now you know it! And ya know
that's why I wish all the manufacturers was in hell
and damnation! It's because I am a mother—Can I
keep a little worm like that alive? I've cried more
than I've breathed, from the moment one of them
tender, little creatures first came into the world, until
death took pity on it, and took it away. You—you
didn't give a damn. Ya prayed and ya sang, and I
walked my feet bloody, for just a drop of skim milk.
How many hundreds of nights I've racked my brains,
just once to cheat the graveyard of a baby of mine.
And tell me, what's the wrong that a little baby like
that has done, huh? That he has to come to such a
miserable end—and over there—at Dittrich's they're
bathed in wine and washed in milk. No, no, I tell
ya, if it starts here, ten horses won't hold me back.
And this I'll say, too, if they was to attack Dittrich's,
I'll be the first one—and God help them that tries to
stop me. I'm fed up—and that's the truth.

OLD HILSE. You're lost—you're past helpin'.

LUISE [*in a frenzy*]. You're the ones that's past helpin'!
You're dishrags—not men! Fools to be spit at. Milk-
sops who'd run away in fright if they so much as
heard a child's rattle. Ya'd say "Thank ya kindly"
three times for every thrashin' ya get. They haven't
left enough blood in your veins so ya can get red in
the face. Somebody ought to take a whip to ya, and

beat some courage into your rotten bones! [*Leaves hurriedly.*]

[*A moment of embarrassment.*]

MOTHER HILSE. What's wrong with Luise, Father?

OLD HILSE. Nothin', Mama. What would be wrong with her?

MOTHER HILSE. Tell me, Father, am I just imagin' it, or are the bells ringin'?

OLD HILSE. I guess they're buryin' somebody, Mother.

MOTHER HILSE. And for me the end never seems to come. Tell me, Father, why don't I ever die? [*Pause.*]

OLD HILSE [*leaves his work, draws himself up, solemnly*]. Gottlieb! Your wife has said such things to us. Gottlieb, look here! [*He bares his breast.*] Here laid a bullet as big as a thimble. And the King himself knows where I lost my arm. It wasn't the mice that ate it. [*He walks back and forth.*] Your wife—before she was even thought of, I shed my blood by the quart for the Fatherland. So let her rave on as much as she wants to.—That's all right with me. I don't give a damn.—Afraid? Me, afraid? What would I be afraid of, I'd like to know. Of the few soldiers who'll be rushin' after the rioters, maybe? Oh, Lord, if that was it—that wouldn't be nothin'! If I'm a bit brittle in my bones, when it comes to action, they're like iron. I wouldn't be scared to stand up against a few miserable bayonets—and, if it comes to the worst? Oh, how glad I'd be to take a rest. I certainly ain't afraid to die. Better today than tomorrow. No. No. And it'd be a good thing. For what would we be leavin'? Nobody'd weep for our poor old tortured bodies. That little heap of fear and pain and drudgery that we call life—we'd be glad enough to leave behind. But afterward, Gottlieb, afterward there's something—and if ya throw that away, too—then everything's really gone.

GOTTLIEB. Who knows what happens when you're dead?

Ain't nobody seen it.

OLD HILSE. I'm tellin' ya, Gottlieb! Don't go and doubt the only thing poor folks have got. Why would I have set here—and worked the treadle like a slave for forty years and more? And watched quietly how that fellow over there lives in pride and gluttony—and makes money out of my hunger and hardship. And for what? Because I've got hope. I've got something, in all this misery. [*Pointing out the window.*] You've got your share here—me, in the world beyond. That's what I've been thinkin'. And I'd let myself be drawn and quartered—I'm that sure. It has been promised to us. Judgment Day is comin', but we are not the judges, no, on the contrary, "Vengeance is mine, saith the Lord."

A VOICE [*through the window*]. Weavers, come on out!

OLD HILSE. I don't care—do what ya want. [*He sits down at the loom.*] You'll have to leave me in here.

GOTTLIEB [*after a short struggle*]. I'll go and work, come what will. [*Leaves.*]

[*Many hundreds of voices are heard near-by singing the "Weavers' Song"; it sounds like a dull, monotonous lament.*]

VOICES OF THE TENANTS. [*in the entrance hall*]. My God! My God! Now they're comin' like ants.—Where'd so many weavers come from?—Don't push—I want to see, too.—Look at that lanky fellow who's walkin' out front. Oh! Oh!—They're comin' in swarms!

HORNIG [*joins the people in the entrance hall*]. It's quite a show, ain't it? Ya don't see the likes of that every day. Ya ought to come around to Dittrich's. What they've done up there is really something. He ain't got no house, no more—no factory, no wine cellar—no nothin' at all. The wine bottles, they're drinkin' them all up . . . they don't even take the time to pull out the corks. One, two, three—the necks come off; nobody cares if they cut their mouths on the broken glass or not. Lots of 'em are runnin' around bleedin' like stuck pigs.—Now they're lookin' for the other Dittrich, the one here.

[*The singing of the crowd has stopped.*]

VOICES OF THE TENANTS. They really don't look so mad.

HORNIG. Don't ya worry. You just wait. Now they're takin' a good look at everything. See how they're lookin' over the place from all sides. Watch that little fat man—him with the stable bucket. That's the blacksmith from Peterswaldau, and a quick worker he is, too. He breaks down doors like they was pretzels—ya can believe me. If that man ever gets a manufacturer in his claws—he'll be done for!

VOICES OF THE TENANTS. Smash! Something happened! That was a stone flyin' through the window!—Now old Dittrich's gettin' scared.—He's hangin' out a sign! —What's on it?—Can't ya read? Where'd I be if I couldn't read?—Well, read it! "Your demands will be met." "Your demands will be met."

HORNIG. He could've spared hisself that. It won't help much. The weavers have their own ideas. Here it's the factory they're after. They want to put an end to the power looms. They're the things that are ruinin' the handweavers—even a blind man can see that. No, no! Those fellows won't stop now. They don't pay no attention to the judge, or to the chief of police—and certainly not to a sign. Anybody who's seen them kick up a riot, knows what it means.

VOICES OF THE TENANTS. All them people! What do they want? [*Hastily.*] They're comin' across the bridge! [*Anxiously.*] Are they comin' over on this side? [*In great surprise and fear.*] They're comin' this way, they're comin' this way.—They're pullin' the weavers out of their houses!

[*Everybody flees; the entrance hall is empty. A disorderly crowd of rioters, dirty, dusty, their faces red with liquor and exertion, wild-looking, exhausted,*

*as if they had been up all night, tattered, pushes its
way in, with the cry, "Come on out, weavers!" The
crowd disperses through the various rooms.* BAECKER
and a few YOUNG WEAVERS, *armed with cudgels and
poles, enter* OLD HILSE'S *room. When they recognize*
OLD HILSE, *they are taken aback and calm down a
little.*]

BAECKER. Father·Hilse, stop that slavin'! Let whoever
wants to work the treadle. Ya don't need to work
till ya've harmed yourself. We'll see to that.

FIRST YOUNG WEAVER. Ya won't have to go to bed hungry another day.

SECOND YOUNG WEAVER. Weavers'll have a roof over
their heads and a shirt on their backs once more.

OLD HILSE. What's the devil makin' ya come in here
for, with poles and axes?

BAECKER. These we're goin' to break in pieces on Dittrich's back.

SECOND YOUNG WEAVER. We'll get 'em red-hot and shove
'em down the manufacturers' throats, so they'll know
how hunger burns.

THIRD YOUNG WEAVER. Come along, Father Hilse. We
don't give no quarter.

SECOND YOUNG WEAVER. They took no pity on us.
Neither God nor man. Now we're makin' our own
justice.

OLD BAUMERT [*comes in, somewhat unsteady on his feet,
with a newly killed chicken under his arm. He
stretches out his arm*]. My dear—dear—br-brother—
we are all brothers! Come to my heart, brother!
[*Laughter.*]

OLD HILSE. Is that you, Willem?

OLD BAUMERT. Gustav!—Gustav, poor, old wretch, come
to my heart. [*Moved.*]

OLD HILSE [*growls*]. Let me alone.

OLD BAUMERT. Gustav, that's the way it is. A man's got
to have luck! Gustav, just look at me. How do I
look? A man's got to have luck. Don't I look like a

count? [*Patting his belly.*] Guess what's in my belly. Food fit for a prince is in my belly. A man's got to have luck. Then he gets champagne and roast hare. I'll tell ya something—we've been makin' a mistake —we've got to help ourselves.

ALL [*speaking at once*]. We've got to help ourselves. Hurray!

OLD BAUMERT. And once ya've had your first good bite to eat, ya feel like a different man. Jesus! Then ya get to feelin' strong like a bull. Then the strength goes through your limbs so ya don't even see no more what ya're strikin' at. Damn it, that's fun!

JAEGER [*in the door, armed with an old cavalry saber*]. We've made a few excellent attacks.

BAECKER. Yes, we've got the hang of it, now. One, two, three, and we're inside the house. Then it goes like wild fire—cracklin' and shiverin'—like sparks flyin' in a forge.

FIRST YOUNG WEAVER. We ought to make a little fire.

SECOND YOUNG WEAVER. We're marchin' on to Reichenbach and burnin' the houses of the rich right over their heads.

JAEGER. I bet they'd like that. Then they'd get a lot of insurance money. [*Laughter.*]

BAECKER. From here we'll march to Freiburg, to Tromtra's.

JAEGER. We ought to string up some of the officials. I've read all the trouble comes from the bureaucrats.

SECOND YOUNG WEAVER. Soon we'll be marchin' to Breslau. The crowd keeps gettin' bigger.

OLD BAUMERT [*to* HILSE]. Have a drink, Gustav? Come on!

OLD HILSE. I never drink.

OLD BAUMERT. That was in the old times—today things is different, Gustav.

FIRST YOUNG WEAVER. Everyday ain't a holiday. [*Laughter.*]

OLD HILSE [*impatiently*]. You infernal firebrands, what do ya want here in my house?

OLD BAUMERT [*somewhat intimidated, overly friendly*]. Now look, I wanted to bring ya a little chicken—so's you can cook some soup for Mother.

OLD HILSE [*perplexed, half-friendly*]. Oh, go and tell Mother.

MOTHER HILSE [*her hand to her ear, has been listening with difficulty. Now she wards BAUMERT off*]. You let me alone. I don't want no chicken soup.

OLD HILSE. You're right, Mother. Me, neither. Not that kind, anyway. And you, Baumert! I'll tell ya one thing. When old men talk like little children, then the devil claps his hands with joy. And let me tell ya this: you and me, we have nothin' in common. You're not here because I want ya here. Accordin' to law and justice and righteousness, you ain't got no business here!

A VOICE. Who ain't with us, is against us.

JAEGER [*threatens brutally*]. You've got the whole thing wrong. Listen here, old man, we aren't thieves.

A VOICE. We're hungry, that's all.

FIRST YOUNG WEAVER. We want to live, and that's all. And that's why we've cut the rope 'round our necks.

JAEGER. And that was right! [*Holding his fist in front of OLD HILSE's face.*] Just say another word! Ya'll get a punch—right between the eyes.

BAECKER. Be quiet, be quiet! Let the old man alone.— Father Hilse, this is the way we look at it. Better dead than start the old life again.

OLD HILSE. Haven't I lived that kind of a life for sixty years or more?

BAECKER. That don't matter. There's got to be a change, anyway.

OLD HILSE. That day'll never come.

BAECKER. What they don't give us willingly, we'll take by force.

OLD HILSE. By force? [*Laughs.*] Ya might as well go and

dig your own graves. They'll show you where the force is. Just wait, young man!

JAEGER. Maybe—because of the soldiers? I've been a soldier, too. We can handle a few companies of soldiers.

OLD HILSE. With your loud mouths, that I'll believe. And if ya chase a couple of them out, a dozen more'll come back.

VOICES [*through the window*]. The soldiers are comin'! Look out! [*Suddenly everyone is silent. For a moment, the faint sound of fifes and drums can be heard. In the stillness a short, involuntary cry.*] Damn it, I'm gettin' out! [*General laughter.*]

BAECKER. Who's talkin' of gettin' out? Who was it?

JAEGER. Who's afraid of a few lousy soldiers? I'll give the commands. I've been in the army. I know the tricks.

OLD HILSE. What'll ya shoot 'em with? With clubs, maybe, huh?

FIRST YOUNG WEAVER. Never mind that old man—he ain't quite right in the head.

SECOND YOUNG WEAVER. Yes, he is a bit crazy.

GOTTLIEB [*has come into the room, unnoticed, and grabs hold of the speaker*]. Ought ya to be so impudent to an old man?

FIRST YOUNG WEAVER. Let me alone. I ain't said nothin' bad.

OLD HILSE [*meditating*]. Oh, let him talk. Don't meddle, Gottlieb. He'll see soon enough who's crazy—me or him.

BAECKER. You goin' with us, Gottlieb?

OLD HILSE. He'll have nothin' to do with it.

LUISE [*comes into the entrance hall, calls in*]. Don't keep hangin' around here. Don't lose no time with such prayer-book hypocrites. Come on out to the square! Ya ought to come on to the square. Uncle Baumert is comin' as fast as he can. The Major's speakin' to the people from horseback. He's tellin' 'em to go home. If ya don't come quick, we're through.

JAEGER [*as he leaves*]. A fine, brave man you have for a husband!

LUISE. A man for a husband? I ain't got no man for a husband.

[*Several in the entrance hall sing.*]

> Once there was a man so small,
> Heigh ho!
> He would have a wife so tall,
> Heigh diddle diddle dum, dum, dum, hurrah!

WITTIG [*has entered from upstairs, a stable bucket in his hand. As he is about to go out, he stops for a minute in the entrance hall*]. Forward! Those that ain't cowards, hurray!

[*He rushes out. A crowd, among them* LUISE *and* JAEGER, *follow him amid shouts of "hurray."*]

BAECKER. Good luck to ya, Father Hilse, we'll be seein' each other again. [*Is about to leave.*]

OLD HILSE. I doubt that. I won't last another five years. And you won't be out before that.

BAECKER [*surprised, standing still*]. Get out of where, Father Hilse?

OLD HILSE. Out of jail—where else?

BAECKER [*laughing wildly*]. That wouldn't be so bad. At least I'd get enough to eat there, Father Hilse. [*Leaves.*]

OLD BAUMERT [*has been sitting slumped on a stool, moodily meditating; now he gets up*]. It's true, Gustav—I am sorta drunk. But even so, my head's clear enough. You've got your opinion in this matter— I've got mine. I say Baecker's right—if it ends in chains and ropes—it's better in prison than at home. There, they at least take care of ya; there, ya don't have to starve. I didn't want to join 'em. But ya see, Gustav, there comes a time when a man has to have a breath of air. [*Going slowly toward the door.*] Good luck to ya, Gustav. If something was to happen, say a prayer for me, will ya? [*Leaves.*]

[*The mob of rioters has now left the stage. The entrance hall gradually fills up with curious tenants.* OLD HILSE *goes about tying knots in his web.* GOTTLIEB *has taken an ax from behind the stove and instinctively is testing its edge. Both* OLD HILSE *and* GOTTLIEB *are agitated, but remain silent. From outside come the buzz and roar of a large crowd.*]

MOTHER HILSE. Tell me, Father, the boards is shakin' so—what's goin' on here? What's goin' to happen? [*Pause.*]

OLD HILSE. Gottlieb!

GOTTLIEB. What do ya want?

OLD HILSE. Put down that ax.

GOTTLIEB. And who'll chop the wood? [*He leans the ax against the stove.—Pause.*]

MOTHER HILSE. Gottlieb, listen to what your father says.

A VOICE [*singing outside the window*].

> The little man at home will stay
> Heigh-ho!
> And wash the dishes all the day
> Heigh diddle diddle, dum, dum, dum, hurrah!

[*It fades out.*]

GOTTLIEB [*leaps up, shakes his fist at the window*]. You son of a bitch, don't make me mad!

[*A volley is fired.*]

MOTHER HILSE [*starts up in alarm*]. Oh, dear Lord, is it thunderin' again?

OLD HILSE [*instinctively folding his hands*]. Dear God in heaven, protect the poor weavers, protect my poor brothers!

[*There is a short silence.*]

OLD HILSE [*to himself, deeply moved*]. Now the blood'll flow.

GOTTLIEB [*when the shots were heard, jumped up and held the ax tight in his hand. He is pale and scarcely able to control his great excitement*]. Well, are we to take it layin' down, even now?

GIRL [*calling into the room from the entrance hall*]. Father Hilse, Father Hilse, get away from that window. A bullet came right through our window upstairs. [*Disappears.*]

MIELCHEN [*puts her head in through the window, laughing*]. Grandpa, Grandpa, they're shootin' with guns. A couple of 'em fell down. One of 'em turned 'round in a circle—'round and 'round like a top. One's all floppin' like a sparrow with its head tore off. Oh, and so much blood spurtin' out—! [*She disappears.*]

A WOMAN WEAVER. They've killed some of 'em.

AN OLD WEAVER [*in the entrance hall*]. Watch out! They're goin' at the soldiers.

A SECOND WEAVER [*beside himself*]. Look at the women! Just look at the women! If they aren't liftin' up their skirts, and spittin' at the soldiers!

A WOMAN WEAVER [*calls in*]. Gottlieb, look at your wife. She's got more courage than you. She's jumpin' around in front of the bayonets like she was dancin' to music.

[FOUR MEN *carry a wounded man through the entrance hall. Silence. A voice is clearly heard saying, "It's Weaver Ullbrich." After a few seconds, the voice says again, "He's done for, I guess—a bullet got him in the ear." The men are heard walking up the wooden stairs. Sudden shouts from outside, "Hurray, hurray!"*]

VOICES IN THE HOUSE. Where'd they get the stones? Ya'd better run for it! From the road construction— So long, soldiers!—Now it's rainin' pavin' stones.

[*Shrieks of terror and yelling are heard outside and continuing in the entrance hall. There is a cry of fear, and the entrance door is banged shut.*]

VOICES IN THE ENTRANCE HALL. They're loadin' again.—
They're goin' to shoot again.—Father Hilse, get away
from that window.

GOTTLIEB [*runs for the ax*]. What! Are we mad dogs?
Are we to eat powder and shot instead of bread?
[*Hesitating a minute with the ax in his hand. To the
old man.*] Am I to stand by and let my wife get shot?
No, that mustn't happen! [*As he rushes out*]. Watch
out—here I come! [*Leaves.*]

OLD HILSE. Gottlieb, Gottlieb!

MOTHER HILSE. Where's Gottlieb?

OLD HILSE. He's gone to the devil.

VOICES [*from the entrance hall*]. Get away from the window, Father Hilse!

OLD HILSE. Not me! Not if ya all go crazy. [*To* MOTHER
HILSE *with mounting excitement.*] Here my Heavenly
Father put me. Right, Mother? Here we'll stay sittin'
and doin' what's our duty—even if the snow was to
catch fire.

[*He begins to weave. A volley is fired. Fatally hit,* OLD
HILSE *rises from his stool and then falls forward over
the loom. At the same time loud cries of "Hurray"
are heard. Shouting "Hurray" the people who have
been standing in the entrance hall rush outside. The
old woman asks several times: "Father—Father—
What's wrong with ya?" The steady shouting grows
more and more distant. Suddenly* MIELCHEN *comes
running into the room.*]

MIELCHEN. Grandpa, Grandpa, they're drivin' the soldiers out of town. They've attacked Dittrich's house.
They did like at Dreissiger's, Grandpa! [*Frightened,
the child sees that something is wrong—sticks her
finger in her mouth and cautiously steps close to the
dead man.*] Grandpa!

MOTHER HILSE. Come now, Father—say something!
You're scarin' me!

Curtain

ANTON CHEKHOV

Gerhart Hauptmann lived to be eighty-four years old. Anton Chekhov died when he was forty-four. The German playwright's collected works fill close to a dozen volumes. The Russian's half-dozen full-length plays can be contained in a single rather slender one. Yet, it is safe to say that Chekhov's influence has been as profound as Ibsen's and Strindberg's and certainly more profound than Hauptmann's.

I have already touched upon the sources of the Chekhovian magic in my Introductions to Dell's *Great Russian Short Stories* and *Great Russian Plays,* and I am loath to repeat myself. Let me now, then, instead of generalizing, look at the single play representing Chekhov in this collection, *The Sea Gull,* and examine it in some detail to see how the generalizations may become specifics.

This play, like all of Chekhov's, takes place somewhere in the country, where people of some means (though in this case not great wealth), surrounded by their neighbors, servants and friends, live what appear on the surface to be rather humdrum existences. Little happens. The talk is casual and prosaic—or so it seems until you begin to examine it. Then you discover that beneath their words lies "something unspoken" (to borrow from Tennessee Williams). These people's lives are inextricably tangled up in one another's.

"Everybody seems to be in love," murmurs Doctor Dorn as the curtain falls on the first of the play's four acts. How right he is! But how frustrating and un-requited most of it appears to be. Medvedenko loves. Masha, but Masha loves Konstantin, who in turn loves Nina, but Nina loves Trigorin. Round the circle it goes. But Konstantin also loves his mother who in her turn is in love with Trigorin too, and then Trigorin falls in love with Nina. Then there is Polina who loves the Doctor unrequitedly. Only Sorin and Shamraev have thoughts that seem not to be amorous!

Although *The Sea Gull* unfolds this complicated tale of unrequited loves, it does far more than that, else it would be hardly worthy of republication, save in the Sunday supplements. Arthur Miller, who con-sulted with me during the rehearsals of the Phoenix Theatre revival of this play in 1954, remarked, I recall, at the extraordinary revelation of the tortures of artis-tic creation which Trigorin expresses at such length in Act II. For Miller this scene was the apex of the play. For others, Konstantin's impassioned plea for "new forms" of art in Act I suggests that the author was using this play as a polemic against the old-fashioned melodramas so popular in the 1890s in Russia (and elsewhere). To still others it is the devastatingly accu-rate portrayal of the rather shallow artist, Irina Arka-dina, that attracts and repels and gives the play its main interest. Certainly, all three of these people (and they come alive as real people as few characters cre-ated by other dramatists ever do): Trigorin, Arkadina, Treplev, are fascinating characters. The former two so challenged the imaginations of Alfred Lunt and Lynn Fontanne that they undertook to revive the play with themselves in those roles. Treplev so intrigued Montgomery Clift that he was drawn to portray that part on the Phoenix Theatre stage. But for me it is Nina, after whom Chekhov named the play, who comes closest to expressing what the author had in mind, and it is she who provides the affirmative view of life that is the key to Chekhov.

"While I've been here," she confides to Konstantin in their last confrontation, "I've spent a lot of time walking and thinking . . . thinking . . . and I feel that my spirit's growing stronger every day. I know now, Kostya, that what matters most for us, whether we're writers or actors, isn't fame or glamour, or any of the things I used to dream of. What matters most is knowing how to endure, knowing how to bear your cross and still have faith. I have faith now and I can stand my suffering. . . . I'm not afraid of life."

It is this reconciliation with life, this final acceptance, despite the frustrations and tribulations one endures, that gives *The Sea Gull* its upward thrust. You must find that in this play or you will have mistaken Chekhov, as so many have done, for a morbid and melancholy Slav.

The Sea Gull was Chekhov's first major work for the stage and it was a failure when it was initially produced in 1896. Two years later Stanislavski restaged it as the second production of the newly established Moscow Art Theatre and the play was revealed as the truly profound human document it is. Then followed Art Theatre presentations of *The Three Sisters, Uncle Vanya* and *The Cherry Orchard,* Chekhov's other masterpieces. But the playwright was already suffering from incurable tuberculosis and in a few months after the première of *The Cherry Orchard* in 1904 he was dead. In this brief quartet of dramas he had managed, however, to instill into the theatre a new way of presenting the enigma of life—a way that seemed naturalistic on the surface, but that made all other naturalists look melodramatic and theatrical. People have undertaken ever since to emulate him, and our modern American theatre is filled with playwrights who are dubbed "Chekhovian." But no one yet has managed to capture the true rhythm of life using his oblique and elusive means.

The Sea Gull

by ANTON CHEKHOV

Translated by Robert W. Corrigan

From SIX PLAYS OF CHEKHOV.
Translated by Robert W. Corrigan.
Copyright © 1962 by Robert W. Corrigan.
All rights reserved.

Application for any use of this play should be made to Applause Theatre Book Publishers, 211 W. 71st Street, New York, NY 10023

CHARACTERS

Irina Nikolayevna Arkadina, an actress
Konstantin Gavrilovich Treplev, her son
Pyotr Nikolayevich Sorin, her brother
Nina Mihailovna Zarechny, a young girl,
daughter of a wealthy landowner
Ilya Afanasyevich Shamraev, Sorin's steward
Polina Andreyevna, his wife
Masha, his daughter
Boris Alexeyvich Trigorin, a famous writer
Yevgeny Sergeyevich Dorn, a doctor
Semyon Semyonovich Medvedenko, a school-
teacher
Yakov, a worker
Cook
Housemaid

*The action takes place in Sorin's house and garden. Be-
tween the third and fourth acts two years have passed.*

ACT ONE.

The lawn of SORIN'S *estate. A wide avenue of trees leads toward the lake. A roughly made stage has been erected and blocks the audience's view of the lake. Rushes surround the stage platform and there are chairs about. The sun is just setting and* YAKOV *is working on the stage behind the drawn curtain.* MASHA *and* MEDVEDENKO *enter, returning from a walk.*

MEDVEDENKO. Why do you always wear black?

MASHA. I'm in mourning for my life. I'm unhappy.

MEDVEDENKO. Why? [*Thinking.*] I don't understand. I mean, your health's good, and even if your father's not rich, he's pretty well off. My life's much harder than yours. I get only twenty-three rubles a month, before deductions, and yet I don't wear mourning.

MASHA. Money isn't everything. Even a beggar can be happy.

MEDVEDENKO. In theory he can, but in practice it's altogether different. For instance, I've got to support my mother, two sisters, my younger brother, and myself—all on twenty-three rubles a month. We have to eat and drink, don't we? And then we have to get tea and sugar; and what about tobacco? It isn't easy.

MASHA [*glancing at the stage*]. The play will be starting soon.

MEDVEDENKO. Yes. Nina's going to act, and Konstantin wrote the play. They're in love and tonight their souls will be united as they try to give expression to a work of art. But our souls aren't united. I'm in love with you. I long for you so desperately that I can't stand staying at home. Every day I walk four miles over here and four miles back, and all I ever get from you is cold indifference. Oh, I understand! I haven't any money, and I've got a large family to take care of . . . who'd want to marry a man who can't even feed himself?

MASHA. Don't be silly! [*Taking snuff.*] I'm touched by your love, but I can't return it, that's all. [*Offering him the snuff box.*] Help yourself.

MEDVEDENKO. No thanks. I don't feel like any right now.

[*Pause.*]

MASHA. My, how close it is! It will probably rain tonight. All you ever do is philosophize or talk about money. You think there's no greater misfortune than poverty, but I think it's a thousand times easier to wear rags and be a beggar than . . . but you wouldn't understand. . . .

[*Enter* SORIN *and* TREPLEV.]

SORIN. For some reason living in the country doesn't agree with me, my boy. Obviously, I'll get accustomed to it. Last night I went to bed at ten and I got up this morning at nine feeling as though my brain were glued to my skull from sleeping so long. [*Laughing.*] And, then, after dinner I accidentally fell asleep again, and now I'm a wreck—as though I'd had a horrible nightmare.

TREPLEV. You're right, Uncle, you ought to live in town. [*Noticing* MASHA *and* MEDVEDENKO.] We'll call you when the play's ready to begin, my friends, but you shouldn't be here now. Please go.

SORIN [*to* MASHA]. Marya Ilyinishna, I wish you'd ask your father not to tie up the dog. It keeps howling all the time. It kept my sister awake again last night.

MASHA. Why don't you tell him yourself? I won't, so don't ask. [*To* MEDVEDENKO.] Come, let's go.

MEDVEDENKO. You'll call us before the play starts, won't you?

[MASHA *and* MEDVEDENKO *go out.*]

SORIN. So the dog will howl all night again tonight. The strange thing is that I've never done anything I really wanted to do in the country. I used to come down here on my month's vacation for a rest, but no sooner had I gotten here when people began bothering me with all sorts of nonsense, and I was ready to leave almost as soon as I arrived. [*Laughs.*] I'm always glad when I leave. But that's the way it goes, now I'm retired and I haven't anywhere else to go. I've got to live here whether I want to or not. . . .

YAKOV. We're going for a swim, Konstantin Gavrilovich.

TREPLEV. Alright, but be sure to be back in ten minutes. [*Looking at his watch.*] We're going to start soon.

YAKOV. Yes, sir. [*Goes out.*]

TREPLEV [*looking at the stage*]. Now, here's a theatre for you! Nothing but a curtain and two wings. And beyond it . . . open space. No scenery, just a view of the lake and the horizon. We'll raise the curtain at eight-thirty when the moon comes up.

SORIN. Wonderful!

TREPLEV. But if Nina's late, then the whole effect will be ruined. She should be here by now. Her father and stepmother watch her so closely, it's almost impossible for her to get out of the house, it's like being in prison. [*Straightening his Uncle's tie.*] Your hair and your beard are never combed, Uncle, and you ought to have them cut, or at least trimmed.

SORIN [*combing his beard*]. That's the tragedy of my life. My appearance . . . Why, even when I was

younger I looked as if I were drunk. Women have
never liked me. [*Sitting down.*] Why's your mother
in such bad humor, today?

TREPLEV. She's bored, that's why! [*Sitting next to*
SORIN.] Bored, and jealous, too! She's annoyed with
me and doesn't want me to put my play on because
Nina's playing the part, and she's not. Why, she
hasn't even read my play, and still she hates it.

SORIN [*laughing*]. Really! What an idea!

TREPLEV. It makes her angry to think—even on this
tiny stage—that Nina and not she will triumph.
[*Looking at his watch.*] My mother's a real case, a
psychological freak. There's no doubt about it, she's
talented and intelligent; she can weep over a novel,
recite all of Nekrasov's poetry by heart, and nurse
the sick with the patience of an angel. But you just
try praising Duse—just one word. Watch out! You
can't praise anyone but her, you have to rave about
her, and go into ecstasy about her wonderful performance in *Camille* or *The Fumes of Life*. But such
intoxicating admiration isn't to be had here in the
country, so she's bored, and cross, and thinks that
we're all her enemies—that it's all our fault. And
she's superstitious too—afraid of three candles and
the number thirteen. *And* she's stingy! She's got seventy thousand rubles in the bank—I know it for a
fact—but just try to borrow some money and she'll
burst into tears.

SORIN. Somehow, you've gotten into your head that your
mother doesn't like your play and you're upset about
it. Don't worry, she worships the ground you walk on.

TREPLEV [*pulling petals from a flower*]. She loves me
. . . she loves me not . . . she loves me . . . loves me not
. . . loves me . . . loves me not. [*Laughing.*] See, my
mother doesn't love me. But, then, why should she?
She wants to live, have love affairs, and wear pretty

clothes; and here I am—twenty-five—always remind-
ing her that she's getting older. When I'm not
around, she's thirty-two; when I am, she's forty-
three . . . and she hates me for it. And she knows
that I despise the theatre! She *loves* the theatre, and
thinks she's serving humanity! But in my opinion our
theatre's in a rut. It's nothing but clichés and shop-
worn conventions. When the curtain opens on those
three-walled "living rooms," and I see those famous
and talented actors, those high priests of that sacred
art, parade about in their costumes in front of the
footlights showing the way people eat, drink, make
love, and walk about; when I hear them try to
squeeze a moral out of commonplace phrases and
meaningless events—some cliché that everyone knows
and is suitable for home consumption; when they
give me a thousand variations of the same old thing
over and over again . . . I have to leave! I want to
run away as Maupassant ran away from the Eiffel
Tower because its vulgarity was destroying him.

SORIN. But we can't do without the theatre.

TREPLEV. No, of course not! But we need new forms,
and if we can't have them, then it's better to have
nothing at all! I love my mother, love her very much,
but she leads a meaningless kind of life, always running around with that novelist, her name always
being tossed about in the newspapers. It disgusts me.
And sometimes, being just an ordinary, selfish person, I resent having a famous actress for a mother,
and wish she were an ordinary woman. I'd be a lot
happier! Uncle, can you imagine anything more impossible, more hopeless, than to be alone—a nonentity—in a room full of celebrities, writers and actors,
and know that you were being tolerated only because
you are her son? Who am I? What am I? I left the
University at the end of my junior year due to
"circumstances," as our editors put it, "over which

we have no control." I haven't any talent, no money, and I'm described on my passport as a shopkeeper from Kiev. Well, my father was a shopkeeper from Kiev, but he was a famous actor, too. So whenever all those famous artists who come to my mother's drawing room noticed me, I always knew from the looks on their faces that they thought I was an insignificant runt. I could read their thoughts and I had to suffer their humiliation. . . .

SORIN. By the way, what kind of person is this writer? I can't figure him out; he never says anything.

TREPLEV. Oh, I don't know. I think he's intelligent, pleasant, and a bit on the melancholy side. Really, a very decent fellow. He's well under forty, but he's already famous, and he can't complain about not having his share of everything. As for his work, well, let's say it's clever, it's charming, but after Tolstoi or Zola, you don't feel much like Trigorin.

SORIN. Well, my boy, I like writers. Years ago, there were just two things I wanted more than anything else in the world. One was to get married and the other was to be a writer. I never did either one. Even at that, it must be nice to be even a minor writer.

TREPLEV [*listening*]. I hear someone coming . . . [*Embracing his Uncle.*] I can't live without her . . . just the sound of her footsteps is beautiful . . . I'm insanely happy. [*He goes quickly to meet* NINA ZARECHNY *as she enters.*] Oh, it's you, my enchantress . . . my dream. . . .

NINA [*upset*]. Am I late? Oh, I hope I'm not late?

TREPLEV [*kissing her hands*]. No, no, no . . .

NINA. I've been so worried all day, and so afraid! I was afraid father wouldn't let me come, but he went out with my stepmother. The sky was red and the moon was coming up, and I had to race my horse faster and faster. [*She laughs.*] But I'm here! Oh, I'm so happy! [*She shakes* SORIN's *hand warmly.*]

SORIN [*laughing*]. Why, you've been crying! That isn't fair, you know.

NINA. It's nothing. . . . Oh, I'm so out of breath. I've got to leave in half an hour, so we'll have to hurry. I can't, I really can't, so don't ask me to stay. My father doesn't know I'm here.

TREPLEV. It's time to begin, anyhow. I'll go and call everybody.

SORIN. I'll go! I'll go at once! [*Goes off singing "The Two Grenadiers," and then stops and turns back.*] Once I started singing this, and the Assistant County Attorney said to me, "Your Excellency, you certainly have a powerful voice." Then he thought for a minute and said, "And a bad one, too!" [*Goes out laughing.*]

NINA. My father and stepmother won't let me come here. They say it's Bohemian . . . and they're afraid I'll go on the stage. But I feel pulled to this place, to this lake, as if I were a sea gull.

TREPLEV. We're alone.

NINA. I think someone's coming.

TREPLEV. Nobody's there.

[*They kiss.*]

NINA. What kind of tree is this?

TREPLEV. An elm.

NINA. Why is it so dark?

TREPLEV. It's late, everything's getting dark. Don't go early, please.

NINA. I have to.

TREPLEV. What if I followed you home, Nina? I'd stay in the garden all night looking up at your window.

NINA. No! You mustn't! The watchman would see you and Tresor isn't used to you yet. He'd bark.

TREPLEV. I love you.

NINA. Ssh . . .

TREPLEV [*hearing footsteps*]. Who's there? Is that you, Yakov?

YAKOV [*behind the stage*]. Yes, sir.

TREPLEV. Have you got the alcohol and the sulphur? Be sure to burn the sulphur when the red eyes appear! [*To* NINA.] You'd better get on stage, everything's ready. Are you nervous?

NINA. Yes, terribly. Your mother doesn't frighten me so much, but Trigorin terrifies me. I'm so ashamed of acting in front of him . . . a famous writer. Tell me, is he young?

TREPLEV. Yes.

NINA. His stories are so wonderful!

TREPLEV [*coldly*]. I wouldn't know; I haven't read them.

NINA. It's hard to act in your play. There aren't any living characters in it.

TREPLEV. Living characters! We don't have to show life as it is, or even as it ought to be, but as we see it in our dreams!

NINA. But there's hardly any action in your play—just speeches. And, then, I think there should be some love in a play.

[*Both go behind the stage. Enter* POLINA *and* DORN.]

POLINA. It's getting damp out here. Please go back and put on your galoshes.

DORN. I'm hot.

POLINA. Why don't you take care of yourself? You're just being obstinate. You're a doctor, and you know perfectly well that the damp air is bad for you; you just want to make worry. You stayed on the patio last night on purpose.

DORN [*hums*]. "Please don't say that youth is gone . . ."

POLINA. You were so absorbed in your conversation with Irina, that you didn't even notice the cold. Admit it, you find her attractive.

DORN. I'm fifty-five.

POLINA. So! A man's not old at that age. You're still

good looking and attractive to women.

DORN. Well, what am I to do about it?

POLINA. You're all so anxious to worship an actress. Every one of you!

DORN [*hums*]. "Once more I stand before you . . ." People always admire artists, they always have. That's why they treat them with more respect than, say, salesmen. It's a kind of idealism.

POLINA. And I suppose it's idealism that makes women fall in love with you and throw themselves at you.

DORN. All I can say is, that in my relationship with women there's been a great deal that was fine and good. Anyway, they liked me mostly for my skill as a doctor. You must remember that ten or fifteen years ago, I was the only decent obstetrician in the whole county. And, besides, I've always been honest with people.

POLINA [*taking his arm*]. Oh, you dear man.

DORN. Ssh! They're coming.

[*Enter* MADAME ARKADINA *on* SORIN'S *arm,* TRIGORIN, SHAMRAEV, MEDVEDENKO, *and* MASHA.]

SHAMRAEV. I remember seeing her at the Poltara Fair in '73. She was a marvelous actress! A sheer delight. Just marvelous! By the way, do you happen to know where Chadin—Pavel Semyonich Chadin—the comedian, is now? He was unmatchable as Raoplyvev, even better than Sadovsky, I can assure you, my dear lady. But where is he now?

IRINA. You keep asking me about all those old fossils. How in the world should I know where he is? [*She sits.*]

SHAMRAEV [*sighing*]. Ah, Pashka Chadin—we don't have actors like that any more. Yes, Irina Nikolayevna, the theatre's declining! Where are the mighty oaks of the past? Today we've nothing but stumps!

DORN. You're right, we don't have many great actors today, but the average actor is much more competent. On the whole, the level of acting is higher.

SHAMRAEV. I can't agree with you there, but that's a matter of taste, *De gustibus aut bene aut nihil.*

[TREPLEV *enters from behind the stage.*]

IRINA. When's it going to start, dear?

TREPLEV. In a minute. Please be patient.

IRINA [*reciting from "Hamlet"*].

"Oh, Hamlet, speak no more!
Thou turn'st mine eyes into my very soul;
And there I see such black and grained spots
As will not leave their tinct."

TREPLEV [*reciting from "Hamlet"*].

"And let me wring thy heart, for so I shall,
If it be made of penetrable stuff."

[*A horn is sounded off stage.*] Ladies and gentlemen, we are ready to begin! Your attention, please! [*Pause.*] We'll begin! [*Tapping the floor with a stick and reciting in a loud voice.*] Oh, venerable shadows of olden days, ye shades that float over this lake at night, lull us to sleep and bring us dreams of what will be in two hundred thousand years.

SORIN. There'll be nothing in two hundred thousand years!

TREPLEV. Then, let the actors show us that nothing!

IRINA. Yes, please do. We're almost asleep already.

[*The curtain opens, revealing the view of the lake, with the moon above the horizon casting its reflection on the water.*]

NINA [*dressed in white, is sitting on a huge rock*]. Men, lions, eagles, and partridges, horned deer, geese, spiders, and the silent fish of the deep, starfish and creatures which cannot be seen by the eye—all living things, all living things, all living things, having completed their cycle of sorrow, are now extinct. For thousands of years the earth has given birth to no living thing, and this poor moon now lights its lamp in vain. In the meadows, the cranes no longer waken with a cry, and the sound of the May beetles, humming in the lime groves, can no longer be heard. It is cold, cold, cold! Deserted, deserted, deserted! Frightening, frightening, frightening! [*Pause.*] All living creatures have turned to dust and the eternal matter has transformed them into rocks, water, and clouds, while the souls of all beings have been merged into one soul. The common soul of the world is I . . . I. . . . In me is the soul of Alexander the Great, of Caesar, of Shakespeare, of Napoleon, and of the lowest form of worm. In me the consciousness of men is fused with the instincts of the animals. I remember all things, all, all, all, and in me every single life shall live anew!

[*Will-of-the-Wisps appear.*]

IRINA [*in a whisper*]. This is right out of the decadent school of the symbolists.

TREPLEV [*imploring and reproaching her*]. Mother!

NINA. I am alone. Once in a hundred years I open my lips to speak, and then my voice echoes mournfully in the void, unheard by all. . . . You, too, pale spirits, do not hear me. The stagnant marsh gives birth to you before the rising of the sun, and you wander until the day breaks . . . without thought, without will, without a tremor of life. The Prince of Darkness, the father of Eternal Matter, fearing that life should be born again in you, has created in you, as in the rocks and water, a continuum of atoms, so that your being is in constant flux. In the whole of the universe, the spirit alone remains constant and unchanged. [*Pause.*] Like a prisoner thrust into a deep and empty well, I know not what I am nor what lies before me. All I know is that I am destined to struggle with the Prince of Darkness, and that in that cruel and bitter battle I shall emerge victorious over the forces of matter, and then the spirit will join with matter in a triumphant harmony, and the Kingdom of the Cosmic Will will have arrived. But this must come gradually, little by little, through countless millennia when the moon, and bright Sirius, and all the earth are slowly turned to dust. Until then, only horror, horror . . . [*Pause. Two red spots appear in front of the lake.*] Look! My all-powerful enemy, the Prince of Darkness, is approaching. I see his terrible bloody eyes. . . .

IRINA. That's the smell of sulphur, isn't it?

TREPLEV. Yes.

IRINA [*laughing*]. That's a good effect. Fine!

TREPLEV. Mother!

NINA. He is lost without Man. . . .

POLINA [*to* DORN]. You've taken off your hat. Put it on again before you catch cold.

IRINA. The doctor's taken his hat off to the Prince of Darkness, the Father of Eternal Matter.

TREPLEV [*flaring up angrily*]. That's enough! The play's over! Curtain!

IRINA. But what are you so cross about?

TREPLEV. Enough! Enough, I say! Close the curtain! [*Stamping his feet.*] Curtain! [*The curtain closes.*] Forgive me! I forgot that only the élite are permitted to write plays and act in them. I've encroached on the rights of the monopoly! I . . . I mean . . . I . . . [*Tries to say more, but cannot; waves his hand and goes off.*]

IRINA. What's wrong with him?

SORIN. Irina, my dear, you must have more respect for a young man's pride!

IRINA. But what did I say?

SORIN. You hurt his feelings.

IRINA. He told us that it was only a joke, so that's the way I took it.

SORIN. All the same . . .

IRINA. And now it seems he's written a masterpiece.

Imagine that! He didn't concoct this little show and stink up the air with sulphur as a joke, but to teach us something. He wanted to show us how to write plays and what kind of plays we should act in. Really, this is getting a little tiresome! These everlasting attacks at my expense, these pinpricks; why it's enough to make a saint lose patience. Really, you must admit he's a conceited, impossible boy!

SORIN. But he wanted so much to please you.

IRINA. Did he really? Well, he didn't choose an ordinary play; instead he made us listen to these decadent outbursts. I'll even listen to the ravings of a madman, if it's a joke, but here we have only pretentiousness— new forms of art, a new era of creativeness! As far as I'm concerned, it's not a matter of new forms, but of bad temper.

TRIGORIN. Everyone writes what he wants to write and as best he can.

IRINA. Let him write whatever he likes and as he can, I don't care. Only just don't let him bother me with it. That's all I ask.

DORN. Jupiter, you're angry. . . .

IRINA. I'm not Jupiter, I'm a woman! [*Lighting a cigarette.*] And I'm not angry, I'm just annoyed that the boy wastes his time that way. I certainly didn't mean to hurt his feelings.

MEDVEDENKO. There's no basis for making a distinction between matter and spirit. After all the spirit is nothing more than a combination of atoms. [*Excitedly to* TRIGORIN.] But you know, someone ought to write a play about how teachers live. That ought to be put on the stage! Did you know we lead a very hard life?

IRINA. That's true, but let's not talk of it now; or about plays or atoms either. It's such a pleasant evening. Listen! Do you hear the singing?

[*All listen.*]

POLINA. It's on the other side of the lake.

[*Pause.*]

IRINA [*to* TRIGORIN]. Sit down here beside me, my dear. You know, ten or fifteen years ago you could hear music and singing almost every night. There are six estates on the lake. Oh, and I remember such laughter, and noise, and there were shootings too—and the love affairs, love affairs all the time. . . . And the idol and favorite of all those estates, was our dear friend here. . . . [*Turning to* DORN.] May I present, Dr. Yevgeny Sergeyevich. He's still a charming, delightful man, but in those days he was irresistible. But my conscience is beginning to bother me. Why did I hurt the poor boy's feelings? Now, I'm all upset about it. [*Calling.*] Kostya! Oh, Kostya, dear!

MASHA. I'll go and look for him.

IRINA. Will you please, my dear.

MASHA [*going out*]. Yoo-hoo! Konstantin Gavrilovich! Yoo-hoo!

NINA [*coming from behind the stage*]. I guess we're not going on, so I might as well join you. Hello, everybody! [*Kisses* IRINA *and* POLINA.]

SORIN. Bravo! Bravo!

IRINA. Bravo! Bravo! You were wonderful. You know, with your good looks and lovely voice you oughtn't to stay out here in the country. It's a sin. You have real talent. Believe me, you owe it to yourself to become an actress . . . and to the rest of us, too.

NINA. Oh, that's my one and only dream! [*Sighing.*] But it'll never come true.

IRINA. Who knows? But, forgive me, let me introduce you to Mr. Trigorin. Boris Alexeyvich Trigorin . . .

NINA. Oh, I'm so glad. . . . [*Overcome with embarrassment.*] I love your books. . . . I've read everything you . . .

IRINA. Here now, my dear, don't be shy. Yes, he's a

famous man, but he's a gentle one, too. You notice, he's shy himself.

DORN. We might as well open the curtain again, don't you think? It has a rather strange effect the way it is now.

SHAMRAEV [*shouting*]. Yakov, open the curtain, will you!

[*The curtain opens.*]

NINA [*to* TRIGORIN]. It's a strange play, isn't it?

TRIGORIN. I didn't understand a word of it, but I enjoyed watching it. And you acted very well—with great sincerity. And the scenery was very beautiful. [*Pause.*] There must be a lot of fish in that lake.

NINA. Yes.

TRIGORIN. I love to fish. There's nothing I'd rather do than sit on the bank of a river in the evening and fish.

NINA. That's so strange. I can't see how anyone who'd experienced the joy of true creation could ever find pleasure in anything else.

IRINA [*laughing*]. Hush, child! When people talk like that to him, he doesn't know what to say.

SHAMRAEV. I remember one night at the opera in Moscow I heard the famous Silva hit low C. By a strange coincidence, one of the basses in our church choir was in the gallery, and suddenly—to everyone's amazement—we heard from the gallery, "Bravo, Silva!" . . . But a whole octave lower. Like this: [*In a deep bass.*] "Bravo, Silva!" Why the audience was thunderstruck! You could actually hear a pin drop. [*Pause.*]

DORN. The angel of silence has flown over us!

NINA. Well, it's time for me to go. Good-bye, everyone.

IRINA. Where are you off to so soon? You mustn't go!

NINA. My father's expecting me.

IRINA. What a man, really. . . . [*Embracing.*] Well, if you must . . . We're terribly sorry you have to go.

NINA. If you only knew how much I hate to go.

IRINA. Someone really ought to take you, child.

NINA [*frightened*]. Oh, no, no!

SORIN [*to* NINA, *pleading*]. Please stay.

NINA. I just can't, Pyotr Nikolayevich.

SORIN. Just for an hour, that's all.

NINA [*thinking a moment, and then tearfully*]. I can't [*Shakes hands with him and goes off.*]

IRINA. How unfortunate she is. They say her mother left her huge fortune to her husband—every bit of it—and now the girl has nothing, because her father married again and is leaving all the money to his new wife. It's terrible!

DORN. Yes, her father's a real beast. I grant you that.

SORIN [*rubbing his hands to keep warm*]. I think we'd better go in, too, my friends. It's awfully damp and my legs are beginning to ache.

IRINA. Oh, your poor legs! They're so stiff you can hardly walk—just like wood. Here, let me help you. Come along, my dear. [*Taking his arm.*]

SHAMRAEV [*offering his arm to his wife*]. Madame?

SORIN. The dog's howling again. [*To* SHAMRAEV.] Ilya Afanasyevich, will you be good enough to have him taken off his chain?

SHAMRAEV. It's impossible, Pyotr Nikolayevich. Thieves might break into the barn and I've just brought the grain in. [*To* MEDVEDENKO, *who's beside him.*] Imagine, a whole octave lower. Bravo, Silva! And he wasn't really a singer, he just sang in the choir.

MEDVEDENKO. How much do they pay to sing in the choir?

[*All leave but* DORN.]

DORN [*alone*]. I don't know, perhaps I don't know anything about it, and maybe I'm crazy . . . but I liked that play. It's got something about it. When that girl talked about loneliness, and later when those red eyes appeared, why I was so moved that my hands were trembling. It was new, fresh, naïve . . . ah, but here he comes. I must tell him lots of nice things about it.

TREPLEV [*entering*]. So, they've gone already!

DORN. I'm here.

TREPLEV. Masha's been looking all over for me. I can't stand her!

DORN. Kostya, I liked your play very much. It's a strange piece, and of course I haven't heard it all, but it did make a deep impression on me. You're a talented man and you must go on writing. [TREPLEV *shakes his hands and embraces* DORN *impulsively*.] That's enough now. You're so nervous; and there are tears in your eyes. . . . What I mean to say is this: You're dealing with abstract ideas, and that's good and as it should be, because a work of art must express some great idea or it will fail. Only the sublime, those things conceived with great seriousness, can ever be truly beautiful. . . . How pale you are!

TREPLEV. So you think I should go on writing?

DORN. Why, of course, I do. But you must only write about things that are significant and permanent. You know, my boy, I've lived a full life and had many experiences. I've enjoyed myself and I am satis-fied. But if it had been my good fortune to experi-ence the exaltation that an artist must feel at the moment of creation, I think I'd have come to despise this body of mine, and all of its pleasures, and my soul would fly off into the heights.

TREPLEV. Excuse me, but where's Nina?

DORN. Just one more thing. There must be a clear and definite idea in a work of art—you must know why you're writing—if not, if you walk along this en-chanted highway without any definite aim, you will lose your way and your talent will ruin you.

TREPLEV [*impatiently*]. Where's Nina?

DORN. She's gone home.

TREPLEV. What am I going to do? I've got to see her. . . . I've got to! I'm going.

[*Enter* MASHA.]

DORN [*to* TREPLEV]. Calm down a bit, my friend.

TREPLEV. But I'm going! I must go.

MASHA. Please come in, Kostya. Your mother's terribly worried and she's waiting for you.

TREPLEV. Tell her I've gone. And please, I beg of you— all of you—let me alone! Just let me alone! Don't follow me about.

DORN. Come, come, my dear boy . . . you shouldn't carry on like this. . . . It's not right.

TREPLEV [*in tears*]. Good-bye, Doctor. Thank you . . . [*Leaves.*]

DORN [*sighing*]. Ah, youth! It always has its own way.

MASHA. When people don't know what else to say, they say, "Ah, youth!" [*Taking some snuff.*]

DORN [*taking the snuff box from her and throwing it into the bushes*]. How disgusting! [*Pause.*] I think I can hear them singing in the house. We'd better go in.

MASHA. Wait just a minute.

DORN. What is it, child?

MASHA. There's something I've got to tell you again. . . . I've got to talk . . . [*Very upset.*] I really don't like my father, and you've always seemed more of one than he. For some reason I've always felt very close to you. Please help me. Help me, or I'll do something foolish that will mock life and ruin it. . . . I can't go on like this. . . .

DORN. But what is it, my child? How can I help you?

MASHA. Oh, I'm so unhappy. Nobody, nobody knows how unhappy I am. [*Leaning against* DORN, *and speaking very softly.*] I love Kostya.

DORN. How upset everyone is! How upset! And every-

body seems to be in love. . . . It must be the magic
of the lake! [*Tenderly*.] But what can I do, my child?
What can I do?

Curtain

ACT TWO.

A lawn on the SORIN *estate. In the background on the right, a house with a large patio. On the left, a view of the lake with bright sunlight reflected in the water. It is about noon and hot. On one side of the lawn* IRINA, DORN, *and* MASHA *are sitting on a garden seat in the shade of an old lime tree.* DORN *has an open book on his lap.*

IRINA [*to* MASHA]. Come, let's stand up. [*Both get up.*] Stand by my side. You're twenty-two and I'm nearly twice your age. Doctor, which of us looks younger?

DORN. Why, you, of course.

IRINA. There, you see! And why is it? Because I work, I'm involved in things, I'm always on the go, while you sit in the same place all the time, you aren't really living. . . . And I make it a rule never to think about the future! And I never think of getting old, or of death. What will be, will be.

MASHA. And I feel as though I'm a thousand years old, and I'm dragging my life behind me like a dress with an endless train. . . . And most of the time I don't have the slightest desire to go on living. Of course, that's all nonsense. I must pull myself out of this depression.

DORN [*humming quietly*]. "Tell her, pretty flowers . . ."

IRINA. And let me tell you one more thing—I am very particular about my appearance. You must never let yourself go, and that's why I'm always properly dressed and have my hair done in the latest fashion. Do you think I'd ever go out, even into the garden, in my dressing-gown or without combing my hair?

Never. I've stayed young because I've never been sloppy or let myself go, as most women do. . . . [*Walking up and down the lawn, her hands on her hips.*] There! you see? I'm as free as a bird. Why, I could play the part of a fifteen-year-old tomorrow!

DORN. Well, I might as well get on with the reading. [*Picking up the book.*] We stopped at the place where the corn merchant and the rats . . .

IRINA. Yes, the rats. Go on. [*Sits down.*] No, wait! Give it to me, I'll read. It's my turn. [*Takes the book and is looking for the place.*] The rats . . . yes, here we are. [*Reads.*] "And it's also true that it is as dangerous for the people in the higher circles of society to pamper and encourage novelists, as it is for corn merchants to breed rats in their granaries. And yet novelists are always pursued. Once a woman has chosen a writer whom she wishes to capture, she besieges him with compliments, flattery and favors." Well, that may be true of the French, but nothing like that goes on here. We don't plan and connive. Here a woman is usually head over heels in love with a writer long before she ever decides to capture him. You see that of course? For instance, take Trigorin and myself . . .

[SORIN *enters leaning on his stick with* NINA *walking beside him.* MEDVEDENKO *follows, wheeling an empty wheel chair.*]

SORIN [*fondly, as to a child*]. Indeed? So we're happy today, are we? We're feeling cheerful at last? [*To his sister.*] We're happy because our father and stepmother have gone to Tver, and now we're free for three whole days.

NINA [*sitting down beside* IRINA, *embraces her*]. I'm so happy! Now I can be with you.

SORIN [*sitting down in his wheel chair*]. Doesn't she look pretty today?

IRINA. Beautifully dressed and her face is just glowing

. . . She's such a fine girl. . . . [*Kisses her.*] But we mustn't praise her too much. It's bad luck. Where's Boris Alexeyvich?

NINA. He's down at the bathing house . . . fishing.

IRINA. I'm amazed he doesn't get bored with it! [*Prepares to go on reading.*]

NINA. What are you reading?

IRINA. Maupassant's "On the Water," darling. [*Reading a few lines to herself.*] Oh, well, this next bit isn't interesting. We'll skip it . . . and besides it's not true. [*Closes the book.*] I'm so worried. I wish somebody would tell me what's the matter with Kostya? Why is he so sullen and depressed? He's out on the lake day after day and I never see him.

MASHA. His heart's troubled. [*To* NINA, *shyly.*] Please, Nina, won't you read us something from his play?

NINA [*shrugging her shoulders*]. If you'd like, but it's so dull.

MASHA [*restraining her enthusiasm*]. When he reads it, his eyes shine and his face turns pale. He has a beautiful sad voice and he looks like a poet.

[SORIN *snores.*]

DORN. Good-night, everybody!

IRINA. Petrusha!

SORIN. Eh? What's that?

IRINA. You've fallen asleep!

SORIN. Why, I have not.

[*A pause.*]

IRINA. You're not taking your medicine. You know you should.

SORIN. I'd be glad to take my medicine, but the good doctor here won't give me any.

DORN. Medicine! At sixty!

SORIN. Even at sixty a man wants to live.

DORN [*annoyed*]. Oh, all right then, take some valerian drops.

IRINA. I think it would do him a lot of good to go to

the springs for a while.

DORN. Well, he might go . . . or he might not.

IRINA. And what does that mean?

DORN. Nothing at all. It's perfectly clear.

[A pause.]

MEDVEDENKO. Pyotr Nikoláyevich, you ought to stop smoking.

SORIN. Nonsense.

DORN. No, it isn't nonsense. Wine and tobacco destroy one's individuality. After a cigar or a glass of vodka you're no longer just Pyotr Nikolayevich, but Pyotr Nikolayevich plus somebody else. You lost your sense of identity, and instead of seeing yourself as you are, you begin to feel like you are someone else . . . a kind of third person.

SORIN [laughing]. It's all very well for you to talk. You've had a good life, but what about me? I've worked in the Department of Justice for twenty-eight years, but I haven't really lived, I haven't really experienced anything, I want to go on living. You've had a full life and don't care any more, that's why you can be so philosophical—but I want to live. That's why I drink sherry at dinner and smoke cigars, and all that. . . . And that's that. . . .

DORN. Certainly, life has to be taken seriously, but when it comes to taking cures at sixty and regretting that you didn't get enough pleasure out of life when you were young—all that, forgive me, is just a waste of time.

MASHA [gets up]. It must be almost lunch time. [Walking languidly and with an effort.] My leg's gone to sleep. [Goes out.]

DORN. She'll go in and have a couple of drinks before lunch.

SORIN. She's not very happy, poor girl.

DORN. Oh, nonsense, your Excellency!

SORIN. That's easy for you to say. You've had everything you've ever wanted.

IRINA. Oh, what can be more boring than being in the country. It's so hot and muggy, and nobody does anything but sit around and philosophize . . . Oh, it's pleasant to be here with you, my friends, I like to listen to you, but . . . how wonderful it is to sit alone in a hotel room learning a part!

NINA [*enthusiastically*]. Oh, yes! I know just what you mean!

SORIN. Yes, of course it's better in town. You can sit in your study, and the doorman doesn't let anyone come in unannounced and bother you, you have a telephone. . . . There are cabs on the streets, and all that sort of thing. . . .

DORN [*humming*]. "Tell her, pretty flowers . . ."

[SHAMRAEV *comes in, followed by* POLINA ANDREYEVNA.]

SHAMRAEV. Here you all are! Good morning! [*Kisses* IRINA's *hand, then* NINA's.] Glad to see you looking so well. [*To* IRINA.] My wife tells me that you're planning on going to town with her today. Am I right?

IRINA. Yes, we are thinking of going.

SHAMRAEV. Why, that's splendid. But—my dear lady, how do you propose to get there? We're hauling rye today, and all the men are busy. And besides, what horses are you going to use?

IRINA. What horses? How should I know what horses?

SORIN. Why, we'll use the carriage horses.

SHAMRAEV [*getting excited*]. The carriage horses? And where am I to get harnesses for the carriage horses? Just tell me, where am I to get harnesses? You people amaze me! It is really more than I can understand! My dear lady! Please forgive me. I have the greatest respect for your talent, I'd give ten years of my life for you—but I can't let you have any horses.

IRINA. But it so happens I *have* to go! Do you understand?

SHAMRAEV. My dear lady! Do you realize the problems there are in farming?

IRINA [*angrily*]. The same old story! All right, then, order me some horses from the village, or else I'll walk to the station. I'm leaving for Moscow today!

SHAMRAEV [*angrily*]. In that case, I resign. You can look for another manager. [*Goes out.*]

IRINA. Every summer it's like this, every time I come here I'm insulted! I'll never set foot in this place again! [*Going out in the direction of the bathing shed which is offstage; a moment later she is seen entering the house, followed by* TRIGORIN, *who is carrying fishing-rods and a pail.*]

SORIN [*flaring up*]. This is the limit! Such insolence! I'm sick and tired of it, once and for all! Harness every horse we've got and bring them here! This minute!

NINA [*to* POLINA]. To say not to Irina Nikolayevna, the famous actress! Even her slightest wish, her smallest whim, is more important than your silly old farming. It's simply incredible.

POLINA [*in despair*]. But what can I do? Put yourself in my place, what can I do?

SORIN [*to* NINA]. Let's go in and try to persuade my sister not to leave. [*Looking in the direction in which* SHAMRAEV *has gone.*] You're insufferable, man! Tyrant!

NINA [*preventing him from getting up*]. Sit still, sit still. . . . We'll take you in. [*She and* MEDVEDENKO *push the wheel chair.*] All this is just terrible!

SORIN. You're right, it is terrible! But he won't leave, I'll talk to him right away.

[*They go out;* DORN *and* POLINA *are left alone.*]

DORN. People are so tiresome. Quite frankly, your husband ought to be thrown out. But of course, like always, that old woman, Pyotr Nikolayevich, and his sister will go begging his forgiveness. You'll see.

POLINA. He's even sent the carriage horses out into the

fields. And this sort of thing goes on every day. If you only knew how it upsets me! It makes me ill; see how I'm shaking. . . . I can't stand his rudeness. [*Pleading with him.*] Yevgeny, my darling, please let me come with you. . . . Time is passing us by; we're not young any longer. . . . If . . . if we could only . . . at least for the rest of our lives . . . stop pretending, stop hiding the way we feel . . .

DORN. My dear, I'm fifty-five; it's too late to change now.

POLINA. I know, you refuse me because you've got other women, too. You can't live with us all. I understand. Forgive me . . . you're tired of me.

[NINA *appears near the house; she is picking flowers.*]

DORN. No, that's not so.

POLINA. I'm wracked with jealousy. Of course, you're a doctor, you can't avoid women. I understand. . . .

DORN [*to* NINA, *who approaches*]. Well, have things quieted down in there?

NINA. Irina's crying and Pyotr's had an attack of asthma.

DORN [*getting up*]. I suppose I'd better go in and give them both some valerian drops.

NINA [*handing him the flowers*]. For you!

DORN. *Merci bien!* [*Going up to the house.*]

POLINA [*going with him*]. Such beautiful flowers! [*Near the house, in a low voice.*] Give them to me!

[*He gives them to her and she tears them to pieces and throws them aside. Both go into the house.*]

NINA [*alone*]. How strange it is to see a famous actress crying . . . and over nothing! And isn't it strange that a famous writer spends all his time fishing. Here he is, a best seller, written about in all the papers, his pictures everywhere, his books translated into foreign languages, and . . . he gets all excited if he catches a couple of perch. I always thought that famous people were proud and aloof and that they despised the crowd; I thought they used their glory and fame to get revenge on people who put wealth and position above everything else. But here they are crying, and fishing, and playing cards, and laughing and getting upset like everyone else.

TREPLEV [*enters, carrying a gun and a dead sea gull*]. Are you all alone?

NINA. Yes. [TREPLEV *lays the sea gull at her feet.*] What does this mean?

TREPLEV. I was rotten enough to kill this sea gull to-day. I lay it at your feet.

NINA. What's wrong with you? [*Picks up the sea gull and looks at it.*]

TREPLEV [*after a pause*]. And soon I'm going to kill myself in the same way.

NINA. What *is* wrong with you? This isn't like you at all!

TREPLEV. That's true! I began to change when you did. You've changed toward me and you know it. . . . You're cold to me, and my very presence bothers you.

NINA. You've been so irritable lately, and most of the time you talk in riddles and I don't understand a word you're saying. And I suppose now that this sea gull, here, is some kind of symbol too. Well, forgive me, I don't understand that either. . . [*Putting the sea gull on the seat.*] I'm too simple-minded to understand you.

TREPLEV. It all began the night my play failed. Women never forgive failure. Well, I burnt it! Every bit of it! Oh, if you only knew how unhappy I am! And the way you've rejected me, I can't understand it! . . . It's as if I woke up one morning and found the lake suddenly drying up. You just said that you're too simple-minded to understand me. Tell me, what's there to understand? Nobody liked my play, so now you despise my talent, and think I'm ordinary and insignificant, like all the rest of them. . . . [*Stamping his foot.*] Oh, how well I understand. How well! It's like a nail in my head. . . . Oh, damn it. . . . And my pride . . . sucking my life blood . . . like a snake. . . . [*Sees* TRIGORIN, *who enters, reading.*] But here comes the real genius, he walks like Hamlet himself, and with a book, too. [*Mimics.*] "Words, words, words." . . . The sun has hardly touched you, and already you're smiling and your eyes are melting in its rays. I won't bother you any more . . . [*Goes out quickly.*]

TRIGORIN [*making notes in his book*]. Takes snuff and drinks vodka. Always wears black. A schoolmaster in love with her . . .

NINA. Good morning, Boris Alexeyvich!

TRIGORIN. Good morning. It seems that unexpectedly we're going to leave today. I don't suppose we'll meet again. I'm sorry. I don't often get a chance to meet young and interesting girls like you. I've forgotten what it feels like to be eighteen or nineteen; in fact, I can't even imagine it any more. That's why the young girls in my novels and stories usually ring false. I wish I could change places with you, just for an hour, so I could know your thoughts and the kind of person you are.

NINA. And I'd like to be in your place for a while.

TRIGORIN. What for?

NINA. So I'd know what it feels like to be famous, to be a talented writer. What does it feel like to be famous? What does it do to you?

TRIGORIN. What does it feel like? I don't know, I've never thought about it. [*After a moment's thought.*] It's one of two things, I suppose: either you exaggerate my fame, or it's nothing at all.

NINA. But you must read about yourself in the papers?

TRIGORIN. When they praise me I'm pleased, and when they attack me I'm in bad humor for a couple of days.

NINA. What a wonderful world you live in! How I envy you—if only you knew! . . . How different people's destinies are! Most people are all alike—unhappy. This obscure, tedious existence just drags on and on. And, then, there are others—like you, one in a million—who have a bright and interesting life, a life that has significance. Yours is a happy destiny.

TRIGORIN. Mine! [*Shrugs his shoulders.*] You talk about fame and happiness, and this bright and interesting life I lead. But—to me all these fine words of yours, you must forgive me, are like great delicacies which I never eat. You are very young and very kind.

NINA. Your life is beautiful.

TRIGORIN. What's beautiful about it? [*Looking at his watch.*] I've got to go and write. Excuse me, I can't stay. . . . [*Laughs.*] You've stepped on my favorite corn, as the saying goes, and here I'm beginning to get excited and even angry. But let's talk. Let's talk about my bright and beautiful life. Where should we begin? [*After a moment's thought.*] Do you know what it is to have a compulsion? You know, when a man thinks about the same thing night and day, about . . . say, the moon. Well, I have my moon. I'm obsessed by one thought: I must write, I must write, I must. . . . For some reason, no sooner have I finished one novel, when I feel I've got to start another, then another, then another. . . . I write without stopping. Now, what's so bright and beautiful about that? It's absurd! Here I am with you, I'm excited, and yet I can never forget for a moment that there's an unfinished novel waiting for me. I look up and I see a cloud that looks like a grand piano. . . . Immediately I think I've got to put it into a story. There's the scent of heliotrope in the air. I make a mental note: "sickly scent . . . a widow's flower . . . use it when describing a summer night." . . . I take every word, every sentence I speak, and every word you say, too, and quickly lock them up in my literary warehouse —in case they might come in handy sometime. When I finish my work, I go off to the theatre, or on a fishing trip, hoping to relax and forget myself. But no; there's a new subject rolling around in my head like a cast iron ball. So immediately I drag myself back to to my desk again, and I keep on writing and writing. . . . And it's always like that, always. . . . I have no rest from myself. I feel as though I'm devouring my own life, and that for the sake of the honey I give to everybody else I strip my best flowers of their pollen, tearing them up, and trampling on their roots. Do you think I'm crazy? Do you think my relatives and friends treat me like a normal person? "What are you writing down now? What's that for?" It's the same thing over and over again, until I begin to think that my friends' attention, their praise and admiration, is nothing but phony, that they're trying to fool me just as if I were insane. Sometimes I think they are going to come up to me from behind and put me into an insane asylum. And when I was younger and just starting out, then my writing was a constant torment. A minor writer, especially if he hasn't had much luck, feels clumsy, and awkward, and unnecessary. He's nervous and can't resist being around people connected with literature and the arts. But when he's with them, they don't notice him and he just wanders about afraid to look them straight in the eyes, like a passionate gambler without any money. I'd never seen any of my readers, but for some reason I always imagined them to be unfriendly and skeptical. I was frightened to death of people and public occasions, and it terrified me. Whenever a new play of mine was produced, I always felt that the dark-haired people in the audience were hostile to it, and the fair-haired ones coldly indifferent. It was awful! Such agony.

NINA. But surely you have moments of happiness and exaltation—times when you feel inspired and your work's going well?

TRIGORIN. Yes, while I'm writing I enjoy it. I enjoy

reading the proofs, too, but . . . as soon as it's published, I can't stand it. Suddenly, I see that it wasn't what I intended, that I'd missed here, and that I should have cut there, and then I feel angry and get depressed. . . . [*Laughing.*] And then the public reads it and says: "Yes, it's charming, very well done. . . . Charming, but, of course, it's not Tolstoi." . . . Or "A fine piece, but Turgenev's *Fathers and Sons* is better." And that's the way it will be until my dying day . . . everything will be charming and well done —and nothing more. And after I'm dead my friends will pass by my grave, and say: "Here lies Trigorin. He was a good writer, but no Turgenev."

NINA. Please forgive me, but I refuse to understand. You're simply spoiled by success.

TRIGORIN. What success? I've never liked myself. I don't like what I write. And worst of all I live in a sort of daze, and I often don't even understand what I'm writing. I love this lake, the trees and the sky. I have an affinity for nature, it arouses a sort of passion in me, an irresistible desire to write. But, you see, I'm not just a landscape painter, I'm also a citizen. I love my country. I love its people. As a writer, I feel it's my duty to write about my people and their sufferings and their future—and about science and the rights of man, and so on, and so forth. And so I write about everything, always in a great hurry rushing to meet deadlines, having people angry with me, dashing about from one side to the other like a fox cornered by the hounds. I see science and society moving onward, while I drop further and further behind, like a peasant who's just missed his train, and finally, I come to feel that all I can do is to paint landscapes, and that everything else is false—false to the core.

NINA. You've been working too hard, and you just don't want—or haven't the time—to recognize just how important you really are. You may be dissatisfied with yourself, but to the rest of us you're a great and wonderful person! If I were a writer like you, I'd give my whole life to the people, knowing that their happiness consisted in striving to rise to my level—and that they'd harness themselves to my chariot.

TRIGORIN. A chariot, is it! . . . Am I an Agamemnon, or what?

[*Both smile.*]

NINA. For that kind of happiness—the happiness of being a writer or an actress—my family could disown me; I'd live in a garret with nothing to eat but rye bread; I could stand disappointment; I'd put up with the knowledge of my own weaknesses. . . . But in return I'd demand fame . . . real, resounding fame. . . . [*Covering her face with her hands.*] Oh, it makes me dizzy even to think of it.

IRINA'S VOICE [*from the house*]. Boris Alexeyvich!

TRIGORIN. She's calling me. . . . I've got to pack, I suppose. But I don't feel like going. [*Looks round at the lake.*] What a beautiful sight! How lovely it is!

NINA. Do you see that house over there, with the garden?

TRIGORIN. Yes.

NINA. It was my mother's. I was born there and I've spent all my life on this lake. I know every island on it.

TRIGORIN. It's a beautiful place! [*Seeing the sea gull.*] What's that?

NINA. A sea gull. Kostya killed it.

TRIGORIN. What a beautiful bird! Really, I don't want to go. Try to persuade Irina Nikolayevna to stay. [*Writes in his notebook.*]

NINA. What are you writing?

TRIGORIN. Just making a note . . . An idea for a story suddenly came into my head. A young girl, like you, has lived in a house on the shore of a lake since she

was a little girl; she loves the lake like a sea gull,
and she's as free and happy as a sea gull. Then a
man comes along, sees her, and having nothing better to do, destroys her, like this sea gull here.

[*A pause.* IRINA *appears in the window.*]

IRINA. Boris Alexeyvich, where are you?

TRIGORIN. I'm coming! [*Goes, then looks back at* NINA.
To IRINA *at the window.*] What is it?

IRINA. We're staying.

[TRIGORIN *goes into the house.*]

NINA [*moves forward; after a few moments' medita-
tion*]. It's a dream!

Curtain

ACT THREE.

The dining-room in SORIN'S *house. Doors right and left. A sideboard and a medicine cupboard. In the middle of the room, a table. A trunk and some cardboard hat boxes indicate people are preparing to leave.* TRIGORIN *is having his breakfast while* MASHA *stands beside the table.*

MASHA. I'm telling you all this because you're a writer. You can use it if you want to. Honestly, if he had seriously wounded himself, I couldn't have gone on living for another minute. But I'm getting courageous. I've just decided that I'd tear this love of mine out of my heart by the roots.

TRIGORIN. How?

MASHA. I'm going to marry Medvedenko.

TRIGORIN. The schoolmaster?

MASHA. Yes.

TRIGORIN. But why?

MASHA. Why love without hope, why wait years for something . . . when you can't be sure of what it is you're waiting for? . . . Anyway, when I'm married there won't be any time for love, new responsibilities will take the place of . . . Anyhow, it'll be a change, you know. Let's have another.

TRIGORIN. Do you think we should?

MASHA. Oh, come! [*Fills two glasses.*] Don't look at me like that. Women drink a lot more than you think. A few of us drink openly, but most of them do it in secret. Yes. And it's always vodka or cognac. [*Clinks glasses.*] Well, here's to you! You're a fine man—I'm sorry you're leaving. [*They drink.*]

TRIGORIN. I don't feel like going myself.

MASHA. Why don't you ask her to stay?

TRIGORIN. No, she'd never stay now. Her son is behaving very tactlessly. First he shoots himself, and now they say he's going to challenge me to a duel. What for? He sulks and groans, and preaches new art forms. . . . But there's room for all kinds—new and old. Why make such a fuss about it?

MASHA. He's jealous, too. But that's not my affair. [*A pause.* YAKOV *comes in carrying a suitcase.* NINA *comes in and stands by the window.*] My schoolteacher's not very bright and he's poor, but he's kind and very fond of me. I'm sorry for him and for his old mother, too. Well, I wish you all the best. Please remember me kindly. [*Shakes his hand.*] I'm grateful to you for your interest and your friendship. . . . Send me your books and be sure to inscribe them. Only don't write: "To the highly respected" and all that, just put "To Marya, who has no place and no object in life." Good-bye! [*Goes out.*]

NINA [*holds out her hand toward* TRIGORIN, *with her fist clenched*]. Odd or even?

TRIGORIN. Even.

NINA [*with a sigh*]. Wrong. I only had one pea in my hand. I was trying to guess my fortune—should I go into the theatre or not. If only someone would advise me!

TRIGORIN. One can't give advice about that kind of thing.

[*A pause.*]

NINA. You're going to leave and . . . perhaps we'll never meet again. I want you to have this little medallion to remember me by. Please take it! I had your initials engraved on it . . . and on the back the title of your book—*Days and Nights.*

TRIGORIN. How exquisite! [*Kisses the medallion.*] It's a beautiful gift!

NINA. Think of me sometimes.

TRIGORIN. Of course, I will. I'll think of you as you were on that sunny day—do you remember?—a week ago, when you were wearing that white dress . . . we talked . . . there was a white sea gull lying on the seat.

NINA [*pensively*]. Yes, a sea gull. . . [*A pause.*] We can't talk any more, someone's coming. Let me see you for just two minutes before you go, please. . . .

[*Goes out. At the same time* IRINA *and* SORIN *come in, the latter wearing a frock-coat with the star of an order on it.* YAKOV *follows with luggage.*]

IRINA. You really ought to stay here, dear. Do you think you're up to so much visiting with your rheumatism as bad as it is? [*To* TRIGORIN.] Who just left—Nina?

TRIGORIN. Yes.

IRINA. I'm sorry we disturbed you. . . . [*Sits down.*] Well, I guess everything's packed. I'm worn out.

TRIGORIN [*reading the inscription on the medallion*]. *Days and Nights,* page 121, lines 11 and 12.

YAKOV [*clearing the table*]. Should I pack your fishing rods too, sir?

TRIGORIN. Yes, I'll be wanting them again. But you can give the hooks away.

YAKOV. Yes, sir.

TRIGORIN [*to himself*]. Page 121, lines 11 and 12. What can they be? [*To* IRINA.] Are any of my books in the house?

IRINA. Yes, in Pyotr's study, in the corner bookcase.

TRIGORIN. Page 121 . . . [*Goes out.*]

IRINA. Really, Petrusha, you'd better stay here.

SORIN. You are going away—I couldn't stand it without you here.

IRINA. But what is there to do in town?

SORIN. Oh, nothing in particular, but just the same . . . [*Laughs.*] There'll be the laying of the cornerstone of the City Hall at Zemstvo. . . . I'd like to do something! Live for a change! If only for an hour or two.

For a long time now, I've felt that I've just been lying around, like an old cigarette-holder on a shelf. The horses are coming at one, so we can get started then.

IRINA [*after a pause*]. You'd better stay here. Don't be bored and don't catch cold. Look after my son. Take care of him. Advise him. [*A pause.*] Here I am going away, and I'll never know why he tried to shoot himself. Probably jealousy, so the sooner I take Trigorin away from here, the better.

SORIN. That's part of it, but there were other reasons, too. It's not surprising, really. He's young, he's intelligent, but he's stuck out here in the country with no money, no position, and no future. He hasn't anything to do, really, and he's ashamed and afraid of his idleness. I am extremely fond of him, and he's fond of me too, but that doesn't change the fact that he feels he's a charity case and doesn't really belong here. After all, he does have his pride.

IRINA. He's caused me a great deal of anxiety! [*Pondering.*] He really ought to get a job. . . .

SORIN [*begins to whistle, then speaks irresolutely*]. I think maybe the best thing would be for you to give him some money. In the first place, he needs clothes. Just look at him, he's been wearing the same old jacket for the last three years, and he runs around without a topcoat. . . . [*Laughs.*] Yes, and it wouldn't hurt him to have a little fun, either . . . go abroad. . . . It wouldn't cost too much.

IRINA. Well, I might be able to afford the suit, but as for going abroad . . . That's out of the question. As a matter of fact, right now I haven't the money for a suit. [*Resolutely.*] I haven't got the money. [SORIN *laughs.*] Well, I don't!

SORIN [*whistling*]. Why, of course! Forgive me, my dear, I didn't mean to annoy you. I believe you. . . . You're a generous, kind-hearted woman.

IRINA [*tearfully*]. I haven't any money!

SORIN. If I had any money I'd give it to him, but I haven't got a penny. [*Laughs.*] My manager takes every bit of my pension and spends it on the farm —buying cattle and bees. It's just a waste of money! The cows and the bees die, and he never lets me use the horses. . . .

IRINA. Well, of course, I have some money, but after all, I'm an actress: my dress bill alone is enough to ruin me.

SORIN. You're a fine woman, my dear. . . . I respect you. . . . Yes . . . But something's the matter with me again. . . . [*Sways.*] I'm getting dizzy. [*Holds on to the table.*] I feel faint.

IRINA [*alarmed*]. Petrusha! [*Trying to support him.*] Petrusha, my dear! . . . [*Calling.*] Help! Help! . . .

[TREPLEV, *with a bandage round his head, and* MEDVE-DENKO *come in*] He's fainting!

SORIN. It's all right, it's nothing. . . . [*Smiles and drinks some water.*] It's better already. . . .

TREPLEV [*to his mother*]. Don't be frightened, Mamma, it's not serious. Uncle's been having these attacks a lot lately. [*To his uncle*]. You'd better go and lie down for a while, Uncle.

SORIN. Yes, for a while . . . But I'm going to town just the same. I'll lie down for a bit, then I'm going. . . . That's definite. . . . [*Goes out, leaning on his stick.*]

MEDVEDENKO [*supporting him by the arm*]. Here's a riddle for you: what walks on four legs in the morning, two at noon, and three in the evening. . . .

SORIN [*laughing*]. That's right. And at night on its back. I can manage alone, thank you. . . .

MEDVEDENKO. Come, come, let's not stand on ceremony. [*Goes out with* SORIN.]

IRINA. How he frightened me!

TREPLEV. It's not good for him to go on living out here. He gets depressed. Why don't you be generous, Mother, and lend him a couple of thousand? Then he could stay in town all year round.

IRINA. I haven't any money. I'm an actress, not a banker.

[*A pause.*]

TREPLEV. Mamma, will you change my bandage for me? You do it so well.

IRINA [*takes some iodine and a box of bandages out of the medicine cabinet*]. The doctor's late.

TREPLEV. He promised to be here by ten, and it's noon already.

IRINA. Sit down. [*Takes the bandage off his head.*] This looks like a turban. Yesterday some stranger was asking in the kitchen what nationality you were. It's almost healed; Just a tiny bit still open here. [*Kisses him on the head.*] Promise me you won't play with guns while I'm away?

TREPLEV. I promise, Mamma. I just lost control of myself I was in such despair. It won't happen again. [*Kisses her hands.*] You've got such wonderful hands. I remember long ago, when you were still touring— I was a little boy then—there was a fight in our courtyard. A washerwoman was badly beaten. Do you remember? She was unconscious . . . and you went to see her several times and took medicine to her, and bathed her children. Don't you remember?

IRINA. No. [*Puts on a fresh bandage.*]

TREPLEV. Two ballet dancers lived in the house then, too. . . . They used to come and have coffee with you. . . .

IRINA. I remember that.

TREPLEV. Weren't they pious! [*A pause.*] During these last few days, Mother, I've loved you as tenderly and as dearly as I used to when I was a little boy. I have no one left but you now. Only why, why, are you under the influence of that man?

IRINA. You don't understand him, Konstantin. He's one of the most honorable men I've ever known. . . .

TREPLEV. And yet, when he was told I was going to challenge him, his honor didn't prevent him from acting like a coward. He's leaving. Such ignominy!

IRINA. What nonsense! I asked him to go myself.

TREPLEV. One of the most honorable men you've ever known! Here you and I are practically quarreling over him, and at this very moment he's probably in the garden or the drawing-room laughing at us . . . cultivating Nina's potential, doing his best to convince her finally that he's a genius.

IRINA. You seem to enjoy saying these unpleasant things to me. I admire him, so please don't speak badly of him in my presence.

TREPLEV. Well, I don't! I know. You want me to think he's a genius too, but I'm sorry, Mother. I don't like telling lies. His books make me sick.

IRINA. You're jealous! Mediocrities who have grand ideas about themselves have to run down people with real talent. I hope it comforts you!

TREPLEV [ironically]. Real talent! [Angrily.] I have more talent than any of you if it comes to that! [Tearing the bandage off his head.] It's conventional, stiff-necked people like you who've usurped the highest places in the arts today. You regard only what you do yourselves as genuine and legitimate. Everything else you stifle and suppress! I refuse to accept your authority! I refuse to accept you or him!

IRINA. You decadent upstart!

TREPLEV. Go on back to your precious little theatre and act in your lousy, third-rate plays!

IRINA. I've never acted in lousy, third-rate plays! Let me alone! You can't even write a decent scene! You're nothing but a hack from Kiev! A parasite!

TREPLEV. Miser!

IRINA. Tramp! [TREPLEV sits down and weeps.] Nonentity! [Walks up and down in agitation, then stops.] Don't cry. . . . You mustn't cry! . . . [Weeps.] You mustn't. . . . [Kisses his forehead, then his cheeks and his head.] Please, forgive me, my darling.

... Forgive your wicked mother. Forgive a very unhappy woman.

TREPLEV [*embraces her*]. Oh, Mother, if only you knew! I've lost everything. She doesn't love me, and I can't write any more ... all my hopes are gone.

IRINA. Don't despair. ... Everything will work out. He's, leaving today, and then she'll love you again. [*Wipes away his tears.*] That's enough. We've made up now.

TREPLEV [*kissing her hands*]. Yes, Mamma.

IRINA [*tenderly*]. Make up with him, too. There's no need for a duel. ... Is there, really?

TREPLEV. All right, Mamma, if you say so. Only I don't want to see him. It hurts too much ... I just couldn't stand it. ... [TRIGORIN *comes in.*] There he is. ... I've got to go. ... [*Quickly puts away the dressings in the cupboard.*] The doctor will take care of the bandage. ...

TRIGORIN [*paging through the book*]. Page 121 ... lines 11 and 12. Here it is. ... [*Reads.*] "If you ever need my life, come and take it."

[TREPLEV *picks up the bandage from the floor and goes out.*]

IRINA [*glancing at her watch*]. The carriage will be here soon.

TRIGORIN [*to himself*]. "If you ever need my life, come and take it."

IRINA. I hope you're packed!

TRIGORIN [*impatiently*]. Yes, yes ... [Musing.] Why is it I feel so sad about the plea of that dear, pure soul? Why is it that my heart aches with such pity? ... "If ever you need my life, come and take it." [*To* IRINA.] Why don't we stay one more day? [IRINA *shakes her head.*] Please, let's stay!

IRINA. Darling, I know what keeps you here. But please, try to control yourself. She's intoxicated you, but now it's time to sober up.

TRIGORIN. You should try to be sober, too—be sensible, be reasonable. Try to understand this like a real friend, please, my dear. . . [*Takes her hand.*] You're capable of sacrifice. . . . Be my friend, let me go. . . .

IRINA [*very upset*]. Is she that fascinating?

TRIGORIN. I'm terribly drawn to her! Perhaps it is just what I need.

IRINA. The love of a little country girl? Oh, how little you know yourself!

TRIGORIN. Sometimes people go to sleep on their feet, and that's what's happened to me. Here I am, I'm talking to you, but all the time I'm dreaming of her. I'm possessed by sweet and wonderful dreams. . . . You must let me go. . . .

IRINA [*trembling*]. No, no . . . What do you think I am? I'm just an ordinary woman, you can't talk to me that way. . . . Don't torture me, Boris. . . . I'm so afraid. . . .

TRIGORIN. If you wanted to, you could be so much more than that! The only thing in this life that is worth having and makes you truly happy . . . is love—a love that's young and beautiful, a love that's poetic, a love that carries you off into the world of dreams. I've never known that kind of love. When I was young I didn't have time; I was always sitting around in some editor's office, struggling to get just enough money to eat on. And suddenly, it's happened! That love has come to me. . . . It calls me on and bids me to follow it. . . . How can I run away from it now? . . . And why should I?

IRINA [*angrily*]. You're out of your mind!

TRIGORIN. And why not?

IRINA. Everyone's in a conspiracy to torture me today! [*Weeps.*]

TRIGORIN [*taking his head in his hands*]. You don't understand! You don't want to understand!

IRINA. Am I really so old and ugly that you can talk to me about other women? [*Embraces and kisses him.*] Oh, you've gone out of your mind! My beautiful, my wonderful you. The last page of my life! [*Falls on her knees.*] My joy, my pride, my happiness! . . . [*Embraces his knees.*] If you leave me even for a single hour I won't survive it, I'll go out of my mind —my wonderful, marvelous, magnificent man, my master. . . .

TRIGORIN. Someone might come in. [*Helps her to her feet.*]

IRINA. Let them, I'm not ashamed of my love for you. [*Kisses his hands.*] My darling reckless boy, you may want to be mad, but I won't let you, I won't let you. . . . [*Laughs.*] You're mine . . . mine. . . . This forehead is mine, and these eyes, and this lovely silky hair. . . . All of you is mine. You're so gifted, so talented—you're the best of all the modern writers, Russia's only hope. . . . You have such sincerity, simplicity, freshness, envigorating humor. . . . With one touch you capture the essence of a character or a landscape; people in your books are alive. It's impossible to read them and not be moved. Oh, you think this is just hero-worship, that I'm flattering you! Come, look into my eyes . . . look. . . . Do I look like a liar? There, you see—I'm the only one who truly appreciates you, I'm the one person in the world who always tells you the truth, my darling, my wonderful man. . . . You are coming? Yes? You won't leave me?

TRIGORIN. I haven't any will of my own . . . I've never had a will of my own. Flabby, feeble, submissive— how can a woman want that kind of man? All right, take me, carry me off, but don't let me ever move a step away from you. . . .

IRINA [*to herself*]. He's mine! [*Casually, as if nothing had happened.*] But, of course, darling, you can stay if you want to. I'll go by myself, and you can come later next week, if you want. After all, there's no need for you to hurry.

TRIGORIN. No, we'll go together.

IRINA. Just as you like. Let's go together then. . . . [*A pause.* TRIGORIN *writes in his notebook.*] What are you writing?

TRIGORIN. I heard a good phrase this morning—"The Maiden's Forest." . . . Might use it sometime. [*Stretches.*] So we're going? More trains, stations, restaurants, chops, conversations . . .

SHAMRAEV [*coming in*]. It's with regret that I've come to say that everything's ready. It's time, my dear lady, that we leave for the station: the train gets in at five minutes after two. Will you do me a favor, Irina Nikolayevna? Will you find out where Suzdaltzev is now? Is he alive? Is he well? We used to drink together years ago. . . . He was wonderful in *The Mail Robbery.* . . . I remember at that time there was a tragedian, Izmailov, who always played with him at Elizavetgrad. . . . He was a remarkable person too. Don't rush, my dear lady, we don't have to start for another five minutes. Once they were playing the villains in some melodrama, and when they were suddenly discovered they had the line: "We're caught in a trap." But Izmailov said, "We're taught in a cap." [*Laughs loudly.*] "Taught in a cap!"

[*While he's speaking,* YAKOV *is busy with the suitcases; a* MAID *brings* IRINA's *hat, coat, umbrella, and gloves, and everyone helps her to put them on. The* CHEF *looks in through the door at left, and after some hesitation enters.* POLINA, *then* SORIN *and* MEDVEDENKO *also come in.*]

POLINA [*with a small basket in her hand*]. Here's some fruit for the trip . . . very ripe. You might feel like having something refreshing.

IRINA. You are very kind, Polina Andreyevna.

POLINA. Good-bye, my dear! If everything hasn't been just as you like it, please forgive us. [*Weeps.*]

IRINA [*embracing her*]. Everything was fine! Don't cry!

POLINA. Time flies so fast!

IRINA. There's nothing we can do about it.

SORIN [_wearing an overcoat with a shoulder cape and a hat, and carrying a cane, comes in from the door at left. He speaks as he walks across the room_]. You'd better hurry, Sister, if you don't want to miss the train. . . . I'm going to get into the carriage. [_Goes out._]

MEDVEDENKO. I'll walk to the station . . . to see you off. I'll be there in no time. [_Goes out._]

IRINA. Good-bye, everyone. . . . If all goes well, we'll.be here next summer. . . . [_The_ MAID, _the_ CHEF, _and_ YAKOV _kiss her hand._] Don't forget me. [_Gives the_ CHEF _a ruble._] Here's a ruble for the three of you.

CHEF. Thank you very much, madam. Have a pleasant journey. Thank you for your kindness.

YAKOV. God speed!

SHAMRAEV. Perhaps you'll write to us, it would make us very happy! Good-bye, Boris Alexeyvich.

IRINA. Where is Kostya? Tell him I'm leaving. We must say good-bye. Think kindly of me. [_To_ YAKOV.] I gave a ruble to the chef. It's for the three of you.

[_All go out. The stage is empty. There is the noise off-stage of people being seen off. The_ MAID _returns to fetch the basket of fruit from the table and goes out again._]

TRIGORIN [_returning_]. I've forgotten my cane. I think I left it out here on the patio. [_Walks toward the door at left and meets_ NINA, _who comes in._] It's you! We're going. . . .

NINA. I knew we'd see each other again. [_Excitedly._] Boris Alexeyvich, I've decided, the die is cast—I'm going into the theatre. I'm going tomorrow, I'm leaving my father and everything else, and I'm going to begin a new life. . . . I'm going to Moscow . . . like you. . . . And then I shall see you there.

TRIGORIN [_glancing behind him_]. Stay at the Slavansky Bazaar. Let me know as soon as you get there . . . at

Molchanovka, Groholsky House. . . . I've got to hurry. . . .

[*A pause.*]

NINA. Just one minute . . .

TRIGORIN [*in an undertone*]. You're so beautiful. . . . Oh, how happy I am when I think that we'll be with each other soon! [*She leans her head on his breast.*] That I'll see these wonderful eyes again, this inexpressibly beautiful, tender smile . . . these soft features, the expression of angelic purity! My darling . . . [*A prolonged kiss.*]

Curtain

[*Between the* THIRD *and the* FOURTH ACTS *there is an interval of two years.*]

ACT FOUR

One of the drawing-rooms in SORIN'S *house, converted into a study for* KONSTANTIN TREPLEV. *Doors right and left leading to other rooms. In the middle, French doors opening on to the terrace. There is a desk in the corner on the right and a sofa by the door on the left; also a bookcase and the usual drawing-room furniture. Books are lying on the window sills and on chairs. It is evening. The room is dimly lit by a shaded table lamp. There is the noise of wind in the trees and the chimneys. A* WATCHMAN *is tapping. Enter* MEDVEDENKO *and* MASHA.

MASHA [*calling*]. Konstantin Gavrilovich! Konstantin Gavrilovich! [*Looking round.*] No, there's no one here. The old man keeps on asking where's Kostya, where's Kostya? . . . He can't get along without him. . . .

MEDVEDENKO. He's lonely. [*Listening.*] What horrible weather! It's been like this for nearly two days now.

MASHA [*turning up the lamp*]. And the waves on the lake are getting bigger, too.

MEDVEDENKO. And it's so dark out. By the way, we might as well tell them to tear down that stage in the garden. It stands there like a skeleton—naked and ugly with its curtains flapping in the wind. You know, last night as I was walking past it, I was sure I heard someone crying there.

MASHA. What next . . .

[*A pause.*]

MEDVEDENKO. Masha, let's go home.

MASHA [*shaking her head*]. No, I'm going to stay here tonight.

MEDVEDENKO [*imploringly*]. Please, Masha, let's go! The baby'll be hungry.

MASHA. Nonsense! Matryona will feed him.

[*A pause.*]

MEDVEDENKO. But I feel sorry for him. This is the third night now that he's been without you.

MASHA. Oh, don't be so tiresome! At least you used to philosophize once in a while. Now all you ever do is talk about the baby and home, baby and home—that's all I hear.

MEDVEDENKO. Please, come, Masha!

MASHA. Go by yourself.

MEDVEDENKO. Your father won't give me a horse..

MASHA. Yes, he will. Ask him.

MEDVEDENKO. I suppose I could. . . . And you'll come home tomorrow?

MASHA [*takes snuff*]. All right . . . tomorrow. Now stop pestering me! [*Enter* TREPLEV *and* POLINA. TREPLEV *carries pillows and a blanket and* POLINA *some sheets, which they put on the sofa.* TREPLEV *then goes to his desk and sits down.*] Who's this for, Mother?

POLINA. It's for Pyotr Nikolayevich. He wants to sleep in Kostya's room.

MASHA. Here, let me. . . . [*Makes the bed.*]

POLINA [*sighing*]. Old people are like children. . . . [*Walks over to the writing desk and, leaning on her elbow, looks at a manuscript.*]

[*A pause.*]

MEDVEDENKO. Well, I'd better go. Good-bye, Masha. [*Kisses his wife's hand.*] Good-bye, Mother. [*Tries to kiss his mother-in-law's hand.*]

POLINA [*with irritation*]. Well, then go if you're going.

MEDVEDENKO. Good-bye, Konstantin Gavrilovich [TREPLEV *gives him his hand without speaking;* MEDVEDENKO *goes out.*]

POLINA [*looking at the manuscript*]. Who'd have guessed that you would turn out to be a real writer,

Kostya? And now, thank God, the magazines are paying you for your work. [*Strokes his hair.*] You've gotten so handsome, too. . . . Kostya, my dear, you're so good, won't you try to be kinder to Masha?

MASHA [*making the bed*]. Leave him alone, Mother.

POLINA [*to* TREPLEV]. She's a fine girl. . . . [*A pause.*] All a woman wants, Kostya, is that sometimes a man give her a kind look. Believe me, I know.

[TREPLEV *gets up from his desk and goes out without speaking.*]

MASHA. Oh, Mother, now you've made him angry! Why pester him like that?

POLINA. I feel so sorry for you, Mashenka!

MASHA. A lot of good that does me!

POLINA. My heart aches for you. I see it all, you know. . . . I understand it all.

MASHA. Nonsense. Love without hope—that doesn't exist except in novels. It's nothing really. You've just got to keep a firm grip on yourself, stop yourself from hoping . . . from hoping that things will change. . . . If you begin to feel love, you just forget it! Anyway, they've promised to transfer my husband to another county. As soon as we get there, I'll forget all about it . . . tear it out of my heart by the roots.

[*A melancholy waltz is played two rooms away.*]

POLINA. Kostya's playing again. He must be very sad.

MASHA [*dancing two or three waltz steps*]. The most important thing, Mother, is not to see him all the time. Just wait till Semyon get's his transfer . . . you'll see, I'll forget it in a month. The whole thing's nonsense.

[DORN *and* MEDVEDENKO *enter, wheeling in* SORIN.]

MEDVEDENKO. I've got six people to take care of now, and flour's two kopecks a pound.

DORN. Yes, you've got to work hard to make ends meet.

MEDVEDENKO. That's easy for you to say. You've got more money than you know what to do with.

DORN. Money? My friend, after thirty years of practice —thirty years of being on call night and day—all I've managed to save is two thousand rubles, and I've just spent them on my trip abroad. I haven't got anything either.

MASHA [to her husband]. So you haven't gone yet?

MEDVEDENKO [apologetically]. Well . . . how could I? They wouldn't give me a horse.

MASHA [bitterly, in an undertone]. I can't stand the sight of you!

[SORIN is wheeled to the side of the room; POLINA, MASHA and DORN sit down beside him; MEDVEDENKO, looking depressed, stands to one side.]

DORN. My, what a lot of changes you've made! You've turned this drawing-room into a study.

MASHA. It's more convenient for Konstantin Gavrilovich. This way he can walk out into the garden whenever he feels like it, and he can think there.

[The WATCHMAN taps.]

SORIN. Where's my sister?

DORN. She's gone to the station to meet Trigorin. She'll be back soon.

SORIN. I must be very sick, if you had to send for my sister. [Pause.] It's a funny thing, here I'm very sick, and no one gives me any medicine.

DORN. Well, what would you like to have? Valerian drops? Soda? Quinine?

SORIN. The same old thing! Now, I suppose you're going to begin philosophizing! Oh, it's so trying! [Jerks his head in the direction of the sofa.] Is my bed ready yet?

POLINA. Yes, Pyotr Nikolayevich, it's all ready.

SORIN. Thank you.

DORN [hums]. "The moon is floating in the midnight sky . . ."

SORIN. You know, I'm going to give Kostya a subject for a story. I'd call it: "The Man Who Wished."

"L'homme qui a voulu." When I was young I wanted to be a writer—and I didn't; I wanted to be a good speaker—and I spoke miserably— [*Mimicking himself.*] "and all that sort of thing, and all the rest of it, and so on, and so forth." . . . When I tried to sum up a case, I'd go plodding on and on until I broke out into a terrible sweat. . . . I wanted to get married —and I didn't, I always wanted to live in town—and here I am finishing my life in the country, and so and so on . . .

DORN. You wanted to become a state's attorney, and you did.

SORIN [*laughs*]. I didn't want that, it just happened.

DORN. Imagine, being dissatisfied with life at sixty-two! You've got to admit that's a bit indecent.

SORIN. Won't you ever stop! Can't you understand someone wanting to live?

DORN. Don't be foolish. Every life has to end—that's the law of nature.

SORIN. That's talk from a man who's had everything he's ever wanted. You've had your fill, so you don't have to worry. But when death comes, you'll be afraid of it, too.

DORN. The fear of death is an animal fear. You've got to overcome it. Only religious people should fear death. They believe in a future life, so they're afraid they'll be punished for their sins. You're different; first of all, you're not religious, and secondly, what sins have you committed? You served in the courts for twenty-five years . . . and that's all.

SORIN [*laughs*]. Twenty-eight years . . .

[*Enter* TREPLEV, *who sits down on a stool at* SORIN's *feet.* MASHA *gazes at him continuously.*]

DORN. We're keeping Konstantin Gavrilovich from his work.

TREPLEV. Oh, it doesn't really matter.

[*A pause.*]

MEDVEDENKO. Excuse me, Doctor, but what city did you like best?

DORN. Genoa.

TREPLEV. Why Genoa?

DORN. Because everything's so alive. You go out of your hotel at night, and the street is crowded with people. You can go anywhere you want, and there's always that crowd. Pretty soon you become part of it, you live with it, and before long you come to believe that a world-soul really does exist. It's something like the world-soul in your play, Kostya; you know, the one Nina Zarechny acted in a couple of years ago. By the way, where is she now? How is she?

TREPLEV. I believe she's quite well.

DORN. Someone told me she'd been leading a rather strange life. What happened?

TREPLEV. Well, it's a long story, Doctor.

DORN. All right, make it short then.

[A pause.]

TREPLEV. Well, she ran away from home and had an affair with Trigorin. You knew that, didn't you?

DORN. Yes, that I did know.

TREPLEV. She had a child and it died. Trigorin got tired of her and went back to his old attachments, as might have been expected. Not that he'd ever given them up; for, being the spineless character he is, he somehow managed to make the best of both worlds. As far as I can gather, Nina's personal life has turned out a complete failure.

DORN. And what about her career in the theatre?

TREPLEV. I guess that's even worse. She began in a small theatre at some resort near Moscow, then she went to the provinces. At that time I never lost track of her, and for months I followed her wherever she went. She always played big parts, but her acting was crude and lacked taste—she tended to rant and over-gesture. She had some good moments—when she cried or played a death scene—that showed she had some talent, but they were only moments.

DORN. Then she has some talent, after all?

TREPLEV. It's very hard to say. Suppose she must have. I saw her of course, but she wouldn't see me, and I never got to see her at her hotel. I knew how she felt so I didn't insist on seeing her. [*A pause.*] Well, what else is there to say? Afterward, when I got back here, I had some letters from her, affectionate, intelligent letters. . . . She never complained, but I could tell that she was very unhappy, every line showing that her nerves were on edge. And then her mind seemed to be a little unbalanced. She always signed herself "Sea Gull." You remember, in Pushkin's *The River Nymph* the miller calls himself a raven. Well, in her letters, she always called herself "The Sea Gull." By the way, she is here now.

DORN. How do you mean—here?

TREPLEV. I mean she's staying at a hotel in town. She's been there for the last five days. I went to see her, and Masha went too, but she won't see anybody. Semyon insists that he saw her yesterday afternoon walking in the fields a mile or so from here.

MEDVEDENKO. Yes, I saw her. She seemed to be walking toward town. I bowed to her and asked her why she didn't come and see us. She said she would.

TREPLEV. She won't! [*A pause.*] Her father and stepmother won't even see her. They've got watchmen all over to see that she doesn't come to the house. [*Goes with the* DOCTOR *toward the writing desk.*] It's so simple to be philosophical on paper, Doctor, but it's so hard in real life.

SORIN. She was a charming girl.

DORN. What?

SORIN. I said she was a charming girl. You know, I was actually in love with her for a while.

DORN. Why, you old philanderer!

[*Offstage* SHAMRAEV *can be heard laughing.*]

POLINA. I think they're back from the station. . . .

TREPLEV. Yes, I can hear mother.

[*Enter* IRINA *and* TRIGORIN, *followed by* SHAMRAEV.]

SHAMRAEV [*as he comes in*]. We all get older and fade like leaves in winter, but you, my dear lady, you're still as young as ever . . . vivacious, graceful, a white dress.

IRINA. You're still trying to bring me bad luck, aren't you, you boring old man!

TRIGORIN [*to* SORIN]. How are you, Pyotr Nikolayevich? Still not feeling well, that's too bad! [*Seeing* MASHA, *happily.*] Ah, Marya Ilyinishna!

MASHA. You remember me? [*Shakes hands with him.*]

TRIGORIN. Of course— Married?

MASHA. Long ago.

TRIGORIN. Happy? [*Bows to* DORN *and* MEDVEDENKO—*who bow in return—then hesitatingly approaches* TREPLEV.] Irina Nikolayevna's told me that you've forgotten the past, and aren't angry with me any more.

[TREPLEV *holds out his hand.*]

IRINA [*to her son*]. Look, Boris Alexeyvich has brought the magazine that has your latest story in it.

TREPLEV [*taking the magazine, to* TRIGORIN]. Thanks, that was kind of you.

TRIGORIN. Your public sends its greetings. . . . People all over Petersburg and Moscow are very much in-tested in your work. They keep asking me what you're like, how old you are, and what you look like. Strangely enough, they all seem to think you're an old man. And no one knows your real name! Why do you always write under a pseudonym? You're as mysterious as the Man in the Iron Mask.

TREPLEV. Will you be here long?

TRIGORIN. No, I've got to be back in Moscow tomorrow. I've just got to finish this novel, and then I've promised to do something for an anthology. You know, the same as ever. [*While they talk,* IRINA *and* POLINA *move a card table into the middle of the room and open it.* SHAMRAEV *lights the candles and puts the chairs in place. A game of lotto is brought out of the cupboard.*] The weather's certainly given me a poor welcome. That's a bad wind. In the morning if it calms down a bit, I think I'll go fishing for a while. Besides, I want to have a look around the garden and see the place where your play was put on—you remember? I've got a good subject for a story, only I'll have to refresh my memory about the setting.

MASHA [*to her father*]. Father, please let Semyon take one of the horses. He's got to get home.

SHAMRAEV [*mimics her*]. He needs a horse . . . he must get home. . . . [*Sternly.*] You know the horses have just been to the station. They can't go out again!

MASHA. But there are other horses . . . [*Seeing that her father says nothing, she gestures impatiently.*] Oh, you're hopeless. . . .

MEDVEDENKO. That's all right, Masha, I can walk.

POLINA [*with a sigh*]. Walk in this weather! . . . [*Sits down at the card table.*] Come, everybody, let's get started.

MEDVEDENKO. After all, it's only four miles. . . . Good-bye . . . [*Kisses his wife's hand.*] Good-bye, Mother. [POLINA *reluctantly holds out her hand for him to kiss.*] I wouldn't have bothered you if it weren't for the baby. . . . [*Bows to the group.*] Good-bye . . . [*Goes out guiltily.*]

SHAMRAEV. Of course, he can walk! Who does he think he is, a general?

POLINA [*tapping on the table*]. Come along, please! Let's not waste any time, they'll be calling us for supper soon.

[SHAMRAEV, MASHA, *and* DORN *sit down at the table.*]

IRINA [*to* TRIGORIN]. When the long autumn evenings

come, we always play lotto when we're here. Look, this is the same set my mother had when she played with us as children. Why don't you play with us before supper? [*Sits down at the table with* TRIGORIN.] It's a dull game, but it's not so bad when you get used to it. [*Deals three cards to everyone.*]

TREPLEV [*turning over the pages of the magazine*]. He's read his own story, but he hasn't even cut the pages of mine. [*Puts the magazine down on his desk and walks toward door at left. As he passes his mother, he kisses her on the head.*]

IRINA. Aren't you going to play, Kostya?

TREPLEV. No thanks, I don't feel like it. . . . I think I'll go for a walk. [*Exits.*]

IRINA. Everyone puts in ten kopecks. Put it in for me, will you, Doctor?

DORN. Certainly.

MASHA. Everybody in? I'm starting. Twenty-two!

IRINA. I've got it.

MASHA. Three.

DORN. Right!

MASHA. Did you play three? Eight! Eighty-one! Ten!

SHAMRAEV. Slow down.

IRINA. What a reception they gave me in Karkhov! It makes me dizzy even when I think of it.

MASHA. Thirty-four!

[*A melancholy waltz is heard offstage.*]

IRINA. Why, the students gave me a regular ovation. . . . Three baskets of flowers and two wreaths, and this little brooch as well. . . . [*Unfastens a brooch on her throat and tosses it on the table.*]

SHAMRAEV. That's really something.

MASHA. Fifty!

DORN. Fifty, did you say?

IRINA. And my dress was beautiful! If there's one thing I know to do, it's how to dress!

POLINA. Kostya's playing the piano again. He's depressed, poor boy.

SHAMRAEV. They've been attacking him quite a bit lately in the papers.

MASHA. Seventy-seven!

IRINA. That shouldn't bother him!

TRIGORIN. It's too bad. His things never quite come off. There's something vague and mysterious about his style; it's like the ravings of a madman. And, then, none of his characters seems to have any life.

MASHA. Eleven!

IRINA [*looking round at* SORIN]. Petrusha, are you bored? [*A pause.*] He's asleep.

DORN. Our great lawyer's asleep.

MASHA. Seven! Ninety!

TRIGORIN. If I lived in a place like this, beside a lake, I don't think I'd ever write. I'd get over this compulsion of mine and do nothing but fish.

MASHA. Twenty-eight!

TRIGORIN. Just to catch perch . . . how wonderful that would be!

DORN. Well, I've got faith in Konstantin Gavrilovich. He's got some real talent! He thinks in images, and his stories are vivid and full of color, and personally I'm deeply moved by them. It's a pity he doesn't have a definite aim. He makes an impression and that's all, but just making an impression doesn't get you very far. Irina Nikolayevna, are you glad that your son's a writer?

IRINA. Can you imagine it?—I haven't read anything he's written. It seems there's never any time.

MASHA. Twenty-six!

[TREPLEV *comes in quietly and walks over to his desk.*]

SHAMRAEV [*to* TRIGORIN]. By the way, Boris Alexeyvich, we've still got something of yours.

TRIGORIN. What's that?

SHAMRAEV. Konstantin Gavrilovich shot a sea gull once, and you asked me to get it stuffed for you.

TRIGORIN. Did I really? [*Pondering.*] I don't remember it.

MASHA. Sixty-six! One!

TREPLEV [*opens the window and listens*]. How dark it is! I can't understand why I'm feeling so restless.

IRINA. Kostya, please shut the window, there's a draught!

[TREPLEV *shuts the window.*]

MASHA. Eighty-eight!

TRIGORIN. I win!

IRINA [*gaily*]. Bravo, bravo!

SHAMRAEV. Well done!

IRINA. That man's lucky in everything! [*Gets up.*] Now it's time to eat. Our celebrity hasn't eaten all day. We'll play some more after supper. [*To her son.*] Kostya, you'd better stop writing and come and eat.

TREPLEV. I don't want to, Mother, I'm not hungry.

IRINA. Just as you like. [*Wakes* SORIN.] Petrusha, supper is ready! [*Takes* SHAMRAEV's *arm.*] Let me tell you about the reception they gave me at Karkhov. . . .

[POLINA *blows out the candles on the table, then she and* DORN *wheel out* SORIN's *chair. Everyone goes out but* TREPLEV, *who remains alone sitting at his desk.*]

TREPLEV [*getting ready to write, he reads through what he has already written*]. I used to talk so much about new forms in art, and now I feel that little by little I'm getting into a rut myself. [*Reads.*] "The poster announced . . . A pale face framed by dark hair . . ." Announced . . . framed by dark hair . . . That's horrible! [*Crosses out.*] I'll begin again where the hero's awakened by the sound of the rain. I'll cut out the rest. And the description of the moonlight is no good either. Trigorin's worked out his own techniques, so it comes easily for him. . . . He'd just mention the neck of a broken bottle glittering in a mill stream and the black shadow of the mill wheel—and he's got a moonlight night. But for me it's the shimmering light, the silent twinkling of the stars, and the distant sounds of a piano, dying away in the still, fragrant air. . . . It's terrible! [*A pause.*] Yes, I'm more and more convinced that it isn't old or new forms that matter—what matters is that one should write without thinking of forms at all, and that whatever one has to say should come straight from the heart. [*There is a tap on the window nearest to his desk.*] What's that? [*Looks through the window.*] I can't see anything. . . . [*Opens the French doors and looks out into the garden.*] Someone's running down the steps. [*Calls.*] Who's there? [*Goes out and is heard walking rapidly along the patio, then returns half a minute later with* NINA.]

Nina! Nina!

[NINA *leans her head against his breast and sobs quietly.*]

TREPLEV [*deeply moved*]. Nina! Nina! It's you . . . it's you. . . . I knew you'd come! All day my heart's been pounding. . . . [*Takes off her cape and hat.*] Oh, my darling, precious girl, you've come at last! Don't cry, darling, don't cry!

NINA. Someone's here.

TREPLEV. No there isn't.

NINA. Lock the doors, so no one can get in.

TREPLEV. No one will come in.

NINA. I know Irina Nikolayevna is here. Lock the doors.

TREPLEV [*locks the door on right, then crosses to the left*]. This one doesn't have a lock, I'll have to put a chair against it. [*Puts an armchair against the door.*] Don't be afraid, darling, no one will come in.

NINA [*looks intently at his face*]. Let me look at you for a minute. [*Looking round.*] How nice and warm it is here! . . . Didn't this used to be the drawing-room? Have I changed a lot?

TREPLEV. Yes . . . You're thinner and your eyes seem

bigger. Nina, how strange it is to be seeing you! Why wouldn't you let me see you before? Why did you want to come here? I know you've been in the town almost a week. . . . I've been to your hotel every day, sometimes several times a day, and I stood under your window like a beggar.

NINA. I was afraid that you might hate me. Every night I dream that you look at me and don't recognize me. If only you knew! Ever since I came I've been walking round here . . . by the lake. I've been near the house many times, but I was afraid to come in. Let's sit down. [*They sit down.*] Let's just sit and talk and talk. . . . It's nice here, warm and comfortable. . . . Do you hear the wind? There's a passage in Turgenev: "Fortunate is the man who, on stormy nights, has a roof over his head and a warm corner of his own." I am a sea gull. . . . No, that's not it. [*Rubs her forehead.*] What was I saying? Yes . . . Turgenev . . . "And Heaven help the homeless wanderers!" . . . But it doesn't matter. . . . [*Sobs.*]

TREPLEV. Nina, you're crying again! . . . Nina!

NINA. Never mind, it does me good . . . I haven't cried for two years. Yesterday, late in the evening I came into the garden to see whether our stage was still there. It's still standing! I cried for the first time in two years then, and it was like taking a great weight off my heart, and I felt better. See, I'm not crying any more. [*Takes his hand.*] So you've become a writer. . . . You're a writer and I'm an actress. We've been drawn into the whirlpool together. I used to live here, happily, as a child—I'd wake up in the morning singing. I loved you and dreamed of fame. . . . And now? Tomorrow, I leave early in the morning on a coach for Yelietz . . . traveling with peasants; and at Yelietz, merchant lotharios will pester me with their attentions. Life is really very ugly.

TREPLEV. Why go to Yelietz?

NINA. I've taken a job for the winter. It's time I went.

TREPLEV. Nina, I used to curse you; I hated you, I tore up the pictures of you and your letters, but all the time I knew that I loved you heart and soul, and that I always would! I can't stop loving you, Nina. Ever since I lost you, ever since I began to get my work published, my life's been unbearable. I'm so unhappy. . . . I feel as if my youth has been suddenly torn away from me, as if I've lived for ninety years. I call out your name, I kiss the ground where you've walked; wherever I go I see your face, that tender smile that brightened the days when I was happy. . . .

NINA [*confused*]. Why does he talk like this, why does he talk like this?

TREPLEV. I am lonely. There is no love to warm me, I feel as cold as if I were in a dungeon—and everything I write turns out lifeless and gloomy and bitter. Please, stay, Nina! I beg you, or else let me come with you! [NINA *quickly puts on her hat and cape.*] Nina, why—what's wrong, Nina? . . . [*Looks at her as she puts on her clothes. A pause.*]

NINA. The horses are waiting at the gate. Don't bother to come with me, I'll go by myself. . . . [*Tearfully.*] Give me a glass of water.

TREPLEV [*gives her water*]. Where are you going now?

NINA. To town. [*A pause.*] Irina Nikolayevna's here, isn't she?

TREPLEV. Yes . . . My uncle had an attack last Thursday, so we wired for her to come.

NINA. Why did you say you kissed the ground where I walked? I ought to kill me. [*Droops over the table.*] Oh, I am so tired. I wish I could rest . . . just rest! [*Raising her head.*] I'm a sea gull. . . . No, that's not it. I'm an actress. But what difference does it make? [*She hears* IRINA *and* TRIGORIN *laughing offstage, listens, then runs to the door at left and looks through the keyhole.*] So he is here, too! . . . [*Returning to*

TREPLEV.] So he is . . . it doesn't matter. . . . Yes . . . He didn't believe in the theatre, he laughed at all my dreams, and so gradually I didn't believe them either, and I lost faith. . . . And then there was the strain of love and jealousy, and the constant worry about my baby. . . . I dried up, and my acting was very bad. . . . I didn't know what to do with my hands or how to stand or how to use my voice. . . . You can't imagine what it feels like when you know that you're doing a bad job. I'm a sea gull. No, that's not it. . . . Do you remember you shot a sea gull once? A man came along by chance, and he saw it and destroyed it, just to pass the time. . . . A subject for a short story . . . That's not it. [*Rubs her forehead.*] What was I saying? . . . Oh, yes, about the stage. I'm different now . . . I've become a real actress. I enjoy acting! I revel in it! The stage intoxicates me, and on it I feel very beautiful. While I've been here, I've spent a lot of time walking and thinking . . . thinking . . . and I feel that my spirit's growing stronger every day. I know now, Kostya, that what matters most for us, whether we're writers or actors, isn't fame or glamour, or any of the things I used to dream of. What matters most is knowing how to endure, knowing how to bear your cross and still have faith. I have faith now and I can stand my suffering when I think of my calling, I'm not afraid of life.

TREPLEV [*sadly*]. You've found your road, you know where you're going—but I'm still floating about in a maze of dreams and images, without knowing what it is I am to do. . . . I have no faith, and I have no calling.

NINA [*listening*]. Sh-sh! . . . I'm going now. Good-bye. When I become a great actress, come and see me act. Promise? But now . . . [*Presses his hand.*] It's late. I'm so tired I can hardly stand up. . . . I'm tired and hungry. . . .

TREPLEV. Do stay! I'll get you some supper.

NINA. No, no . . . Don't come with me, I'll go by myself.
. . . My horses are close by. . . . So she brought him
with her? Oh, well, it doesn't matter. . . . When you
see Trigorin don't say anything. . . . I love him. I love
him even more than before. A subject for a short
story . . . Yes, I love him, I love him passionately, I
love him desperately! Do you remember how nice it
used to be, Kostya? Do you remember? How peaceful
and warm, how joyous and pure our life was then,
what feelings we had? . . . like tender, exquisite
flowers. . . . Do you remember? . . . [*Recites.*] "Men,
lions, eagles, and partridges, horned deer, geese,
spiders, and the silent fish of the deep, starfish and
creatures which cannot be seen by the eye—all living
things, all living things, all living things, having
completed their cycle of sorrow, are now extinct. For
thousands of years the earth has given birth to no
living thing, and this poor moon now lights its lamp
in vain. In the meadows, the cranes no longer waken
with a cry, and the sound of the May beetles, humming in the lime groves, can no longer be heard."
. . . [*Impulsively embraces* TREPLEV *and runs out
through the French doors.*]

TREPLEV [*after a pause*]. I hope no one sees her in the
garden and tells mother about it. It might upset her!
[*He spends the next two minutes silently tearing up
all his manuscripts and throwing them under the
table, then unlocks the door at right and goes out.*]

DORN [*trying to open the door at left*]. That's funny,
the door seems to be locked. . . . [*Comes in and puts
the armchair in it place.*] What have we got here, a
regular obstacle course.

[*Enter* IRINA *and* POLINA, *followed by* YAKOV *carrying
drinks, then* MASHA, SHAMRAEV *and* TRIGORIN.]

IRINA. Put the red wine and the beer on the table for
Boris Alexeyvich. We'll want to drink while we play.

Let's sit down, everyone.

POLINA [*to* YAKOV]. Bring the tea, too. [*Lights the candles and sits down at the card table.*]

SHAMRAEV [*leads* TRIGORIN *to the cupboard*]. Here's the thing I was telling you about before. . . . [*Takes the stuffed sea gull out of the cupboard.*] This is what you ordered.

TRIGORIN [*looking at the sea gull*]. I don't remember. [*Musing.*] No, I don't at all!

[*There is a sound of a shot offstage on right. Everyone starts.*]

DORN. Don't worry. Something must have gone off in my medicine case. Don't worry. [*Goes out through door at right, returns in half a minute.*] Just as I thought. A bottle of ether blew up. [*Hums.*] "Again I stand before you, enchanted . . ."

IRINA [*sitting down to the table*]. Oh, how it frightened me! It reminded me of how . . . [*Covers her face with her hands.*] Everything went black for a minute.

DORN [*thumbing through a magazine, to* TRIGORIN]. There was an article in here about two months ago . . . a letter from America that I wanted to ask you about. . . . [*Puts his arm around* TRIGORIN'S *waist and leads him downstage.*] You see, I'm very much interested in this question. . . . [*Dropping his voice, in a lower tone.*] Somehow get Irina Nikolayevna away from here. The fact is, Konstantin Gavrilovich has shot himself. . . .

Curtain

CHEKHOV:
THE MAJOR PLAYS
English Versions by
Jean-Claude van Itallie

Despite the abundant variety of Chekhov translations available in bookstores and libraries, American directors and actors have sought out these versions by Jean-Claude van Itallie to make them the most often performed renditions on the American stage today. The van Itallie versions are favored and prized for their fresh clarity, subtle construction and supple colloquial rhythm. Van Itallie goes beyond the literal translation and shapes and invigorates the scholarly text until Chekhov's spirit feels present and familiar.

Reviews of the van Itallie versions:

THE CHERRY ORCHARD

"A classic restored to the hands, mind and blood of the creator."
—The New York Times

THE SEAGULL

"Sublimely understood Chekhov. . . absolutely true to the original."
—The New York Post

THREE SISTERS

"Captures Chekhov's exhuberance, music and complexity."
—The Village Voice

UNCLE VANYA

"The crispest and most powerful version extant."
—The New Republic

ISBN: 1-55783-162-9

THE MISANTHROPE
and other FRENCH Classics
Edited by Eric Bentley

"I would recommend Eric Bentley's collection
to all who really care for theatre."
—Harold Clurman

THE MISANTHROPE

by Molière
English version by Richard Wilbur

PAEDRA

by Racine
English version by Robert Lowell

THE CID

by Corneille
English version by James Schevill

FIGARO'S MARRIAGE

by Beaumarchais
English version by Jacques Barzun

ISBN: 0-936839-19-8

THEATRE AND DRAMA IN THE MAKING:
The Greeks to the Elizabethans

by John Gassner and Ralph Allen
Revised by Ralph Allen

"One of the absolutely essential resource books for both the theory and practice of the art form. Allen has done a masterful job in revising and updating the material. A must for practitioners, scholars and casual playgoers."

—Paul Antoine Distler
Distinguished Professor of Theatre
Virginia Tech

"A Classic. The definitive source book in the history and theory of western theatre. No serious student can afford to be without it."

—Gil Lazier
Dean, School of Theatre
Florida State

ISBN: 1-55783-073-8